THE COM

ARLIDGE, EADY & SMITH ON CONTEMPT

SECOND SUPPLEMENT TO THE FOURTH EDITION

THE COMMON LAW LIBRARY

ARLIDGE, EADY & SMITH ON CONTEMPT

SECOND SUPPLEMENT TO THE FOURTH EDITION

Up-to-date until 1 October, 2015

by

DOCTOR PATRICIA LONDONO, LL.B., MSc (Oxon), D.Phil.
Barrister, Red Lion Chambers

and

PROFESSOR A.T.H. SMITH, LL.D.
Barrister, 5 Raymond Buildings. Professor of Law, Victoria University of Wellington. Fellow of Gonville and Caius College, Cambridge and Arthur Goodhart Visiting Professor, University of Cambridge 2015–16

and

SIR DAVID EADY, M.A., LL.B.
Former Judge of the Queen's Bench Division

CONTRIBUTORS

Caroline Addy, Barrister, One Brick Court
Aidan Eardley, Barrister, One Brick Court
David Glen, Barrister, One Brick Court
Ian Helme, Barrister, One Brick Court
Clara Hamer, Barrister, One Brick Court
Sarah Palin, Barrister, One Brick Court
Hannah Ready, Barrister, One Brick Court
Jonathan Scherbel-Ball, Barrister, One Brick Court
Kate Wilson, Barrister, One Brick Court
Clare Kissin, Barrister, Government Legal Service

SWEET & MAXWELL

THOMSON REUTERS

Published in 2015 by Thomson Reuters (Professional) UK Limited, trading as Sweet & Maxwell, Friars House, 160 Blackfriars Road, London SE1 8EZ
(Registered in England & Wales, Company No 1679046. Registered Office and address for service: 2nd Floor, 1 Mark Square, Leonard Street, London EC2A 4EG

Typeset by YHT Ltd, London
Printed and bound by CPI Group (UK) Ltd, Croydon, CR0 4YY

For further information on our products and services, visit www.sweetandmaxwell.co.uk

No natural forests were destroyed to make this product; only farmed timber was used and replanted.

A CIP catalogue record of this book is available from the British Library.

ISBN 978 0 414 05269 7

HOW TO USE THIS SUPPLEMENT

This is the Second Supplement to the Fourth Edition of *Arlidge, Eady & Smith on Contempt*, and has been compiled according to the structure of the main volume.

At the beginning of each chapter of this Supplement the mini table of contents from the main volume has been included. Where a heading in this table of contents has been marked with a square pointer (■), this indicates that there is material that is new to the work in the Supplement to which the reader should refer.

Within each chapter, updating information is referenced to the relevant paragraph in the main volume.

PREFACE

Since publication of the First Supplement, there has been a good deal of activity over a wide front. There have been a number of significant legislative reforms following the recommendations of the Law Commission in their reports: *Contempt of Court (1): Juror Misconduct and Internet Publications* (Law Comm 340) and *Contempt of Court (2): Court Reporting* (Law Comm 344). The Law Commission's final report in this area *Contempt of Court: Contempt in the face of the Court* is due to be published late in 2015. Additionally, the pursuit of transparency and open justice continues to impact upon practice and procedure, and especially in the Family Court. Moreover, there have been a number of further comments by judges calling for the uncertainties to be resolved in relation to the provision of legal aid in contempt proceedings.

The earliest of the recent reforms, shaped by the recommendations of the Law Commission Report No 335, was the abolition of the branch of the law dealing with "scandalising", which took effect on 25 June 2013. In England and Wales it has had little impact, if any, because it was already in effect a dead letter, but it has been interesting to observe how the doctrine has continued to be applied in other jurisdictions, not only in younger democracies such as Fiji (where the administration of justice has been perceived as "more vulnerable than in the United Kingdom"), but also in Australia: see *State v Citizen's Constitutional Forum Ltd and Yabaki* [2013] FJHC 220, at [63], and *Tate v Duncan-Strelec* [2014] NSWSC 1125, at [223]. Meanwhile, in New Zealand, an Issues Paper has been published by the Law Commission seeking feedback but expressing the preliminary view, at [6.62], that the retention of such an offence has become "untenable in the light of freedom of expression, rule of law concerns and the views of modern New Zealand society". These matters are discussed at 5–271A *et seq.*

It has been necessary to follow through the recommendations made by the Law Commission in its Report 340 of December 2013 and the extent to which they have or have not been implemented by Parliament. In particular, the suggestion of new offences in respect of disclosing jury deliberations has led to significant legislative changes. The provisions of s.8 of the Contempt of Court Act 1981 have been revoked in England and Wales and there is now instead a new indictable offence of disclosing a jury's deliberations contrary to s.20D of the Juries Act 1974 (as amended). There are, however, a number of detailed exceptions contained in ss. 20E to 20G of the 1974 Act. There is a list of persons or bodies to whom such a disclosure *may* be made which includes, for example, the police—but not the Criminal Cases Review Commission, despite the Law Commission's recommendation to the contrary. Provision has also been made by way of s.20E(2) of the 1974 Act for a judge to disclose information 'about statements made, opinions expressed, arguments advanced or votes cast by members of a jury in the course of their deliberations' for the purpose of either dealing with the case or investigating whether an offence or a contempt of court has been committed. In addition, it is not an offence for a person to disclose such information after a jury has been discharged if they believe reasonably that an offence or contempt of court has been committed, or if the conduct of a juror in connection with the proceedings may provide grounds for an appeal against conviction or sentence. These provisions were considered important in remedying potential miscarriages of justice. There is a new offence of 'research by jurors' contrary to s.20A of the Juries Act 1974 (as amended) where a juror 'intentionally seeks information' and 'when doing so, knows, or reasonably ought to know that the information is or may be relevant to the case'. Section 20B of the 1974 Act (as amended), creates an offence of 'sharing research with other jurors'. Section 15A permits a judge to order that a jury trying a case, 'surrender any electronic communication devices for a period'. The Law Commission final report *Juror Misconduct and Internet Publications* had also recommended, at 4.31 to 4.57, that an exception be allowed for "authorised academics" to conduct research into jury deliberations, but it was announced in Parliament on 30 July 2014 that this proposal was not to be taken forward, at least for the time being.

A number of human rights decisions relating to the role of jurors and the effect of prejudicial reporting are discussed at paras 2–147A to 2–147D below. In *Abdulla Ali v United Kingdom* (Application No 30971/1/12), 30 June 2015, the ECtHR expressed the view, consistently with previous decisions in this regard, that where prejudicial media coverage appears some time before a jury is empanelled, it is unlikely that a potential or prospective juror will pay particular attention to the details of press reports, and a direction from the judge will usually be sufficient to counter any negative consequences for the defendant: it is reasonable to assume that the jury will follow the judge's directions.

The Law Commission, in its March 2014 Report *Contempt of Court (2): Court Reporting*, recommended that there be made generally available online a list of s.4(2) orders, identifying the relevant cases, but that the detailed content was only to be available on a subscription basis. The Government is currently considering how the proposals for such a database can be taken forward.

Another statutory development, in relation to court reporting, has been that the changes envisaged by ss.45 and 45A of the Youth Justice and Criminal Evidence Act 1999 have finally come into effect: see the discussion in chapter 8 of the main text. There is a power to protect young and vulnerable witnesses in criminal proceedings by restricting reporting not only in the conventional media but also online and, if necessary, for life. From 13 April 2015, s.39 of the Children and Young Persons Act no longer applies to criminal proceedings but it survives in relation to civil litigation: see s.79 of the Criminal Justice and Courts Act 2015. These changes were reviewed in the Divisional Court in *Aitken v DPP* [2015] EWHC 1079 (Admin), at [70]–[73], and certain discrepancies pointed out, which might require the further attention of the legislature.

Perhaps the most important judicial decision on the general principle of open justice, and the extent of the courts' powers to derogate from it, is to be found in the judgment of Lord Reed in *A v BBC* [2015] AC 588. This is discussed in chapters 7 and 16. These topics were also canvassed, and not least by the Court of Appeal in relation to criminal proceedings in *Re Guardian News & Media Ltd* [2015] 1 Cr App R 4. They were also considered, in the context of a court martial, in *R v Marine A* [2014] 1 WLR 3326 and in that of employment tribunal proceedings in *BBC v Roden* [2015] UKEAT 0385 14 1205.

The principle of open justice has been restated in a number of practice directions and in other guidance, covering both access to court hearings and the wider publication of judgments. In relation to committal applications, a new Practice Direction was promulgated by the Lord Chief Justice in March 2015: *Practice Direction (Committal for Contempt: Open Court) (Senior Courts)* [2015] 1 WLR 2195. This not only emphasises the importance of openness in relation to committal hearings but also provides for judgments to be made available on an expedited basis on the judicial website and also, as in Scotland, by way of the CopyDirect service. These provisions are discussed more fully at 7–38A and 7–106. The limitations of the CopyDirect service have been noted by Sir James Munby P in *P (A Child)* [2013] EWHC 4048 (Fam) in that the system does not serve all media organisations. This is discussed at 8–96.

Under the heading *Transparency in the Family Courts* there was issued on 16 January 2014 further Practice Guidance on the publication of judgments: [2014] 1 WLR 230. This was at the same time as similar guidance governing the Court of Protection: *Transparency in the Court of Protection: Publication of Judgments* (16 January 2014). These moves were intended to have an immediate and significant impact on the availability of judgments in those courts, while it was also recognised that there would often be a specific need for anonymity. Reference was made both to Sir Nicholas Wall's July 2011 paper *Media Access and Reporting* and to Sir James Munby's *View from the President's Chambers: the Process of Reform* [2013] Fam Law 548, which had expressed the intention to improve access to and reporting of the Family Court (as renamed from April 2014) and the Court of Protection. So far as possible the same rules were to apply in both jurisdictions, while accepting the need to protect the personal privacy of relevant children and vulnerable adults.

Hitherto, in the light of s.12 of the Administration of Justice Act 1960, it had been normal practice, where judgments were given in open court or made available with the judge's permission, for the parties to be protected by anonymity. Now, however, it was to be recognised that there would need to be exceptions to that general principle in certain cases. Parents might wish, for example, to discuss their experiences of the court system using their real names, or the court may decide that the public interest requires that the identity of some person(s) would need to be revealed following adverse findings in relation to their conduct. In such circumstances, it would be appropriate to obtain permission to reveal the relevant identities and to vary the rubric on the judgment: see *Media Access and Reporting*, at [83], and *Re B (Adult) (No 4)* [2012] 1 FLR 466, at [17] and [19], discussed at para 2–

63G and 8–97B The new regime took effect from 3 February 2014 with reference to the family court and to all High Court judgments where the inherent jurisdiction was being exercised in relation to children or vulnerable adults. These provisions are discussed at 2–63 A–J and 8–83A *et seq*.

There were to be two classes of judgment; namely, those which the judge *must* ordinarily allow to be published, and those which *may* be published. The first category embraces those in which the judge concludes that publication would be in the public interest (whether or not requested to do so by the parties or by the media) and those which relate to matters listed in Schedules 1 and 2 (and where there is a judgment available in publishable form or one has been ordered). Schedule 1 was to cover Family Court (or inherent jurisdiction) judgments following the determination of certain specified issues, of which a more detailed summary is to be found at 2–63D, 8–97B and 8–108. Schedule 2 concerns proceedings involving the inherent jurisdiction in relation to vulnerable adults and covers judgments dealing with the deprivation of liberty, medical treatment, removal to a residential establishment, a declaration as to capacity to marry or to consent to sexual relations, or restraint as to publication.

As to the second category, the starting point is that permission may be given on application by a party or an accredited member of the media. The judge will have regard to a number of factors in exercising the discretion including rights under the ECHR and the effect on any criminal proceedings. Where permission is given for a judgment to be published, it follows that (i) public authorities and experts *should* be named in the absence of compelling reasons; (ii) children or family members, or vulnerable adults, should *not* normally be named unless otherwise ordered; (iii) anonymity should not normally extend beyond protecting the privacy of children and adults who are the subject of the proceedings, or family members, unless there are compelling reasons to do so. The judge has a discretion in relation to the costs of transcribing the judgment. Judgments which are to be published should normally be made available on BAILII.

After six months, a consultation paper was published on 15 August 2014 called *Transparency—The Next Steps*. This was part of a continuing programme of reform, which the President intends should be informed at every stage by the views obtained from consultation. It was revealed that there had already been a significant increase in the number of judgments published on BAILII since the issue of the Practice Guidance in January. One of the matters canvassed in the consultation was that of possibly making the court's listing of cases more informative (or, as one sceptic has put it, more "enticing") for the media. Some commentators have suggested that the media are likely to be mainly interested in providing entertainment rather than enlightenment. While this may be true, at least in some cases, it is not necessarily an argument in favour of less transparency. The same argument could be raised about other forms of litigation, such as public or commercial law. There has been no official response to the consultation paper as yet. This is likely to take place during the Autumn of 2015.

Sir James Munby P also set up the Vulnerable Witnesses & Children Working Group, which reported in March 2015 and addressed some of the issues raised in *View from the President's Chambers*. The primary focus of its

20 recommendations was not so much to deal with court reporting, but rather with improving the obtaining of evidence from vulnerable witnesses and children by the most effective means. Transparency was not forgotten, however, but was indeed recognised as a "leitmotif" in the recent modernisation of family justice. It was, therefore, recommended that the Family Courts should hold open days every year with a view to demystifying the system of family justice and educating the public in the process, including children and young people.

At 8–85 below we add a new section 'The Abolition of the Family Proceedings Court'. Since the coming into effect, from 22 April 2014, of Pt 2 s.17(3) of the Crime and Courts Act 2013, the Family Proceedings Court no longer exists and all family work is dealt with by the single Family Court (subject to transitional provisions specified in SI 2014/954 art.3): see *The Single Family Court: A Joint Statement by the President of the Family Division and the HMCTS Family Business Authority* (April 2013) [2013] Fam. Law 600.

Scotland chose to address the familiar problems associated with contempt in the face of the court, and not least that of apparent bias, by way of legislation. The Act of Sederunt (Contempt of Court in Civil Proceedings) 2011 applies to civil proceedings in the sheriff court and to proceedings in the Court of Session. But it has been necessary in various criminal cases to give further reminders of the guidance given in *Robertson and Gough v HMA* [2007] HCJAC 63. See e.g. *Stephanie Bowie v The Procurator Fiscal, Paisley* [2014] ScotHC HCJAC 65, *Owen Hood v HMA* [2014] ScotHC HCJAC 85 and *Petition of Leanne Martin to the Nobile Officium of the High Court of Justiciary* [2014] ScotHC HCJAC 15. These are covered at 16–58 below.

There had been some uncertainty as to the appropriate extent of media coverage of settlement hearings in personal injury and professional negligence cases but, in *X v Dartford & Gravesham NHS Trust* [2015] EWCA Civ 96; [2015] C.P. Rep 22; [2015] E.M.L.R 14; [2015] P.I.Q.R P14 the Court of Appeal indicated that the default position should be that the claimant and his family are protected by anonymity, unless the court is satisfied that it is unnecessary. Questions have also been raised as to the well known problem of jigsaw identification. Although the intention has been to retain protection for personal privacy, once public attention is drawn to any interesting or "entertaining" aspects of a case, the danger is that readers will be able to piece together parts of the evidence and deduce the identities of the people concerned. This is clearly a problem which the court will have to address on a case by case basis, so as to minimise the risks.

Meanwhile, the trend continues towards wider television coverage of court proceedings. The advocates invariably emphasise the need for the public to be informed and for the courts to be kept under scrutiny, although inevitably coverage is likely to be dominated by the "news agenda". In Scotland, Lord Gill announced in January 2015 (and appropriately on television) the outcome of the consultation on the subject and of the enquiry carried out under Lady Dorrian. The central conclusion reached was that there should be wider opportunities for coverage, especially of appellate proceedings, but that clear guidelines should be worked out and especially for the protection of vulnerable witnesses. We mentioned in the preface to the First Supplement that the experience of televising courts in New Zealand had not been wholly positive. The issue was accordingly reconsidered, and in July 2015, a final report to the Chief Justice on *In-Court Media Coverage* was published. It concluded that there was room for improvement, particularly in the procedures and the quality and detail of the publications. New *In-Court Media Coverage Guidelines 2015* have been produced which aim to secure greater liaison between the press and the courts, and an increased role for the Media and Courts Committee in monitoring compliance with existing guidelines.

In chapter 6, there is extensive discussion about the court's power to grant *contra mundum* injunctions and the extent to which it might be appropriate to restrict the reporting of criminal proceedings. The authorities in this context have been considered in *Surrey County Council v ME* [2014] EWHC 489 (Fam), where it was recognised that such a power has only been (and should only be) exercised in exceptional circumstances: see 6–119C below. An unusual point arose before the Court of Protection, in *PA v Newcastle on Tyne Hospitals Federation Trust* [2014] EWCOP 6, as to whether a reporting restriction might legitimately survive the death of the person whom it was intended to protect. The answer was by no means straightforward, but on the facts it was held that it need not and that the anonymity order should be lifted.

A number of recent contempt cases have concerned the making of false statements or documents in the course of litigation and specifically in the context of fraudulent claims for compensation. The Supreme Court had made clear in *Summers v Fairclough Homes Ltd* [2012] 1 WLR 2004 that it would ordinarily be appropriate to impose a custodial penalty and this approach has been illustrated in a number of cases summarised in Appendix 3: see e.g. *Royal & Sun Alliance Insurance Plc v Fahad* [2015] EWHC 1092 (QB), *R (on the application of Saleem) v Serwan* [2015] EWCA Civ 123, *Aziz v Ali* [2014] EWHC 4003 (QB), *Bate v Aviva Insurance UK Ltd*, 18 November 2014, unreported, *Liverpool Victoria Insurance Co Ltd v Thumber* [2014] EWHC 3051 (QB), *Solicitor-General v Dodd* [2014] EWHC 1285 (QB), *Surface Systems Ltd v Wykes* [2014] EWHC 422 and *Homes for Haringey v Fari* [2013] EWHC 3623 (QB).

Freedom of expression was considered in the specific context of journalism by the Divisional Court in *R (Miranda) v Home Secretary* [2014] 1 WLR 3140. It was emphasised that journalistic freedom of expression serves the public interest as well as benefitting those individual journalists whose article 10 rights are primarily in issue. That has to be borne in mind when any balancing exercise has to be carried out. Source protection was further considered in Strasbourg in *Nagla v Latvia* (2013) ECHR 688 and *Tillack v Belgium* (2012) 55 EHRR 25, where again the Court drew attention to the fact that the principle is closely linked to the right of the public to be informed under article 10 which must be treated with the utmost caution. It was also stressed, however, in *Keena v Ireland* (29804/10, 30 September 2014) that the task of implementing the right of source protection is reserved to the courts, and that it is not compatible with the rule of law for journalists to choose to destroy documents which they had been ordered to disclose.

Following the emergence of reports that the provisions of Part 1 Chapter II of RIPA had been used by a number of police forces to identify journalistic sources, a report by the Interception of Communications Commissioner's Office found that the Home Office Code of Practice did not provide adequate safeguards to protect journalistic sources. In light of this, amendments were made to s.71 of RIPA requiring Codes of Practice to include provisions designed to protect the public interest in the confidentiality of journalist sources (s 71 (2A). This was followed by the new *Code of Practice on the Acquisition and Disclosure of Communications Data.* These developments are considered in chapter 9.

Freedom of expression has even been acknowledged for barristers in the Bar Standards Board Handbook (2nd edn April 2015) and its *Media Comment Guidance* discussed at 1–70A below. They are recognised as being free to comment even on cases in which they are instructed, although they are reminded of the law of strict liability contempt, which is the subject of chapter 4.

It has been noted at regular intervals that there remains undesirable uncertainty about the important subject of public funding and the circumstances in which it is available to those alleged to be in contempt. Judges have pointed out the lack of clarity and the need to do something about it. In particular, attention should be given to Regulation 21 of the Criminal Legal Aid (General) Regulations 2013 (SI 2013/9) and to Regulation 39 of the Criminal Legal Aid (Financial Resources) Regulations 2013 (SI 2013/471). See *King's Lynn and West Norfolk Council v Bunning* [2013] EWHC 3390, [2015] 1 WLR 531, *per* Blake J; *Inplayer v Thorogood* [2014] EWCA Civ 1511; *Brown v LB Haringey* [2015] EWCA Civ 483, *per* McCombe LJ and *Ramet, Re* [2014] EWHC 56 (Fam), Sir James Munby P. The cumulative effect of these decisions is that public funding is available to all those alleged to be in contempt, whether the contempt is 'civil' or 'criminal' in nature. The potential for loss of the contemnor's liberty as a result of being committed to prison for contempt means that the proceedings are for the purpose of Article 6 criminal in nature. The basis of the criminal scheme is found in r 9 (v) of the Criminal Legal Aid (General) Regulations 2013 (SI 2013/9). However, what remains unclear is whether any such funding is subject to a means test. In *National Farmers' Union v Tiernan* 16 July 2015, unreported, the Court of Appeal did not attempt to resolve the remaining uncertainties, while acknowledging them, as it was not necessary to do so for the case in hand. This remains, however, a fundamentally important issue: it arises almost every time contempt proceedings are contemplated against an individual. The courts have emphasised regularly over the past decade how central the question of funding is to ensuring a fair and efficient hearing and thus for complying with the obligations imposed by Article 6. Yet it should be relatively straightforward to set out a code of practice to resolve the remaining uncertainties and, especially, as to whether there is to be a means test (bound to take up time and to cause delay in determining and resolving the issues to be tried). Indeed, we would suggest that it is now the most pressing of the outstanding problems requiring the attention of Parliament in this field.

Again, we express our gratitude all the contributors to this supplement.

DE
ATHS
PIL

September 2015

TABLE OF CASES

TABLE OF INTERNATIONAL CASES

TABLE OF STATUTES

TABLE OF STATUTORY INSTRUMENTS

TABLE OF INTERNATIONAL LEGISLATION

TABLE OF PRACTICE DIRECTIONS & GUIDANCE

TABLE OF CIVIL PROCEDURE RULES

CHAPTER 1

HISTORY OF THE LAW OF CONTEMPT

VI. OTHER NINETEENTH CENTURY DEVELOPMENTS

C. Strict liability for contempt in the eighteenth century

[Add to note 172] **1–67**

The provisions set out at para 7–188 have been superseded, and the current provisions are to be found in the Criminal Procedure Rules 2015 (SI 2015/1490) in force with effect from 5 October 2015. On the same day, the new Criminal Practice Directions 2015 came into force [2015] EWCA Crim 1567. Part 6 of the Rules deals with "Reporting, Etc. Restrictions", Practice Direction 6B2 states that "it remains the responsibility of those reporting a case to ensure that restrictions are not breached". This appears to echo the sentiments of Lord Edmund Davies in *Att-Gen v Leveller Magazine* [1979] AC 440, cited in the main text. The complete edition of the Criminal Procedure Rules and Criminal Practice Directions 2015 is to be found at *https://www.justice.gov.uk/courts/procedure-rules/criminal/rulesmenu-2015* [accessed 17 October 2015].

D. The gradual demise of attachment

[Add to note 201] **1–84**

See now CPR Pt 81.

VIII. THE CONTEMPT OF COURT ACT 1981

D. Some "miscellaneous amendments"

1–119 *[Add to note 261]*

Section 8 of the 1981 Act has been repealed by the Criminal Justice and Courts Act 2015, which amends s 20 of the Juries Act 1974: see 11–408 *et seq* below.

1–119 *[Add to note 262]*

Section 9 of the Contempt of Court Act 1981 has been amended by s.31 of the Crime and Courts Act 2013: see para.10–197 below.

IX. DEVELOPMENTS SINCE THE 1981 ACT: A SUMMARY

F. Prominence of contempt in the family law cases

1–138 *[Add to note 308]*

The case of *L-W, Re* was cited and discussed by Sir James Munby P in *Jones, Re*; [2014] 1 FLR 852 at [25]–[27].

H. Developments in other common law jurisdictions

1–144A *[Insert new paragraph]*

The New Zealand Law Commission produced an Issues Paper no 36, *Contempt in Modern New Zealand* (May 2014). A final Report, which is likely to recommend that Parliament should legislate in this area, is expected imminently. See also the paper by A.T.H. Smith, *Reforming the New Zealand Law of Contempt: An Issues/Discussion Paper* (Crown Law Office, April 2011). *http://www.crownlaw.govt.nz/uploads/contempt_of_court.pdf*.

I. Technological developments

1–145 *[Add to note 322]*

See also J.R. Spencer, "*Contempt of Court and Misbehaving Jurors*" [2014] Crim L.R. 245; A.J. Ashworth, "*Contempt of Court: Juror Misconduct and Internet Publications*" [2014] Crim L.R. 169; C. Thomas, *Avoiding the Perfect Storm of Juror Contempt*, [2013] Crim LR 483; P. Humpherson, "*Contempt of Court and internet publications — the Law Commission's recommendations and the Criminal Courts and Justice Bill*" (2014) *Arch Rev.* 4; A. Kervick, "*Strict Liability in the age of the internet*" (2013) *Arch Rev* 5;

E. Robinson, *Jury Instructions for the Modern Age: A 50-State Survey of Jury Instructions on Internet and Social Media*, [2011] *1 Reynolds Court and Media Law Journal*; E. Brickman, J. Blackman, R. Futterman, J. Dinnerstein, (2008) *How Juror Internet Use Has Changed the American Jury, Jo of Court Innovation*, Vol 1, No.2.

[Add new paragraph] **1–146A**

The misuse by jurors of the search capacities of the internet is now regulated by the Criminal Justice and Courts Act 2015, ss.69–71, discussed below at 10–188B. Facebook and Twitter provide other means by which communications can be made very quickly, and without much thought, while giving rise to a risk of contempt; for example, by making threats to jurors or potential jurors as in *R v N* [2013] EWCA 989, [2013] 1 W.L.R. 3900, [2013] 2 Cr. App. R. 25 or breaching anonymity orders by posting photographs as in *Att-Gen v Harkins and Liddle* [2013] EWHC 1455 (Admin), [2013] A.C.D. 103. In the light of these developments, the Attorney-General announced in December 2013 that he proposed to publish advisory notes from time to time on the gov.uk website and Twitter to help prevent social media users from running the risk of committing contempt of court.

[Add to note 329] **1–148**

There is a 4th edition of the work cited, now entitled *Collins on Defamation* (2014).

[Add to note 336] **1–151**

See also *R v Harwood (Re Associated Newspapers Ltd)* [2012] EW Misc 27 (CC), July 20, 2012, Central Criminal Court (Fulford J.).

J. Other legislative developments

[Add to note 341] **1–152**

Seckerson v United Kingdom (32844/10 and 33510/10) (2012) 54 E.H.R.R. SE19.

[Add to end of paragraph] **1–152**

Section 51(1) of the Criminal Justice and Public Order Act 1994 has been repealed by the Criminal Justice and Courts Act 2015. The replacement provision is set out and discussed below at 11–152.

X. ISSUES CURRENTLY REQUIRING ATTENTION IN THE LAW OF CONTEMPT

B. Public statements by legal representatives and the police

1–165A *[Add new paragraph]*

Several high profile individuals have been arrested following the exposure of the late Jimmy Savile's long term sexual offending. Also, in August 2015, a police officer stood outside the former home of the late Sir Edward Heath and announced that enquiries were being carried into allegations of historic sex abuse made against him. There had already been considerable concern that some of the people arrested had likewise been publicly identified by the police. Some also had been made the subject of police bail over a long period without any charges ever being laid against them. Accordingly, the Home Affairs Select Committee conducted an investigation into police practices surrounding such arrests. Its 17th report *Police Bail*, dated March 2015, is available at *http://www.publications.parliament.uk/pa/cm201415/cmsele/ct/cmhaff/962/96208.htm* (accessed 13 July 2015). It recommended, in relation to those suspects still living, that their names should not be revealed unless and until they are charged with an offence, and that the police should not release any such information to the media in "an informal, unattributed way".

1–165B *[Add new paragraph]*

The Government's very prompt Response to the Committee's Report was published on 26 March 2015: *http://www.parliament.uk/documents/commons-committees/home-affairs/150324%20Home%20Sec%20to%20KV%20re%20Police%20Bail%20Govt%20Response.pdf*. In it, the Government agreed to propose legislative and other changes that would afford greater judicial scrutiny of the use of bail generally, and introduce a presumption of anonymity for persons during the pre-charge phase of the investigation.

1–166 *[Add to end of paragraph]*

In *Att Gen's Ref No.38 of 2013; sub nom R v Hall* [2013] EWCA Crim 1450 (26 July 2013) at [66]–[69] and [84], the then Lord Chief Justice mentioned, on an Attorney's reference, that it was relevant and "a seriously aggravating feature" that the accused had made public statements alongside his solicitor (long before he had pleaded guilty to a number of historic sexual offences) that the charges had no substance, in a way that suggested that the victims had made up the allegations. Not only would this have added to the distress of the victims and their families, but Lord Judge specifically added that the remarks may have been "for the purpose of possibly influencing potential jurors". The overall sentence was, for a variety of reasons, effectively doubled. But it is noteworthy that the possible impact on the trial should have been mentioned as an aggravating factor. It is conceivable (although perhaps unlikely) that it may have a discouraging effect on the relatively recent proliferation of public statements by parties and/or their legal advisers canvassing the merits of forthcoming cases.

[Add new paragraph] **1–170A**

Shortly before the introduction of the Bar Standards Board (BSB) Handbook on 6 January 2014 (second edition April 2015) the old Code of Conduct had been updated to remove the prohibition on media comment by barristers on cases in which they were instructed. This is given effect at section gC22 of the Code. The BSB's *Media Comment Guidance* explains the new position as follows:

> "The Bar Standards Board believes that, consistent with the rights of freedom of expression that are enjoyed by all, the starting point is that barristers are free to make comments to or in the media (this includes both conventional media — speaking to newspapers or broadcasters — and new media — social media, blogs and websites). However, because of the special position they occupy, certain rules will continue to limit the circumstances in which it will be appropriate for barristers to comment on cases in which they have been instructed and what they can properly say.
>
> .... Media comment which causes a substantial risk of serious prejudice to current or pending proceedings may lead to proceedings for contempt of court."

C. Payments to witnesses

[Add to note 395] **1–174**

The Leveson Inquiry addressed this issue of payments by journalists to the police for information: see The Report into the Culture, Practices and Ethics of the Press which was published on Thursday 29 November 2012, vol 2, Part F, Chapter 6, s.10 and Vol 2, Part G, Chapters 3 and 4. See main volume, 11–281.

D. Reporting court proceedings

[Add new paragraph] **1–178A**

Significant efforts have been made to make the proceedings of the Family courts more accessible to the public. The President of the Family Division issued draft *Practice Guidance on Transparency in the Family Courts and the Court of Protection* on July 12, 2013. It proposed that there should be, so far as possible, unification of the rules governing access to hearings in those courts. This was followed by further Practice Guidance *Transparency in the Family Courts* (16 January 2014) as well as further guidance concerning the publication of judgments. This was at the same time as similar guidance governing the Court of Protection: [2014] COPLR 78. These moves were intended to have an immediate and significant impact on the availability of judgments in those courts, while it was also recognised that there would often be a need for anonymity (see 2–63B below).

1–181 *[Add to end of paragraph]*

It has become increasingly apparent in the most recent decisions on court reporting, and in particular in the context of requests for anonymity couched in terms of Article 8, that the balancing exercise is likely to be resolved in favour of an individual's privacy only in exceptional circumstances: see e.g. *A v BBC* [2014] UKSC 25, *OPO v MLA* [2015] UKSC 32, [2015] 2 WLR 1373, *R v Marine A* [2014] 1 WLR 3326 and *Re Guardian News & Media Ltd* [2015] 1 Cr App R 4; see too the general discussion under chapters 6 and 7 below and in E Grant, *Injunctions and the Right to Privacy in the United Kingdom*, (2014) 19 M and A Law Rev 205. This trend is also true in the context even of the traditionally more "secretive" proceedings held in family courts and in the Court of Protection: see the commentary at 2–63B and in chapters 7 and 8 below.

1–183A *[Add new paragraph]*

The proposals canvassed in the Law Commission's Consultation Paper No.209 included the introduction of statutory offences to deal with examples of juror misconduct such as, in particular, carrying out independent research into the facts or background of cases they are trying: see below at 10–188A. It was suggested that such offences should be tried on indictment in the usual way. It was thought that this procedure would afford greater protection for any accused person's rights under arts 5 and 6 of the ECHR. The position as to the availability of public funding might, it was hoped, also be clearer.

1–183B *[Add new paragraph]*

Parliament has legislated in the Criminal Justice and Courts Act 2015 to take account of some of the problems highlighted by the Law Commission, and specifically the risk that jurors might disobey judicial directions not to search the internet for information relating to the trial before them. There are new criminal offences of engaging in such a practice (s.71) and of sharing the results of such a search with other jurors (s.72). There is a further offence of engaging in conduct from which it may reasonably be concluded that the person intends to try an issue otherwise than on the basis of the evidence presented (s.73). The secrecy of jury deliberations is preserved. Section 74 of the 2015 Act is in similar terms to those of the repealed s.8 of the Contempt of Court Act 1981, but it creates certain exemptions from liability, principally in cases where a jury irregularity constituting contempt arises and is being officially investigated, although notably not in respect of academic research (as the Law Commission had proposed), nor in relation to disclosures to the Criminal Cases Review Commission, as the Law Commission had also proposed. These provisions are now to found in the amended ss.20A–20G of the Juries Act 1974. See further at 11–372 *et seq* below.

G. The implications of the world wide web

[Add new paragraph] **1–190A**

The implications of the Internet and of social media for the future of jury trial, especially in criminal cases, have continued to be a focus of concern. The problems have been further illustrated in cases such as *Att Gen v Dallas* [2012] EWHC 156 (Admin); [2012] 1 W.L.R. 991, [2012] 1 Cr. App. R. 32; *R. v Harwood (Re Associated Newspapers Ltd)* [2012] EW Misc 27 (CC), July 20, 2012 (Fulford J.); *Att Gen v Pardon* [2012] EWHC 3402 (Admin); and *Att Gen v Davey; Att Gen v Beard* [2013] EWHC 2317 (Admin), [2014] 1 Cr. App. R. 1. It was one of the main subjects to receive attention from the Law Commission in its Consultation Paper No.209 and in the responses to it. (It is illuminating, in particular, to consider the response from the senior judiciary, dated March 4, 2013, and available on its website. The document was prepared by Treacy L.J. and Tugendhat J.) See also L. Whitney Lee, *Silencing the 'Twittering Juror': The Need to Modernize Pattern Cautionary Jury Instructions to Reflect the Realities of the Electronic Age*, (2010) 60 De Paul Law Review 181; N. Haralambous, *Educating Jurors: Technology, the Internet and the Jury System*, (2010) 19(3) Information and Communications Technology Law 255; C. Thomas, *Avoiding the perfect storm of juror contempt*, [2013] Crim. L.R. 483; R. Clarke, *Juries and Contempt — Compensating for the Internet* [2013] 177 J.P.N. 85.

In December 2013, the Law Commission published its Report, "Contempt of Court (1): Juror Misconduct and Internet Publications" (Law Com. No. 340). The main concern about the way the previous regime operated centered around the potential for inconsistency: the potential to prosecute for contempt was dependent on the words used by the judge at the start of the trial when telling jurors not to conduct research into the case they are trying [3.13]. In addition, there was concern that a layperson may not necessarily understand what a 'contempt of court' meant [3.17]. Furthermore, the Law Commission took the view that it was unclear whether the contempt would be as a result of research *per se* or as a result of breaching the directions given by the judge [3.19]. Finally, there was some concern that any threat to imprison jurors who breach the directions given to them by the judge concerning extraneous research would interfere with their attempts to build a rapport with the jury at the early stages of the trial [3.25]. The recommendations of the Law Commission have largely been implemented by Parliament in the Criminal Justice and Courts Act 2015, discussed at 11–372 below.

[Add new paragraph] **1–190B**

There are two fundamental propositions advanced by protagonists in the course of the debate. On the one hand, since jury trial has long been perceived by many in this jurisdiction as an aspect of democracy, and as being the foundation of our criminal justice system, some have asked why we should no longer trust jurors to deliberate and bring in a verdict solely upon the evidence before them. The other argument, however, is that it is unrealistic to expect jurors *not* to search the web for information about the case before them, or to communicate via social media, since it has become so much part of everyday life to do so for a large section of the population. There is clearly a tension between these points of view since, if jurors really are to be trusted, why is it reasonable to suppose that they will routinely ignore the standard judicial directions not to consult extraneous material? It is clear that this has proved a problem in all those jurisdictions reliant upon jury trial: see e.g. E. Robinson, *Jury Instructions for the Modern Age: A 50-State Survey of Jury Instructions on Internet and Social Media*, [2011] 1 Reynolds Court and Media Law Journal; E. Brickman, J. Blackman, R. Futterman, J. Dinnerstein, (2008) *How Juror Internet Use Has Changed the American Jury*, Journal of Court Innovation, Vol.1, No.2; *Juror's iPhone Causes Mistrial in Manslaughter Case*, Gizmodo Australia, September 17, 2010.

1–190C *[Add new paragraph]*

Optimistic assertions are sometimes made about the sterling qualities of jurors, to the effect that they are well aware of their responsibilities and have proved over generations how they can be trusted to discharge them effectively and in accordance with their oaths: see e.g. *R. v Ali (Ahmed)* [2011] EWCA Crim 1260 at [89]–[92]; *R. v H* [2012] EWCA Crim 1797. Yet there are undoubted concerns, as illustrated by the issuing of the Protocol, *Jury Irregularities in the Crown Court*, by the President of the Queen's Bench Division in November 2012 (which is now to be found consolidated in the Criminal Practice Directions 2015, at 26M). Generalities are unhelpful, as it must be acknowledged that those selected for jury service are no better or worse than the rest of us. In this context, it is often claimed that it is vital to carry out research into the experience and attitudes of those who have actually served in criminal trials and, indeed, that changes to s.8 of the Contempt of Court Act 1981 might be desirable in order to obtain fuller and more reliable information. Would not conclusions about jurors' behaviour which was based on such evidence be more reliable than if they were founded on speculation, assumption or prejudice? Again, however, it is difficult to see how general conclusions can be drawn from limited information derived from sample jurors about their own behaviour and reactions (even if what they say about them is to be taken at face value). Jurors are not a class apart. The fact that one juror or one jury may have behaved in a certain way helps little in establishing a general picture. Each jury is unique in its combination of persons and personal characteristics. In any event, it is by no means clear that anyone interviewed about experiences of jury service is going to speak frankly about any disclosures that may have been made, or admit having carried out Internet searches (in apparent defiance of judicial directions), or to having been influenced by media publications. The Law Commission recommendation that an exemption to the offence of disclosing juror deliberations be created to allow approved academic research was rejected by the Government (Law Commission's 49th Annual Report. Law Com No 359, HC 295, 43).

[Add new paragraph] **1–190D**

Various proposals have been canvassed in the attempt to meet these challenges. One problem, because of readier access to potentially prejudicial material, is that jurors will now be more likely to come across it than in the past. Whether there is "a substantial risk of serious prejudice", in accordance with s.2(2) of the 1981 Act, has traditionally been assessed, mainly by reference to newspapers and television, in the light of such factors as the scale and geographical area of publication: see e.g. *Att Gen v News Group Newspapers* [1987] QB 1 and *Att Gen v Independent Television News Ltd* [1995] 2 All E.R. 370, discussed at 4–75 *et seq*. Where relevant information is continually accessible on the web, such criteria diminish in significance and the risk of prejudice is correspondingly greater.

[Add new paragraph] **1–190E**

There has been much discussion of a "single publication rule", a phrase that is used in various senses, but although it is proposed that material placed on the Internet should be deemed to have been published (and published only) when it is first made available, that does not mean that its continued availability can or should be regarded as free of risk. Hence the proposal by the Law Commission that there might be a statutory power for trial judges to order temporary removal (or "take down") for so long as it is necessary to avoid prejudice arising in the course of a particular trial, as was done by Fulford J. (as he then was) in *R. v Harwood (Re Associated Newspapers Ltd)* [2012] EW Misc 27 (CC) 20 July 2012. See discussion at para 4–30A *et seq* below.

[Add new paragraph] **1–190EE**

The matter was considered by the Law Commission in its Report. The Commission endorsed the view adopted by Fulford J in *Harwood* and by the Scottish Court in *Beggs (No 2)* (2002) SLT 139 that an internet publication is continuing in nature. Therefore, even if published before proceedings became 'active' prejudicial words could give rise to a risk thereafter of strict liability contempt. The Commission recognised that, in practice, this would place an enormous monitoring burden upon publishers. A suggested solution was put forward by the Commission to the effect it should be a defence to proceedings for a strict liability contempt that the offending material had been published before the proceedings had become "active" for the purposes of the strict liability rule. However, the Attorney-General should be given a power to issue a formal warning that material in the archives was likely to have a prejudicial effect upon a forthcoming trial, and was at risk of proceedings for contempt if it continued to be published. This suggestion proved unpopular with, inter alia, the press (and in particular, the Society of Editors) and the Joint Parliamentary Committee on the Human Rights Act, both of which took the view that the arrangement would give the Attorney-General too great a role in affecting the freedom of the press, and the Attorney-General announced in Parliament that the clause giving effect to this suggestion would be withdrawn. For the sake of completeness, it might be added that the Commission proposed that the common law power to order the removal of material as exercised by Fulford J should be put on a statutory basis, but this was not adopted. See also discussion at 4–30 *et seq*.

1–190F *[Add new paragraph]*

Another preliminary ruling by the same Judge, in *R. v April Casburn*, 9 December 2012 (Southwark Crown Court), illustrates that especially in high profile cases the grant of an order to postpone publication, far from being "necessary", could prove in practical terms to be futile. The defendant was a senior police officer who was to be tried on a charge of misconduct in a public office. Her counsel sought an order, under s.4(2) of the Contempt of Court Act, to postpone publication of the fact that she had been charged separately with an offence under the Official Secrets Act (which was not relied on by way of bad character evidence in the forthcoming trial). The Judge declined to make the order "because the court does not have jurisdiction over many of the websites that host the articles that are revealed by internet searches relating to the defendant". He referred, by way of example, to a *New York Times* article on the case. He concluded that any risk of prejudice would have to be addressed by means of judicial directions in due course. He emphasised that the decision was based on the particular facts before him; specifically, in order to give it utility, any order would have involved securing the removal of a large number of internet reports already in existence.

1–190G *[Add new paragraph]*

The power of removal proposed by the Law Commission was not taken forward by the government. See the Law Commission, Annual Report 2014–2015, p 43. There were a number of difficulties with it. It could have been wide enough to embrace persons who are not "publishers", in any conventional sense, but who nonetheless have a degree of control over whether material remains accessible on the web or not. This might to some extent alleviate the problems of seeking to restrain persons outside the jurisdiction. There may conceivably be cases in which such a power, although not available in respect of persons or websites based abroad, would be effective to at least reduce the availability of the offending material to jurors. After all, the tests of necessity and proportionality would have to be assessed, as in *Casburn*, on the individual circumstances of the case. One of the risks in giving such a power, however, is that it would be used excessively, at least initially, as happened with the power to postpone reporting under s.4(2) of the 1981 Act: see the discussion at 7–149 *et seq* of the main text. Applications would tend to arise at short notice at the beginning of, or during, a criminal trial when minds are likely to be focussed on other issues. They would sometimes lead to delay and the cost for any third parties involved would be considerable. Moreover, even where an order is held to be appropriate, it may be ineffective for a variety of reasons. For example, those with the capacity to remove the offending item may be out of the jurisdiction, or the material may have already been spread on by means of blogging or tweeting.

[Delete paragraph] **1–190H**

CHAPTER 2

CONTEMPT OF COURT: THE CONSTITUTIONAL DIMENSION

I. THE CONTINUING ROLE OF THE CONTEMPT JURISDICTION

A. The purpose of the Contempt Jurisdiction

2–1 *[Add to note 2]*

The Law Commission has made a number of proposals for reform in the law of contempt, which had been foreshadowed in *Contempt of Court: a Consultation Paper* (2012) LCCP No. 209. This had been reviewed by I. Cram and N. Taylor in *The Law Commission's Contempt Proposals — Getting the Balance Right* [2013] Crim. L.R. 465 and by C. Thomas in *Avoiding a Perfect Storm of Juror Contempt* [2013] Crim L.R. 483. The first of three reports was *Contempt of Court: Scandalising the Court* (2012) Law Com No 335, which led to the abolition of "scandalising", in June 2013, by the Crime and Courts Act 2013, s.33. The second was *Contempt of Court (1): Juror Misconduct and Internet Publications* (2013) Law Com. No. 340. This gave rise to the reforms introduced by the Criminal Justice and Courts Act 2015, dealing with juror misconduct, which are discussed below at 11–408A *et seq.* The third, *Contempt of Court (2): Court Reporting* (2014) Law Com. No. 344, is considered below at 7–198 *et seq.* A yet further report relating to contempt in the face of the court is in preparation, and its publication is expected in 2016.

F. The overlap between contempt and the general criminal law

2–14 *[Add to note 25]*

See also *R v Kenny (Mark)* [2013] EWCA Crim 1, [2013] Q.B. 896, where the overlap between contempt of court and the offence of perverting the course of justice is considered. See below at 11–1.

[Add to note 26] **2–14**

See also *Att Gen v Dallas* [2012] EWHC 156 (Admin), [2012] 1 W.L.R. 991 at [7] ("It should now be clearly understood that trials for contempt on indictment are obsolete, and of historical interest only. Neither the Attorney General, nor the alleged contemnor, has any right to seek trial by jury on indictment"). And see *R. v Kayani; R. v Solliman* [2011] EWCA Crim 2871, [2012] 1 W.L.R. 1927, [2012] 1 Cr.App.R. 16.

[Add to end of paragraph] **2–14**

This "overlap" was mentioned by Laws LJ in *Accident Exchange Ltd v George-Broom* [2015] EWHC 2205 (Admin). He pointed out that the court and the prosecuting authorities are concerned with different, though no doubt overlapping, aspects of the public interest. The specific duty of the court under the contempt jurisdiction is to protect the integrity of the justice process, whereas the police and CPS are concerned to investigate crime and bring criminals to justice. Moreover, the evidential test under the Code for Crown Prosecutors has no application to contempt proceedings.

[Add to end of paragraph] **2–14**

Both these statutory regimes have been the subject of recent changes. Section 51 of Criminal Justice and Public Order Act 1994 has been repealed and replaced from a date to be appointed. The text of the new provision is set out below, at 11–152. Also, following the repeal of s.8 of the Contempt of Court Act, which addressed disclosures of jury discussions, s.20 of the Juries Act 1974 has been supplemented by new ss.20A–20G inserted by the Criminal Justice and Courts Act 2015. The new provisions are discussed below at 11–408A *et seq.*

G. The missing safeguards

[Add to end of paragraph] **2–20**

See now CPR Pt 81.

[Add to note 37] **2–23**

The Defamation Act 2013 came into effect on 25 April of that year. Jury trials had become rare prior to that — only two having taken place since 2009. Section 11 of the Act removed the presumption in favour of that mode of trial (contained in s.69 of the Senior Courts Act 1981) and none has taken place since October 2012. In *Gregory v Metropolitan Police Commissioner* [2014] EWHC 3922 (QB), Cranston J. commented at [22]: "Any constitutional right to trial by jury in a defamation case disappeared overnight following the Defamation Act 2013". See now CPR 26.11(2).

2–23 *[Add to note 39]*

Following the decision of the Supreme Court in *Siemer*, discussed further below at 3–76 *et seq*, s. 24 (e) of the New Zealand Bill of Rights Act 1990 was amended by the New Zealand Bill of Rights Amendment Act 2011. This increased the original period of three months' imprisonment that gave a right to jury trial to two years.

2–24 *[Add to note 40]*

See now CPR Pt 81.

2–24 *[Add to note 42]*

See the discussion of the decision of the Supreme Court in *Siemer v Solicitor-General* [2010] NZSC 54, [2010] 3 N.Z.L.R. 767 at 3–76 *et seq*.

H. Factors justifying the use of the summary procedure

2–29 *[Add to note 51]*

See now CPR Pt 81. See also *Att Gen v Dallas* [2012] EWHC 156 (Admin); [2012] 1 W.L.R. 991 at [7] ("It should now be clearly understood that trials for contempt on indictment are obsolete, and of historical interest only. Neither the Attorney General, nor the alleged contemnor, has any right to seek trial by jury on indictment".)

II. FREEDOM OF INFORMATION AND THE LAW OF CONTEMPT

B. The law of contempt as a fetter on freedom of speech

2–42 *[Add to note 82]*

See *Att-Gen v Harkins and Liddle* [2013] EWHC 1455 (Admin), where the defendants had compromised the safety of two notorious young child killers (Thompson and Venables) by posting material on social media websites, in breach of a *contra mundum* anonymity order. The court decided to enforce the order by imposing custodial penalties of nine months, although the exceptional course was taken of suspending them because of mitigating factors.

E. The "constitutional" role of the press

2–52 *[Add to note 103]*

See also *Foreign Secretary v Assistant Deputy Coroner for Inner North London* [2013] EWHC 3724 (Admin), [2014] A.C D. 43, at [20].

[Add new paragraph] **2–63A**

The willingness of the courts to make available to the media such documents as are deployed in court for the purposes of litigation, civil or criminal, was further illustrated by the decision of the Court of Appeal in *R (Guardian News and Media Ltd) v City of Westminster Magistrates' Court and other* [2012] EWCA Civ 420 [2013] Q.B. 618 [2012] 3 W.L.R. 1343 [2012] C.P. Rep. 30 [2012] E.M.L.R. 22. See also at 12–230A. See also *the Practice Direction: Committal for Contempt of Court: Open Court* [2015] 1 WLR 2195. The importance of open justice is nowadays continually emphasised in the context of family proceedings — not least because of the widespread impression given by the media and others that there is a sinister process of "secret justice". The President of the Family Division issued draft *Practice Guidance on Transparency in the Family Courts and the Court of Protection* on July 12, 2013. It proposed unification of the rules governing access to hearings in those courts. The Guidance meant that more judgments in those categories will be made generally available in due course. This developing process is borne out by *View from the President's Chambers: The Process of Reform* [2013] Fam. Law 548, in which the President reaffirmed his determination to improve access to and the reporting of family proceedings. The same objectives were further discussed, in the context of media access and reporting by Baker J. in *Al-Hilli (Children), Re* [2013] EWHC 2190 (Fam). Shortly afterwards there came the President's reserved judgment in *J (A Child), Re* [2013] EWHC 2694 (Fam). This concerned the right of "disgruntled parents" to speak out about the justice and care systems and also, more widely, as to the need for the courts to adapt to the realities of the internet and social media.

[Add new paragraph] **2–63B**

Under the heading *Transparency in the Family Courts* there was issued on 16 January 2014 further Practice Guidance on the publication of judgments. This was at the same time as similar guidance governing the Court of Protection: [2014] COPLR 78. These moves were intended to have an immediate and significant impact on the availability of judgments in those courts, while it was also recognised that there would often be a need for anonymity. Reference was made both to Sir Nicholas Wall's July 2011 paper *Media Access and Reporting* and to *View from the President's Chambers: the Process of Reform* [2013] Fam Law 548, which had expressed the intention to improve access to and reporting of the Family Court (as renamed from April 2014) and the Court of Protection. So far as possible the same rules were to apply in both jurisdictions, while accepting the need to protect the personal privacy of relevant children and vulnerable adults.

[Add new paragraph] **2–63C**

Hitherto, in the light of s.12 of the Administration of Justice Act 1960, it had been normal practice, where judgments were given in open court or made available with the judge's permission, for the parties to be protected by anonymity. Now, however, it was to be recognised that there would need to be exceptions in certain cases. Parents might wish, for example, to discuss their experiences of the court system using their real names, or the court may decide that the public interest requires that the identity of some person(s) would need to be revealed following adverse findings in relation to their conduct. In such circumstances, it would be appropriate to obtain permission to reveal the relevant identities and to vary the rubric on the judgment: see *Media Access and Reporting*, at [83], and *Re B (Adult) (No 4)* [2012] 1 FLR 466, at [17] and [19]. The new regime was to take effect from 3 February 2014 with reference to the family courts and to all High Court judgments where the inherent jurisdiction was being exercised in relation to children or vulnerable adults.

2–63D *[Add new paragraph]*

There were to be two classes of judgment; namely, those which the judge *must* ordinarily allow to be published, and those which *may* be published. The first category embraces those in which the judge concludes that publication would be in the public interest (whether or not requested to do so by the parties or by the media) and those which relate to matters listed in Schedules 1 and 2 (and where there is a judgment available in publishable form or one had been ordered). Schedule 1 was to cover Family Court (or inherent jurisdiction) judgments following the determination of issues relating to significant harm; the making or refusal of care or supervision orders under Pt 4 of the Children Act 1989; the making or refusal of placement or adoption orders under the Adoption and Children Act 2002; orders relating to deprivation of liberty, including secure accommodation under s.25 of the Children Act 1989; the granting or withholding of serious medical treatment; and an application for restraint of publication.

2–63E *[Add new paragraph]*

Schedule 2 concerns proceedings involving the inherent jurisdiction in relation to vulnerable adults and covers judgments dealing with the deprivation of liberty, medical treatment, removal to a residential establishment, a declaration as to capacity to marry or to consent to sexual relations, or restraint as to publication.

2–64F *[Add new paragraph]*

As to the other cases, the starting point is that permission may be given on application by a party or an accredited member of the media. The judge will have regard to a number of factors in exercising the discretion including rights under the ECHR and the effect on any criminal proceedings. Where permission is given for a judgment to be published, it follows that (i) public authorities and experts should be named in the absence of compelling reasons; (ii) children or family members, or vulnerable adults, should not normally be named unless otherwise ordered; (iii) anonymity should not normally extend beyond protecting the privacy of children and adults who are the subject of the proceedings, or family members, unless there are compelling reasons to do so.

[Add new paragraph] **2–63G**

Where a judgment is released, the rubric will be a matter for the judge, but there is a standard from available:

> "This judgment was delivered in private. The judge has given leave for this version of the judgment to be published on condition that (irrespective of what is contained in the judgment) in any published version of the judgment the anonymity of the children and members of their family must be strictly preserved. All persons, including representatives of the media, must ensure that this condition I strictly complied with. Failure to do so will be a contempt of court."

The judge has a discretion in relation to the costs of transcribing the judgment. Judgments which are to be published should normally be made available on BAILII.

[Add new paragraph] **2–63H**

After six months, a consultation paper was published on 15 August 2014 called *Transparency — The Next Steps*. There has been no official response to the President's consultation on transparency but it is currently expected to become available in the autumn of 2015. This was part of a continuing programme of reform which is intended to be informed at every stage by the views obtained from consultation. It was revealed that there had been a significant increase in the number of judgments published on BAILII since the issue of the Practice Guidance in January.

[Add new paragraph] **2–63I**

One of the matters canvassed in the consultation was that of possibly making the court's listing of cases more informative (or, as one cynic has put it, more "enticing") for the media.

Some commentators have suggested that the media are likely to be mainly interested in providing entertainment rather than enlightenment. While this may be true, at least in some cases, it is not necessarily an argument in favour of less transparency. The same argument could be raised about other forms of litigation, such as public or commercial law.

Questions have also been raised as to the well known problem of jigsaw identification. Although the intention has been to retain protection for personal privacy, once public attention is drawn to any interesting or "entertaining" aspects of a case, the danger is that readers will be able to piece together parts of the evidence and deduce the identities of the people concerned. This is clearly a problem which the court will have to address on a case by case basis, so as to minimise the risks.

2–63J *[Add new paragraph]*

Sir James Munby P also set up the Vulnerable Witnesses & Children Working Group, which reported in March 2015 and addressed some of the issues raised in *View from the President's Chambers.* The primary focus of its 20 recommendations was not so much to deal with transparency or media reporting, but rather with improving the obtaining of evidence from vulnerable witnesses and children by the most effective means. They included proposals for two new Practice Directions (PD 3D and PD 3C) in relation to the identifying of vulnerable witnesses and the arrangements for pre-recording evidence along the lines of a Crown Court pilot scheme. Transparency as not forgotten, however, but was indeed recognised as a leitmotif of the recent modernisation of family justice. It was, therefore, recommended that the Family Courts should hold open days every year with a view to demystifying the system of family justice and educating the public in the process, including children and young people.

2–65A *[Add new paragraph]*

The role of the press was extensively examined in the course of an enquiry chaired by Sir Brian Leveson and in his *Report into the Culture, Practices and Ethics of the Press* published on 29 November 2012. In the course of the hearings, it became apparent that there had been widespread wrongdoing by some members of the press, and in particular through phone hacking and the paying of public officials (including members of the police) for official information. Misconduct by the police in their dealings with members of the press was also uncovered. As a result, the Director of Public Prosecutions formulated guidance for prosecutors and a number of high profile prosecutions took place — in most cases leading to jury acquittals. See A.T.H. Smith, *'Assessing the Public Interest in Cases Affecting the Media' — The Prosecution Guidelines* [2013] Crim L.R. 449.

F. Provision for criminal proceedings in private

2–66A *[Add new paragraph]*

The language in which the current provision in the Criminal Procedure Rules (r.6.6(2)) is expressed is slightly different to that quoted in para 2–66 of the main text, but to the same practical effect. The then current provision was discussed in *Re Guardian News and Media Trust Ltd v Incedal* [2014] EWCA Crim 1861, [2015] 1 Cr App R 4, [2015] EMLR 2, considered in this supplement below, at 7–13A. See Archbold 2015, ch 4.

III. FREE PRESS AND FAIR TRIAL

C. Developments in other jurisdictions

[Add to note 189] **2–101**

See the article by D Milo and S. Scott, *South Africa: Access to court papers is part of open justice*, Inforrm blog 20 July 2015, which makes the point that South Africa is a jurisdiction where trial is by judge alone, rather than by jury, and that the Deputy Chief Justice has asserted extra-judicially that the law of contempt surrounding the *sub judice* rule is, at the very least "on the verge of extinction." A similar point was made in the European Court of Human Rights, if rather more cautiously expressed, in *Abdulla Ali v The United Kingdom* (Application No 30971/1/12), 30 June 2015:

> "[88] The Court has previously identified various matters that it considers relevant to the assessment of the impact of adverse publicity on the fairness of the trial or on respect for the presumption of innocence. Thus, it has made clear that there is unlikely to be any arguable complaint under Article 6 where the criminal charges are determined by professional judges, since their professional training and experience allow them to disregard any external influence (see, for example, *Priebke v. Italy* no. 48799/99, 5 April 2001 and *G.C.P. v. Romania*, no. 20899/03, § 48, 20 December 2011)."

D. Minimising the risk of prejudice without restricting free press

1. *Postponement of the trial*

[Add to note 206] **2–106**

See now *Archbold.* 2015, 4–79 *et seq* A. L.-T. Choo, *Abuse of Process and Judicial Stays of Criminal Proceedings* (OUP, 2nd ed, 2008), "Delay".

[Add to note 208) **2–106**

There is now a greater willingness to pursue historical cases, e.g. in relation to allegations of sexual abuse or of war crimes. As to some of the difficulties, see J. McEwan, *Vulnerable Defendants and the Fairness of Trials* [2013] Crim L.R. 100; Lyndon Harris and Dan Bunting, *Has the approach to sentencing historical offences changed?, Archbold Review* (2015) 4, 5–6 discussing *inter alia* the case of *R. v Clifford (Frank Maxwell)* [2014] EWCA Crim 2245. The authors point to the difficulty that the maximum current sentences are considerably higher than were prevalent at the time when the offences were committed, and that the courts have increasingly sentenced according to the higher more contemporary sentences available to them unless this exceeds the maximum sentence available to the courts at the time the offence was committed.

2. *Change of venue*

2–109 *[Add to note 215]*

The Magistrates' Courts Act 1980, s.7 has now been repealed.

2–109 *[Add to note 216]*

See now the Criminal Practice Directions 2015 [2015] EWCA Crim 1567, CPD XIII: Listing, C.7 (v). There is nothing specific about local prejudice in the Directions, but C.7(v) provides that the relevant presiding judge should be consulted about a case which for any reason "is likely to attract exceptional media attention".

4. *Jury vetting and selection by the use of a voir dire*

2–115 *[Add to note 227]*

By virtue of the Criminal Justice Act 2003, Sched 33, jury service became obligatory for all persons aged 18 to 70, other than mental patients and convicted persons. A challenge to the presence of a serving police officer who knew some of the prosecution witnesses was unsuccessful in the UK domestic courts, but it succeeded before the European Court of Human Rights in *Hanif v United Kingdom (52999/08)* [2012] 3 Costs L.O. 355 (ECHR) on the basis that it was a breach of the right to a trial by an independent and impartial tribunal, as guaranteed by Article 6. See J.R. Spencer *Police Officers on Juries* (2012) 71 C.L.J. 254.

2–118 *[Add to note 235].*

On the other hand, in *R v Skelton* [2008] NZCA 382 at [118], Priestly J ruled that in the course of the empanelling process, potential jurors should be asked to identify themselves as being, for example, friends of the parties to the proceedings, or people who have encouraged one or other of the parties through means such as telephone calls or other communications. See also *R v Smail* [2009] NZCA 549, Young P.

IV. THE IMPACT OF THE EUROPEAN CONVENTION

2–124 *[Add to note 244]*

The cross-reference should be to 1–133.

2–124 *[Add to note 246]*

See J. Beatson, S. Grosz, T. Hickman, R. Singh and S. Palmer, *Human Rights: Judicial Protection in the United Kingdom* (2008), especially chapters 1 to 3. See also T. Hickman, *Public Law after the Human Rights Act* (2010).

A. "Incorporation" into United Kingdom law

[Add to note 247] **2–125**

See generally J. Beatson, S. Grosz, T. Hickman, R. Singh and S. Palmer, *Human Rights: Judicial Protection in the United Kingdom* (2008), especially chap 1. The part played by the ECHR and its implementation by the Human Rights Act 1998 have not been uncontroversial. There have been proposals for radical change, such as by repealing the Human Rights Act and substituting "a British Bill of Rights". Matters such as the voting rights of prisoners (*Hirst v United Kingdom (74025/01)* (2006) 42 E.H.R.R. 41, Grand Chamber) and the power to deport dangerous non-nationals (*Chahal v United Kingdom (22414/93)* (1997) 23 E.H.R.R. 413) have been politically divisive. Indeed, sometimes the national courts have found themselves at odds with Strasbourg. For discussion of these and other issues arising from the enactment of the Human Rights Act, see A.L. Young, *Parliamentary Sovereignty and the HRA* (2009), reviewed by A Bradley, [2011] PL 203, CJS Knight, (2009) 68 CLJ 479, Adam Tomkins (2010) Edin L. R. 154; I. Leigh and R. Masterman, *Making Rights Real: The Human Rights Act in its First Decade* (2009), reviewed by E Prochaska (2009) 125 L.Q.R. 355; E. Bates, *British Sovereignty and the European Court of Human Rights* (2012) 128 L.Q.R. 382; M. Amos, *The dialogue between the United Kingdom courts and the European Court of Human Rights* (2012) ICLQ 557; A. Young, *Is dialogue working under the Human Rights Act 1998?* (2011) PL 773; H. Fenwick, *The Human Rights Act or a British Bill of Rights: creating a down-grading recalibration of rights against the counter-terrorism backdrop* (2012) PL 468; C. Chandrachud, *Reconfiguring the discourse on political responses to declarations of incompatibility* (2014) PL 624. See also T. Hickman, *Public Law after the Human Rights Act* (2010).

B. The relevance of the Convention to the law of contempt

[Add to footnote 248] **2–126**

See Clayton and Tomlinson, *The Law of Human Rights: Privacy and Freedom of Expression* (2nd ed 2010) Raymond Wacks, *Privacy and Media Freedom* (2014), chapters 4 and 5. For an extended discussion of the impact of the ECHR on the law of contempt, see the Law Commission, *Consultation Paper* No 209 (2012), Appendix B.

[Add to note 250] **2–128**

See *Siemer v Solicitor-General* [2010] NZSC 54, [2010] 3 N.Z.L.R. 767, discussed at 2–23 and 2–24, where it was held that, in spite of the fact that the New Zealand Bill of Rights Act 1990, s.24(e), afforded a right to trial by jury where the available penalty for the relevant offence was at least three months imprisonment, this did not apply to the law of contempt.

2–129 *[Add to note 251]*

See, however, *Abdulla Ali v The United Kingdom* (Application No 30971/1/12), 30 June 2015, where it was held that the circumstances were such that the pre-trial publication of a good deal of prejudicial material did *not* give rise to a violation of Article 6. See above at 2–101 and at 2–131A below. It was explained as follows:

"88. The Court has previously identified various matters that it considers relevant to the assessment of the impact of adverse publicity on the fairness of the trial or on respect for the presumption of innocence. Thus, it has made clear that there is unlikely to be any arguable complaint under Article 6 where the criminal charges are determined by professional judges, since their professional training and experience allow them to disregard any external influence (see, for example, *Priebke v. Italy* no. 48799/99, 5 April 2001; and *G.C.P.* v. *Romania*, no. 20899/03, § 48, 20 December 2011).

89. Even in cases involving jury trials, an appropriate lapse of time between the appearance of any prejudicial commentary in the media and the subsequent criminal proceedings, together with any suitable directions to the jury, will generally suffice to remove any concerns regarding the appearance of bias (see Beggs, cited above, § 124–128; and, as regards in particular the importance of jury directions, *Pullicino v. Malta* (dec.), no. 45441/99, 15 June 2000; and Mustafa (*Abu Hamza*), cited above, §§ 39–40). In particular, where the impugned newspaper reports appeared at a time when the future members of the jury did not know that they would be involved in the trial process, the likelihood of any appearance of bias is all the more remote, since it is highly unlikely that the jury members would have paid any particular attention to the detail of the reports at the time of their publication (see Beggs, cited above, § 126). In such cases, a direction to the jury to disregard extraneous material will usually be adequate to ensure the fairness of the trial, even if there has been a highly prejudicial press campaign (for an example where such a direction was sufficient, see Beggs, cited above, § 128). It is essential to underline in this respect that it is reasonable to assume that a jury will follow the directions given by the judge in the absence of any evidence suggesting the contrary (Beggs, cited above, § 128; and *Szypusz* v. *the United Kingdom*, no. 8400/07, § 85, 21 September 2010)."

2–130 *[Add to note 254]*

See the discussion at 1–181 above.

Recent Strasbourg cases relevant to the law of contempt

2–131A *[Add new paragraph]*

There have been a number of decisions of the European Court of Human Rights, arising from the United Kingdom and elsewhere, which illustrate the various points at which the Convention is relevant to the law of contempt.

[Add new paragraph] **2–131B**

In *Gough v United Kingdom (49327/11)* (2015) 61 E.H.R.R. 8, 28 October 2014, the Court was concerned with "the naked rambler" who believed in "social nudity" and in 2003 decided to walk naked from Land's End to John O'Groats. He was prosecuted for numerous breaches of the peace between 2003 and 2012 and appeared naked on a number of occasions in court. He received custodial sentences for contempt, by reason of his refusal to dress in court, varying between two and four months' imprisonment. He complained of alleged breaches under Articles 8, 9 and 10, but no violations were found.

[Add new paragraph] **2–131C**

The Court was asked in *Beggs v United Kingdom* (Application Number 15499/10),16 October 2012, to consider what was said to have been a virulent and prejudicial press campaign against applicant. It was held that the complaint was manifestly ill-founded and inadmissible. The Court referred to its own previous jurisprudence which:

> "regularly emphasised the importance of directions given to the jury regarding their approach to various matters arising in the case (see as recent examples *Adetoro v. the United Kingdom*, no. 46834/06, § 49, 20 April 2010; *Szypusz v. the United Kingdom*, no. 8400/07, § 84, 21 September 2010; and *Al-Khawaja and Tahery v. the United Kingdom* [GC], nos. 26766/05 and 22228/06, §§ 150151, ECHR 2011)." [124]. The judge had directed the jury appropriately about not taking in to account any extraneous material, explicitly referring to material in the press and on television. The conclusion was reached, at [128], that "There is nothing in the circumstances of the case to suggest that the jury could not be relied upon to follow the judge's instructions and it is therefore reasonable to assume that the jury would follow the directions given (see the Court's similar conclusion in *Szypusz*, cited above, § 85)".

[Add new paragraph] **2–131D**

Another complaint was made of a "virulent" press campaign in *Abdulla Ali v The United Kingdom* (App No 30971/1/12, 30 June 2015. It was alleged to have violated the applicant's right to a fair trial. The Court declared the application admissible, being satisfied that the application raised "arguable issues" under Article 6(1). Such a campaign *could* adversely affect the fairness of a trial by influencing public opinion and, consequently, jurors called to decide upon the guilt or innocence of an accused. In this way, it would risk having an impact on the impartiality of the court under Article 6(1) as well as the presumption of innocence enshrined in Article 6(2). Despite this, the Court said that "what is decisive is not the subjective apprehensions of the subject but whether, in the particular circumstances of the case, his fears can be held to be objectively justified." It was held not to be. See 2–101 and 2–129 above.

C. Constitutional protection of rights: the common law approach

2–134 *[Add to note 259]*

See J. Beatson, S. Grosz, T. Hickman, R. Singh and S. Palmer, *Human Rights: Judicial Protection in the United Kingdom* (2008), especially chaps 1 to 3. See also T. Hickman, *Public Law after the Human Rights Act* (2010).

2–139A *[Add new paragraph]*

The "shift" in attitude towards the protection of rights, following the enactment of the Human Rights Act, was aptly summed up by Lord Bingham in *R (Laporte) v Chief Constable of Gloucestershire* [2007] 2 A.C. 105, at 126–7, paragraph [34]:

> "The approach of the English common law to freedom of expression and assembly was hesitant and negative, permitting that which was not prohibited. Thus although Dicey in *An Introduction to the Study of the law of the Constitution*, 10th ed (1959), in Part II on the 'Rule of Law', included chapters VI and VII entitled 'The Right to Freedom of Discussion' and 'The Right of Public Meeting', he wrote of the first (at pp 239–240) that 'At no time has there in England been any proclamation of the right to liberty of thought or to freedom of speech' and of the second (at p 271) that 'it can hardly be said that our constitution knows of such a thing as any specific right of public meeting'. Lord Hewart CJ reflected the then current orthodoxy when he observed in *Duncan v Jones* [1936] 1 KB 218, 222, that 'English law does not recognise any special right of public meeting for political or other purposes.' The Human Rights Act 1998, giving domestic effect to articles 10 and 11 of the European Convention, represented what Sedley LJ in *Redmond-Bate v Director of Public Prosecutions* (1999) 163 JP 789, 795, aptly called a 'constitutional shift'."

D. A matter of balance? Contrasting approaches to rights adjudication

2–141 *[Add to note 271]*

Laura Hoyano, *What is balanced on the scales of justice? In search of the essence of the right to a fair trial* [2014] Crim L.R. 4 (The courts should act "unclouded by nebulous balancing"); G Webber *Proportionality: Constitutional Rights and their Limitations* [2013] Public Law 433; H Fenwick, *The Human Rights Ac tor a British Bill of Rights: Creating a Down-Grading Recalibration of Rights Against the Counter-Terror Backdrop?* [2012] Public Law 468; G Anagnostaras, *Balancing conflicting fundamental rights* [2014] 39 E.L. Rev 111; J. Rozenberg, *Balancing Exercise* (2012) Law Soc Gaz 109.

E. Open Justice: Articles 6 and 10

[Add to note 282] 2–146

In *A v BBC (Scotland)* [2014] UKSC 25, [2015] AC 588 at [27], open justice was said to be "a constitutional principle to be found in the common law". See also *BBC v Roden* [2015] I.C.R. 985.

[Add new paragraph] 2–146A

In *Seckerson v United Kingdom* (32844/10 and 33510/10), (2012) 54 E.H.R.R. SE19, it was argued that s.8 of the Contempt of Court Act 1981 which forbids jurors from disclosing the secrets of the jury room, violated art.10 of the Convention. The Court held that the application was inadmissible and that the absolute prohibition imposed by s.8 was neither disproportionate nor unreasonable. The provision has now been repealed and replaced. See 2-1 above and the discussion in chapters 10 and 11 below.

[Add new paragraph] 2–146B

The Law Commission in its Report No.335, *Contempt of Court: Scandalising the Court* (2012), took the view that the law of scandalising was not necessarily of itself offensive to the European Convention, but doubted whether its existence could be said to be "necessary" in the requisite test under the Convention.

[Add new paragraph] 2–147A

Article 6 — Right to a fair trial

In *Mustafa Abu Hamza (No.1) v UK* (31411/07), (2011) 52 E.H.R.R. SE11, the Court rejected as "manifestly ill-founded" the claim that a trial had been affected by the adverse publicity surrounding it, saying that "this Court's approach has been to examine whether there are sufficient safeguards to ensure that the proceedings as a whole are fair", and took the view that the judge's direction, in particular, constituted a sufficient safeguard.

[Add new paragraph] 2–147B

In *R. v Ali (Ahmed)* [2011] EWCA Crim 1260; [2011] 2 Cr. App. R. 22, complaint was made that a fair trial had not been possible because of adverse publicity that had been generated at an earlier trial of the same defendants which was still available on the internet at the time of the second trial. There was, however, no evidence that any of the jurors had looked at that material, and the court took the view it was impossible to infer that any juror had done so, since any attempt by the juror to influence fellow jurors as a result of what had been found on the internet would have been bound to be revealed by other jurors.

2–147C *[Add new paragraph]*

In *R. v Pouladian-Kari (Ramin)* [2013] EWCA Crim 158, a conviction for unlawfully exporting goods which could be used for military purposes was quashed as being unsafe. The trial judge had failed to discharge the jury after a juror had written to him, following the prosecution opening, disclosing that he that was professionally employed in the customs sector, saying that there were "definite red signals" in the material presented by the prosecution, and that he was not sure that he could base a decision solely upon the evidence, as was his duty.

2–147D *[Add new paragraph]*

In *Taxquet v Belgium* Application No.926/05 (2012) 54 E.H.R.R. 26, it was held that there had been a violation of art.6(1). The Second Section of the Court had held that "judgments of courts and tribunals should adequately state the basis on which on which they are based". The Grand Chamber held, however, that there is no Convention requirement that lay jurors should give reasons for their decision, so long as there were sufficient safeguards in place for accused and the public to understand the jury's verdict. These safeguards could be found in the instructions given by a judge to the jury, or in questions posed by the judge for the jury.

H. The significance of the right of individual petition

2–152 *[Add to note 299]*

See also J. Beatson, S. Grosz, T. Hickman, R. Singh and S. Palmer, *Human Rights: Judicial Protection in the United Kingdom* (2008), especially chapter 1, and T. Hickman, *Public Law after the Human Rights Act* (2010).

I. The so called "margin of appreciation"

2–153 *[Add to note 305]*

See now eds Harris, O'Boyle, E.P. Bates, C.M.Buckley, *Law of the European Convention on Human Rights,* 3rd ed (2014).

2–153 *[Add to note 305]*

But see *Seckerson v United Kingdom* (32844/10 and 33510/10), (2012) 54 E.H.R.R. SE19 at [40] where the continued vitality of the margin of appreciation was affirmed in the context of an art.10 challenge to s.8 of the Contempt of Court Act 1981. Another case in which the margin of appreciation was recently considered was that of *Animal Defenders International v United Kingdom (Application No. (48876/08))* [2013] E.M.L.R. 28. The ECtHR considered prior restraint in the context of advertising. The NGO applicant wished to broadcast an advertisement against the practice of carrying out experiments on animals. The Broadcast Advertising Clearance Centre refused to permit it, because the NGO's objectives were "wholly or mainly of a political nature" and therefore the advertisement was prohibited by s.321(2) of the Communications Act 2003. (The advertisement was available on the internet.) The applicant argued that the decision was unjustifiable prior restraint. The Court observed that, as the subject matter was one of general public interest, the margin of appreciation afforded to the state was limited and, furthermore, the NGO was acting in a way comparable to that of the media in its "public watchdog role" which added weight to its position. Nonetheless, a distinction was drawn between "a general measure" imposed by a state (such as the restrictions imposed by the Communications Act 2003 on types of advertising), which may result in unfair outcomes for particular parties, and prior restraint imposed on an individual act of expression. In the circumstances, this measure was not disproportionate.

[Add to end of paragraph] **2–153**

The "margin of appreciation" was referred to by Lord Reed in *A v BBC (Scotland)* [2014] UKSC 25, [2015] AC 588, at [46]:

> "The court therefore allows a margin of appreciation to national authorities in striking a fair balance between the interest in publicity of court proceedings, on the one hand, and the interests protected by article 8, on the other hand: *Z v Finland* (1997) 25 EHRR 371, para 99".

For commentary, see See Eirik Bjorge, "Fundamental Rights at English (and European) Common Law" (2015) 131 LQR 196.

N. Contempt cases in which reliance was placed upon the European Convention

[Add to note 348] **2–179**

See now the 17th Report of the Home Affairs Select Committee, *Police Bail* (March 2015), on the subject *inter alia* of police naming suspects before charge. See also 1–165A above.

O. The enactment of the Human Rights Act 1998

[Add to note 356] **2–183**

See now CPR Pt 81 and the associated Practice Direction.

V. THE ROLE OF THE ATTORNEY GENERAL

A. The initiation of contempt proceedings

2–184 *[Add to note 360]*

As Sir James Munby P observed in *Jones, Re* [2013] EWHC 2579 (Fam) at [14],

> "It is quite clear, in my judgment, that the Law Officers have *locus* to apply for the committal of an alleged contemnor even if the contempt is civil and involves the breach of an order obtained, as in the present case, by a private individual in the course of proceedings between private individuals. The Law Officers act to safeguard the public interest and the administration of justice."

C. Doubts as to the locus standi of other persons

2–192 *[Add to note 372]*

See also *Bedfordshire Police v RU and FHS* [2013] EWHC 2350 (Fam), at [30] *et seq.* and *Jones, Re* [2013] EWHC 2579 (Fam), at [16].

E. Considering the public interest

2–195 *[Add to note 380]*

See now CPR Pt 81.

2–197 *[Add to end of paragraph]*

The Law Commission has proposed that the Attorney General should publish a "prosecution" policy to promote transparency and consistency: Consultation Paper No.209 at 2.60–2.63. That suggestion has some academic support: See I. Cram & N. Taylor, "*The Law Commission's Contempt proposals — getting the balance right?*" Crim. L.R. 2013 6 465–482. (Traditionally, courts have tended to eschew the term "prosecution" in the context of the Attorney's role in upholding the law of contempt: see 2–185 *et seq* and following, 3–67 and 3–82 *et seq* in the main text. But that does not affect the point of substance, which is the need for maximum clarity.) The article by Cram and Taylor also suggests that consideration should now be given to making amenable to judicial review any decision by the Attorney General refusing consent to initiate proceedings. For the current position, see *R. v Solicitor-General, Ex p. Taylor* [1996] C.O.D. 61 and the discussion in the main text at 2–200 *et seq*.

As JR Spencer has noted in the Cambridge Law Journal, [2012] 71 C.L.J. 27, "the law now imposes on the Director of Public Prosecutions the duty to publish his prosecution policy and, influenced by this, the courts now treat the decision to prosecute as susceptible of judicial review". See also D. Ormerod, [2012] Crim. L.R. 653, who has made essentially the same point:

> "The courts' position is clear: 'only in highly exceptional cases will the court disturb the decisions of an independent prosecutor and investigator': Lord Bingham in *R (Corner House Research) v Director of Serious Fraud Office* [2008] UKHL 60, [2009] A.C. 756 at [30]. The simple fact is, however, that the more policies there are and the more specific their content, the greater opportunity for challenging the lawfulness of the content and/or the application in a given case."

Whether this trend will extend in due course to the Law Officers remains to be seen.

F. The Attorney's role in relation to civil contempts

[Add to note 401] **2–205**

See also *Bedfordshire Police v RU and FHS* [2013] EWHC 2350 (Fam) at [30] *et seq.* It was held by Holman J. that the police had no locus to apply for committal in relation to the alleged breach of a protection order made in respect of forced marriage. The Judge concluded, at [32]–[33]:

> "The hierarchy of recognised applicants is as follows —
>
> (a) the party who obtained the order;
> (b) if he decides not to, the Attorney General, if the public interest requires him to intervene in order to enforce the order;
> (c) the court will act of its own volition ... in exceptional cases of clear contempts ... in which it is urgent and imperative to act immediately.
>
> It would not be an incremental step for me to add in the police as a category of applicants in this situation. It would be a huge leap in a legal framework that has been regarded as settled for many decades."

In *Jones, Re* [2013] EWHC 2579 (Fam) at [16], Sir James Munby P expressed his agreement.

G. The court's power to act of its own initiative

[Add to note 402] **2–207**

And see *Balli, Re* [2011] EWHC 1736, at [7].

VI. CONTEMPT OF COURT AND THE CROWN

A. Contempt of Court by Ministers of the Crown: M, Re

2–211 *[Add to note 412]*

See also *Kenneth Smith v Scottish Ministers* [2015] CSOH 15; 2015 S.L.T. 131, another case where a prisoner's privileged correspondence was opened at the orders of prison officers without authority. Undertakings had been given by the Scottish Ministers at previous judicial review proceedings not to interfere with Mr Smith's correspondence. The Lord Ordinary had no difficulty in finding the Ministers to be in contempt, saying that the "leading authority is the decision of the Inner House in *Beggs v Scottish Ministers*" 2005 1 S.C 342, 2005 S.L.T. 305. See also 14–2 below.

CHAPTER 3

THE DISTINCTIONS BETWEEN CRIMINAL AND CIVIL CONTEMPT

I. THE DISTINCTION EXPLAINED

A. The essence of the distinction

[Add to note 1] 3–1

The distinction was reaffirmed and explained by the Supreme Court in *R v O'Brien* [2014] UKSC 23, [2014] AC 1246: see e.g. at [37]–[39] and the words of Lord Toulson, at [42]

> "The question whether a contempt is a criminal contempt does not depend on the nature of the *court* to which the contempt was displayed; it depends on nature of the *conduct*. To burst into a court room and disrupt a civil trial would be a criminal contempt just as much as if the court had been conducting a criminal trial. Conversely, disobedience to a procedural order of a court is not in itself a crime, just because the order was made in the course of criminal proceedings. To hold that a breach of a procedural order made in a criminal court is itself a crime would be to introduce an unjustified and anomalous extension of the criminal law. "Civil contempt" is not confined to contempt of a civil court. It simply denotes a contempt which is not itself a crime."

See also 13–35A below. The distinction is also reflected in legislation: See s.13 of the Administration of Justice Act 1960 and the current Criminal Procedure Rules 2015 (SI 2015/1490) r.48.2 and 48.3.

[Add to note 8] 3–4

See too *JSC BTA Bank v Ablyazov* [2012] EWCA Civ 639 at [27] and *Forrester Ketley v Brent* [2012] EWCA Civ 324 (although a committal hearing may be regarded as "criminal" in the context of art.6, hearings are rightly conducted in accordance with the CPR rather than the Criminal Procedure Rules). See the general discussion at 2–13 *et seq* of the main text. In the context of whether contempt proceedings are criminal for the purpose of public funding, see para.15–118 below *et seq*.

3–9 *[Add to note 13]*

See also *Dar Al Arkan Real Estate Development Co v Al-Refai* [2015] 1 WLR 135 at [42], where reference was made to *JSC BTA Bank v Solodchenko (No 2)* [2011] EWCA Civ 1241, [2012] 1 WLR 350 (cited *inter alia* at 3–69, 3–116 and 3–188 below), and it was stated that "... it is thus clear that it is for the public good that the order of the court should not be disregarded".

3–11A *[Add new paragraph]*

In *Director of Serious Fraud Office v B* [2012] EWCA Crim 67, the court decided that breach of a proceeds of crime order should be treated as civil contempt, at least in part, because an application for committal has a coercive as well as a punitive purpose.

B. Illustrations of the dual nature of civil contempts

3. *Breaches treated in England as civil contempt*

3–21 *[Add to note 27]*

A person who commits a civil contempt does not acquire a criminal record, since it would not equate to a criminal offence: *R v O'Brien* [2014] UKSC 23, [2014] AC 1246, at [38]. See too the observations of Lord Toulson cited at 3–1 above and 13–35A below.

3–22 *[Add to note 30]*

In *Button v Salama* [2013] EWHC 4152 (Fam), a father was refusing to disclose the whereabouts of his daughter despite having served almost two years in prison. The court considered that prison had lost its coercive effect and that there was no point in imposing a further custodial penalty.

C. Points of comparison between civil and criminal contempt: an overview

3–27 *[Add to note 35]*

In *Ealing London Borough Council v Connors* [2013] EWHC 3493 (Fam), the children were the subject of an emergency protection order. Nothing was said as to the classification of the contempt as criminal or civil. It is not yet clear whether this is reflective of a shift in categorisation or merely that the court considered the matter so well-established it needed no mention.

3. *Waiver*

3–32 *[Add to end of paragraph]*

In *Williams v Minnock*, 24 June 2015 (unreported a decision in the Family Court) the respondent mother had failed to hand her child over in accordance with an order of the court, and had gone into hiding with him. Whilst in hiding she had contacted media agencies and there had been a great deal of public and media interest in the case. In their absence, the father applied to commit the mother to prison for breach of the order. When the mother subsequently broke her cover, and returned her son to his father, he applied to the court to withdraw the committal application on the basis that it was no longer in the child's best interests. Despite stating that the mother could not have escaped a finding of contempt and a term of imprisonment if the committal application had gone ahead, the court permitted its withdrawal. The judge was of the view that the father was also a victim of the mother's actions and that his wish to withdraw the application was to be respected.

5. *Sanctions*

[Add to note 41] **3–34**

But note that contemnors can be released before the conclusion of their fixed term. See *Solicitor General v Dodd* [2014] EWHC 1285 (QB). The contemnor, who was sentenced to six months' imprisonment, was being held at HMP Pentonville, a category B/C prison. Section 33 of the Criminal Justice Act 1991 entitled him to be released at the half way point, namely 12 weeks. On an application to purge his contempt the court noted that the conditions of imprisonment there had had a far greater effect on him than had been anticipated at the time he was sentenced. The Court granted his application and released him from prison once he had served eight weeks of the original 12.

11. *Extra-territorial jurisdiction*

[Add to end of paragraph] **3–40**

But the jurisdiction to make a finding of contempt would not be affected by the inability to enforce any sanction on a contemnor who was abroad: *Re Demesne Investments* [2013] NICh 2 at [47].

12. *Hearsay evidence*

[Add to end of paragraph] **3–41**

The Criminal Procedure Rules 2015 (SI 2015/1490) in force 5 October 2015 r.48.11, provides that hearsay evidence is admissible for civil contempt proceedings which take place in a criminal court: for an example, see under the previous provisions *Director of Serious Fraud Office v B* [2012] EWCA Crim 67, cited above at 3–11A

[Add to note 48] **3–41**

See also *Archbold*, 2015, at para 28–95 where it is submitted that summary proceedings for contempt would amount to criminal proceedings and that hearsay evidence would be admissible in relation to which the 'strict rules of evidence apply' in line with the Criminal Justice Act 2003 ss.114 (1) and 134 (1). But see the words of Lord Toulson cited above at 3–1, from which it is clear that proceedings for civil contempt may take place in a criminal court.

16. *The availability of public funding*

3–45 *[Add to note 51]*

Now largely replaced by the Legal Aid, Sentencing and Punishment of Offenders Act 2012. See ss.14, 15, and 16 for the provision of advice and representation for "contempt committed, or alleged to have been committed, by an individual in the face of the court". This is noted also at 10–10 and 15–115 *et seq*. See particularly para 15–118 *et seq* for the discussion on the uncertainties that remain in relation to whether the public funding available to those said to be in contempt is subject to a means test.

E. Continuing criticisms of the distinction

3–48 *[Add to end of paragraph]*

On the other hand, the distinction was noted and appears to have been reaffirmed by the Supreme Court in *R v O'Brien* [2014] UKSC 23, [2014] AC 1246: see e.g. at [37]–[39] and the words of Lord Toulson, at [42], cited at 3–1 and 13–35A below.

II. THE JURIDICAL NATURE OF CONTEMPT

A. Criminal contempt and the general criminal law framework

3–55 *[Add to note 66]*

See now CPR Pt 81 and the associated Practice Direction.

3–58 *[Add to note 70]*

See *Kyprianou v Cyprus* (2007) 44 EHRR 27, where on the facts it was held by the European Court of Human Rights that the use of a summary procedure had involved a breach of Article 6: See *inter alia* at 10–40, 10–52, 10–55, 10–57, 10–139, 10–151, 10–161 of the main text

2. *The variable application of general sentencing provisions to contempt cases*

3–60 *[Add to note 74]*

See now s.83 of the Powers of Criminal Courts (Sentencing) Act 2000, which replaced s.21 of the 1973 Act, referred to in the text.

[Add to note 76] **3–60**

See now the Criminal Procedure Rules 2015 (SI 2015/1490) in force with effect from 5 October 2015, r.48.

4. *The right to silence*

[Add to note 82] **3–64**

See now *Archbold* 2015, paras 15–361—15–389.

5. *The relevance of general principles of criminal liability*

[Add to note 87] **3–66**

See also *Attorney General v Davey* [2013] EWHC 2317 (conduct was calculated to interfere with or prejudice the due administration of justice if there was a real risk, as opposed to a remote possibility, that interference or prejudice would result.)

6. *Criminal contempts as "misdemeanours"*

[Add to note 91] **3–67**

See also *Att Gen v Dallas* [2012] EWHC 156 (Admin); [2012] 1 W.L.R. 991 at [7]:

> "It should now be clearly understood that trials for contempt on indictment are obsolete, and of historical interest only. Neither the Attorney General, nor the alleged contemnor, has any right to seek trial by jury on indictment."

See also at 2–14 and 2–29 above. In New Zealand, the argument that the Bill of Rights entitled a person accused of contempt to have the issue tried by jury was rejected in *Siemer v Solicitor-General* [2010] NZSC 54; [2010] 3 NZLR 767 (noted in the main text at 2–23).

B. The nature of civil contempt

[Add to note 95] **3–69**

See also *JSC BTA Bank v Solodchenko* [2012] EWCA Civ 1241 at [45].

[Add to note 97] **3–70**

See *Broxbourne Borough Council v Robb* [2011] EWHC 1626 at [52]. See also *Dar Al Arkan Real Estate Development Co v Al-Refai* [2015] 1 WLR 135 at [42], where reference was made to *JSC BTA Bank v Solodchenko (No 2)* [2011] EWCA Civ 1241, [2012] 1 WLR 350 (cited *inter alia* at 3–69, 3–116 and 3–188 below), and it was stated that "... it is thus clear that it is for the public good that the order of the court should not be disregarded".

3–71 *[Add to note 99]*

The Supreme Court decided in *R v O'Brien* [2014] UKSC 23, [2014] AC 1246, that the breach of an order under s.41 of the Proceeds of Crime Act 2002 was not an "offence" for the purposes of s.151A of the Extradition Act 2003. See at 13–35A below.

3–71 *[Add to note 100]*

See also *South Cambridgeshire DC v Buckley* [2012] EWHC 1669.

3–71 *[Add to note 101]*

See also *R v O'Brien* [2014] UKSC 23, [2014] AC 1246.

C. The adoption of some criminal safeguards for civil contempt

3–74 *[Add to note 104]*

See also *Jones, Re* [2013] EWHC 2579 (Fam) where the court reiterated that a mandatory order is not enforceable by committal unless it specifies a time for compliance and that it was impossible to read implied terms into a court order in relation to committal.

3–75 *[Add to note 110]*

See also *Forrester Ketley v Brent* [2012] EWCA Civ 324 (it is appropriate that committal hearings should be conducted in accordance with the CPR rather than the Criminal Procedure Rules).

E. Civil contempts as "misdemeanours"

3–85 *[Add to note 124]*

It would seem that today the maximum sentence of two years' imprisonment for contempt would often be regarded as inadequate in child kidnapping cases. The maximum under the Child Abduction Act 1984 is seven years, whereas the offence of kidnapping itself carries the possibility of life imprisonment: see the discussion in *R. v Kayani; R. v Solliman* [2011] EWCA Crim 2871.

3–87 *[Add to note 130]*

See now *Archbold* 2015, [28–27]–[28–131].

F. Is contempt of court a wrong sui generis?

[Add to note 138] **3–91**

See also the historical summary in *Att Gen v Dallas* [2012] EWHC 156 (Admin); [2012] 1 W.L.R. 991.

[Add to note 139] **3–91**

See also *Att Gen v Dallas* [2012] EWHC 156 (Admin); [2012] 1 W.L.R. 991, where it was confirmed that trials on indictment have become obsolete and "of historical interest only".

[Add to note 140] **3–91**

For the modern approach to sentencing in child kidnapping cases, see *R. v Kayani; R. v Solliman* [2011] EWCA Crim 2871.

G. The practical importance of the distinction gradually minimised

[Add to note 147] **3–94**

See also *Bedfordshire Police v RU and FHS* [2013] EWHC 2350 (Fam) at [30] *et seq*. It was held by Holman J. that the police had no locus to apply for committal in relation to the alleged breach of a protection order made in respect of forced marriage. In *Jones, Re* [2013] EWHC 2579 (Fam) at [16], Sir James Munby P expressed his agreement.

[Add to end of paragraph] **3–96**

Furthermore, the distinction between civil and criminal contempt appears to have been reaffirmed in *R v O'Brien* [2014] UKSC 23, [2014] AC 1246.

H. How do the contempts created by the 1981 Act fit into the framework?

2. *The secrecy of jury deliberations: s.8*

[Add to note 161] **3–98**

See now *Seckerson v UK* (2012) 54 E.H.R.R. SE19.

[Add to note 162] **3–98**

See the explanatory notes to the Bill, which state at para 447, in respect of the exceptions for disclosure after the conclusion of the trial, "The purpose of these exceptions is to ensure that irregularities in relation to jury deliberations can be investigated." See also para 211 of the Ministry of Justice Circular No 2015/01: "The provisions therefore create exceptions so that a juror with real concerns about specific issues affecting the fairness of the deliberation process, such as the commission of offences or contempt, can make the disclosure in certain situations."

3–98 *[Add to end of paragraph]*

Section 8 of the Contempt of Court Act 1981 was repealed in England and Wales (only) on 13 April 2015 by s.74 (2) Criminal Justice and Courts Act 2015. This inserts ss.20D–20G in the Juries Act 1974. By s.20D it is an indictable offence for a person intentionally '(a) to disclose information about statements made, opinions expressed, arguments advanced or votes cast by members of a jury in the course of their deliberations in proceedings before a court, or (b) solicit or obtain such information' save in so far as the disclosure or solicitation occurs in the circumstances set out in ss.20E-G. See the further discussion at 10–181 *et seq* and 11–408A *et seq*.

3. *Tape recording in court: s.9*

3–99 *[Add to end of paragraph]*

This would appear to be consistent with the Criminal Procedure Rules 2015 (SI 2015/1490) in force with effect from 5 October 2015, r.48.5(1)(d) and (e). Section 9 of the 1981 Act has been amended by s.31 of the Crime and Courts Act 2013: see 10–197 below.

3–110 *[Add to note 175]*

Delete the reference to *Archbold* 2013, para.28–113.

4. *Breaches of s.4(2) and s.11 orders*

3–102 *[Add to note 170]*

And see *Masri v Consolidated Contractors International* [2011] EWHC 1024 (Comm) at [150] and [155], also referred to at 7–244, 12–96A and 15–24.

3–103 [*Add to note 171]*

Note should be taken of the more restrained approach of the Court of Protection in *Re M (Incapacitated Adult) (Best Interests Declaration: Potential Contempt)* [2015] EWCOP 3 (It is not the case that *anything* hampering the Court of Protection in the exercise of its duty, or done in wanton defiance of its objectives, is capable of being an interference with the administration of justice and therefore a criminal contempt.)

3–110 *[Add to note 175]*

Delete the reference to *Archbold* 2013, para 28–113.

I. Breaches classified as criminal at common law

2. *Failing to answer questions when ordered to do so*

[Add to note 184] 3–116

See *JSC BTA Bank v Solodchenko* [2011] EWCA Civ 1241 at [56], where it was suggested, in the context of civil contempt, that a sentencing court might appropriately give an indication as to the portion of a custodial term which could potentially be remitted in the event of subsequent compliance with the relevant order. See also at 14–14A and 14–45 below. See also *Smith v Doncaster Metropolitan Borough Council* [2014] EWCA Civ 16.

J. Orders relating to wards of court

[Add to note 195] 3–122

It is interesting to note that the Official Solicitor sought to argue that this principle applied by analogy to the Court of Protection in *M,Re (Incapacitated Adult) (Best Interests Declaration: Potential Contempt)* [2015] EWCOP 3. The judge disagreed, stating, at [48], both that the wardship jurisdiction has a paternalistic quality which does not easily equate to protection of vulnerable adults, and that the law in relation to wardship "is, to my mind, largely anomalous" This would appear to confirm wardship as a special category in contempt.

[Add to end of paragraph] 3–123

In *W (A Child) (Abduction: Committal), Re* [2011] EWCA Civ 1196, a father abducted his daughter who was a ward of court and refused to comply with orders to return her, and to provide information as to her whereabouts. The court did not expressly characterise the contempt as criminal, but in considering the penalty referred to the need for "regard to the likely sentence that might be imposed for similar conduct in the criminal court". See at 12–8 and 14–21A below and the discussion in *R. v Kayani* [2011] EWCA Crim 2871, cited at 3–85 above.

III. POINTS OF COMPARISON BETWEEN CIVIL AND CRIMINAL CONTEMPTS

B. Appeals

[Add to note 235] 3–144

See also *Att Gen v Dallas* [2012] EWHC 156 (Admin); [2012] 1 W.L.R. 991.

D. Waiver

1. *The nature of the issue*

3–163 *[Add to note 273]*

But see *Williams v Minnock*, 24 June 2015 (unreported). There Judge Wildblood allowed the father to withdraw committal proceedings, and waive the mother's failure to hand over their child in accordance with a court order. The mother had gone "on the run" with the child, and the case had generated a lot of media interest. When the mother and child were found, the court noted that the father was also a victim of the mother's breach, and his wish to withdraw the application had to be respected ("It is only the mercy of the father that spares this mother.").

3. *Public interest can exclude waiver*

3–169 *[Add to end of paragraph]*

Similar considerations were addressed in *Williams v Minnock* [2015] All ER (D) 174 (Jun), Judge Wildblood at [4]:

> "However, the public knowledge of this case has come at a price. Mr Williams now wishes to end the public displays of the difficulties that affect Ethan's upbringing and wishes the remaining disputes to be heard away from the glare of publicity. If the committal application is continued, he feels that there will be a dramatic increase in the emotional focus that has been directed to him, Ethan and the family as a whole. He wishes that to stop and that is why he does not wish to pursue this application. Once again I commend him for his decision. His decision is, in my opinion, a strong and commendable display of parental responsibility and is plainly based on the best interests of Ethan. He does not wish Ethan to be exposed to the continuing publicity that Ms Minnock has caused. The guardian and the child's solicitor have indicated that they would not wish to initiate any contempt proceedings on behalf of Ethan."

The court accordingly allowed the committal application to be abandoned on the basis that this was in the child's best interests.

E. Institution of proceedings

3–176 *[Add to note 295]*

See now CPR r.81.3(3). The Law Commission in its Consultation Paper No.209 proposed, at 2.60–2.63, that it would be useful for the Attorney General to publish from time to time a "prosecution" policy. This proposal has some support: see the discussion at 2–197 above. See at 4–325B below.

3–176 *[Add to end of paragraph]*

The Law Commission has proposed that the Attorney General should publish a "prosecution" policy to promote transparency and consistency:

Consultation Paper No.209 at 2.60–2.63. See also I. Cram & N. Taylor, "*The Law Commission's Contempt proposals — getting the balance right?*" [2013] Crim. L.R. 6 465–482. The article suggests too that consideration should be given to making any decision by the Attorney General refusing consent to initiate proceedings amenable to judicial review. This is discussed further at 2–197 above.

[Add to note 297] **3–178**

See also *Bedfordshire Police v RU and FHS* [2013] EWHC 2350 (Fam), [2014] 1 FLR 286, [2013] All ER (D) 22 (Aug) at [30] *et seq*. It was held by Holman J that the police had no *locus standi* to apply for committal in relation to the alleged breach of a protection order made in respect of forced marriage. Agreement with this conclusion was expressed by Sir James Munby P in *Jones, Re* [2013] EWHC 2579 (Fam), [2014] 2 FCR 354, [2014] 1 FLR 852, [2013] All ER (D) 202 (Aug) at [16].

[Add to 301] **3–181**

See now CPR Pt 81.

F. Sanctions

[Add to note 310] **3–183**

See also *Back Office Ltd v Percival* [2013] EWHC 3776 (QB), *R v Savva* [2014] EWCA Crim 1386.

[Add to end of paragraph] **3–184**

The court can impose a fresh penalty for a subsequent contempt, which may give rise to an overall total in excess of two years: see *W (A Child) (Abduction: Committal), Re* [2011] EWCA Civ 1196. When imposing penalties in such circumstances, the court should naturally have regard to the total period already spent in prison. See the discussion at 14–21A below.

G. Release *ex debito justitiae* no longer available

[Add to note 316] **3–188**

See now CPR Pt 81. See also *JSC BTA Bank v Solodchenko* [2012] EWCA Civ 1241 at [56], where it was suggested that, at least in the case of civil contempt, the court imposing a penalty might indicate what portion of a custodial term could potentially be remitted in the event of subsequent compliance with the relevant order. In *Doncaster MBC v Elizabeth Watson* [2011] EWHC 2376 (Fam) at [15], Sir Nicholas Wall P had made an order for suspension on an application to purge. After *Harris v Harris* had been drawn to his attention, on the same day, he handed down a further judgment: [2011] EWHC 2498. He substituted an order for the applicant's immediate and unconditional release. The correct reference for *Harris v Harris* in the Court of Appeal is [2001] EWCA Civ 1645.

3–188 [*Add to note 318]*

In *Solicitor General v Dodd* [2014] EWHC 1285 (QB) the fact the contemnor had been sent to serve his sentence at HMP Pentonville, a category B/C prison with harsh conditions that had had a greater effect on the contemnor than had been anticipated by the court at the time of sentence, was sufficient reason to justify his early release.

3–189 *[Add to note 319]*

See now CPR r.81.31 for the early release provisions. This does not adopt the phrase "any contempt of court", but simply refers to "a person committed to prison for contempt of court ...". Part 81 applies, unless otherwise stated, to the Court of Appeal, High Court and county courts. See 14–29 and 14–32 below.

3–189 *[Add to note 320]*

The Supreme Court Act is now referred to as the Senior Courts Act 1981. It would seem that CPR r.81.31 does not on its face apply to Crown Courts, but s.45(4) of the Senior Courts Act confers on the Crown Court the like powers to those of the High Court in relation to contempt. See at 6–45A below.

3–190 *[Add to note 321]*

CPR r.81.31 applies to county courts.

I. Exercise of the Royal prerogative

3–192 *[Add to note 334]*

See now CPR r.81.31 and at 14–29 *et seq* below.

J. The privilege against self-incrimination

3–195 *[Add to note 340]*

See the reference to this privilege in *Invideous v Thorogood* [2014] EWCA Civ 1511 (finding of contempt quashed on appeal because the contemnor had not been told of his right to remain silent and it was not enough that he was reminded of his right not to incriminate himself.)

[Add to note 345] **3–195**

See now *Archbold* 2015, para.15–361 *et seq.*

[Add to note 351] **3–199**

So far as civil proceedings are concerned, see CPR 81.28(2)(a), which provides that a respondent is entitled to give oral evidence whether or not the respondent has filed and served written evidence and, if doing so, may be cross-examined. Criminal Procedure Rules 2015 (SI 2015/1490) in force with effect from 5 October 2015, only make express provision for cross-examination of a person "who made a statement which another party wants to introduce as hearsay": r.48.14. See the general discussion of self-incrimination by Roth J in *Milsom v Ablyazov* [2011] EWHC 1846 (Ch), at [9] *et seq* and also by the Court of Appeal in *Mohan v Mohan* [2013] EWCA Civ 586, [2013] Fam Law 959, at 15–62 below.

1. *Senior Courts Act: s.72*

[Add to note 358] **3–203**

The standard form of order has been amended. CPR PD 25A now states expressly that there is no privilege against self-incrimination in intellectual property cases to which s.72 applies. The current form of search order requires the supervising solicitor to explain the terms and effect of the order to the respondent "in everyday language" and to advise him in respect of a number of matters, including the privilege against self-incrimination: PD25A para 7.4(4)(b)(ii). If the case concerns an intellectual property dispute, it would therefore have to be explained that the privilege does not apply.

[Add to note 360] **3–205**

See also *Tchenguiz v Serious Fraud Office* [2014] EWCA Civ 1409 (absent special circumstances the court would not ordinarily permit use of documents disclosed in civil proceedings for a collateral purpose).

[Add new paragraph] **3–211A**

One of the cases forming part of the "phone hacking" litigation, which came before the Chancery Division from 2008 onwards, gave rise to a self-incrimination point: *Coogan and Phillips v NGN Ltd and Mulcaire* [2012] UKSC 28. A defendant relied on this doctrine and the Claimant argued that s.72 excluded any such defence. She was successful before Mann J. ([2010] EWHC 2952 (Ch)) and the Court of Appeal ([2012] EWCA Civ 48). Lord Neuberger M.R. had expressed the general view, at [18], that privilege against self-incrimination had "had its day in civil proceedings" but that nevertheless it remained part of the common law, despite certain statutory qualifications imposed upon it, and that it would be for the legislature to remove it or cut it down further. It was recognised that, in achieving an appropriate balance, it would be right to provide some protection corresponding to that contained in s.72(3), to the effect that disclosed material should not be admissible against the discloser in criminal proceedings (i.e. "proceedings for any related offence or for the recovery of any related penalty"). See also *Kensington International Ltd v Republic of Congo* [2008] 1 W.L.R. 1144 at [36], per Moore-Bick L.J. As already noted, s.72(4) makes specific reference to perjury and contempt of court: in any such context, relevant disclosed material will *not* be rendered inadmissible. (See also the discussion of *Mohan v Mohan* [20113] EWCA Civ 586; [2013] Fam. Law 959 at 15–62 below.)

3–211B *[Add new paragraph]*

In the Supreme Court, two issues fell for determination: first, as to the meaning of the words in s.72(2)(a) "proceedings for infringement of rights pertaining to ... intellectual property" and, secondly, whether proceedings for conspiracy should be regarded as being "for a related offence" within the meaning of s.72(5). As to the first, it so happened that Ms Phillips' mobile phone contained information of a commercially confidential nature: it was thus held that her proceedings were indeed in respect of rights pertaining to intellectual property. The result might have been different if the information had related to confidential matters of a purely personal character. As Lord Walker put it, at [30], at the time the provisions were enacted in 1981 the law on confidence had not become "bifurcated", as it later did under the influence of the Human Rights Act 1998. At that time, Parliament was concerned to prevent remedies against commercial piracy from being frustrated by pleas of privilege. This policy came about in response to the decision of the House of Lords in *Rank Film Distributors Ltd v Video Information Centre* [1982] A.C. 380, where it had been reluctantly held that a search order could not be made because of the defendant's potential exposure to a charge of conspiracy to defraud: see at pp.441, 448 and 455–6.

3–211C *[Add new paragraph]*

Turning to the second issue, Lord Walker observed that for practical purposes the conspiracy point was raised as a new issue in the Supreme Court. The statute referred to any offence committed by or in the course of the relevant infringement. Conspiracy is a continuing offence. If there was an agreement to intercept, then the offence of conspiracy would continue for so long as it was being performed: any interception would be in the course of the infringement.

3 *The provisions in CPR r.35.9*

3–213 *[Add to note 374]*

See now CPR PD 81 para 14.3(3).

4. *The need to file evidence notwithstanding the privilege*

[Add to note 375] **3–214**

See the wording of CPR r.81.28(3): "The court may require or permit any party or other person (other than the respondent) to give oral evidence at the hearing". The court cannot *require* a respondent to give evidence.

[Add to note 376] **3–214**

See also *Forrester Ketley v Brent* [2012] EWCA Civ 324. (The Civil Procedure Rules, rather than the Criminal Procedure Rules, are appropriate for a contempt hearing.)

K. *Autrefois acquit* and *convict*

[Add to end of paragraph] **3–220**

The point was illustrated in *Re W (A Child) (Abduction: Committal)* [2011] EWCA Civ 1196 at [37]. But whether the Court will commit the contemnor to a further sentence on a fresh application will depend on whether it is necessary and proportionate: see *Button v Salama* [2013] EWHC 4152 (Fam). The application before the Court was for a contemnor father to be remanded in prison for a further 12 months for a continuing failure to comply with an order to reveal his daughter's whereabouts. The Court held that, although there could lawfully be successive terms of imprisonment for further and repeated breaches of orders, the court should not lose sight of Parliament's aim in enacting s.14 Contempt of Court Act 1981 or attempt to subvert that purpose by way of successive sentences for an aggregate total in excess of two years. It appeared that prison had lost its coercive effect on this contemnor.

[Add to note 390] **3–221**

See now also the discussion by Sir James Munby P in *Jones, Re* [2013] EWHC 2579 (Fam), [2014] 2 FCR 354, [2014] 1 FLR 852, [2013] All ER (D) 202 (Aug) at [18]–[24].

[Add to note 402] **3–231**

See also *Jones, Re* [2013] EWHC 2579 (Fam), [2014] 2 FCR 354, [2014] 1 FLR 852, [2013] All ER (D) 202 (Aug)at [18]–[24].

L. Extra-territorial jurisdiction

3–233 *[Add to note 405]*

See now *Archbold* 2015, paras 2–33 and 2–34. See also G Williams, *Venue and the Ambit of Criminal Law (Part 3)* (1965) 81 LQR 518; M Hirst, *Jurisdiction and the Ambit of the Criminal Law* (2003); M Goode, *The Tortured Tale of Criminal Jurisdiction* (1997), 21 Melbourne University Law Review, 411; C Ryngaert, *Territorial Jurisdiction over Cross-Frontier Offences: Revisiting a Classic Problem of International Criminal Law* (2009), 9 International Criminal Law Review, 187. The Law Commission considered the problems caused by the Internet and social media in a number of contexts, including the fact that many of those communicating by these means, and those who host websites, are based outside the jurisdiction. This means that it is especially difficult to shelter jurors from prejudicial material emanating from such sources. One proposal canvassed was to create a statutory power for the courts to grant restraining orders against persons within the jurisdiction, who would not have been regarded traditionally as "publishers", but who have a sufficient degree of control over accessibility to enable them to remove any offending material on at least a temporary basis. This would obviously not provide a fool-proof means of overcoming jurisdictional problems, but it might in some circumstances afford the means of reducing the risks significantly. Whether any such order would be granted would naturally depend on showing to the court's satisfaction that such a restraint was necessary and proportionate. If it could, in the particular case, only amount to a futile gesture, then it would not be appropriate to grant it. The extent of the court's reach in relation to property located abroad was considered in the context of Pt 5 of the Proceeds of Crime Act 2002 in *SOCA v Perry (Nos 1&2)* [2012] UKSC 35; [2013] 1 AC 182 and in *SOCA v O'Docherty* [2013] EWCA Civ 518. The Supreme Court held by a majority that the definition of "property wherever situated" in s.316(4) of the statute should not be interpreted as including property abroad because of the presumption against extra-territorial reach. In the later case of *O'Docherty* the Court of Appeal was concerned with the effect of the *Perry* decision in relation to orders already made. By a majority (Mummery LJ dissenting), it was held that the court should vary a property freezing order which had been made (prior to the *Perry* decision) in relation to property abroad — even though it was merely ancillary to a final civil recovery order (made even earlier). See also *Cadder v HMA* [2010] 1 WLR 2601, where it had been held that once a final order has been made, it would not be liable to be set aside or varied purely because a later court decision has interpreted the law differently. See, however, the discussion of that case by Lord McClusky in "*Supreme Error*" [2011] 15 Edin LR 276 and by PR Ferguson in "*Repercussions of the Cadder Case*" [2011] Crim LR 743. See also Pamela R Ferguson and Fiona Raitt, "*A Clear and Coherent Package of Reforms? The Scottish Government Paper Upon the Carloway Report*" [2012] Crim. L.R. 909. See also D. Giannoulopoulos, "'*North of the Border and Across the Channel': Custodial Legal Assistance Reforms in Scotland and France*" [2013] Crim. L.R. 369. The Law Commission's proposals to grant restraining orders were not included in the Criminal Justice and Courts Act 2015, which instead made new offences relating to juror research, and granted the courts power to order jurors to surrender electronic communication devices — see Criminal Justice and Courts Act 2015 s.69–74.

[Add to end of paragraph] **3–235**

It is clear from the decision in *Demesne Investments, Re* [2013] NICh 2 that it is not necessarily inappropriate to make a finding of contempt merely because there would be difficulty in enforcing any penalty imposed.

M. Hearsay evidence

2. *Reform of hearsay law in criminal cases*

[Add to end of paragraph] **3–237**

Criminal Procedure Rules 2015 (SI 2015/1490) in force with effect from 5 October 2015, r.48.11 provides that hearsay evidence is admissible under the Civil Evidence Act 1995 for civil contempt proceedings which take place in a criminal court: for an example, see *Director of Serious Fraud Office v B* [2012] EWCA Crim 67, cited above at 3–11A. See also *Archbold* 2015, at para 28–95, where it is submitted that summary proceedings for contempt would amount to criminal proceedings in relation to which the "strict rules of evidence apply", and thus that hearsay would be admissible in line with the Criminal Justice Act 2003 ss.114 (1) and 134 (1), see 3–41 above.

3. *Civil contempts*

[Add to note 417] **3–243**

The Family Proceedings (Amendment No.4) Rules 2005, Family Proceedings Rules 1991 and Family Proceedings Rules 2010 have all been replaced. Provisions on hearsay evidence in family proceedings are now to be found in the current Family Procedure Rules Pt 23.

4. *The Civil Evidence Act 1995*

[Add to note 422] **3–245**

See also *Masri v Consolidated Contractors International* [2011] EWHC 1024 (Comm) at [157].

[Add to note 427] **3–247**

See also *Al-Khawaja v UK* (2012) 54 E.H.R.R. 23.

N. Fresh evidence on appeal

3–248 *[Add to note 428]*

See now *Archbold* 2015 para.7–205 *et seq.*

O. The standard of proof

3–255 *[Add to note 441]*

See also *Airbus Operations v Roberts* [2012] EWHC 3632 (Admin).

P. The approach to mens rea in civil and criminal contempt

3–256 *[Add to note 446]*

See also *Masri v Consolidated Contractors International* [2011] EWHC 1024 (Comm) at [155].

Q. A possible distinction as to the relevance of duress

3–260 *[Add to note 453]*

See also *JSC BTA Bank v Shalabayev* [2011] EWHC 2903 (Ch).

CHAPTER 4

THE STATUTORY REGIME FOR STRICT LIABILITY

I. THE STRICT LIABILITY RULE

C. The uncertain scope of strict liability at common law

[Add to note 16] **4–5**

See now *Gatley on Libel and Slander*, 12th ed (2013), para.6–30.

[Add to note 17] **4–5**

Section 10 of the Defamation Act 2013 extends the protection from libel actions to anyone who is not an "author, editor or publisher". It simply provides that there is no jurisdiction to bring a defamation action against such a person unless it is "not reasonably practicable" to bring a claim against the author, editor or publisher. Thus the legal position in respect of publication so far as contempt is concerned would appear to be diverging from that applying in the context of defamation, rather than converging. See now Gatley on Libel and Slander, 12th ed (2013), para.6–31.

D. The statutory terminology further examined

3. *"Publications"*

[Add new paragraph] **4–27A**

The Law Commission considered the definition of "publication" in the context of new (online) media. It took the position that "communication in whatever form" was a wide definition that "seemed on its own to cover comprehensively or near comprehensively the new media": Consultation Paper No.209 at 3.20. Its preliminary view was that the definition of publication in s.2(1) of the Act was broad enough to cover all, or almost all, material on the internet, including on social media sites, photo sharing websites, microblogging services and video sharing websites. The senior judiciary, in its response to the consultation, favoured putting the definition of "publication" (including the place of publication) on a statutory footing: "A Judicial Response to the Law Commission Consultation Paper No 209" at para.28: *https://www.judiciary.gov.uk/wp-content/uploads/JCO/Documents/Consultations/sen-judiciary-response-to-law-comm-on-contempt-court.pdf* [accessed 14 July, 2015]. The Law Commission published its final report in December 2013: see "*Contempt of Court (1): Juror Misconduct and Internet Publications*" (Law Com No. 340) at *http://www.lawcom.gov.uk/wp-content/uploads/2015/06/lc340_contempt_of_court_juror_misconduct.pdf*. The report recommended the maintenance of the current statutory definition of 'publication' under s.2 (1) of the 1981 Act. See further the discussion at 4–30E below.

4. *"Publication" on the internet*

4–29 *[Add to note 63]*

HMA v Beggs (No.2) 2002 S.L.T 139; S.C.C.R 879 was applied in respect of online publications in *R. v Harwood* [2012] EW Misc 27 (CC), July 20, 2012 (Fulford J.). A police officer was on trial for manslaughter. The judge had ruled that the prosecution could not adduce evidence of two previous incidents of bad character. Yet articles referring to previous allegations of wrongdoing by the defendant remained available online. It was held that two such articles about the defendant which remained on a newspaper's website gave rise to a substantial risk of serious prejudice and would thus amount to contempt. See also *R. v Sheppard* [2010] EWCA Crim 65 at [34]–[35], which was a case concerning s.19 of the Public Order Act 1986.

4–30A *[Add new paragraph]*

The interpretation in *HMA v Beggs (No.2)* 2002 S.L.T 139; S.C.C.R 879 of the words "the time of the publication" in s.2(3) of the Act, as including material which was previously published and remains available on the internet, prompted the Law Commission to propose changes to the Act: Consultation Paper No. 209 at 3.63 to 3.86. Its consultation paper asked whether s.2(3) should be amended, so that "the time of the publication" would be expressed to be the time of first publication only. Part of the rationale for the law to be changed in that way is that the current situation imposes a potentially onerous burden on those operating websites to review them proactively, in case circumstances have changed, for example because a person has been arrested and the website contained previously published articles about bad character. The consultation notes that, presently, a publisher could be liable for contempt merely because of a change of circumstances which are outside its control and without any specific (active) conduct on its part, which is an unusual foundation for even strict liability. A suggested solution was put forward by the Commission to the effect it should be a defence to proceedings for a strict liability contempt that the offending material had been published before the proceedings had become "active" for the purposes of the strict liability rule. However, the Attorney-General should be given a power to issue a formal warning that material in the archives was likely to have a prejudicial effect upon a forthcoming trial, and was at risk of proceedings for contempt if it continued to be published. This suggestion proved unpopular with, inter alia, the press (and in particular, the Society of Editors) and the Joint Parliamentary Committee on the Human Rights Act, both of which took the view that the arrangement would give the Attorney-General too great a role in affecting the freedom of the press, and the Attorney-General announced in Parliament that the clause giving effect to this suggestion would be withdrawn. (see 1–190E above and 4–30 E below).

[Add new paragraph] **4–30B**

It was recognised that prejudicial material previously published on the internet could pose a risk to a defendant's art.6 rights because of the ease with which it could come to the attention of a juror. It therefore proposed that, in the event of s.2(3) being amended, the courts should have a corresponding power to order a publisher to remove or disable access to any previously published articles which, because of a change in circumstances, had come to create a substantial risk of serious prejudice. Such orders would be for a specific period, e.g. the duration of the trial, and could be made against the primary publisher or, if necessary, anyone with sufficient control over the material. It would then be a contempt if the person failed without lawful excuse to comply with the order. See also the discussion at 1–190A above.

[Add new paragraph] **4–30C**

The Law Commission recommended these changes having concluded that they would afford some protection for a defendant's art.6 rights, that they would impose no more than a proportionate burden on publishers, and that they would be compliant with art.10. It proposed that either the prosecution or a defendant could apply for an order, without the permission of the Attorney General. The Law Commission is due to publish its final report in the Spring of 2014. Its authors recommend the proposal as giving "clarity to publishers" and "adequate protection for defendants": see A. Kervick, *Archbold Review* 2013 1, 5. The Law Commission published its final report in December 2013. See para.4–30E below.

[Add new paragraph] **4–30D**

The response of the senior judiciary expressed reservations about the proposed new "take down" orders. It was inclined to favour the solution that trial judges should use practical measures during the trial process, specifically tailored to the circumstances, to address any problems arising from prejudicial material remaining available online. It was suggested that the take down orders would (or should) rarely be used because old material would normally be unlikely to meet the threshold of creating a substantial risk of serious prejudice. In any event, the court would first have to consider adopting other measures which would interfere less with freedom of expression, including enquiring of the jurors what they had read online: "A Judicial Response to the Law Commission Consultation Paper No 209" at paras 10 and 32–49: *http://www.judiciary.gov.uk/Resources/JCO/Documents/Consultations/sen-judiciary-response-to-law-comm-on-contempt-court.pdf* [Accessed 15 September 2015].

4–30E *[Add new paragraph]*

Commentators have also expressed reservations. In "*The Law Commission's Contempt proposals — getting the balance right?*" Crim. L.R. 2013 6 465–482, I. Cram & N. Taylor advocate focussing on measures designed to restrict jurors accessing archive material online. On a practical level, they argue that such measures could provide effective means of meeting the risks to a defendant's art.6 rights, whereas take down orders risk being ineffective because, in respect of intermediaries, many are likely to be outside the jurisdiction. They also raise the principled objection that such orders against intermediaries would risk making them criminally liable for the exercise of freedom of speech by other people.

Following the Law Commission's consultation (No. 209), in December 2013 it recommended amending the law of contempt, as it affected publications on the internet: see "*Contempt of Court (1): Juror Misconduct and Internet Publications*" (Law Com No. 340) at *http://www.lawcom.gov.uk/wp-content/uploads/2015/06/lc340_contempt_of_court_juror_misconduct.pdf*. Those recommendations were largely adopted by the Government in 2014 and it proposed amendments to the Contempt of Court Act 1981 (as it applied to England and Wales) in the Criminal Justice and Courts Bill. The proposals would have meant that publications which had been first published on the internet prior to the active period, and remained available after proceedings became active, would still fall within the ambit of strict liability: the defences available to a publisher/Distributor would have been amended accordingly. The defence of innocent dissemination under s.3 would have been available to a publisher or Distributor who continued to make material available to the public after proceedings had become active *unless* he knew or had reason to suspect that proceedings were active, or that the material fell within s.2(2). By a proposed new section, a publisher would have had a defence in relation to any material uploaded onto the internet prior to proceedings becoming active and which remained available, unless he failed to remove that material in response to notification by the Attorney General that the material should be removed because it was prejudicial. On 30 June 2014, however, the Attorney General informed the House of Commons in a written statement that the Government would not pursue the proposals and would be seeking to remove clauses 51 and 52, which by that stage contained the relevant proposals, from the bill. See *http://www.*

publications.parliament.uk/pa/cm201415/cmhansrd/cm140630/wmstext/140630 m0001.htm#14063013000002 (last accessed July 8, 2015).

[Add new paragraph] **4–30F**

Separately, the Law Commission also questioned whether the Act needed amendment to add a statutory definition of the *place* of publication (at 3.87–3.95).

7. *"Includes" is equivalent to "means"*

[Add to end of paragraph] **4–35**

The contrast between the term "publication" in the 1981 Act and private communications was considered (in the context of an order made pursuant to s.11 of the Act) in *R(Yam)* [2014] EWHC 3558 (Admin), [2015] 1 Cr. App. R. 10. (See 4–52B, 7–110A, 7–142A below).

D. The statutory terminology further examined

9. *"... or any section of the public"*

(c) *The context of the communication*

[Add new paragraph] **4–52A**

In the context of new media, it is possible that a tweet would be found to have been addressed to a "section of the public" because of the open nature of Twitter's platform, even if the Twitter user had a limited number of followers all of whom were known to him. In *Chambers v DPP* [2012] EWHC 2157 (Admin); [2013] 1 W.L.R. 1833, the Court was considering the use of Twitter in the context of s.127 of the Communications Act 2003. The defendant had posted a tweet which he may have intended only to be read by his followers, who would know him and have been limited in number. The Court, nonetheless, accepted the prosecution's case that the *potential* recipients of the message would include the public as a whole. It is anticipated that, in considering the effect of any particular tweet in the context of s.2, regard would be had to the ephemeral nature of Twitter and the number and nature of followers.

In *R (Yam) v Central Criminal Court* [2014] EWCA 3558 (Admin); [2015] **4–52B** 1 Cr. App. R. 10, the Divisional Court was concerned with the ambit of an order made by a trial judge under s.11 of the 1981 Act and other powers. The order prohibited the publication of evidence and submissions which had been heard in camera (in order to protect national security) during the applicant's trial for murder and other offences. The applicant wanted to use the protected information in support of his application to the European Court of Human Rights, complaining that the conduct of his trial had infringed his Article 6 rights. While disagreeing with the trial judge's analysis of the meaning of "publication" (which would have included private communications), Elias LJ was inclined, at [50], to the view that a communication to "the court staff and judges in Strasbourg as a body" would be a publication to a "section of the public" within the Act. It was not, however, necessary to determine the issue because the order preventing publication had also been made pursuant to other powers (not specified in the order). Further, under s.12(1)(c) of the Administration of Justice Act 1960, the communication to the court in Strasbourg would be a contempt. (The wider meaning of the word "publication" in the 1960 Act is discussed in the main text at 8–130 to 8–135.) The court considered how different types of risks would require different degrees of prohibition on reporting/communicating the relevant information and highlighted the apparent inability of the 1981 Act to protect against some types of risk to national security (which could arise from limited communications, even to one person).

On 29 May 2015, the Supreme Court granted the applicant permission to appeal the Divisional Court's refusal to allow him to disclose the material.

(e) *General conclusions on the meaning of "section of the public"*

4–54 *[Add to note 100]*

See *Aitken v DPP* [2015] EWHC 1079 (Admin), for a consideration of editorial responsibility for publication in the context of s.39 of the Children and Young Persons Act 1933 (remaining in force until 13 April 2015), which imposed potential liability on "any person who publishes". There is also a review of an editor's potential liability for breaches of other statutory reporting restrictions. It was held (unsurprisingly) that an editor did not fall outside the scope of "any person who publishes". Section 39 is amended by s.79 of the Criminal Justice and Courts Act 2015 in force with effect from 13 April 2015.

4–54 *[Add to note 107]*

See now *Gatley on Libel and Slander*, 12th ed (2013), para 6–53.

4–54A *[Add new paragraph]*

The Law Commission did not consider that the term "section of the public" in s.2(1) would itself require amendment or definition in order to deal with new media. Any specific internet service or publication could be considered on a case by case basis, whether the court is addressing an email, a website or a posting on a social networking site where the poster has utilised privacy settings: Consultation Paper No.209 at 3.29; "*Contempt of Court (1): Juror Misconduct and Internet Publications*" (Law Com No. 340) at *http://www.lawcom.gov.uk/wp-content/uploads/2015/06/lc340_contempt_of_court_juror_misconduct.pdf* at 2.45.

E. Intention to publish required

[Add to note 109] 4–55

See, in the context of providing a platform for blogs, *Tamiz v Google Inc* [2012] EWCA Civ 68; [2013] E.M.L.R 14 at [23]–[36]. A provider of a website which hosted a popular internet discussion forum was held to be a secondary publisher in *Oriental Press Group Ltd v Fevaworks Solutions Ltd* [2013] HKCFA 47, although it was entitled to rely on a defence of innocent dissemination at common law (at least for so long as it had no knowledge of the defamatory posts). See also the discussion of the potential liability of internet intermediaries and of the Law Commission's Consultation Paper No.209 at 4–204A and *Contempt of Court (1): Juror Misconduct and Internet Publications* (Law Comm No 340), at 2.18–2.20.

II. RESTRICTIONS ON THE ACTUS REUS OF STRICT LIABILITY CONTEMPTS

D. The principles summarised

[Add to note 163] 4–89

See also the approach of the European Court of Human Rights (Fourth Chamber) in *Abdulla Ali v United Kingdom* (Appn No. 30971/12), June 30, 2015. It rejected the application that prejudicial pre-trial publicity amounted to a violation of the applicant's Art 6 rights to a fair trial. The applicant was convicted of conspiracy to murder, but the jury failed to return verdicts on other counts. Following the verdict there was widespread media coverage which a judge later described as "an avalanche of objectionable material". A retrial of the other counts then became necessary. The applicant argued that the earlier publicity had rendered the retrial unfair. This was rejected. The Court referred to the lapse of time between the publicity and the retrial, as well as the ability of the jury to follow the trial judge's directions and the practical steps taken by the trial judge to ensure a fair trial. It was held that the steps taken were sufficient to ensure a fair trial. The Court noted that no decision of the European Court of Human Rights had been drawn to its attention in which it had found that prejudicial pre-trial publicity had made a fair trial wholly impossible.

[Add new paragraph] 4–93A

The above principles were applied in *Att Gen v Times Newspapers Ltd* [2012] EWHC 3195 (Admin). A woman (NE), who had recently been released from a secure mental health unit, stabbed and killed another woman in the street. *The Times* reported that NE had previously been convicted of manslaughter, having stabbed her mother a few years earlier. The Court rejected the newspaper's argument that, on the facts, there was no likelihood of NE entering a not guilty plea. It held that the reporting of NE's previous conviction was undoubtedly potentially seriously prejudicial, and warned that the media should not "second guess" whether or not there would be a trial. To do so, would be to pay insufficient regard to the primary need to maintain the integrity of the trial process, as a publisher would inevitably be reaching a conclusion with incomplete knowledge of the relevant facts.

4–93B *[Add new paragraph]*

Nevertheless, the Court found (narrowly) that the publication did not amount to a contempt. It could not be sure that the publication had caused a substantial risk of serious prejudice in light of a number of factors, including the limited circulation of the newspaper in the area from which jurors would be drawn, the largely unsensational nature of the coverage and the potential operation of the fade factor by the time of any trial. The decision illustrates the application of principles 6 to 10 identified in *Att Gen v MGN Ltd* [1997] 1 All E.R. 456. The court rejected the Attorney General's alternative argument based on "impeding" for the same reasons.

4–93C *[Add new paragraph]*

In *Att Gen v Associated Newspapers Ltd* [2012] EWHC 2029 (Admin), the publishers of the *Daily Mail* and the *Daily Mirror* were found to be in contempt in respect of articles which formed part of an "avalanche" of prejudicial media coverage which had led a trial judge to discharge the jury. The defendant faced charges of the kidnap and murder of one girl and the kidnapping of another. The jury returned a guilty verdict on the murder charge prior to the offending publication, but were still deliberating on the kidnapping charge in respect of the second girl. The murder conviction received extensive coverage in the media. In light of television coverage following the verdict, the CPS emailed various media organisations reminding them that proceedings were still active and the jury was still deliberating. The next morning, both newspapers published background material about the defendant which had not been before the jury. The trial judge discharged the jury (although that fact in itself would not determine the issue of liability for contempt). On contempt proceedings brought by the Attorney General, the court held that even though the jury knew that the defendant had previously been convicted of murder and had itself convicted him of another murder, the additional material published by each of the newspapers was highly prejudicial. The fact that the jury had already heard serious bad character evidence did not mean that other information could not create a substantial risk of serious prejudice. Furthermore, although the television coverage had been prejudicial, the additional material in each of the newspapers was sufficient — by itself — to meet the s.2(2) test, applying *Att Gen v Independent Television News* [1995] 2 All E.R. 370 at 381.

E. The application of the common law when s.2(2) does not apply

[Add to note 169] **4–94**

See the decision of Newton J in *A Healthcare NHS Trust v P* [2015] EWCOP 15, at [56]-[59] and [67]. The judge considered that, were a media organisation to publish information supplied to it for the purpose of enabling it to decide whether to oppose an application for a reporting restriction order, such conduct would amount to contempt at common law, even if the publication was not a strict liability contempt (which, in any event, the judge thought it would be). This would be an interference with the administration of justice, in thwarting the court's order, quite apart from the matter of any prejudice caused to the particular proceedings.

H. "Impeded"

[Add new paragraph] **4–116A**

The Law Commission has consulted on whether the test in s.2(2) is suitable: Consultation Paper No.209 at 2.44–2.49. It questioned whether (i) the threshold for prejudice/ impediment is too high, and whether publication creating less serious prejudice should suffice for contempt; (ii) whether "substantial" risk was too low a threshold and whether "likelihood" of risk should be required to prove contempt; and (iii) whether the Act should be amended to make the tests for impediment and prejudice distinct.

The senior judiciary response did not recognise any need to amend the Act to distinguish further between the notions of prejudice and impediment: "A Judicial Response to the Law Commission Consultation Paper No 209" at para.17: *http://www.judiciary.gov.uk/Resources/JCO/Documents/Consultations/ sen-judiciary-response-to-law-comm-on-contempt-court.pdf* [Accesssed July 14, 2015]. The recent cases of *Att Gen v Times Newspapers Ltd* [2012] EWHC 3195 (Admin) and *Att Gen v Associated Newspapers Ltd* [2012] EWHC 2029 (Admin) may betoken a trend for proceedings to be advanced expressly on both footings in the alternative. The Law Commission published its final report in December 2013 *"Contempt of Court (1): Juror Misconduct and Internet Publications"* (Law Com No. 340 at: *http:\\www.lawcom.gov.uk/wp-content/uploads/2015/06/lc340_contempt_of_court_junor_misconduct.pdf*

The authorities would seem to suggest that the test in s.2(2) remains appropriate and is not creating any difficulties in practice which would justify reform. A substantial body of case law now exists where the criteria articulated in older cases, especially in *Att Gen v MGN Ltd* [1997] 1 All E.R. 456, have been applied without too much difficulty.

III. CATEGORIES OF PERSONS THOUGHT SUSCEPTIBLE TO INFLUENCE

Who is thought susceptible to influence?

1. *Jurors*

4–121 *[Add to note 206]*

The case of *R. v H* [2012] EWCA Crim 1797 provides a further example of the confidence placed in juries to focus only on admissible evidence. A juror had disclosed prejudicial information to other members of the jury. The defendant appealed against his conviction on the ground that the trial judge had been wrong not to discharge the jury. His appeal was dismissed. It was held that the trial judge had properly managed the risk of prejudice when he discharged the juror who had disclosed the prejudicial information, and then asked the remaining jurors whether they were able to disregard the information they had been given: each claimed to be able to do so.

4–121 *[Add to note 208]*

See now *Mustafa Abu Hamza (No.1) v UK* (31411/07), (2011) 52 E.H.R.R. SE11.

4–121A *[Add new paragraph]*

The response of the senior judiciary to the Law Commission's Consultation Paper No.209 emphasised the confidence which can be placed in juries to consider only the evidence which they have heard. It pointed to the numerous examples of juries having to consider multiple charges and acquitting on some while convicting on other more serious ones: "A Judicial Response to the Law Commission Consultation Paper No.209" at paras 20–21: *http://www.judiciary.gov.uk/Resources/JCO/Documents/Consultations/sen-judiciary-response-to-law-comm-on-contempt-court.pdf* [Accessed 14 July, 2015].

3. *Professional judges generally*

4–128 *[Add to text at end of paragraph]*

The Law Commission has proposed amending Sch.1, so that the "active" period would end with the final verdict; a proposal which has the support of the senior judiciary: see Consultation Paper No.209 at 2.23–2.24; "A Judicial Response to the Law Commission Consultation Paper No.209" at para.6 *http://www.judiciary.gov.uk/Resources/JCO/Documents/Consultations/sen-judiciary-response-to-law-comm-on-contempt-court.pdf* [Accessed 14 July, 2015].

[Add to note 226] **4–135**

The prohibition is now found in CPR r.36.16.

4. *The Judicial Committee of the House of Lords and now the Supreme Court*

[Add to note 230] **4–139**

See also *A Healthcare Trust v P* [2015] EWCOP 15. Although it was not a case concerned with influencing the judiciary, the court was satisfied that the publication to the world at large of material contained in an application for a reporting restriction order would amount to a contempt at common law because it would be "thwarting the very purpose of the application, thereby making the application for reporting restrictions redundant" (at [59]).

IV. STRICT LIABILITY CONTEMPT AND ABUSE OF PROCESS

The interrelationship between strict liability contempt and abuse of process

[Add to note 261] **4–160**

See now the Criminal Procedure Rules 2015 (SI 2015/1490) in force with effect from 5 October 2015, r.3.20 (application to stay case for abuse of process). Abuse is addressed in *Archbold* 2015 at 4–75 to 4–100. Procedural matters are now covered in the Criminal Practice Directions 2015 [2015] EWCA Crim 1567, Division I at 3C. See also *Mustafa Abu Hamza (No1) v UK* (31411/07), (2011) 52 EHRR SE11.

[Add to note 282] **4–172**

See the decision of the ECtHR (Fourth Chamber) in *Abdulla Ali v United Kingdom* (Appn No 30971/12), June 30, 2015, summarised at 4-89, note 163 above. See also paragraph 4–121A.

[Add to note 292] **4–180**

See also *R. v Harwood* [2012] EW Misc 27 (CC), July 20, 2012, Central Criminal Court (Fulford J.).

The courts must not "speak with two voices"

[Add to text at end of paragraph] **4–187**

The approach was subsequently applied in *Att Gen v Associated Newspapers Ltd* [2012] EWHC 2029. The facts are summarised in 4–93C above.

4–187A *[Add new paragraph]*

In its consultation on the law of contempt, the Law Commission advocated keeping distinct the tests for contempt and for abuse of process. The two doctrines serve separate functions and involve different standards of proof: Consultation Paper No. 209, at 2.48–2.49. The response of the senior judiciary expressed agreement, concluding that "the tests must remain different": A Judicial Response to the Law Commission Consultation Paper No 209", at para 18 *https://www.judiciary.gov.uk/wp-content/uploads/JCO/Documents/Consultations/sen-judiciary-response-to-law-comm-on-contempt-court.pdf* [accessed July 14, 2015]

See also I. Cram & N. Taylor "*The Law Commission's Contempt proposals — getting the balance right?*" [2013] Crim L.R. 6 465–482. The authors argue that the sanction of contempt is an important safeguard for the fair trial process in respect of risks created by a publication prospectively — even though in the event the trial did not have to be abandoned and any such risk was effectively managed or neutralised by the trial judge.

V. WHEN ARE PROCEEDINGS "ACTIVE"?

A. Schedule 1 of the 1981 Act

4–189 *[Add to end of paragraph]*

One of the problems that has arisen in the light of modern developments in communication and, in particular, the continuing availability of archived material on the internet is that of *when* any such material should be deemed to have been published for the purpose of judging inter alia whether it gives rise to a substantial risk of prejudice. One suggestion canvassed by the Law Commission in its Consultation Paper No.209 is that it might be helpful to introduce a "single publication" rule, so that the material would be treated as published only once, when it first appeared, and those responsible for its publication or with control over its accessibility should not be treated as having some continuing obligation to monitor it in order to establish whether any legal problem has arisen such as, for example, that some criminal proceedings have subsequently become "active" in respect of which it might be said to be prejudicial. As the law stands for the time being, it would appear that the courts would regard the availability of archived material as representing a continuing publication: see e.g. *HMA v Beggs (No.2)* 2002 S.L.T. 139; *R. v Sheppard* [2010] EWCA Crim 65; and *R. v Harwood* [2012] EW Misc 27 (CC), July 20, 2012 (Fulford J.). Even if that is to remain the position, one possible solution would be to provide that any such continuing publication should only be regarded as capable of giving rise to strict liability contempt with regard to any proceedings that were "active" at the time of the original publication. That would alleviate any difficulties of monitoring, but in order to achieve balance by giving protection to the integrity of the trial process, the Law Commission has canvassed the possibility of creating a statutory power to direct the temporary removal of any seriously prejudicial allegations pending the outcome of the relevant proceedings. This would obviously require safeguards as to the art.10 rights of those affected (who might well include persons who would not ordinarily have been considered as "publishers" in the past, but who nonetheless have a degree of control over the continuing accessibility). Also, it gives rise to the interesting point of principle, to which the Law Commission has drawn attention, that the court would in such circumstances *ex hypothesi* be restraining publication, albeit only temporarily, of material when that publication would not otherwise itself be unlawful. These are issues which will need to be resolved in due course. The Law Commission made recommendations in December 2013 which were initially adopted by the government, but they were subsequently abandoned. See above at 4–30E.

B. The general scheme

[Add to each of notes 311, 312, 313 and 315] **4–191**

The provision came into force from 28 November 2011.

[Add to Schedule 1] **4–191**

Schedule 1 to the 1981 Act was amended by the Crime and Courts Act 2013 Sch. 17(3), para 34 which inserted a new sub-paragraph (ab) into para 7. It came into force on February 24, 2014 (subject to transitional provisions and savings) and provides:

> "(ab) in England and Wales, if they are discontinued by virtue of paragraph 11 of Schedule 17 to the Crime and Courts Act 2013 (deferred prosecution agreements);"

[Add new paragraph] **4–192A**

The Law Commission consulted on whether the commencement of the active period should remain as set out in Sch.1 or only be triggered by a later event, e.g. when a suspect is charged. It favoured maintaining the present law: Consultation Paper No.209 at 2.9 to 2.19. More contentious was its proposal that all police forces should adopt a policy of giving the names of arrestees to the media, except in circumstances when identifying the arrested person would be inappropriate. It suggested that this would remove uncertainty for the media about whether the active period had commenced in respect of a particular person. The Home Affairs Select Committee, in its report published on March 17 2015, adopted an approach similar to that of Leveson LJ in his *Report into the Culture, Practices and Ethics of the Press*, November 29, 2012, namely that arrestees should be granted anonymity: see 4–192B below.

4–192B *[Add new paragraph]*

Leveson L.J. in his *Report into the Culture, Practices and Ethics of the Press*, November 29, 2012 proposed that the names of persons arrested should not be disclosed to the media save in exceptional and clearly identified circumstances (G Ch. 3 para.2.39). That position was supported by the response of the senior judiciary to the Law Commission's consultation (to which Leveson L.J. contributed). Any decision to name or withhold the name of someone arrested should take account of competing interests, including the arrested person's right to reputation. The Information Commissioner also said that naming an arrestee should be decided on a case by case basis. He opposed a policy whereby the names of arrestees would "generally" be released to the media and questioned whether such a policy would comply with the Data Protection Act 1998. The Information Commissioner's opinion was that in order for the processing of sensitive personal data — by disclosing the fact of a person's arrest to the media — to be lawful, the disclosure would probably have to be "necessary" in accordance with one of the conditions in Sch.3 to the 1998 Act (unless the arrestee consented to the disclosure). The Information Commissioner expressed the view that, unless there was a policing purpose which justified disclosing an arrestee's name, it was not obvious that such disclosure would be compliant with the DPA or properly take account of privacy rights: see *http://www.ico.org.uk/about_us/consultations/~/media/documents/consultation_responses/ico_response_to__Law_Commission_Contempt _of_Court_Consultation_20130225.ashx* [Accessed 19 July 2015]. The House of Commons, Home Affairs Select Committee's 17th Report, published on March 17, 2015, essentially adopted a similar position to that of Leveson LJ in relation to anonymity for arrestees. It recommended that "The police should not release information on a suspect to the media in an informal, unattributed way. If the police do release the name of a suspect it has to be limited to exceptional cases, such as for reasons of public safety." *http://www.publications.parliament.uk/pa/cm201415/cmselect/cmhaff/962/96204.htm* [accessed 19 July 2015]

4–192C *[Add new paragraph]*

In contrast, the media have voiced concerns about "secret arrests" if the police cannot identify to them the names of persons arrested. For a contrary argument, based on the provisions of the Police and Criminal Evidence Act 1984 and an arrested person's right to inform a nominated person of his arrest, see *Criminal Law & Justice Weekly* (2013) 177 J.P.N. 303 May 4, 2013.

4–192D *[Add new paragraph]*

The Law Commission also put forward two other proposals for changes to the active period in the Act. First, that it should be triggered by the issue of an arrest warrant in extradition cases and, secondly, that the active period should come to an end at the delivery of the verdict (rather than on sentencing): Consultation Paper No.209 at 2.20–2.24. The latter proposal received support from the senior judiciary response: "A Judicial Response to the Law Commission Consultation Paper No.209" at para.6. See *http://www.judiciary.gov.uk/Resources/JCO/Documents/Consultations/sen-judiciary-response-to-law-comm-on-contempt-court.pdf* [Accessed 19 July 2015]. The former gives rise to the possibility of inhibiting publications even where no proceedings in the jurisdiction are imminent. It is submitted that such a reform is not necessary.

VI. SECTION 7 AND THE ATTORNEY-GENERAL

Role of the Attorney General under the strict liability rule

[Add new paragraph] **4–196A**

The Law Commission has proposed that the Attorney General should publish a "prosecution" policy to promote transparency and consistency: Consultation Paper No.209 at 2.60–2.63. That suggestion has some academic support: see I. Cram & N. Taylor, "*The Law Commission's Contempt proposals — getting the balance right?*" [2013] Crim. L.R. 6 465–482. The article also suggests that consideration should be given to making amenable to judicial review any decision by the Attorney General refusing consent to initiate proceedings: see discussion at para 2–197 above.

VII. WHO MAY BE LIABLE FOR PUBLICATION AND UPON WHAT BASIS?

A. Liability under s.2 of the 1981 Act

[Add to note 338] **4–203**

See, in the context of providing a platform for blogs, *Tamiz v Google Inc* [2012] EWCA Civ [2013] E.M.L.R 14 at paras [23]–[36]. In Hong Kong, a provider of a website hosting a discussion forum was held to be a (secondary) publisher at common law: *Oriental Press Group Ltd v Fevaworks Solutions Ltd* [2013] HKFCA 47.

[Add to note 339] **4–203**

See now *Gatley on Libel and Slander*, 12th ed (2013), especially paras 6–31 to 6–37.

[Add new paragraph] **4–204A**

The potential liability of intermediaries in the context of electronic communications has been considered by the Law Commission (Consultation Paper No.209). Intermediaries, including internet access providers and internet platform providers whose roles are primarily technical, may be publishers within the 1981 Act and, arguably, because their business is to provide a platform for publication, could be held to have the necessary intention to publish (discussed in para.4–55). Yet, as the Law Commission observed, such persons may have a defence (under s.3(1) of the 1981 Act) or in reliance on the Electronic Commerce (EC Directive) Regulations (SI 2002/2013). Although noting the lack of clarity, the Commission did not make any specific proposals with regard to such operators (see at 3.30–3.49). In its response to the consultation, the senior judiciary favoured prescribing a statutory test for who is responsible for publication: "A Judicial Response to the Law Commission Consultation Paper No.209" at para.28, *http://www.judiciary.gov.uk/Resources/JCO/Documents/Consultations/sen-judiciary-response-to-law-comm-on-contempt-court.pdf* [Accessed 19 July, 2015].

G. Editorial responsibility

4–225 *[Add to note 369]*

See *Aitken v DPP* [2015] EWHC 1079 (Admin) for a consideration of editorial responsibility for publication in the context of s.39 of the Children and Young Persons Act 1933 and a review of other statutes concerned with reporting restrictions.

I. The analogy with the law of libel

4–238 *[Add to note 386]*

Section 33 of the Crime and Courts Act 2013 abolished scandalising the judiciary as a form of contempt of court in England and Wales, which became effective on June 25, 2013: see s.61(6).

4–240 *[Add to note 388]*

See now *Gatley on Libel and Slander*, 12th ed (2013), paras 6–47 to 6–57.

4–241 *[Add to note 389]*

See now *Gatley on Libel and Slander*, 12th ed (2013), Chapter 6, especially at paras. 6–23 to 6–29.

J. Printers

4–242 *[Add to note 390]*

See now *Gatley on Libel and Slander*, 12th ed (2013) Ch 6, especially at paras 6–30.

K. "Distributors"

[Add to note 396] **4–246**

See *Tamiz v Google Inc* [2012] EWCA Civ 68, [2013] E.M.L.R 14 at [23]–[36] in respect of provision of a blog platform. See also the somewhat different analysis of Justice Ribeiro P.J. in *Oriental Press Group Ltd v Fevaworks Solutions Ltd* [2013] HKCFA 47.

[Add to note 398] **4–246**

See now *Gatley on Libel and Slander*, 12th ed (2013) Ch 6, especially at paras 6.30.

VIII. INNOCENT PUBLICATION OR DISTRIBUTION

A. Innocent publication and distribution: Section 3

[Add to note 403] **4–248**

See *Aitken v DPP* [2015] EWHC 1079 (Admin) for a consideration of editorial responsibility for publication in the context of s.39 of the Children and Young Persons Act 1933 and a review of other statutes concerned with reporting restrictions.

[Add new paragraph] **4–249A**

The Law Commission has noted in its Consultation Paper No.209 at 3.30, that the s.3 defence is very narrow, given that many things could give rise to a "reason to suspect". In the context of archived material, it may be that a media organisation would know that certain proceedings have at some point become "active", but the individual(s) who had such knowledge may not be aware that the organisation had published, some time earlier, material which would or could give rise, if viewed during the "active" period, to a substantial risk of serious prejudice. One proposal to deal with this situation was that strict liability should only come into effect if the proceedings in question were active at the time of initial publication. Any reliance on s.3 would be assessed as at that date. As to proceedings becoming active after that time, liability could only arise on the basis of the Law Commission's proposed "second" form of contempt; namely, if the organisation had been informed of the risk, through the formal notification procedure proposed, and failed to take down the material to avoid that risk. See 4–30E above. The Law Commission made recommendations in December 2013 which were initially adopted by the government, but they were subsequently abandoned.

D. Vicarious liability and s.3

4–269 *[Add to note 421]*

See *Aitken v DPP* [2015] EWHC 1079 (Admin) at note 4–248 above.

4–270 *[Add to note 423]*

See now *Gatley on Libel and Slander*, 12th ed (2013), para 8.30.

E. The burden of proof

4–273 *[Add to note 426]*

See also *R. v Williams (Orette)* [2012] EWCA Crim 2162; [2013] 1 W.L.R 1200; [2013] 1 Cr. App. R. 11, which considered the statutory burden of proof in the context of a strict liability firearms offence.

IX. THE RIGHT TO REPORT COURT PROCEEDINGS

A. Contemporaneous Reporting of Court Proceedings: the general principle

4–275 *[Add to note 430]*

See also *Apex Global Management Ltd v Fi Call Ltd* [2013] EWCA Civ 819.

4–275 *[Add to note 431]*

See now *Gatley on Libel and Slander*, 12th ed (2013), paras 15–35 and 16–10.

B. Section 4(1)

4–277 *[Add to end of paragraph]*

This defence was considered by the Law Commission in its investigations into the law of contempt: Consultation Paper No.209. One of the proposals canvassed, which may find its way into statute in due course, related to the vexed question of archived material continuing to be available online. The main problem envisaged was that criminal proceedings might become "active" after the original publication in respect of which the archived material could give rise to a substantial risk of serious prejudice (or impediment). Suppose, for example, that there remained accessible a (fair and accurate) report of earlier criminal proceedings in respect of the same defendant. Suppose that he had been convicted at the earlier trial. Whether or not that conviction had later been overturned by the Court of Appeal, it may well be that it would not be admissible in the later trial. Accordingly, its continuing accessibility could give rise to prejudice. The Law Commission would deal with that situation by means of its proposal to introduce a notification and take down procedure regarding the archived material. Obviously, if it remained available in defiance of any order so made, there could be a prima facie contempt of court. The Law Commission made clear that in such circumstances there could be no defence available in relation to the original court report under s.4(1). See 4–30E above. The Law Commission made recommendations which were initially adopted by the government, but were subsequently abandoned.

What is a report?

[Add to note 435] **4–279**

Lord Judge CJ issued updated guidance for live text-based communications on December 14, 2011: *Practice Guidance (Court Proceedings: Live Text-based Communications) (No.2)* [2012] 1 W.L.R. 12. See now the Criminal Practice Directions 2015 [2015] EWCA Crim 1567, in force with effect from 5 October 2015, Division I, 6C. "The use of live text-based forms of communication (including Twitter) from court for the purposes of fair and accurate reporting". The position remains as set out in the First Supplement: members of the public require permission from the judge, but representatives of the media (and legal commentators) do not need to make an application.

See also *Gatley on Libel and Slander*, 12th ed (2013), para 13–38, fn.353.

[Add to note 437] **4–280**

See now *Gatley on Libel and Slander*, 12th ed (2013), para 13–39.

[Add to note 438] **4–280**

See now *Gatley on Libel and Slander*, 12th ed (2013), para 13–40.

[Add to note 439] **4–280**

See now *Gatley on Libel and Slander*, 12th ed (2013), paras 13–35 and 15–35.

[Add to text at end of paragraph] **4–281**

In 2012 the Scottish High Court gave permission for remotely-operated cameras to film a murder trial and the subsequent footage was used in a documentary broadcast in July 2013. (See at 16–430A below.) But following the announcement of a review into current practice as to television cameras, in October 2012, no further applications for filming in courts were to be considered until the outcome is known. In Scotland, Lord Gill announced in January 2015 (and appropriately on television) the outcome of the consultation on the subject and of the enquiry carried out under Lady Dorrian. The central conclusion reached was that there should be wider opportunities for coverage, especially of appellate proceedings, but that clear guidelines should be worked out and especially for the protection of vulnerable witnesses.

The experience of television in court rooms in New Zealand has not so far been auspicious, as emerges clearly from the discussion in *Law Talk*, 26 October 2012 (a journal published by the New Zealand Law Society). The problems have clearly been noted by Elias CJ, who on 9 August 2013 instituted a review by a panel of judges of "in-court television coverage, photography and sound recording by mainstream media". It will address current guidelines, any changes that may be required in the light of continuing developments in the available technology, and whether appropriate safeguards are in place to protect the fair trial process. On 20 July 2015, a final Report to the Chief Justice on In-Court Media Coverage was published. The Report concluded that it did not recommend any fundamental changes to the existing system, saying at [6] that "We consider it better to have the present coverage than none at all. There is room for improvement, particularly in the procedures, and the quality and detail of the publications. Lawyers and judges want more accuracy and balance in reporting". New "In-Court Media Coverage Guidelines 2015" have been produced to reflect these aspirations. See further the discussion of these issues at 10–213 above. The experience of television in court rooms in New Zealand has not so far been auspicious: see e.g. the discussion in *Law Talk*, October 26, 2012 (a journal published by the New Zealand Law Society). The problems have clearly been noted by the Chief Justice, who on August 9, 2013 instituted a review by a panel of judges of "in-court television coverage, photography and sound recording by mainstream media". It will address current guidelines, any changes that may be required in the light of continuing developments in the available technology, and whether appropriate safeguards are in place to protect the fair trial process. On 20 July 2015, a final Report to the Chief Justice on In-Court Media Coverage was published. The Report concluded that it did not recommend any fundamental changes to the existing system, saying at [6] that "We consider it better to have the present coverage than none at all. There is room for improvement, particularly in the procedures, and the quality and detail of the publications. Lawyers and judges want more accuracy and balance in reporting". New "In-Court Media Coverage Guidelines 2015" have been produced to reflect these aspirations. See further at 10–213 below.

C. The requirement that the report be contemporaneous

4–288 *[Add to note 449]*

Paragraphs (b) and (c) came into force on June 18, 2012: Criminal Justice Act 2003 (Commencement No.28 and Saving Provisions) Order, SI 2012/1320, subject to saving provisions in arts 5 and 6(2).

4–290 *[Add to notes 450 and 451]*

See now *Gatley on Libel and Slander*, 12th ed (2013), para 13–37.

F. Fair and accurate reporting

[Add to note 460] **4–298**

For a more recent consideration of fairness and accuracy in the context of defamation, see *Qadir v Associated Newspapers Ltd* [2012] EWHC 2606 (QB); [2013] E.M.L.R 15. See now Gatley on Libel and Slander, 12th ed (2013), para 13–38.

[Add to note 462] **4–299**

See now *Gatley on Libel and Slander*, 12th ed (2013), paras 13–49 and 34–21.

X. DISCUSSING PUBLIC AFFAIRS

A. Discussion of public affairs: s.5

[Add to end of paragraph] **4–304**

As in so many areas, it is necessary now to consider the potential relevance of archived material available online in the context of s.5. One of the Law Commission's proposals in its Consultation Paper No.209 was that strict liability under the 1981 Act should only arise if the relevant proceedings had been "active" at the time the material was first published: see paras 3.7 to 3.86. If proceedings become "active" later, any archived material giving rise at that point to a risk of serious prejudice would have to be addressed through its proposed notification and take down procedure. Thus, any reliance on s.5 would be judged in the light of the circumstances prevailing at the time of original publication. In its final report, the Law Commission recommended that where the communication was first published before proceedings became active, the person responsible for such publication should be exempt from liability under s 2 unless they had been formally put on notice by the Attorney General of the existence and location of the publication which first appeared before proceedings were active, the fact that relevant proceedings had become active since then, and the offending contents. No recommendations were made in relation to s.5 itself: "*Contempt of Court (1): Juror Misconduct and Internet Publications*" (Law Com No. 340) at *http://www.lawcom.gov.uk/wp-content/uploads/2015/06/lc340_contempt_of_court_juror_misconduct.pdf* at 2.151 and 2.152 [accessed on the 19 July 2015].

C. The issues addressed in *Attorney General v English*

4. *Later developments*

4–325A *[Add new paragraph]*

The Law Commission supports retaining s.5 in its present form (Consultation Paper No.209 at 2.54). The senior judiciary response expressed the same view: "A Judicial Response to the Law Commission Consultation Paper No.209", at para.22: *http://www.judiciary.gov.uk/Resources/JCO/Documents/Consultations/sen-judiciary-response-to-law-comm-on-contempt-court.pdf* [Accessed 14 July, 2015].

4–325B *[Add new paragraph]*

The Law Commission has proposed that the Attorney General should publish a "prosecution policy". It appears to suggest that such a policy would assist publishers in making decisions about whether a publication would be protected by s.5. That suggestion has some academic support: see I. Cram & N. Taylor "*The Law Commission's Contempt proposals — getting the balance right?*" [2013] Crim. L.R. 6 465–482. See the discussion at 2–197 above.

WHAT ARE THE "DEFENCES" PRESERVED BY SECTION 6?

B. Possible candidates

1. *Protection from "gagging" writs*

4–339 *[Add to end of paragraph]*

With the effective demise of trial by jury in defamation, and especially following the enactment of s.11 of the Defamation Act 2013, the risk of committing strict liability contempt in relation to defamation actions is now reduced in any event.

3. *Parliamentary privilege*

4–346 *[Add to note 526]*

See now *Gatley on Libel and Slander*, 12th ed (2013), paras 13–29 to 13–31.

4. *No defence of public good or benefit*

4–352 *[Add to note 536]*

The *Reynolds* defence has now been replaced by the provisions of s.4 of the Defamation Act 2013.

Chapter 5

CONTEMPTS BY PUBLICATION AT COMMON LAW

I. Questions Unresolved by the 1981 Act

A. Introduction: the outstanding questions

[Add to note 1] 5–1

See now s.3 of the Defamation Act 2013. The defence is to be known as "honest opinion".

[Add to note 251] 5–166

The comments of Lloyd LJ were recently cited in the Court of Appeal's judgment in *In re West (Ian Stuart)* [2014] EWCA Crim 1480; [2015] 1 W.L.R. 109 at [44].

[Add a note 283A at end of paragraph] 5–198

For an example of when the requisite intent is likely to be inferred from "all the circumstances", see the findings of Newton J in *A Healthcare NHS Trust v P* [2015] EWCOP 15 (Fam) at [59].

V. Scandalising the Court

A. Introduction

[Add to end of paragraph] 5–204

The form of contempt known as "scandalising" was abolished in this jurisdiction by s.33 of the Crime and Courts Act 2013. The statute received the royal assent on 25 April and came into effect on 25 June 2013. Nonetheless, the history remains of significance not least because the notion survives in other jurisdictions addressed in the following paragraphs. Similar provision has been made in Northern Ireland in s.12 of the Criminal Justice Act (Northern Ireland) 2013. The Scottish concept of "murmuring", which is discussed at 16–88 and 16–288 *et seq* of the main text, has not been affected by legislation either at Westminster or Holyrood.

5–207 *[Add to note 302]*

It was an attempt to rely on the doctrine in Northern Ireland which prompted Parliament's attention to the issue of whether "scandalising" should be formally abolished. Proceedings had been authorised by the Attorney General in that jurisdiction in respect of a politician (a member of the Westminster Parliament) who had published memoirs in which criticism was directed at a northern Ireland judge concerning a judicial review case in 2006. The view had apparently been taken that the relevant passages amounted to "unwarranted abuse of a judge in his judicial capacity", but those proceedings came to a conclusion in May 2012, at which time the politician acknowledged that his remarks had not been intended to undermine the administration of justice.

M. Other jurisdictions

2. *Australia*

5–271A *[Add new paragraph]*

The doctrine was considered again by the Family Court of Australia in *Xuarez v Vitela* [2012] FamCA 574. A father who was a party in family proceedings had established a website where he posted disparaging remarks about the mother, the experts and the lawyers involved in the litigation. Forrest J. made the following observations at [56]–[57]:

> "Furthermore, in my view at least, the content clearly contemptuously scandalises this Court ... Although the Court has to consider that the good sense of the community might be a sufficient safeguard against the damage these attacks can do to the rule of law in this country, in the specific context of this case, where I am satisfied, at least, that the publication otherwise contravenes section 121 [of the Family Law Act] and identifies the particular proceedings in this Court, I am satisfied that the continuous contemptuous scandalising of this Court should be restrained."

That approach was also adopted in the Federal Magistrates Court in *Lackey & Mae* [2013] FMCAfam 284, where it was said, at [11], that a number of Facebook postings denigrated the court and the litigious process, as well as containing detail and critical comment about information regarding the case, including information that could only have been impermissibly taken from affidavits filed.

[Add new paragraph] **5–271B**

In *Tate v Duncan-Strelec* [2014] NSWSC 1125, the defendant had unsuccessfully brought proceedings against the plaintiff in the Supreme Court of New South Wales. She was said to have subsequently published material on the Internet which was critical of both the trial judge who had heard those proceedings and the New South Wales judicial system.

Bergin CJ was satisfied that the relevant website was calculated to assert that an injustice had been perpetrated against the defendant; that the trial judge had dealt with the defendant callously and unfairly in circumstances of a family crisis; that the decision reached by the trial judge was unjustified; and that it was impossible to obtain justice before the court because it failed to bring criminals to account. The statements made by the defendant were found "beyond reasonable doubt" (at [223]) to amount to scandalising the court, since they were calculated to impair the confidence of the people in the court's judgments and to lower its authority.

[Add new paragraph] **5–271C**

In *O'Shane v Harbour Radio* [2013] NSWCA 315, radio-show host Alan Jones was said to have made defamatory statements about the plaintiff, including that she had failed in her duties as a magistrate by delivering diabolically bad decisions which were wrong in law. One issue before the New South Wales Court of Appeal was whether the plaintiff was debarred from bringing defamation proceedings with respect to criticism of the performance of her function as a judicial officer.

The majority (Beazley P, McColl JA and Tobias AJA) found that the plaintiff was not debarred from bringing defamation proceedings. Rather than being directed towards the institutional integrity of the magistracy or the judicial system, the criticisms of Mr Jones were said to have constituted "a direct, personal attack on the plaintiff for allegedly making wrong and diabolically bad decisions" (at [66]).

The minority (Basten JA and McCallum J) held that the pleaded imputations related to the conduct, competence and capacity of the plaintiff in carrying out her functions as a judicial officer, and that she had no cause of action in defamation. One of the factors of relevance identified by Basten JA was "the principle underlying contempt for scandalising the court" (at [228]), namely, the protection afforded to the courts from false or unfair allegations which tended to bring the administration of justice into disrepute. As summarised by Tobias AJA, the factors identified by Basten JA were relied upon as constituting:

> ".. policy reasons which preclude the existence of a cause of action in tort of the suit of a judicial officer with respect to statements relating to his or her conduct or capacity as such an officer in carrying out his or her judicial functions." (at [251])

3. *New Zealand*

5–273A *[Add new paragraph]*

The New Zealand Law Commission has published the Issues Paper 'Contempt in Modern New Zealand' (IP 36, 2014), in which it seeks feedback on a number of reforms, including in relation to scandalising the court. The Commission's preliminary view is said to be that the retention of the common law offence of scandalising is untenable in the light of freedom of expression issues, rule of law concerns and the views of modern New Zealand society (at [6.62]).

4. *Singapore*

5–275A *[Add new paragraph]*

The Court of Appeal heard conjoined appeals from the decisions in *Att Gen v Shadrake Alan* [2011] 2 S.L.R. 445 ("Shadrake 1") and *Att Gen v Shadrake Alan* [2011] 2 S.L.R. 506 ("Shadrake 2"). In Shadrake 1, it had been held that 11 out of 14 impugned statements amounted to contempts and, in Shadrake 2, a sentence of six weeks imprisonment was imposed (together with a fine of $20,000 with two weeks in default). On appeal, the sentence was upheld, although only nine of the statements were held to be in contempt. It was accepted, at [149], that the judge had aptly characterised the allegations of judicial impropriety as being "without precedent in terms of their specificity, the number of judges targeted (the whole Supreme Court bench in [one] case) and their gravity, pertaining as they did to cases concerning the life and liberty of those who come before the courts". In July 2011, he was deported to the UK, having been released from prison for "good behaviour".

5–275B *[Add new paragraph]*

The concept of "scandalising" was again considered by the Court of Appeal in *PT Makindo (formerly known as PT Makindo TBK) v Aperchance Co Ltd* [2011] SGCA 19. Following the setting aside of freezing orders which it had obtained, Aperchance placed advertisements in Indonesian newspapers to the effect that an injunction had been granted against "the entire assets/capital of PT Makindo". The Court of Appeal upheld the judge's conclusion that these advertisements did not amount to contempt. They did not impugn the impartiality, integrity or independence of the judiciary. Nor did they interfere with the administration of justice. The legal position was summarised at [17]:

> "... it is possible to damage the fountain of justice at any time by undermining public confidence in the administration of justice by baseless and unwarranted attacks on the integrity and impartiality off the courts and judges. Scurrilous abuse of a judge qua judge has the same effect. Scurrilous and unwarranted attacks on the judiciary as an institution are certainly an aggravated form of contempt. Hence, in the present case, the advertisements would only amount to a

contempt of court if they amounted to scandalising the court, which they could not possibly do since they carried no suggestion as to the conduct of the court. Any person reading the advertisements in Indonesia without any knowledge of the background would be none the wiser as to the truth or otherwise of what they purported to say."

5. *Mauritius*

[Add new paragraph] **5–277A**

On October 17, 2011, the editor of the newspaper *Samedi Plus*, Dharmanand Dhooharika was convicted of scandalising the court in a series of articles concerning what was known as the "Paradise litigation" and the role of the Chief Justice in that connection. The sentence imposed was one of three months' imprisonment against the editor and a fine against the publisher Contact Press Ltd. In December 2012, the judicial Committee of the Privy Council gave permission to appeal: *DPP of Mauritius v Dhooharika.*

[Add new paragraph] **5–277B**

In *Dhooharika v DPP (Commonwealth Lawyers' Association intervening) [on appeal from the Supreme Court of Mauritius]* [2014] UKPC 11; [2015] A.C. 875, Mr Dhooharika's appeal against his conviction was allowed.

The Board first considered whether the offence of scandalising the court still existed in Mauritius. It was noted that the European Court of Human Rights had not declared the existence of the offence to be incompatible with Article 10 of the European Convention on Human Rights, provided that the restrictions on free speech were proportionate. The Board concluded that it would be inappropriate to depart from the decision in *Ahnee v DPP* [1999] 2 AC 294 and held that, if the offence were to be abolished in Mauritius, this should be done by way of statute.

As to the ingredients of the offence, the Board confirmed that it exists solely in order to protect the administration of justice rather than the feelings of judges, and that there must be a real risk of undermining public confidence in the administration of justice. It was held that the relevant mens rea should be related to the creation of such a risk and, with regard to the generality of a defendant's bad faith, the Board concluded as follows:

> "... while it makes sense to hold that the defendant commits the offence if he intends to undermine public confidence in the administration of justice or is subjectively reckless as to whether he did so, it is not easy to see that any other, more general, state of mind would amount to relevant bad faith sufficient to support a conviction." (at [49])

The Board found that that Mr Dhooharika was, as a matter of practical fact, deprived of his right to give evidence on his own behalf and that he had not received a fair trial. Even assuming that it had been permissible to determine the issue of bad faith without hearing evidence from Mr Dhooharika, the Board concluded that the Supreme Court had not been justified in holding that he had acted in bad faith:

"The Board does not agree with the Supreme Court that the various articles and their presentation, taken as a whole, were intended to convey the message that the allegations of Mr Hurnam were justified and that the Chief Justice should resign and appear before a tribunal. The thrust of them was rather that the allegations were such that they should be investigated and that the Chief Justice should put his position before the tribunal. The editorial expressly conceded that the paper was not equipped to judge a Chief Justice. It was for that reason that it expressed the view that the allegations should be judged by a tribunal, concluding that "in alleged cases of misconduct, it is incumbent on the accused judge to defend his integrity by agreeing to appear before a competent court named by the President of the Republic". It was properly conceded on behalf of the defendant before the Board that some of the comments were perhaps ill-judged. The Board would go further and say that they were plainly ill-judged but the Board does not think that they prove bad faith on the part of the defendant." (at [57])

7. *Swaziland*

5–281A *[Add new paragraph]*

In April 2013, the editor of the *Nation* magazine and its publishing company were found guilty of scandalising the court in relation to two articles (appearing in 2009 and 2010) which were critical of the judiciary and, in particular, of the Chief Justice: *The King v Swaziland Independent Publishers (Pty) Ltd* [2013] SZHC 88. The first article was said to have been a "scurrilous attack" on the judges of the Supreme Court and the second to have been calculated or intended to bring into contempt and disrepute and to lower the authority of the Chief Justice. The conviction was upheld on appeal [2014] SZSC 25 (30 May 2014).

8. *Fiji*

5–281B *[Add new paragraph]*

The respondents in *State v Citizens' Constitutional Forum Ltd and Akuila Yabaki* [2013] FJHC 220; HBC195.2012 (3 May 2013) were a Fijian non-governmental organisation ('CCF') and its then director. The case concerned a summary in CCF's *Tutaka* newsletter of a report published by the Law Society Charity which had concluded that there was no rule of law or freedom of expression in Fiji and that the independence of its judiciary could not be relied upon.

Justice Calanchini noted that the constitutional history of Fiji since its independence in 1970 had resulted in the administration of justice being, at times, more vulnerable than in the United Kingdom. The need for the offence of scandalising the court in a developing Island state was said to be "greater than in a developed state such as the United Kingdom" (at [63]).

The judge was satisfied that the words published in the newsletter did represent a real risk of undermining public confidence in the administration of justice. They were said to have the effect of "raising doubts" (at [77]) in the minds of the public that their disputes would not be resolved by impartial and independent judges. As a result, the authority and integrity of the judiciary in Fiji was said to be undermined and the offence of scandalising the court established.

In later determining the respondents' punishment ([2013] FJHC 388), Calanchini J stated that the ordeal of court proceedings and an offer to pay costs with an apology was not sufficient. Such an outcome:

> "...would suggest that the court did not take seriously the role of safeguarding the community from attacks on members of the judiciary and the court which have the effect of undermining confidence in the administration of justice." (at [8])

CCF was fined F$20,000 and Yabaki was given a suspended three-month jail term conditional upon him paying a F$2,000 fine. The respondents were also ordered to arrange for an apology directed to the "judiciary of Fiji" to be submitted to the court for approval before being published in the next issue of CCF's newsletter.

CHAPTER 6

COURT ORDERS AFFECTING THE MEDIA

I. QUIA TIMET INJUNCTIONS TO RESTRAIN A CONTEMPT

A. A jurisdiction to be sparingly exercised

6–2 *[Add to note 6]*

See also *Director of the Serious Fraud Office v O'Brien* [2014] UKSC 23; [2014] A.C. 1246; [2014] 2 W.L.R. 902; [2014] 2 All E.R. 798; [2014] Lloyd's Rep. F.C. 401; Times, April 11, 2014 as to the distinction between civil and criminal contempt in the context of s.41 of the Proceeds of Crime Act 2002.

6–5A *[Add new paragraph]*

The Law Commission proposed new powers to enable a court to order an internet publisher, or someone with sufficient control over access to material on the internet, to remove or to disable access to that material during active proceedings: Consultation Paper No.209, paras 3.7 to 3.86. The proposed new statutory provision was considered in the context of the Law Commission's review of parts of the Contempt of Court Act 1981 and its proposals in this regard are addressed more fully in Chapter 4 in the context of the 1981 Act. However, the proposed power was one which could be used against the media to order them to disable access to previously published information on their websites, including any user generated content. The Law Commission envisaged that the power would be applied in accordance with the approach of *Ex p. Cymru (Wales) Ltd* [2002] E.M.L.R. 184 and that it would clarify the existing law. Concerns have been expressed, however, that such powers could be used more frequently than intended (as happened in the early years after the powers contained in s.4(2) of the Contempt of Court Act 1981 were introduced). There could be a temptation to use such powers at or before the commencement of a criminal trial without having taken the painstaking steps required in order for the court to be satisfied that any such order was necessary and proportionate. The Law Commission was of the view that such a power would in practice need to be used only rarely, because it would pre-suppose circumstances in which a juror had become aware of prejudicial material without having disobeyed a judicial direction or having committed one of the proposed new criminal offences which could apply to jurors. It might, for example, occur where a juror has received a summons for jury service but has yet to attend court and has come across the material while conducting a quite innocent online search of some kind. The outcome of these proposals is discussed at paras 4–30A–E above.

B. The traditional reluctance to grant prior restraint

[Add to note 22] 6–8

For the application of the principles in Scotland, where *Bonnard v Perryman* [1891] 2 Ch 269 does not apply, see *Massie v McCaig* [2013] CSIH 14; 2013 S.L.T. 373. The Court must consider s.12 of the Human Rights Act 1998 and conduct a balancing exercise at the interim stage.

C. The relevance of s.12 of the Human Rights Act 1998

[Add new paragraph] 6–22A

It was argued in *A v BBC* [2014] UKSC 25 that before a s.11 order was made it would have been appropriate to give notice to the media in accordance with s.12(2) of the Human Rights Act 1998, on the basis that the BBC was a person against whom relief was being sought. But, at [66], Lord Reed rejected the submission, since there was no such person. Directions made under s.11 operate on a blanket basis: there is no respondent who should be notified or who might be present or represented at the hearing. While existing procedures provide sufficient safeguard to protect Convention rights, improved procedures may be possible and desirable, providing, in some circumstances, those who might be affected by such an order with the opportunity to make representations. Any improvements "should not however make it impossible to obtain orders restricting publicity on an *ex parte* basis" [68].

D. The approach of the Strasbourg jurisprudence towards prior restraint

[Add to text at end of paragraph] 6–24

In *Animal Defenders International v United Kingdom (Application No.48876/08)*, 22 April 2013, the European Court of Human Rights considered prior restraint in the context of advertising. The NGO applicant wished to broadcast an advertisement against the practice of carrying out experiments on animals. The Broadcast Advertising Clearance Centre refused to permit it, because the NGO's objectives were "wholly or mainly of a political nature" and therefore the advertisement was prohibited by s.321(2) of the Communications Act 2003. (The advertisement was available on the internet.) The applicant argued that the decision was unjustifiable prior restraint.

The Court observed that, as the subject matter was one of general public interest, the margin of appreciation afforded to the state was limited and, furthermore, the NGO was acting in a way comparable to that of the media in its "public watchdog role" which added weight to its position. However, the Court distinguished between "a general measure" imposed by a state (such as the restrictions imposed by the Communications Act 2003 on types of advertising), which may result in unfair outcomes for particular parties, and prior restraint imposed on an individual act of expression. It found that the measure was not disproportionate.

E. A comparison with the Canadian Charter

6–25 *[Add to note 56]*

What has become known as the *Dagenais/Mentuck* test is now well established in Canada. For a recent example of its application, to restrain publication of information about a criminal trial, see *R. v Sipes* 2011 BCSC 1329. It was held that a ban on publishing the defendant's name was not justified because there was no "real and substantial risk to [his] right to a fair trial". The court did not need to go on to consider any competing factors (such as open justice).

F. Who may claim an injunction?

6–26 *[Add to note 58]*

The Law Commission saw no reason to change the law so as to make any such application conditional upon the consent or permission of the Attorney General.

J. To which court should an application be made?

6–45A *[Add new paragraph]*

In *R. v Harwood* [2012] EW Misc 27 (CC), July 20, 2012, it was the trial judge at the Central Criminal Court (Fulford J.) who directed that archived material, relevant to the defendant's character, should be temporarily removed from websites pending conclusion of the trial. Reliance was placed on s.45(4) of the Senior Courts Act 1981: see the discussion at 6–2 in the main text. The Law Commission, in its review of contempt of court, has put forward the suggestion that the power exercised by Fulford J. in *Harwood* might be put on a statutory footing. The proposed power would extend to the grant of such an order against anyone having a sufficient degree of control over internet access (e.g. those who cache or host): it would not necessarily be confined to those who have traditionally been characterised as "publishers": see 4–203 *et seq*. above. So far, responsibility for publication on the internet has not been considered in the context of contempt, but only in that of defamation: see e.g. *Tamiz v Google* [2013] EWCA Civ 68; [2013] 1 W.L.R. 2151 and *Oriental Press Group Ltd v Fevaworks Solutions Ltd* [2013] HKCFA 47. The Law Commission has pointed out that if the law were to be changed, so as to reverse the effect of the decision in *HMA v Beggs (No.2)* 2002 S.L.T. 139, the hosting of archived material would no longer give rise to strict liability contempt. Accordingly, there would arguably be nothing unlawful to justify the court's granting a restraining order. Statutory provision would thus be necessary to found the jurisdiction to do so. The proposal is that the relevant persons or entities would be given formal notification (probably through the CPS) of the fact that proceedings have become "active" and of precisely which material, in the light of that, is said to give rise to prejudice or impediment. If the material is *not* removed voluntarily following notification, then the court might, if necessary and proportionate, grant an order along the lines of that granted in *R. v Harwood.* If that were not complied with, then there would potentially arise two alternative modes of proceeding. Either the Attorney General would initiate proceedings for strict liability contempt or one of the parties, or possibly the court of its own motion, could begin committal proceedings in view of the *ex hypothesi* breach. In the case of the former, there would be a defence to the effect that the respondent had not received proper notification (in addition, of course, to any argument based on lack of substantial risk of serious prejudice). The Government however decided not to adopt these proposals: see discussion at 4–30 A–E above.

II. INJUNCTIONS *CONTRA MUNDUM*

A. Injunctions *contra mundum*

3. *Jurisdiction and application in civil and family proceedings*

[Add to text at end of paragraph] **6–53**

In *In the matter of X and Y (Children)* [2012] EWCA Civ 1500; [2013] 1 F.C.R. 1, the Court of Appeal overturned a decision permitting a local authority to publish an executive summary of a Serious Case Review which it had carried out. A parent had been convicted of a serious offence in relation to a child of the family and the media had reported those criminal proceedings. Following the criminal trial, the Local Safeguarding Board carried out a Serious Case Review. The Local Safeguarding Children Boards (Wales) Regulations 2006 and related Guidance required the Board to publish an anonymised executive summary. The local authority recognised that the anonymised summary was likely to identify other children of the family as victims of abuse: people would recognise the family because of the media coverage of the criminal trial. It therefore sought a reporting restriction order in respect of any further publication of the Executive Summary. Peter Jackson J. initially approved the publication by the local authority only of a redacted version of the executive summary. On appeal, the Court of Appeal held that the Judge had struck the wrong balance between the competing interests. While the local authority had a duty to inform the public of its review, it was "necessary" (in the Strasbourg sense) to protect children in the family whom the judge had found were in a fragile state. Further redactions were thought appropriate (see also 6–64A and 7–175).

In *Re J (A Child), Re* [2013] EWHC 2694 (Fam), a *contra mundum* injunction was granted to protect the interests of the child concerned, but carefully designed to maximise the opportunities, otherwise, for discussing important issues of legitimate public interest, such as the administration of justice in family proceedings, the care system and the conduct of social workers (see also 2–63A, 8–83A, 8–96, 8–97A, 8–104, 8–150).

6–54A *[Add new paragraph]*

In *Hutcheson v Popdog Ltd* [2012] 1 W.L.R. 782, Lord Neuberger M.R. observed that it should not be assumed that that Court would in a future case approve the proposition that the *Spycatcher* principle did not apply to final injunctions (as had been held in *The Jockey Club v Buffham* [2002] EWHC 1866; [2003] QB 462: see 6–172 and following).

Separately, Lord Neuberger observed that if parties complied with the *Practice Guidance (Interim Non-disclosure Orders)* [2012] 1 W.L.R. 1003 and cases were actively case managed, the situation which had arisen in *Hutcheson v Popdog* (i.e. that the parties had reached an agreement and allowed the interim injunction to remain undisturbed) should not occur. As a result of those observations a number of claims in which interim injunctions had been granted, but the parties had then not progressed the litigation, came back before the court and were finally disposed of in *JIH v News Group Newspapers Ltd* [2012] EWHC 2179 (QB). Although the Judge permitted the continuation of many anonymity orders, he declined to make any final injunctions *contra mundum*.

An application for a final injunction *contra mundum* was considered in *Ambrosiadou v Coward* [2013] EWHC 58 (QB). There was no dispute that s.37(1) of the Senior Courts Act 1981 gave the Court jurisdiction to make such an order, although Tugendhat J. declined to make an order restraining third parties because there was no evidence of any threat to publish the private information, or even of a third party disputing that the material in question was private. The Judge doubted that the mechanism which the applicant had sought to rely upon to restrain third parties was correct. The applicant had sought to rely merely on a penal notice which referred to the order binding anyone with knowledge of it; the Judge appeared to be of the view that the prohibition would need to be contained within the body of the order.

6. *The need for a public domain proviso*

6–63 *[Add to end of paragraph]*

A contrasting example to *Stedman, Re* [2009] EWHC 935 (Fam); [2009] 2 F.L.R. 852 was *WXY v Gewanter* [2012] EWHC 1601 (QB) (a claim in privacy, breach of confidence and harassment). Some information which fell within the ambit of the interim injunction had appeared on various websites. However, the evidence did not indicate that those websites were popular or widely read. The judge, therefore, prohibited the publication of that material by way of a final injunction because the order would not be futile. The decision also illustrates the need in such cases for the order to identify with particularity what information is deemed to be in the public domain and thus covered by the proviso.

[Add to note 157] 6–63

In *Mahmood v BBC* [2014] EWHC 4207 at [11], the court stressed the importance of including a public domain proviso. It was held, on the facts, that the applicant could not show a materially increased risk posed to him by the broadcast he was seeking to prohibit, as compared to the pre-existing risk from materials already in the public domain.

7. *The approach of appellate tribunals*

[Add to note 158] 6–64

JIH v News Group Newspapers Ltd [2011] EWCA Civ 42; [2011] E.M.L.R 15 was applied in *AAA v Associated Newspapers Ltd* [2013] EWCA Civ 554.

[Add to end of paragraph] 6–64

In *PNM v Times Newspapers Ltd and others* [2014] EWCA Civ 1132; [2014] C.P. Rep. 48; [2015] 1 Cr. App. R. 1; [2014] E.M.L.R 30 at [46], the Court of Appeal described the task of the judge in balancing Convention rights as:

> "an evaluative one, akin to the exercise of discretion. [The Court of Appeal] would not interfere unless the judge erred in principle or reached a conclusion which was plainly wrong, that is, one outside the ambit of the conclusions which a judge could reasonably reach."

See also the similar comments about the role of an appellate court in *Mahmood v BBC* [2014] EWCA Civ 1567 at [5].

[Add new paragraph] 6–64A

In *In the matter of X and Y (Children)* [2012] EWCA Civ 1500; [2013] 1 F.C.R. 1 the Court of Appeal stated that it was "not suggested that [the Judge] misunderstood the law or that he directed himself otherwise than appropriately". Nevertheless, the appeal was allowed because the judge had struck the balance "wrongly". The decisions highlight perhaps a tension between the appellate court, on the one hand, seeking to limit its role to a review of a decision under appeal where it was reached after weighing competing factors (and with which it should thus be slow to interfere) and, on the other hand, complying with its obligation, under s.6 of the HRA, to act compatibly with the Convention. In some cases, the disclosure of information about a claimant will be an "all or nothing" question and the correct balance between competing rights can only be struck in one place. If the decision of the judge was simply "wrong", then the appellate court will not be slow to interfere.

B. The history of the *parens patriae* (or "inherent") jurisdiction generally

(f) *How media rights were addressed before the Human Rights Act*

6–99 *[Add to note 231]*

See *Hunt v Hunt* [2012] All E.R. (D) 217 (Oct), a decision of Macur J. discussed at 8–107 below.

6–108A *[Add new paragraph]*

Section 39 of the Children and Young Persons Act 1933 has been amended by s.79 of the Criminal Justice and Courts Act 2015 with effect from 13 April 2015. The section now applies to proceedings other than criminal proceedings — civil matters and certain hybrid proceedings. The amendments also extend the range of publications in respect of which a discretionary reporting restriction order can be made to include online publications. This remedies the limitations of the statute were identified in *MXB v East Sussex Hospitals NHS Trust* [2012] EWHC 3279 (QB). The discretionary reporting restrictions for criminal proceedings can now be found in s.45 and s.45A of the Youth Justice and Criminal Evidence Act 1999. S.45A provides the court with a discretionary power under specified circumstances to make a lifelong reporting restriction in respect of a victim of witness aged 18 during the proceedings, thereby remedying the lacuna identified in *JC v Central Criminal Court* [2014] EWCA Civ 1777; [2015] 1 W.L.R. 2865; (2015) 179 J.P. 205; at [46] and [49]. See *Aitken v DPP* [2015] EWHC 1079 (Admin); (2015) 179 J.P. 223 at [70]-[73] for a review of these changes. The Divisional Court highlighted certain discrepancies:

(i) Criminal liability for newspaper publications in respect of reporting *criminal* proceedings in breach of a restriction is limited to proprietors, editors and publishers. But this is not the case in relation to breaches of s.39. "*Any person* who includes" matter prohibited by a s.39 order may be liable.

(ii) There is no "due diligence" defence in s.39 cases such as that provided by s.49(9A).

(iii) There is no counterpart in civil proceedings of the power to grant lifelong anonymity conferred on criminal courts by s.45A of the YJCEA.

The three judges agreed that the statutory scheme was in need of further review.

C. Could such a media ban restrict the reporting of criminal proceedings?

[Add new paragraph] **6–119A**

The particular vulnerability of the children justified a reporting restriction order in *A Council v M, F, A, B, C, D* [2012] EWHC 2038 (Fam). The order prevented reporting the defendant's name in her forthcoming trial on charges of child cruelty.

[Add new paragraph] **6–119B**

In *Mr Z v News Group Newspapers Limited* [2013] EWHC 1150 (Fam) (which should be read with the subsequent decision in the same case [2013] EWHC 1371 (Fam)) Cobb J. granted an injunction prohibiting the publication of information which would identify the children of a defendant who was on trial for benefit fraud. The effect of the order was to prohibit the identification of the defendant. The prosecution case was that the defendant had knowingly claimed benefits to which she was not entitled by falsely claiming that a number of her children had various disabilities. The prosecution claimed that she had misrepresented or exaggerated them. Five of the defendant's children were cited in the indictments. An order which had been made in respect of some of the children pursuant to s.39 of the Children and Young Persons Act 1933 had been discharged on the ground that the children did not fall within the jurisdiction of that Act. In the middle of the trial, however, Cobb J. granted the above injunction, holding that the balancing exercise fell in favour of the children's art.8 rights, and in particular in favour of the rights of one of the children who was under the care of the Child and Adolescent Mental Health service. The defence case was going to focus on a detailed analysis of the children's medical records. Cobb J. held that the circumstances were "exceptional" such that the art.8 rights of the children outweighed considerations of open justice and art.10. He also decided that he would reconsider the matter when a verdict was imminent. He subsequently varied the injunction to allow the defendant to be identified if she were found guilty on any count, but prohibited the publication of particular details about the children in order to minimise the impact on them ([2013] EWHC 1371 (Fam) at [30]).

[Add new paragraph] **6–119C**

These authorities were reviewed in *Surrey County Council v ME and others* [2014] EWHC 489 Fam; [2014] 2 F.L.R. 1267; [2014] Fam. Law 815. At [21], the Court stressed that open justice was particularly important in relation to serious criminal behaviour, that members of the public were to entitled to know who was responsible for such behaviour, and that the impact of a story would be significantly reduced without a face and a name. The court noted that in those cases where the Family Division had imposed reporting restrictions in related criminal proceedings the facts were wholly exceptional: see e.g. *A Local Authority v W* [2005] EWHC 1564 (Fam) and *A Council v M* [2012] EWHC 2038. Moreover, there was also detailed evidence in support of each restriction sought. In this case, the court was not prepared to make similar reporting restrictions. There were powerful and compelling reasons for allowing the media to identify a child defendant to a murder charge and thereby fully report on a criminal trial held in public. In respect of other children in the family, Keehan J found that the facts were far from sufficient to outweigh the substantial interference with the media organisations' rights to report the contemporaneous criminal proceedings. In reaching this decision, the judge recognised that the media did not intend to name the other children, and that even a limited reporting restriction in respect of the four children might inhibit media organisations from reporting on the criminal proceedings for fear of inadvertently identifying the parents and defendant, who clearly should be named.

D. Anonymity Orders in Legal Proceedings

1. *Jurisdiction*

6–121A *[Add new paragraph]*

The jurisdiction to make an anonymity order in court proceedings was reviewed by the Supreme Court in *A v BBC* [2014] UKSC 25; [2015] AC 588. Lord Reed, giving the court's judgment, emphasised that common law principles of open justice and the power to derogate from the principles of open justice existed in tandem with the Convention, even where Convention rights were also applicable. The Supreme Court stressed that the principle of open justice is a "constitutional principle to be found in the common law" and therefore the courts had an inherent jurisdiction to determine how the principle should be applied.

2. *Statutory powers to grant anonymity*

6–123 *[Add to end of paragraph]*

The Prevention of Terrorism Act 2005 Sch.1 para.5 was repealed by the Terrorism Prevention and Investigation Measures Act 2011 Sch.4 para.6 of which provides for the grant of anonymity to individuals made subject to an order under the Act. Since 13 April 2015, see also s.45 and s.45A of the Youth Justice and Criminal Evidence Act 1999 and the changes to s.39 and s.49 of the Children and Young Persons Act 1933, as reviewed by the Divisional Court in *Aitken v DPP* [2015] EWHC 1079 (Admin); (2015) 179 J.P. 223 at [70]. See also paras 4–54, 4–248, 4–225, 6–108A, 8–25, 8–50, 8–51 and 8–54.

E. The principles to be applied

[Add new paragraph] **6–127A**

In *A v BBC* [2014] UKSC 25; [2015] AC 588, the Supreme Court upheld an order anonymising a sex offender in an application to prohibit his deportation. The applicant had argued that deportation to his country of origin would amount to an infringement of his Article 2 and 3 Convention rights. The applicant had been anonymised to minimise the risk of publicity which might itself engage those rights were he to be deported. The Supreme Court emphasised, at [41], that the court had to carry out a balancing exercise which was fact-specific:

> "Central to the court's evaluation will be the purpose of the open justice principle, the potential value of the information in question in advancing that purpose and, conversely, any risk of harm which its disclosure may cause to the maintenance of an effective judicial process or to the legitimate interests of others."

The anonymity order was upheld because it was plainly necessary in the interests of justice and in order to protect the safety of a party to proceedings. The publication of A's identity in connection with the proceedings might have rendered those proceedings pointless. Accordingly, the interference with the BBC's rights under Article 10 of the Convention was proportionate and necessary.

[Add new paragraph] **6–127B**

In *R v Marine A* [2013] EWCA Crim 2367; [2014] 1 W.L.R. 3326; [2014] 1 Cr. App. R. 26; [2014] E.M.L.R 10; [2014] Crim. L.R. 536, at [86]-[87], the Divisional Court emphasised that an application to anonymise parties should be approached in a structured manner:

> "The starting point is, in our judgment, the duty of the court, as a public authority, to ensure compliance with the principles (1) of open justice, and (2) that there be no interference with an individual's rights under articles 2 and 3, and (3) no unnecessary or disproportionate interference with (a) the rights of the public under article 10 (having regard to the position of the media under section 12 of the Human Rights Act) 1998, and (b) of any relevant individuals under article 8."

If the court was not obliged to make an under Articles 2 or 3, then the correct approach would be to follow that of Lord Rodger in *Re Guardian News and Media* [2010] 2 AC 697.

[Add to end of paragraph] **6–128**

The question of a balancing exercise in the context of an application for anonymity founded on art.2 and art.3 rights was referred to in *ZY v Higgins* [2013] NIQB 8. McCloskey J. found that there was a real and immediate risk that the applicant would commit suicide if his identity were published in the context of any report of the criminal proceedings which were being brought against him. Having found that art.2 was engaged, McCloskey J. observed that the balancing exercise the court had to carry out had "a certain tinge of unreality". In contrast, in Scotland in *BBC Applicants* [2012] CSOH 185; 2013 S.L.T. 324 (in the context of considering s.11 of the Contempt of Court Act 1981) the court held that there would be no balance to be struck with art.10 rights once an applicant had established a real and not fanciful risk to his rights under art.2 (because of its absolute nature). The appeal to the Supreme Court was dismissed: *A v BBC* [2014] UKSC 25. It was held that the restrictions on the BBC's Article 10 rights were justified because of the physical risks to A, in the event of his deportation, and they were accordingly necessary to protect his rights under Articles 2 and 3. Also, it was the court's intention that he should be deported subject to that protection. The restrictions were thus also necessary in order to uphold the authority of the judiciary in accordance with Article 10(2). (see especially the discussion in the judgment of Lord Reed at [67]–[68]).

6–128 *[Add to note 299]*

In *R. (on the application of M) v Parole Board* [2013] EWHC 1360 (Admin), the Court discharged an anonymity order which had been granted to a claimant (a prisoner serving a life sentence) in judicial review proceedings. M had been convicted of the murder of three young children in 1973. While serving his sentence, he had been attacked and threatened. Three media reports about him had appeared to trigger threats and on one occasion an actual assault by other inmates. The claimant sought anonymity in the judicial review proceedings, relying on his rights under arts 2, 3, 5 and 8. The court approached the matter as a balancing exercise of those rights against the open justice principle and the media's art.10 rights. It found that the risks to the claimant's life and safety were not sufficiently real and imminent to justify anonymity. Any increased risk from a report of the judicial review proceedings could be managed by the prison system and within the Vulnerable Prisoners Unit in which the claimant was housed. The Court rejected the Secretary of State's submission that the fact that the judicial review proceedings were publicly funded materially affected the question of anonymity.

6–129 *[Add to note 300]*

In *PNM v Times Newspapers Ltd and others* [2014] EWCA Civ 1132; [2014] C.P. Rep. 48; [2015] 1 Cr. App. R. 1; [2014] E.M.L.R 30 at [46], the Court of Appeal described the task of the judge as an "evaluative one, akin to the exercise of discretion". See also the similar comments in *Mahmood v BBC* [2014] EWCA Civ 1567 at [5].

6–129 *[Add to text at end of paragraph]*

In *R. (on the application of M and S) v London Borough of Haringey* [2013] EWHC 252 (Admin) Underhill J. expressed doubt that there had been sufficient justification for an earlier order giving anonymity to the claimant but, despite that assessment of the balancing exercise, he continued the order. The claimant had been granted anonymity when she was joined as a party (after the original claimant (M), who had also been given anonymity, encountered problems with obtaining legal aid). Underhill J. took account of S's legitimate expectation of anonymity, on the basis of the previous orders regarding M and herself, when continuing the anonymity order.

[Add new paragraph] **6–131A**

The court observed in *R. (on the application of M) v Parole Board* [2013] EWHC 1360 (Admin) that the question of whether there should be a standard procedure in the Administrative Court for notifying the media in advance of applications for anonymity orders (as in the Family Division) should be considered, although no general guidance was given.

[Add new paragraph] **6–131B**

In *PNM v Times Newspapers Ltd and others* [2014] EWCA Civ 1132; [2014] C.P. Rep. 48; [2015] 1 Cr. App. R. 1; [2014] E.M.L.R 3, the Court of Appeal maintained an order under s.4(2) of the Contempt of Court Act 1981 and anonymised its judgment to protect the appellant's rights pending his application for permission to appeal to the Supreme Court.

[Add new paragraph] **6–131C**

The power of the Court of Appeal to anonymise parties in appeals from the Family Court was considered in *DE v AB* [2014] EWCA Civ 1064; [2015] 1 F.L.R. 1119; [2014] Fam. Law 1530. The court accepted that reporting was *prima facie* not restricted unless an order was made, and that s.97(2) of the Children Act 1989 did not apply in the Court of Appeal. Nevertheless, in light of the decision of the Supreme Court in *A v BBC* [2014] UKSC 25; [2015] AC 588, it was held that the parties to the proceedings should be anonymised, because the very purpose of the hearing would be defeated if the subject-matter could be reported with names.

F. Anonymity orders granted

[Add to note 310] **6–133**

The Claimant was anonymised in *ABC v St George's Healthcare NHS Trust* [2015] EWHC 1394 (QB) where she had brought a claim in negligence against an NHS Trust for allegedly failing to provide her with details of an inherited medical condition.

[Add to note 311] **6–133**

See also *MXB v East Sussex Hospitals NHS Trust* [2012] EWHC 3279 (QB) which briefly considers why in the case of a child an order pursuant to CPR r.39.2(4) may be better than reliance on s.39 of the Children and Young Persons Act 1933. The judge saw force in the argument that s.39 may not give the court jurisdiction to prohibit the making of a report otherwise than in a newspaper, or by way of sound or television broadcast, for example by blogging. He referred to the guidance given by the Court of Appeal in *JIH v News Group Newspapers Ltd* [2011] EWCA Civ 42 at [21] and made an order "pursuant to s.11 Contempt of Court Act 1981, s.6 of the Human Rights Act 1998 and CPR Rule 5.4D and CPR Rule 39.2". There was to be "no publication or other disclosure of any name, address or information tending to identify the Claimant". He pointed out in a "postscript" that the limited wording of s.39 would have clear implications for the restrictions sought to be imposed by judges for the protection of young people involved in criminal trials. The limitation highlighted by the Judge has been addressed to an extent by the legislature in the amendments to the 1933 Act which came into effect on 13 April 2015: see e.g. at 6–108A above.

[Add to note 312]

In *AB Ltd JW, SM and CM v Facebook Ireland* [2013] NIQB 14 anonymity was given to the claimants in an action for misuse of private information even though the dominant claim was for libel.

6–133 *[Add to note 313]*

See also *SPA v TAS* [2014] EWHC 1512 (QB), where similar reasoning was applied in anonymising both parties to a civil claim based on allegations of blackmail.

[Add to note 314]

In *F v G* [2012] ICR 246, the President of the Employment Tribunal gave further guidance on the jurisdiction and practice to be followed when considering anonymity (and reporting restriction) orders in the Employment Tribunal and on appeal, by reference to both the Employment Tribunal Rules of Procedure and Convention rights. In this context, see *BBC v Roden* (UKEAT/0385/14/DA), dated 12 May 2015, in which the EAT overturned a decision of the Employment Tribunal to anonymise a claimant, emphasising that the default position was that judgments of tribunals should be published in full, including the names of the parties.

6–133A *[Add new paragraph]*

In *X v Dartford & Gravesham NHS Trust* [2015] EWCA Civ 96; [2015] C.P. Rep 22; [2015] E.M.L.R 14; [2015] P.I.Q.R P14 at [35] the Court of Appeal ruled, in relation to settlement hearings for personal injury claims, that the default position should be that the judge should make an anonymity order for the protection of the claimant and his or her family, unless satisfied that it is not necessary to do so. Such hearings should, however, be listed in public, and the parties by name, unless an anonymity order has already been made. The media would ordinarily be able to report the hearings, which should be held in open court, subject to any order for anonymity.

[Add to end of paragraph] **6–134**

An application for anonymity was refused in *Graiseley Properties Ltd v Barclays Bank Plc* [2013] EWHC 67 (Comm) because the applicants had not shown that it was "strictly necessary". The claim arose out of the LIBOR-fixing by the defendant bank. Various former and current employees of the bank sought anonymity. Some, but not all, had been identified to the US and UK regulatory authorities as being involved in the rate-fixing. Flaux J. rejected arguments that the principles governing derogations from open justice applied with less force to interim matters than at trial. He observed that the applicants were seeking to avoid identification to protect themselves from reputational harm. There was no general exception to the principle of open justice to protect non-parties from potential unfairness merely because they may not have the opportunity to respond to the alleged wrongdoing.

[Add to note 317] **6–134**

Other recent examples, where applications for anonymity have been refused, include *Birmingham City Council v Riaz and others* [2014] EWHC 4247 (Fam); [2015] Fam. Law 271 (public interest in identifying those involved in child sexual exploitation outweighing any distress embarrassment or anxiety to the applicants or their families); *R (on the application of SF) v Secretary of State for Justice* [2013] EWCA Civ 1275 (no anonymity for a convicted criminal seeking to be released on licence in a different jurisdiction); and *PNM v Times Newspapers Ltd and others* [2014] EWCA Civ 1132; [2014] C.P. Rep. 48; [2015] 1 Cr. App. R. 1; [2014] E.M.L.R 30 (the principle of open justice was not overridden by the presumption of innocence in respect of an individual who had not been charged with any crime; the public can distinguish between someone who had been arrested and someone who had been charged with or convicted of an offence).

[Add new paragraph] **6–134A**

In *R v Marine A* [2013] EWCA Crim 2367; [2014] 1 W.L.R. 3326; [2014] 1 Cr. App. R. 26; [2014] E.M.L.R 10; [2014] Crim. L.R. 536, the Divisional Court declined to overturn the judge's lifting of anonymity in respect of three marines, one of whom was convicted of murder and two cleared of charges. The Divisional Court emphasised that the public interest in open justice in these circumstances did not differ as between individuals who were convicted and those who were acquitted.

[Add new paragraph] **6–134B**

Similarly, the Court of Appeal in *Re Guardian News and Media Ltd* [2014] EWCA Crim 1861; [2015] 1 Cr.App. R.4. [2015] E.M.L.R. 2; [2014]

H.R.L.R. 28, at [47], rejected an application on behalf of the Crown for the anonymisation of defendants on trial for alleged involvement in terrorist offences. It was argued that anonymity might allow greater flexibility in the overall reporting of the trial. The court expressed its "grave concerns" about the cumulative effect of holding a criminal trial in camera, and also anonymising the defendants, and noted that it was difficult to conceive of circumstances in which both departures from open justice would be necessary, even on the grounds of national security.

6–134C *[Add new paragraph]*

Anonymity was lifted in very different circumstances in *Westminster City Council v Manuela Sykes* (2014) 17 C.C.L. Rep. 139. The Court of Protection permitted the reporting of its judgment, without anonymization, in respect of a dementia sufferer was had been deprived of her liberty under the Mental Capacity Act 2005. A critical factor in the decision was the subject's personality; she had played an active role in political and public life when younger, and although she lacked capacity to make such decisions at the date of the hearing, she clearly wanted to contribute to a subject of public concern and debate. These unusual circumstances tipped the balancing exercise in favour of lifting anonymity in the reporting of the Court of Protection judgment.

G. Limited anonymity

6–135A *[Add new paragraph]*

Limited anonymity can be granted in other circumstances. In *CVB v MGN Ltd* [2012] EWHC 1148 (QB) the claimant had been granted dispensation from complying with CPR PD 16 which requires a claim form to include the claimant's name and address. Such orders may affect the media whether or not parties to the litigation (as in that case). Yet it was held that such an order is "permissive" and does not equate to an injunction of any kind or to an "interim remedy" within CPR Pt 25. As such, it was held that there was no requirement under HRA s.12(2) or CPR r.23 to give notice to an intended defendant, or anyone else, of an application to apply for an order dispensing with the requirement. In *A v BBC* [2014] UKSC 25 Lord Reed held that there was no need to give notice in such cases, see para.6–22A above.

6–136A *[Add new paragraph]*

In *Press Association v Newcastle upon Tyne Hospitals Foundation Trust* [2014] EWCOP 6; [2014] C.O.P.L.R 502, the court was faced with the unusual situation where the subject of a reporting restriction application in the Court of Protection died between the making of the application and its hearing. It was accepted that the court had the power to make an order preventing the reporting of the deceased's name in order to uphold the rights of others, including family members. It was disputed whether there was an independent right to protect the deceased person himself. Peter Jackson J rejected the argument that a person's death should lead automatically to all protection being lost. Where anonymity had been granted during an individual's lifetime, the court had a duty to consider whether that should continue following death. This involved considering medical confidentiality and the interests of justice. Specifically, individuals should not be deterred from approaching the court for fear of losing their privacy on death. On the facts of the case, however, the lack of significant intrusion into medical confidentiality, coupled with the public interest in the court's declaration, led to the conclusion that the anonymity order should be lifted. The primary issue confronting the court had been whether it would be lawful to withhold a blood transfusion from a Jehovah's Witness on account of her beliefs.

[Add new paragraph] **6–137A**

The Family Court ([2014] 1 WLR 230; [2014] E.M.L.R 22; [2014] 1 F.L.R 733; [2014] 2 F.C.R. 226) and the Court of Protection ([2014] 1 W.L.R. 235; [2014] E.M.L.R. 21; [2014] C.O.P.L.R. 7) have both issued Practice Guidance about the publication of judgments which took effect from 3 February 2014. The primary purpose was substantially to increase the transparency of the Family Court and the Court of Protection. Where publication is in the public interest, permission to publish a judgment should always be granted. Where a judgment relates to a matter set out in specified categories in each Practice Guidance, the "starting point" is that permission to publish the judgment should be granted unless there are compelling reasons against publication. The Practice Guidance emphasises at [20] that all public authorities and expert witnesses should be named unless there are compelling reasons why they should not. In contrast, children, family members, and vulnerable or incapacitated adults should not normally be named unless the judge otherwise orders. Anonymity in the judgment should not normally extend beyond protecting the privacy of the children and adults who are the subject of their proceedings unless there are compelling reasons to do so. The Practice Guidance states that a standard rubric shall be published with every judgment (unless varied) emphasising that the judgment was delivered in private, and that the court has only given leave to publish the anonymised judgment on the basis that relevant individuals are not to be identified. The rubric states that publication which identifies anonymised individuals will amount to a contempt.

[Add new paragraph] **6–137B**

The consequences of the Practice Guidance for anonymity arose for consideration in *Wigan Borough Council v Fisher & Thomas* [2015] EWFC 34. The court had to consider whether a fact finding judgment, which exonerated a mother and criticised a father for causing injuries which led to a child's death, should be published and, if so, in what form. The father had been acquitted at a criminal trial. The judge ruled that the judgment should be published in full, subject only to the anonymization of the other children. The parents were not anonymised. There was a strong public interest in making accurate information available in a serious case. There was also a strong public interest in allowing the mother to use the judgment to exonerate herself, and for the court's criticisms of the father to be made public. If the judgment were not made public, "the law would be a screen to hide the truth." In light of the extent of material in the public domain, it would be futile to anonymise the parents in any event. The court should not "stultify itself and any attempt to publish anonymously could only lead to bewilderment about what could and could not be reported." The court emphasised, at [34], that the purpose of the Practice Guidance was not the improvement of the image of the Family Court but the wider goal of achieving a proper balancing of all the rights that arise in cases before it.

III. INJUNCTIONS AFFECTING PERSONS WHO ARE NOT DIRECTLY BOUND

B. Injunctions indirectly affecting third parties

Safeguards for third parties? The need to notify persons likely to be affected

6–152A *[Add new paragraph]*

Another safeguard intended to protect third parties' interests is the requirement on parties to progress claims where interim non-disclosure orders have been granted. The *Practice Guidance (Interim Non-disclosure Orders)* [2012] 1 W.L.R. 1003 requires claims to be brought to a conclusion whether by a trial or otherwise (para.41). In *EWQ v GFD* [2012] EWHC 1907 (QB), the court provided for the undertaking not to publish to expire by reference to the timing of a case management conference which the parties were required to fix within a specified period.

6–152B *[Add new paragraph]*

In *A v BBC* [2014] UKSC 25; [2015] AC 588, the Supreme Court ruled that an order to allow a name or matter to be withheld, or an application for ancillary directions, under s.11 of the Contempt of Court Act 1981 was not an application for relief against any person. There was, therefore, no obligation under s.12(2) of the Human Rights Act 1998 to allow the media an opportunity to be heard before such an order was granted. The ability to have a prompt *inter partes* hearing at which the media could make representations was sufficient to provide the media with an effective remedy if they wished to challenge the making of such an order. This approach is consistent with that of Tugendhat J in *JXMX (A Child) v Dartford and Gravesham NHS Trust* [2013] EWHC 3956 (QB); (2014) B.M.L.R. 180, where he ruled that an application for anonymity of a party in civil proceedings did not require an applicant to give notice to the media. On appeal the Court of Appeal ruled that while the media should be given an opportunity to make submissions before any order is made restricting publication of a report of proceedings, it was not necessary to notify the media formally that an application for an anonymity order was going to be made in a settlement case [2015] EWCA Civ 96; [2015] C.P. Rep 22; [2015] E.M.L.R 14; [2015] P.I.Q.R P14 at [34]

C. The nature of the liability of persons not directly bound by an order

[Add to note 353] **6–154**

In *Siemer v Solicitor-General* [2014] 2 LRC 186, Elias CJ (dissenting) held that a third party could challenge the validity of the original order in contempt proceedings (a "collateral challenge") and that such a person should not be held in contempt unless it was shown that he had in fact interfered with the administration of justice. Thus, if it emerged that a restraint on publication had not been reasonably necessary to avoid a risk to the administration of justice, then a publication which was inconsistent with such an order could not be in contempt: see at [33]-[34] and [37]. The majority, however, held that the rule against "collateral challenge" should be reaffirmed. A third party who found that his right of free expression had been adversely affected by a restraining order (i.e. by one made *contra mundum*) should apply to the court for a variation or for rescission of the order.

3. Spycatcher: *the appellate stages*

[Add to note 380] **6–166**

The contrary view was expressed in the New Zealand Supreme Court by Elias CJ in *Siemer v Solicitor-General* [2014] 2 LRC 186, who was of opinion that a third party could not be in contempt unless it were shown that he had actually interfered with the administration of justice. It was not enough that he published while knowing that a restraining order had been made by a judge — he should be able to resist contempt proceedings on the basis that it had not been reasonably necessary to make such an order. This did not accord with the majority view, which was to the effect that a collateral challenge should not be allowed. A third party in these circumstances should apply to vary or rescind the order before publishing.

4. *Att Gen v Punch Ltd*

[Add to text at end of paragraph] **6–172**

In respect of *Jockey Club v Buffham* [2002] EWHC 1866; [2003] Q.B. 462, the Court of Appeal has observed that it should not be assumed that it would, in any future case, approve the conclusion that the *Spycatcher* principle did not apply to final injunctions: see *Hutcheson v Popdog Ltd* [2011] EWCA Civ 1580; [2012] 1 W.L.R 782.

F. The increasing use of "John Doe" injunctions

6–183 *[Add to the end of paragraph]*

The distinct questions of (a) the commission of a contempt and (b) an application to vary an injunction arose on the appeal in *Broxbourne BC v Robb* [2011] EWCA Civ 1355. A refusal to vary the injunction restraining anyone from living at the site was upheld because to accede to it would, in practical terms, have amounted to condoning the applicant's earlier breach. Even on the facts of that case, where the contemnor's conduct had not been of the worst sort, the Court of Appeal was not prepared to send any message that the court will tolerate contempt of its orders or permit those who break them to profit thereby. Compare the reasoning of the various members of the Court of Appeal in *SOCA v O'Docherty* [2013] EWCA Civ 518, where the context was not that of variation but of a new interpretation of the law post-dating a court order. See at 3–233 above.

6–184 *[Add to note 414]*

In *AMP v Persons Unknown* [2011] EWHC 3454 (TCC), an interim injunction was granted against persons unknown in respect of continuing breaches of privacy, namely the sharing and downloading of digital photographic images, including by use of BitTorrent Protocol. The Court was persuaded that an order could be effective to stop distribution of the photographs because there was evidence as to how it was possible to identify internet users, by way of their Internet Protocol addresses, and block them from sharing the identified private material. Relief against intrusion from paparazzi photographers (albeit in a claim brought under the Protection from Harassment Act 1997, rather than as infringement of privacy) was granted in *Hong v XYZ* [2011] EWHC 2995 (QB). Other "celebrities" have obtained similar injunctions against harassment in recent years, such as Lily Allen and Amy Winehouse in 2009 and Cheryl Cole in 2011. See the discussion of this form of relief in various posts on the INFORRM blog by Natalie Peck. See too *Howlett v Holding* [2006] EWHC 41 (QB); *Brett Wilson v Persons Unknown* [2015] EWHC 2628 (QB).

CHAPTER 7

COURT REPORTING I: RESTRICTIONS UNDER THE 1981 ACT

I. THE COMMON LAW BACKGROUND

A. Open justice

[Add to note 2] **7–1**

See also the judgment of Lord Reed in *A v BBC* [2014] UKSC 25, [2015] AC 588, at [23] *et seq.*

[Add new paragraph] **7–4A**

The approach of the common law and the Convention to the principle of open justice was considered by the Supreme Court in *A v BBC* [2014] UKSC 25; [2015] AC 588. Lord Reed, giving the court's judgment, emphasised that common law principles of open justice and the power to derogate from the principles of open justice existed in tandem with the Convention, even where Convention rights were also applicable. The Supreme Court stressed that the principle of open justice was a "constitutional principle to be found in the common law" and therefore the courts had an inherent jurisdiction to determine how the principle should be applied. Although the principle of open justice was expressly protected by Article 6.1 of the Convention, the qualifications set out in the article "broadly reflect the various grounds on which exceptions to the principle of open justice are made in our domestic law, either under the common law or under statute." Qualifications to the open justice principle for the protection of the interests of justice under Article 6.1 were expressly the domain of national courts. In relation to other exceptions from open justice, national states were allowed a margin of appreciation. The Supreme Court emphasised at [57] that the "starting point" was the domestic principle of open justice, as the common law:

> "should normally meet the requirements of the Convention, given the extent to which the Convention and our domestic law in this area walk in step...it is however necessary to bear in mind that, although the Convention and our domestic law give expression to common values, the balance between those values, when they conflict, may not always be struck in the same place under the

Convention as it might have been under our domestic law. In that event, effect must be given to the Convention rights in accordance with the Human Rights Act 1998."

7–6 *[Add to note 15]*

In the context of the media's right to attend hearings in the Family Court, see *Re Al-Hilli (Children)* [2013] EWHC 2190 (Fam); [2014] 1 F.L.R. 403; [2013] Fam. Law 1364. The media's rights to attend and report the Court of Protection were considered in *Re DP* [2014] EWCOP 7, *Westminster City Council v Manuela Sykes* (2014) 17 C.C.L. Rep. 139 and *Press Association v Newcastle upon Tyne Hospitals Foundation Trust* [2014] EWCOP 6; [2014] C.O.P.L.R 502.

7–6 *[Add to note 17]*

See also *Al-Rawi v Security Services* [2011] UKSC 34; [2012] 1 A.C 531 and *A v BBC* [2014] UKSC 25, [2015] AC 588, at [34]–[41].

7–6 *[Add to note 18]*

And see *A v BBC* [2014] UKSC 25, [2015] AC 588, at [44].

7–13A *[Add new paragraph]*

The principle of open justice in the context of reporting criminal proceedings was considered by the Court of Appeal in *Guardian News and Media Ltd, Re* [2014] EWCA Crim 1861; [2015] 1 Cr. App. R.4. [2015] E.M.L.R. 2; [2014] H.R.L.R. 28. On appeal, the court overturned the judge's decision to order both that a terrorism trial take place in private and that the defendants should be anonymised. The court expressed its "grave concerns" about the cumulative effect of holding a criminal trial in camera and also anonymising the defendants, and stated that it was difficult to conceive of circumstances in which both departures from open justice would be necessary, even on the grounds of national security. The Court of Appeal stressed that any departure from the open justice principle should not be greater than was absolutely necessary. There was no risk to the administration of justice in naming the defendants who accordingly should not be anonymised. However, while national security meant that the core of the trial would be held in camera, there was no risk to the administration of justice in holding selected parts of the trial in open court. Further, a limited number of accredited journalists would be permitted to attend but not report on the bulk of the trial with exclusion only from a few small parts. This proposal was not objectionable in principle and was not unworkable. In reaching this conclusion, the Court of Appeal recognised at [41] that:

> "Journalistic presence at a criminal trial fulfils two distinct but related purposes: public scrutiny of the proceedings, coupled with its contemporaneous reporting. We acknowledge that what will be lost is contemporaneous reporting — but that

is an inevitable corollary of an order for an in camera hearing and will, in any event be reviewed at the conclusion of the trial. However, the proposal for the attendance of accredited journalists means that the scrutiny function of the media will be preserved throughout the trial (save for the discrete *ex parte* aspects)."

Some statutory encroachments on the principle

[Add to note 43] 7–19

The same approach applies under the 2009 Act: *R. v Donovan (Reece)* [2012] EWCA Crim 2749.

B. The right of the public to be informed

2. *The need to take account of pre-reading and the diminution of "orality"*

[Add to note 51] 7–22

Reversed on appeal: *R. (on the application of Guardian News and Media Ltd) v City of Westminster Magistrates' Court* [2012] EWCA Civ 420; [2013] Q.B. 618 (discussed in 7–25A).

[Add to note 54] 7–24

Access to court documents was further considered in *Various Claimants v News Group Ltd* [2012] EWHC 397 (Ch); [2012] 1 W.L.R. 2545. The court may order redactions of documents to which a third party has a right of access under CPR r.5.4C if the provision of unredacted documents would create a substantial risk of serious prejudice. In respect of documents to which a third party does *not* have a right of access, Vos J. concluded, at [66], that the court must, in addition,

> "look at the reasons why the documents are sought, and the use to which they will be put. It will also be necessary to consider how far the documents are truly required (in this case in their unredacted form) in order properly to understand and report the court proceedings in which they were referred to and relied upon."

Although he did not accept that *The Guardian* actually needed the documents in order to understand hearings which had taken place, the Judge granted the application because the issues raised in the litigation were of considerable public importance. He ordered limited redactions to some documents.

[Add new paragraph] 7–25A

In *R. (on the application of Guardian News & Media Ltd) v City of Westminster Magistrates Court* (discussed in paragraph 7–25 of the main text), the Court of Appeal allowed an appeal by *The Guardian*: [2012] EWCA Civ 420; [2013] Q.B. 618. It was held that the District Judge had been wrong to conclude that she lacked the power to order the disclosure sought by the newspaper. Because open justice is a common law principle, all courts have an inherent jurisdiction to determine what is required to apply it in any particular case. At [85], Toulson L.J. held:

> "In a case where documents have been placed before a judge and referred to in the course of proceedings, in my judgment the default position should be that access should be permitted on the open justice principle; and where access is sought for a proper journalistic purpose, the case for allowing it will be particularly strong."

He continued:

> "The court has to carry out a proportionality exercise which will be fact-specific. Central to the court's evaluation will be the purpose of the open justice principle, the potential value of the material in advancing that purpose and, conversely, any risk of harm which access to the documents may cause to the legitimate interests of others."

The Criminal Procedure Rules 2015 (SI 2015/1490) in force with effect from 5 October 2015, r.5.8, now provides a specific basis on which third parties can make applications for the supply of information in criminal proceedings. See also the Criminal Practice Directions 2015 [2015] EWCA Crim 1567, CPD I, 5B.

7–25B *[Add new paragraph]*

The South African Supreme Court of Appeal in *City of Cape Town v South African National Roads Authority Limited & others* (20786/14) [2015] ZASCA 58 (30 March 2015) clarified that court documents became public documents when they were filed, even if this predated a court hearing at which they were referred to. However, this approach has not always been followed by some courts in South Africa, see *South Africa: Access to court papers is part of open justice*, D. Milo and S. Scott, 2 July 2015, Inforrm Blog: *https://inforrm.wordpress.com/2015/07/02/south-africa-access-to-court-papers-is-part-of-open-justice-dario-milo/* [Accessed July 9, 2015].

7–25C *[Add new paragraph]*

In the context of the Family Division, the President of the Family Division launched a Consultation Paper on 15 August 2014 *'Transparency — the next steps'*, about the possibility of making documents used in Family Court proceedings available to the media. At the time of writing, there has been no official response to the Consultation Paper and this is now expected some time in Autumn 2015.

3. *The application to public enquiries*

7–27 *[Add to note 64]*

See also *R. (on the application of Associated Newspapers Ltd) v Leveson* [2012] EWHC 57 (Admin), in which the court refused an application for judicial review of the decision of Sir Brian Leveson to receive anonymous evidence in the course of his Inquiry into the Culture, Practice and Ethics of the Press. Certain journalists had been concerned about the impact on their careers of giving evidence publicly. The importance of his being able to pursue the terms of reference was held to outweigh any unfairness to the core participants from the media.

D. The limited power to confer privacy on proceedings

[Add to note 80] 7–36

In *Access Bank v Akingbola* [2012] EWHC 1124 (Comm), the court refused to hold hearings in private because of parallel criminal proceedings in Nigeria. The applicant had argued that a public hearing would be prejudicial to him, as the English trial would be a "dress rehearsal" for the foreign prosecution authorities. Yet his evidence fell short of showing that a private hearing was *necessary*. There was no equivalent of the voluntary undertakings which had been accepted in *Trustor AB v Smallbone*. For a recent example of a limited but pragmatic approach to conferring privacy in criminal proceedings, see *Guardian News and Media Ltd, Re* [2014] EWCA Crim 1861; [2015] 1 Cr. App. R.4. [2015] E.M.L.R. 2; [2014] H.R.L.R. 28, as discussed at paragraph 7–13A above.

[Add to note 84] 7–38

And see *BBC, Applicants* [2013] CSIH 43 at [37]–[38]. The appeal to the Supreme Court was dismissed: *A v BBC* [2014] UKSC 25, [2015] AC 588. (See above at 6–128 and 7–4A.) The Supreme Court upheld an order anonymising a sex offender in an application to prohibit his deportation. The applicant had sought to prevent his deportation on the basis that it would amount to an infringement of his Article 2 and 3 Convention rights, if he was returned to his country of origin. The applicant had been anonymised to minimise the risk of publicity which might in turn engage his Article 2 and Article 3 rights were he to be deported. The principle of open justice had to be balanced against the requirement to do justice.

[Add to note 85] 7–38

In due course, the order had to be enforced by the imposition of custodial penalties (albeit suspended because of the exceptional mitigating circumstances): *Att Gen v Harkins and Liddle* [2013] EWHC 1455 (Admin).

[Add new paragraph] 7–38A

Practice Direction (Committal for Contempt: Open Court)(Sen Cts) [2015] 1 WLR 2195; [2015] 2 All E.R. 541 sets out the limited circumstances in which a court can hear committal hearings for contempt in private and the procedure which should be followed where it is considering sitting in private.

Paragraph 13 of the Practice Direction makes clear that without exception where a court sits in private and finds that a person has committed a contempt, at the conclusion of that hearing it must sit in public and state the name of that person, the nature of the contempt in general terms and the punishment being imposed. The court must also provide details of these matters to the national media and the Judicial Office for publication online.

Criminal Proceedings and hearings in private: Criminal Procedure Rules 2015

7–39A *[Add new paragraph]*

Since 5 October 2015, the Criminal Procedure Rules 2015 have replaced the previous rules governing criminal procedure: The Criminal Procedure Rules 2015(SI 2015/1490) in force with effect from 5 October 2015. The principles described in paragraph 7–39 above which address the circumstances in which a party may make an application for a trial to be heard in private remain substantially unchanged in the new rules (rr.6.6–6.8).

7–40 *[Add to note 91]*

See now Criminal Procedure Rules 2015 (SI 2015/1490) in force with effect from 5 October 2015, Part 40.

Employment Tribunals

7–43 *[Add to note 95]*

The EAT gave guidance as to the approach to be taken under the Regulations in *Eversheds LLP v Gray* (2012) 109(9) L.S.G. 16.

The Court of Appeal

7–47A *[Add to end of paragraph]*

In *DE v AB* [2014] EWCA Civ 1064; [2015] 1 F.L.R. 1119; [2014] Fam. Law 1530, the Court of Appeal considered the appropriateness of sitting in private when a public hearing would defeat the very purpose of the hearing, although in the event this was unnecessary as there were no members of the public in attendance.

E. The distinction between public and private hearings: a change of practice

4. *The provisions of CPR Pt 39*

7–68 *[Add to note 138]*

In *Global Torch Ltd v Apex Global Management Ltd* [2013] EWHC 223 (Ch), an application for interim applications to be heard in private was refused. Allegations of serious wrongdoing had been made against parties and non-parties in the proceedings, but those matters would not be determined in the course of those applications. The applicants were seeking to protect their rights to reputation. The judge proceeded on the basis that their rights under art.8 were indeed engaged, but held that the interference with those rights was not sufficient reason to justify a private hearing in the interests of justice under CPR r.39.2(g). The mere fact that damaging allegations were being made in proceedings was not such a serious interference with the private life of the applicants to displace the open justice principle.

See also *Shuldham, Re* [2012] EWHC 1420 (Ch), a case in which an application for the proceedings to be heard in private, based on a number of different grounds in CPR r.39 and PD 39A, was rejected. Merely because the applicant could bring the claim within the provisions, this did not mean that there was a right to a private hearing. Where the claim involved confidential information, "[t]he court will have to form a view as the nature of the confidential information, its importance to the party, and the damage he will suffer by its disclosure before deciding whether it is necessary to hold a hearing in private".

[Add to text at end of paragraph] **7–70**

A number of recent decisions have emphasised that anonymity will not be granted to parties or non-parties unless it is *necessary*, in the interests of justice, and there is cogent evidence in support: see e.g. *Graiseley Properties Ltd v Barclays Bank Plc* [2013] EWHC 67 (Comm) and *Deripaska v Cherney* [2012] EWCA Civ 1235.

Other rules of court

[Add to note 148] **7–71**

In *Bank Mellat v HM Treasury* [2013] UKSC 38 (a case arising from the Counter-Terrorism Act 2008 and the Financial Restrictions (Iran) Order 2009 made under the Act), the Supreme Court acknowledged that it could hold a closed hearing and consider closed material. Yet Lord Neuberger's judgment emphasised that such a step should be regarded as exceptional. Guidance was given on the use of closed and open judgments as a means of minimising the need for closed hearings on appeal.

F. The traditionally recognised exceptions to the openness principle

[Add new paragraph] **7–78A**

The tension between open justice and the need for secrecy in national security matters has received further attention in *Al-Rawi v Security Service* [2011] UKSC 34; [2012] 1 A.C. 531. The Supreme Court rejected the use of closed material procedures, which are used in terrorism proceedings, in civil claims for damages. The claims had been brought by individuals who had been subject to rendition and detention, including at Guantanamo Bay, and who alleged that the domestic security services were complicit. It was accepted that the court has an inherent power to regulate its own procedures, and that innovations may be introduced in the interests of justice, but it was held that

> "the court cannot exercise its power to regulate its own procedures in such a way as will deny parties their fundamental common law right to participate in the proceedings in accordance with the common law principles of natural justice and open justice."

The same approach was applied by the Supreme Court in *A v BBC* [2014] UKSC 25, [2015] AC 588. (See the discussion at 6–127A above.)

7–80 *[Add to end of paragraph]*

Similarly, in *Re Guardian News and Media Ltd* [2014] EWCA Crim 1861; [2015] 1 Cr. App. R.4. [2015] E.M.L.R. 2; [2014] H.R.L.R. 28, the Court of Appeal ordered that much of a terrorism trial would be heard in private to protect national security, albeit that selected accredited members of the media could attend but not report on the proceedings: see the discussion at paragraph 7–13A above.

Family proceedings

7–85A *[Add new paragraph]*

There has been increased access to and reporting of both the family courts and the Court of Protection. The President of the Family Division issued draft *Practice Guidance on Transparency in the Family Courts and the Court of Protection* on July 12, 2013. It proposed that there should be, so far as possible, unification of the rules governing access to hearings in those courts. The Practice Guidance *Transparency in the Family Courts: Publication of Judgments'* issued by the President of the Family Division has the effect "of increasing the number of judgments available for publication (even if they will often need to be published in an appropriately anonymised form)" [2] *https://www.judiciary.gov.uk/wp-content/uploads/JCO/Documents/Guidance/transparency-in-the-family-courts-jan2014.pdf* [accessed July 14, 2015]. See para 7–85B below.

7–85B *[Add new paragraph]*

The Family Court ([2014] 1 WLR 230; [2014] E.M.L.R 22; [2014] 1 F.L.R 733; [2014] 2 F.C.R. 226) and the Court of Protection ([2014] 1 W.L.R. 235; [2014] E.M.L.R. 21; [2014] C.O.P.L.R. 7) have both issued Practice Guidance about the publication of judgments in the Family Court and Court of Protection which took effect from 3 February 2014, discussed at paragraph 6–137A above. After the introduction of this Practice Guidance, 255 judgments of the Family Court had been published on BAILII between February and July 2014, compared to 115 judgments in the corresponding period for 2013.

In the context of the Family Division, the President of the Family Division launched a Consultation Paper on 15 August 2014 *'Transparency — the next steps'*, about the possibility of making documents used in Family Court proceedings available to the media. At the time of writing, there has been no official response to the Consultation Paper and this is now expected some time in Autumn 2015.

Appellate Proceedings

[Add to end of paragraph] **7–87**

In *DE v AB* [2014] EWCA Civ 1064; [2015] 1 F.L.R. 1119; [2014] Fam. Law 1530, the Court of Appeal considered the appropriateness of sitting in private where sitting in public would defeat the very purpose of the hearing, although in the event this was not necessary as there were no members of the public in attendance. See also *X v Dartford & Gravesham NHS Trust* [2015] EWCA Civ 96; [2015] C.P. Rep 22; [2015] E.M.L.R 14; [2015] P.I.Q.R P14 at [35] where the Court of Appeal ruled that in settlement hearings for personal injury claims, the balancing of the respective rights in issue meant that the default position should be that a judge should make an anonymity order for the protection of the claimant and his or her family unless the court is satisfied that it is not necessary to do so.

[Add to note 186] **7–88**

See also *R (on the application of Willford) v Financial Services Authority* [2013] EWCA Civ 674.

G. The residual discretion: deterrence of witnesses by publicity

[Add to note 190] **7–90**

See also *ZAM v CFW* [2013] EWHC 662 and *SPA v TAS* [2014] EWHC 1512 (QB).

H. Circumstances justifying the withholding of particular items of information in open court

Private hearings, public judgments

[Add to note 217] **7–106**

See the Practice Guidance about the publication of judgments in the Family Court and Court of Protection which took effect from 3 February 2014, discussed at paragraph 6–137A, and 7–85 A and B above. See also *Practice Direction (Committal for Contempt: Open Court)(Sen Cts)* [2015] 1 WLR 2195; [2015] 2 All E.R. 541, discussed at paragraph 7–38A above. Additionally, see "*Lost opportunities: law reform and transparency in the family courts*", Sir James Munby [2010] CFLO 273; "*View from the President's*

Chambers: The Process of Reform" (1) [2013] Fam Law 548 and (4) 16 July 2013; and *The Single Family Court: A Joint Statement by the President of the Family Division and the HMCTS Family Business Authority* (April 2013) [2013] Fam Law 600. See also *Practice Direction (Committal for Contempt: Open Court)(Sen Cts)* [2015] 1 WLR 2195; [2015] 2 All E.R. 541, discussed at paragraph 7–38A above.

I. The continuing relevance of the common law

7–108 *[Add to end of paragraph]*

It is worthy of note, however, that in *A v BBC* [2014] UKSC 25, [2015] AC 588, Lord Reed emphasised that the starting point was the common law principles of open justice: see paragraphs 6–121A and 7–4A above.

II. Section 11 of the Contempt of Court Act

A. The terms of s.11

7–110 *[Add to note 223]*

In Scotland, the Court of Session has an inherent jurisdiction to withhold the name of a party or a third party in order to prevent injustice or protect a third party's rights, and where appropriate to make an order under s.11 to prevent reporting: see *BBC, Applicants* [2013] CSIH 43 at [37]–[38] (doubting Lord Brailsford's reasoning in *SRC v Kemp* [2013] CSOH 56). The appeal to the Supreme Court was dismissed: *A v BBC* [2014] UKSC 25, [2015] AC 588. (See above at 6–128 and 7–4A and below at 16-390.)

7–110 *[Add to note 224]*

In the *Practice Guidance (Interim Non-disclosure Orders)* [2012] 1 W.L.R. 1003, the then Master of the Rolls re-stated the established position that s.11 orders should only be made "when strictly necessary".

C. The Consolidated Criminal Practice Direction

7–110 *[Add to note 229]*

See now the *Criminal Practice Directions* [2013] EWCA Crim 1631 and, in particular, 16B.4(g), (h) and (i) (which require orders to be in precise terms and to state whether it is prohibited to report the existence of the order itself) and 16B.5 which states that the court should generally use the template orders available.

[Add new paragraph] **7–110A**

The purpose of s.11 was reviewed by the Supreme Court in *A v BBC* [2014] UKSC 25; [2015] AC 588. At [59], the Supreme Court noted that s.11 does not itself confer any power on courts to allow information to be withheld from the public, but applies in circumstances where an independent power has been exercised. The purpose of s.11 was to support the exercise of such a power by giving the court a statutory power to make ancillary directions prohibiting the publication in connection with the proceedings of information which had been withheld from the public in the proceedings itself. The directions were such as were necessary for the purpose for which the information was withheld. The purpose of an order under s.11 was not confined to circumstances where an order was necessary to protect the administration of justice.

In *R (on the application of Wang Yam) v Central Criminal Court* [2014] EWHC 3358 (Admin); [2015] 1 Cr. App. R. 10; [2015] Crim. L.R. 224; [2015] A.C.D. 26, the Divisional Court stated that even if an order under s.11 could not prohibit a publication to the European Court of Human Rights,

> "the court must have an inherent power to issue an ancillary order or direction whose express object is to secure the purpose of an order made in court. The common law would be seriously deficient if the order made in the proceedings could be wholly undermined because the judge's writ did not run outside the court room."

[Add to note 235] **7–114**

And see *A v BBC* [2014] UKSC 25, [2015] AC 588, at [58] *et seq.* (See above at 6–128 and 7–4A.)

[Add new paragraph] **7–114A**

The issue of anonymity was also considered in the context of a Court Martial in *R v Marine A* [2013] EWCA Crim 2367; [2014] 1 W.L.R. 3326; [2014] 1 Cr. App. R. 26; [2014] E.M.L.R 10; [2014] Crim. L.R. 536. The judge had made an interim order prohibiting the identification of marines charged with murder on the basis that there was a real and immediate risk to their lives. The order was made under r. 153 of the Armed Force (Court Martial) Rules 2009 and s.11 of the Contempt of Court Act 1981 and remained in place until the Court Martial had delivered its findings. After the conclusion of the Court Martial, the judge ruled that the position had changed and lifted the anonymity orders. Three marines appealed against the lifting of the orders, but the appeals were rejected by the Divisional Court. The judge had ruled that there was no real and immediate risk threat to life posed by naming the marines and the Divisional Court regarded this decision as unassailable. In weighing the competing rights under Article 8 and Article 10, the Divisional Court emphasised the public interest in open justice in these circumstances such as a court martial, and that this did not differ as between Marine A who had been convicted and Marines B and C who had been acquitted.

7–117A *[Add new paragraph]*

These matters are now governed by the new Criminal Practice Directions 2015 [2015] EWCA Crim 1567 which came into force with effect from 5 October 2015. CPD I, 5B deals with third party rights to access documents. Part 6 of the Criminal Procedure Rules [2015] (SI 2015/1490) and the accompanying Practice Directions apply to orders restricting reporting, including orders made under s.11 of the Contempt of Court Act 1981.

7–118A *[Add new paragraph]*

In *BBC, Applicants* [2013] CSIH 43, the Lord President observed that the procedures in Scotland for hearing the media on applications for s.11 orders were inadequate. Although he was not persuaded that the media should necessarily be notified of all such applications in advance, since there may be cases of pressing urgency, he suggested that the Scottish Civil Justice Council consider procedures and provision for ensuring media interests can be addressed. The appeal was dismissed. See now the discussion in *A v BBC* [2014] UKSC 25, [2015] AC 588, at [67]–[68] (See above at 6–128 and 7–4A). Following the decision in *A v BBC* an Act of Sederunt was passed in Scotland amending the Rules of the Court of Session, the Ordinary Cause Rules and the Summary Application rules in respect of orders which restrict the reporting of proceedings. See para 16–203 below.

In *A v BBC* [2014] UKSC 25; [2015] AC 588, the Supreme Court ruled that an order to allow a name or matter to be withheld or an application for ancillary directions under s.11 of the Contempt of Court Act 1981 was not an application for relief against any person and there was therefore no obligation under s.12(2) of the Human Rights Act 1998 to allow the media an opportunity to be heard before such an order was granted. The ability to have a prompt *inter partes* hearing at which the media could make representations was sufficient to provide the media with an effective remedy if they wished to challenge the making of such an order. However, paragraphs 16B.4(e) and (f) of the Criminal Practice Direction 2015 [2015] EWCA Crim 1567 in force with effect from 5 October 2015 which apply to England and Wales do provide that no order should be made without giving the media an opportunity to make representations. Where the media or other interested parties have not been represented on the making of the order, they should have permission to apply within a limited period.

D. Mens rea for breach of s.11 orders

7–122 *[Add to note 254]*

See now the Criminal Practice Directions [2015] EWCA Crim 1567 at CPD I, 6B.7 which warns that it is the responsibility of those reporting proceedings to make enquiries as to the existence of any orders "in case of doubt".

E. Decisions in the light of s.11

2. *Cases where anonymity has been properly granted*

[Add to note 270] **7–134**

See the discussion in *A v BBC* [2014] UKSC 25, [2015] AC 588, at [36] *et seq.* (See above at 6–128 and 7–4A.)

[Add to note 271] **7–134**

See also *BBC, Applicants* [2013] CSIH 43, at [37]-[38], where the Lord President referred to the court's "repeatedly recognised" inherent jurisdiction and observed,

> "... I would regard it as the court's duty to withhold the identity of, say, a female pursuer where the decision turned on intimate medical evidence".

The Supreme Court upheld the decision to grant anonymity: *A v BBC* [2014] UKSC 25, [2015] AC 588. The inherent jurisdiction to withhold information from the public was acknowledged: see 7–4A above.

[Add to end of paragraph] **7–137**

For example, in *A Council v M* [2012] EWHC 2038 (Fam), an order was made in the Family Division prohibiting the identification of members of a family in any reporting of criminal proceedings being taken against the mother for abuse and cruelty to her children. Peter Jackson J. considered that the powers available to the Crown Court to restrict reporting provided insufficient protection for the children of the family. He also held that the Family Division would normally be better placed than the Crown Court to assess all the interests engaged.

[Add new paragraph] **7–140A**

In *BBC, Applicants* [2013] CSIH 43, the BBC sought recall of a s.11 order which had been made in judicial review proceedings. The petitioner had been convicted of sexual offences and, after serving his sentence, the Secretary of State sought to deport him. He resisted deportation for many years, including on the ground that he faced a real risk of being attacked if returned to his home country because of media coverage of his conviction. In judicial review proceedings of the deportation order, a s.11 order was made in respect of his identity. The BBC sought to challenge it on the basis that the petitioner had not shown that anonymity was necessary to protect his rights under arts 2 and 3. The Court did not consider that question afresh. The view was taken, not only that the court below had been entitled to reach the conclusion on the evidence that there was a risk to him, but also that there were good reasons not to discharge the s.11 order which concerned the proper administration of justice; namely that, as deportation had been ordered on the understanding that the petitioner would have anonymity, recalling the s.11 order might subvert the very basis on which that order had been made. The appeal to the Supreme Court was dismissed. See now the discussion in *A v BBC* [2014] UKSC 25, [2015] AC 588, and especially at [67]–[68]. (See above at 6–128 and 7–4A.)

3. *The power to prohibit "other matter"*

7–142A *[Add new paragraph]*

In *R (on the application of Wang Yam) v Central Criminal Court* [2014] EWHC 3358 (Admin); [2015] 1 Cr. App. R. 10; [2015] Crim. L.R. 224; [2015] A.C.D. 26, the Divisional Court had to consider whether an order under s.11 could prohibit the publication of sensitive material by a defendant in criminal proceedings upon an application to the European Court of Human Rights. At his original trial, the defendant had sought to vary the order under s 11 because he wished to use some of the sensitive material to argue in Strasbourg that he had not received a fair trial under Article 6. The Divisional Court expressed its reservations about the appropriateness of the definition of 'publication' under s.2(1) of the Contempt of Court Act 1981 when used in the context of s.11. Orders under s.11 might need to prohibit limited even entirely private publications which might not fall within the scope intended by s.2(1). The Divisional Court was prepared to accept that a publication to the court staff and judges could fall within the scope of s.11, even if it ultimately declined to determine this "difficult issue".

III. POSTPONEMENT ORDERS UNDER SECTION 4(2) OF THE 1981 ACT

B. Section 4(2): Reporting restrictions

7–146 *[Add to note 314]*

The substituted paragraphs (b) and (c) came into force on June 18, 2012, subject to savings in art.6(2): SI 2012/1320.

F. The principal issues raised by s.4 of the Act identified

7–158 *[Add to note 336]*

See now the Criminal Procedure Rules 2015 (SI 2015/1490) in force with effect from 5 October 2015, and the Criminal Practice Directions 2015 [2015] EWCA Crim 1567. Part 6 of the Criminal Procedure Rules and the accompanying Practice Directions applies to orders restricting reporting, including under s.4 (2) of the Contempt of Court Act 1981.

I. Is breach of a s.4(2) order ipso facto a contempt?

[Add to note 351] 7–169

FSMA 2000 ss.18 and 161 have been repealed.

J. The "proceedings" contemplated under s.4(2)

[Add to note 362] 7–174

In *R. v April Casburn*, December 9, 2012, on an application under s.4(2) in pre-trial proceedings relating to a charge of misconduct in a public office, the Judge was asked to order the postponement of any report of a separate charge against the defendant under the Official Secrets Act. He refused to do so, largely because the information was widely available on the internet, including on sites hosted abroad. He did, however, indicate that he had been asked to determine whether the term "proceedings" would be wide enough to cover the mere fact that the defendant had been charged with the other offence. He did not need in the event to decide that point, but it is submitted that in the light of the judgments in the *Horsham Justices* case the fact that she had been charged could in itself fall within the scope of the section and that he would accordingly have had the necessary jurisdiction.

Restricting a report of appellate proceedings

[Add to note 364] 7–175

The Court of Appeal postponed reporting of its own proceedings in *X (Children) (Serious Case Review: Publication), Re* [2012] EWCA Civ 1500. Although the full terms of the order are not included in the judgment, it appears that the postponement was intended to be effective until the Court handed down its decision. The purpose of the order was to avoid having to sit in private while, at the same time, not inhibiting the parties from making full submissions on the material thereby defeating the very purpose of the application for a reporting restriction, which was itself under appeal.

K. What "publications" may be postponed?

[Add text to end of paragraph] 7–177

In *McLuckie v The Coroner for Northern Ireland* [2011] NICA 34, the court quashed a coroner's decision refusing to make a s.4(2) order. The appellant was to give evidence at the inquest of a man he had shot while serving in the army. At the time of the inquest, he was serving a prison sentence for murder, which was unconnected with the matters arising at the inquest. His conviction was referred to during a preliminary hearing and widely reported upon. Nevertheless, he sought an order postponing further publication on the ground it would prejudice the inquest jury. The coroner refused on the basis that the information was already in the public domain. In the subsequent judicial review proceedings, on appeal, it was held that the coroner had been wrong to conclude that the fact the information was in the public domain precluded him from making such an order. It appears that the relevant information was only in the public domain because of the earlier reports of the coroner's proceedings.

M. For how long may a publication be postponed?

7–181 *[Add to note 382]*

See now the identical provision at CPD I, 6B.4(h)(iii) of the Criminal Practice Directions 2015 [2015] EWCA Crim 1567 in force with effect from 5 October 2015.

O. The practical implementation of s.4(2) orders

7–188A *[Add new paragraph]*

See now the provisions at CPD I, 6B of the Criminal Practice Directions 2015 [2015] EWCA Crim 1567. It re-states established principles concerning the making of discretionary reporting restriction orders, which are derogations from open justice. A copy of an order should be provided to anyone interested in reporting the proceedings and to local or national media which regularly report proceedings in the court (6B.6). Court staff should also be prepared to answer enquiries, but responsibility for finding out about any orders remains with those reporting on proceedings (6B.7).

Whether to reveal the existence of a s.4(2) order

7–197A *[Add new paragraph]*

The Law Commission has proposed adopting a system in England and Wales similar to the one operating in Scotland, and referred to in paragraph 7–191. It proposes that a central record of s.4(2) orders — and possibly other reporting restriction orders — could be maintained and that users throughout the United Kingdom could sign up for email notification: Consultation Paper No.209, at 2.100–2.015. The proposal was supported in the response of the senior judiciary (although it entered a note of caution as to the possibility of extending such a service to orders made in relation to children under s.39 of the Children and Young Persons Act 1933 — "where the need for restraint in reporting will be obvious": "A Judicial Response to the Law Commission Consultation Paper No 209" at para 26: *http://www.judiciary.gov.uk/Resources/JCO/Documents/Consultations/sen-judiciary-response-to-law-comm-on-contempt-court.pdf* [Accessed July 14, 2015]. The Law Commission released its final recommendations in March 2014 'Contempt of Court (2): Court Reporting': *https://www.gov.uk/government/uploads/system/uploads/attachment_data/file/295972/9781474101257_HC_*

1162_web.pdf [Accessed July 9, 2015]. The Law Commission maintained its recommendation for a publicly available online database of existing s.4(2) orders similar to that maintained in Scotland. The standard form of order should make clear that that any restriction on reporting the fact of an order does not apply to the publication on this official database. The publicly available online list would be limited to the name of the case and the date on which the order expires. This publicly available database of orders should also be supplemented by an additional database which would contain the terms of s.4(2) orders themselves. There would be restricted access by way of subscription for media organisations. The Law Commission noted that if these recommendations were adopted, they would provide valuable protection for publishers. Although the Law Commission's proposal extends only to s.4(2) orders, it did welcome a planned IT system which would make information regarding all reporting restrictions available to interested parties.

P. The tests to be applied before making an order

3. *A three stage test*

[Add to end of paragraph] **7–208**

This approach was followed by the Divisional Court in *R v Marine A* [2013] EWCA Crim 2367; [2014] 1 W.L.R. 3326; [2014] 1 Cr. App. R. 26; [2014] E.M.L.R 10; [2014] Crim. L.R. 536 at [86]–[87] who emphasised that a similarly structured approach should be adopted when the court was considering making an order for anonymity. See also paragraph 2.28 of the Law Commission's report dated 25 March 2014 'Contempt of Court (2): Court Reporting': *https://www.gov.uk/government/uploads/system/uploads/attachment_data/file/295972/9781474101257_HC_1162_web.pdf* [Accessed 9 July, 2015].

5. *Stage 1: evaluating the risk*

[Add to note 427] **7–213**

See now *Mustafa Abu Hamza (No.1) v UK* (31411/07), (2011) 52 E.H.R.R. SE11. See also the views expressed on the integrity of the jury system in the response of the senior judiciary to the Law Commission Consultation Paper No.209 at paras 20–21: *http://www.judiciary.gov.uk/Resources/JCO/Documents/Consultations/sen-judiciary-response-to-law-comm-on-contempt-court.pdf* [Accessed July 14, 2015].

10. *Two uses of "necessity"*

[Add new paragraph] **7–243A**

The three stage approach in *Ex. p. Telegraph Group Plc* [2001] EWCA Crim 1075; [2001] 1 W.L.R. 1983 was considered by way of analogy in *Mobile Phone Voicemail Interception Litigation, Re* [2012] EWHC 397 (Ch); [2012] W.L.R 2545. A third party media organisation had applied for copies of documents from the court file, presumably to use in its reporting of civil proceedings concerning "phone hacking". The application was resisted by a personal defendant, who had been arrested on suspicion of attempting to pervert the course of justice and unlawful interference in communications. He argued that publishing material from the civil proceedings would prejudice those future criminal proceedings, and that the application for documents should be approached in the same way as if the court were considering ordering a postponement of reporting. In deciding whether and how to exercise the court's discretion to redact parts of the documents, the judge accepted that the factors to be taken into account were much the same as would have to be considered upon an application under s.4(2).

Q. What is the required mental element in the case of the breach of a s.4(2) order?

7–244 *[Add to text at end of paragraph]*

It is relevant here to consider the summary of the law on the mental element for civil contempt generally in *Masri v Consolidated Contractors International* [2011] EWHC 1024. See also at 12–96A below.

2. *Question 1: (b) Will recklessness as to the existence of the order suffice?*

7–251 *[Add to note 484]*

See now paragraphs 6B.6 and 6B.7 of the Criminal Practice Directions [2015] EWCA Crim 1567 in force with effect from 5 October 2015. It remains the responsibility of a publisher to ensure no breach of an order occurs and to make enquiries in case of doubt. See also para.1–67 above.

7–260 *[Add to note 494]*

See now paragraphs 6B.6 and 6B.7 of the Criminal Practice Directions [2015] EWCA Crim 1567 in force with effect from 5 October 2015. See also para.1–67 above.

7–261A *[Add new paragraph]*

The ambiguity of the law in this areas was referred to at paragraph 2.48–2.49 of the Law Commission's Report dated 25 March 2014 'Contempt of Court (2): Court Reporting': *https://www.gov.uk/government/uploads/system/uploads/attachment_data/file/295972/9781474101257_HC_1162_web.pdf* [Accessed July 9, 2015].

The Law Commission noted that the lack of clarity was 'unfortunate'. As the Law Commission stated at paragraph 2.54, s.4(2) orders were:

> "designed to prevent exceptional cases of prejudicial court reporting, by communicating to the publisher that such reporting needs to be postponed to protect

the proceedings. This aim only justifies punishing a breach of the order if it is done with knowledge of the order's existence".

It was to provide greater fairness to publishers that the Law Commission therefore proposed establishing a public database and a subscription database which would identify whether a s.4(2) order had been made in a particular case. As the Law Commission stated in its conclusions, if liability for a breach of a s.4(2) order requires actual knowledge of that order, such databases would provide useful evidence in any contemplated contempt proceedings. If recklessness was sufficient to ground liability for contempt, the Law Commission stated that the presence of an order on the database would "likely to be determinative" of the necessary mens rea. Equally however, the list would provide valuable protection to publishers, because if an order was not contained in the database which a publisher had checked, it was likely that the publisher "would have done enough to avoid liability for contempt in most circumstances".

3. *Question 2: Is there additionally a need to prove intention to interfere with the administration of justice?*

[Add to end of paragraph] **7–262**

This uncertainty was referred to at paragraph 2.44 of the Law Commission's Report dated 25 March 2014 'Contempt of Court (2): Court Reporting', citing this paragraph.

4. *Question 3: Will recklessness as to the consequences suffice?*

[Add to note 506] **7–267**

See now the Criminal Practice Directions 2015 [2015] EWCA Crim 1567 in force with effect from 5 October 2015.

R. Who has the power to punish a breach?

[Add to note 510] **7–269**

See now CPR r.81.13(e). Rule 81.13 indicates to which court an application for permission to commit for contempt is to be made, although, on granting permission, a court may direct the matter to be transferred to another court (CPR r.81.14(6)).

[Add to note 512] **7–269**

The exception in respect of contempt comprising "disobedience to an order of a court", previously in Ord.52 r.1, is preserved in CPR r.81.12(1). Separately, the jurisdiction of the High Court, and that of the Court of Appeal, to make an order for committal of its own motion is now to be found in CPR r.81.2(3).

7–271 *[Add to note 514]*

See now CPR Pt 81.

T. The recognition of journalists' locus standi in relation to such orders

7–293 *[Add to end of paragraph]*

Furthermore, Part 6 of the Criminal Procedure Rules 2015 (SI 2015/1490) in force with effect from 5 October 2015 (which governs reporting restrictions and related matters) and the Criminal Practice Directions 2015 EWCA 1567 provides that the court should hear from parties and "any other person directly affected" before making an order: CPR I, 6B.4. See *R v Jolleys, ex parte Press Association* [2013] EWCA Crim 1135 (where reference was made to the equivalent passage in the 2012 rules).

U. Appeals against s.11 and 4(2) orders: Section 159 of the 1988 Act

1. *The background and the terms of the section*

7–300 *[Add to note 561]*

See however the decisions of *R v McGreechan* [2014] NICA 5 and *JC & RT v Central Criminal Court and others* [2014] EWHC 1041 (QB); [2014] 1 W.L.R. 3697; [2014] 4 All E.R. 319; [2014] 2 Cr. App. R. 13; [2014] E.M.L.R. 20; [2014] 2 F.C.R. 571; [2014] Crim. L.R. 902 discussed at paragraph 7–306 A below.

7–300 *[Add to note 562]*

See also *R v Marine A* [2013] EWCA Crim 2367; [2014] 1 W.L.R. 3326; [2014] 1 Cr. App. R. 26; [2014] E.M.L.R 10; [2014] Crim. L.R. 536 for the approach of the Court Martial Appeal Court.

7–300 *[Add to end of paragraph]*

As subss.(b) and (c) make clear, the reach of s.159 extends beyond appeals from orders made under the 1981 Act. In *R. v ITN News* [2013] EWCA Crim 773, where it provided the basis for an appeal against an order under s.46 of the Youth Justice and Criminal Evidence Act 1999, Lord Judge C.J. held that s.159 should be given the "widest possible construction", given that it was a means for the media to challenge reporting restrictions, and re-emphasised the importance of open justice in criminal proceedings.

[Add to note 565] **7–301**

See now the discussion in *A v BBC* [2014] UKSC 25, [2015] AC 588, at [67]-[68]. See above at 6–128 and 7–4A. In relation to developments in Scotland following this decision, see paras 7–118A and 16–203.

3. *"Person(s) aggrieved"*

[Add to note 569] **7–304**

See also *R. (on the application of Press Association) v Cambridge Crown Court* [2012] EWCA Crim 2434; [2013] 1 W.L.R. 1979.

[Add new paragraph] **7–306A**

The limitations of the right to appeal to the Court of Appeal in s.159 were demonstrated by an appeal considering the corresponding provisions in the Armed Forces (Court Martial) Rules 2009 in *R v Marine A* [2013] EWCA Crim 2367; [2014] 1 W.L.R. 3326; [2014] 1 Cr. App. R. 26; [2014] E.M.L.R 10; [2014] Crim. L.R. 536. Rule 154 of the Court Martial Rules provided corresponding rights of appeal to those contained in s.159 of the Criminal Justice Act.

In *R v Marine A*, various media organisations sought to appeal restrictions placed on their right of access to documents used during the Court Martial. At the same time, three marines sought to appeal the lifting of an order which had granted them anonymity. The Court Martial Appeal Court emphasised that it was necessary to give rule 154 a broad and liberal construction in the same way that the Court of Appeal had done in respect of the corresponding provision in s.159 in *R (on the application of Central Television Plc)* [1991] 1 WLR 4. Accordingly, the Court Martial Appeal Court did have the jurisdiction to hear the media's appeal against the limitations placed on their access to court documents. In contrast however, the Court Martial Appeal Court could not construe the same rule in such a way that would not contradict its express language which limited appeals to orders restricting access or publication. It therefore did not have jurisdiction to hear the marines' appeals against the lifting of the anonymity order and had to reconstitute itself as the Divisional Court to determine these appeals by way of a judicial review.

[Add new paragraph] **7–306B**

In *R v McGreechan* [2014] NICA 5 the Northern Ireland Court of Appeal had to consider the limitations in s.159 when an application was made to challenge an order of the Crown Court which had lifted reporting restrictions concerning the identity of a rapist. An application to judicially review the Crown Court's decision could not proceed because in Northern Ireland, the Crown Court was part of the Court of Judicature, and there was no equivalent to s.29(3) of the Senior Courts Act 1981, which made such decisions susceptible to judicial review. The Northern Ireland Court of Appeal noted that:

> "In this case section 159 of the 1988 Act provides the media with a right of appeal to the Court of Appeal where an order is made restricting reporting of matters relating to a child. No equivalent right is available to the child in the Crown Court. The child would, of course, have protection by way of judicial review if the decision was made in the lower courts. We can well understand why the media should be entitled to pursue the principle of open justice by way of an appeal to the Court of Appeal but there is no reason why the affected child should not have a similar entitlement in relation to his rights."

Instead, and considering that article 6 of the Convention required the applicant to have access to rights of appeal, the Northern Ireland Court of Appeal felt obliged to interpret s159 in accordance with s.3 of the Human Rights Act 1998 so that s.159(c) read that an appeal to the Court of Appeal could lie against:

> "any order restricting the publication of any report of the whole or any part of a trial on indictment or any such ancillary proceedings or any discharge of such order or refusal by the Court to make such order."(new words underlined)

7–306C In contrast, a challenge to the Crown Court's decision not to make an order under s.39 of the Children and Young Persons Act 1933 was made by way of judicial review in England and Wales in *JC & RT v Central Criminal Court and others* [2014] EWHC 1041 (QB); [2014] 1 W.L.R. 3697; [2014] 4 All E.R. 319; [2014] 2 Cr. App. R. 13; [2014] E.M.L.R. 20; [2014] 2 F.C.R. 571; [2014] Crim. L.R. 902. In an addendum to its judgment, the Divisional Court pointed to the inconsistent approaches between Northern Ireland and England and Wales in respect of the appropriate route to challenge the withholding or discharge of a reporting restriction order and stated that there was a need for "urgent legislative intervention" to remedy this disparity of approach.

W. Procedure on s.159 appeals

7–308 *[Add to notes 575 and 576]*

See now Parts 6 and 36 of the Criminal Procedure Rules 2015 (SI 2015/1490) in force with effect from 5 October 2015.

[Add to end of paragraph]

See now the same provisions at Parts 36 and 40 of the Criminal Procedure Rules 2015 (SI 2015/1490) in force with effect from 5 October 2015.

CHAPTER 8

COURT REPORTING II: OTHER STATUTORY RESTRICTIONS

I. JUDICIAL PROCEEDINGS (REGULATION OF REPORTS) ACT 1926

A. The relevant provisions of the Statute

[*Add to note 2*] **8–2**

For a recent summary of the background to the Act, see the judgment of Sir James Munby P in *Rapisarda v Colladon* (also known as *180 Irregular Divorces, Re*) [2014] EWFC 1406; [2014] E.M.L.R. 26; [2015] 1 F.L.R. 584 at [6]-[17].

[*Add to note 7*] **8–3**

In *A v A (Issue of Reporting Restrictions)* [2012] EWHC 4226 (Fam) there was an application by the media to report the evidence given in proceedings held in private with accredited media attending in accordance with FPR r.27.10. The District Judge declined to rely on the 1926 Act ("There being as yet no determination of which I am aware that the Judicial Proceedings (Regulation of Reports) Act 1926 s.1. applies to financial remedy [previously known as ancillary relief] proceedings"). He dealt with the application by balancing Convention rights, guided particularly by the Court of Appeal in *Clibbery v Allan* [2002] EWCA Civ 45; [2002] Fam. 261; [2002] 2 W.L.R. 1511; [2002] 1 All E.R. 865; [2002] 1 F.L.R 565 and *Lykiardopulo v Lykiardopulo* [2010] EWCA Civ 1315; [2011] 1 F.L.R 1427. Reference was made to the importance of the implied undertaking. In *Lykiardopulo* the rationale was set out by Stanley Burnton L.J. at [76]:

> "Parties to a matrimonial dispute who bring before the court the facts and documents relating to their financial affairs may in general be assured that the confidentiality of that information will be respected. They are required by the court to produce the information and documents and it is a general principle, applicable to both civil and family proceedings, that confidential information produced by those who are compelled to do so will remain so unless and until it passes into the public domain. That confidence will in an appropriate case be protected by the anonymisation of any reported judgment."

The restrictions in s.1(1)(b) of the1926 Act were extended to certain other proceedings: see para.8–13 *et seq*.

The ongoing uncertainty as to whether the reporting restrictions in the Judicial Proceedings (Regulation of Reports) Act 1926 s.1(1)(b) apply to the reporting of proceedings for ancillary relief (now known as financial remedy proceedings) was again considered in *Rapisarda v Colladon* (also known as *180 Irregular Divorces, Re*) [2014] EWFC 1406; [2014] E.M.L.R. 26; [2015] 1 F.L.R. 584 and *Cooper-Hohn v Hohn* [2014] EWHC 2314 (Fam); [2015] 1 F.L.R. 19; [2015] 1 F.C.R. 594; [2014] Fam. Law 1528. In *Rapisarda v Colladon* Sir James Munby P held that s.1(1)(b) applied to proceedings to set aside divorce petitions, and served to limit reporting of the proceedings to those matters prescribed by the Act, but that it remained uncertain whether or not s.1(1)(b) applied to limit reporting of financial remedy proceedings. The President suggested that Parliament might wish to consider, with an appropriate degree of urgency, whether retention of the Act was any longer justified. Meanwhile, he held that s.1(4), which excluded from the ambit of the Act the publication of any notice or report in pursuance of the directions of the court, gave the judge an unfettered discretion to give directions in respect of any notice or report. Accordingly, the President made a direction thereunder that the media were free to report the instant proceedings. Similarly, in the financial remedy proceedings in *Cooper-Hohn v Hohn*, the court proceeded on the assumption that the Act applied to restrict publication, save in so far as the court made directions under s.1(4). The decision in *Cooper-Hohn v Hohn* appears not to have been followed in the recent decision of *Appleton v Gallagher* [2015] EWHC 2689 (Fam), [2015] All ER (D) 131 (Sep), Mostyn J.

8–3 [*Add to text at end of paragraph*]

In *Rapisarda v Colladon* (also known as *180 Irregular Divorces, Re*) [2014] EWFC 1406; [2014] E.M.L.R. 26; [2015] 1 F.L.R. 584, Sir James Munby P confirmed that he agreed with the observations of Thorpe L.J. in *Clibbery v Allan* [2002] EWCA Civ 45; [2002] Fam. 261; [2002] 2 W.L.R. 1511; [2002] 1 All E.R. 865; [2002] 1 F.L.R. 565, [88] that "it is clear that the purpose of s.1(1)(b), as indeed of the 1926 Act as a whole, was—and is—the protection of public morality and public decency" and stated that Lord Rodger of Earlsferry J.S.C. had put the point definitively in *In re Guardian News and Media Ltd* [2010] UKSC 1, [2010] 2 AC 697, [24]: "The purpose of the legislation was ... not the protection of the parties' privacy but the prevention of injury to public morals throughout Great Britain: *Friel v Scott*

2000 J.C. 86 [where a prosecution under the 1926 Act failed]". See also at 8–12 of the main text.

[*Add to end of paragraph*] **8–11**

The issue of whether the reporting restrictions in the Judicial Proceedings (Regulation of Reports) Act 1926 s.1(1)(b) applied in proceedings to set aside divorce petitions and financial remedy proceedings (previously referred to as proceedings for ancillary relief) was again discussed in *Rapisarda v Colladon* (also known as *180 Irregular Divorces, Re*) [2014] EWFC 1406; [2014] E.M.L.R. 26; [2015] 1 F.L.R. 584 and *Cooper-Hohn v Hohn* [2014] EWHC 2314 (Fam); [2015] 1 F.L.R. 19; [2015] 1 F.C.R. 594; [2014] Fam. Law 1528. Sir James Munby P held, with a lack of enthusiasm comparable to that of Sir Stephen Brown P in *Moynihan v Moynihan* (No.1) [1997] 1 F.L.R. 59, that he was driven to the conclusion that s.1(1)(b) did apply to proceedings to set aside divorce petitions and served to limit reporting of the proceedings to those matters prescribed by the Act, subject to the discretion in s.1(4) (see 8–3, n 7, above). He made clear that he could not begin to understand how the protection of public morality and public decency, or indeed any other public interest, was facilitated by restraining the reporting of open court proceedings in the case before him or in the *Moynihan* case. Moreover, given the continuing uncertainty as to whether the 1926 Act applies to the reporting of ancillary relief (financial remedy) proceedings, he suggested that Parliament might wish to consider whether the retention of the 1926 Act on the statute book is any longer justified.

II. Restrictions on Publication Under the Criminal Justice Act 2003

A. Prosecution appeals

[*Add to note 31*] **8–15**

At the time of writing, a date remains to be set for the introduction of Criminal Justice Act 2003 s.62.

[*Add to note 33*] **8–15**

Section 71(8)(g) has been amended by the Legal Aid, Sentencing and Punishment of Offenders Act 2012, Sch.5(1) para.65 (in force with effect from 13 April 2013).

[*Add to note 34*] **8–16**

Part 16 of the Criminal Procedure Rules 2011 has now been superseded by Part 6 of the Criminal Procedure Rules 2015 (SI 2015/1490) in force with effect from 5 October 2015.

III. Statutory Anonymity for Complainants of Sexual Offences

F. Anonymity for the accused

8–24 [*Add to text at end of paragraph*]

The Act does not empower a court with jurisdiction to make an express order prohibiting identification of a defendant, even when the purpose of the order is to protect the anonymity of the complainant. In *R. (on the application of Press Association) v Cambridge Crown Court* [2012] EWCA Crim 2434; [2013] 1 All E.R. 1361; [2013] 1 Cr. App. R. 16; [2013] E.M.L.R. 9; [2013] Crim. L.R. 323 the Court of Appeal confirmed that it was for the media to decide how appropriately to report the case so as to ensure the anonymity of the complainant, with the assistance, where appropriate, of non-binding guidance from the court. There are, however, penalties for breaching the order if the media culpably misjudge the practical reach of the prohibition in a specific case. The court held that the absence of a judicial power to restrict publication provided a clear demarcation of responsibility: publication decisions were left to editors and reporters: see e.g. *R. v B* [2006] EWCA Crim 2692; [2007] E.M.L.R. 5. Only an extreme case, where the identification of the defendant would imperil his life or safety or that of his family, or presented a significant threat to the administration of justice, might lead to an anonymity order: see Lord Rodger in *Guardian News and Media Ltd, Re* [2010] UKSC 1; [2010] 2 A.C. 697; [2010] E.M.L.R. 15 at [26] and para.6–128. For an example of a rare case where the court's balancing of arts 2, 8 and 10 justified an injunction restraining reporting of both the trial and conviction of a defendant for engaging in sexual activity with a minor, see *ZY v Higgins* [2013] NIQB 8, one of a number of such orders that have been made in Northern Ireland: see 6–128, 6–133 and 7–177. In *Re BBC* (also known as *A v BBC*) [2014] UKSC 25; [2015] AC 588, the Supreme Court upheld an order anonymising a sex offender in an application to remain in the United Kingdom. It was argued that his deportation would, *inter alia*, violate his rights under articles 2 and 3 rights of the ECHR if he was returned to his country of origin. The court held that in those circumstances it was plainly necessary in the interests of justice to depart from the general principle of open justice. An order was made because publication of his identity would have subverted the very basis of the decision to authorise his deportation, which had been based on an assessment that there was no real risk of violation of his article 3 rights *provided* he was granted anonymity. See paras 6–22A, 6.128, 7–4A, 7–38, 7–118 above and 16–390 below.

IV. PROTECTION FOR JUVENILES (CHILDREN AND YOUNG PERSONS): THE 1933 ACT

I. Protection for children or young persons in adult proceedings: s.39 of the 1933 Act

[*Add new paragraph*] **8–25A**

With effect from 13 April 2015, a new regime has been introduced for reporting restrictions aimed at the protection of children and young persons involved in court proceedings. Under the new regime:

(i) The scheme for discretionary reporting restrictions in any criminal proceedings provided for by s.45 of the Youth Justice and Criminal Evidence Act 1999 was finally brought into force. The power is available in any criminal proceedings in any court (other than a service court), including adult criminal courts. This new statutory provision also remedies the lacuna identified in *MXB v East Sussex Hospitals NHS Trust* [2012] EWHC 3279 (QB); (2013) 177 J.P. 31; [2013] 1 F.L.R. 1152 (see (ii) and 8–67 below) by extending the range of publications in respect of which a discretionary reporting restriction order can be made to include online publications. The offence of breaching such a restriction is subject to a defence that at the time of the alleged offence the defendant was not aware, and neither suspected nor had reason to suspect, that the publication included the material in question (known as a "due diligence" defence): s.50 of the 1999 Act.

(ii) Section 39 of the Children and Young Persons Act 1933 is amended by s.79 of the Criminal Justice and Courts Act 2015. It no longer applies to cases in the criminal courts, except those involving Criminal Behaviour Orders (see para.8–43 below). Section 39 of the 1933 Act continues to apply in relation to civil and family proceedings, but it has been amended by s.79(7) of the Criminal Justice and Courts Act 2015 to widen the definition of publication, thereby ending the anomaly that it did not apply to material published on the internet or social media. As stated in (i) above, this is intended to remedy the lacuna identified in *MXB v East Sussex Hospitals NHS Trust* [2012] EWHC 3279 (QB); (2013) 177 J.P. 31; [2013] 1 F.L.R. 1152.

(iii) Section 49 of the Children and Young Persons Act 1933, which gives automatic anonymity to any young person involved in proceedings in a Youth Court remains in force in relation to Youth Courts and appeals from Youth Courts. Those who may be liable have a "due diligence" defence under s.49(9A).

(iv) A new s.45A of the Youth Justice and Criminal Evidence Act 1999, inserted by the Criminal Justice and Courts Act 2015, gives to adult criminal courts and Youth Courts the same discretionary powers to grant lifelong anonymity to victims and witnesses aged under 18 as they currently have in relation to adults under s.46 of the 1999 Act. This last change was evidently prompted by the observations in *R (JC and RT) v Central Criminal Court*, in which Sir Brian Leveson P, sitting in the Divisional Court, identified "a lacuna in the law" regarding the protection of young victims and witnesses in that, under the law as it stood, anonymity could only last for as long as a person remained under 18. This "require[d] to be addressed as a matter of real urgency": [2014] EWHC 1041 (Admin), [2014] 1 WLR 3697, [36]-[38]. (See too the observations of Laws L.J. in the Court of Appeal at [2014] EWCA Civ 1777, [2015] 1 WLR 2865 at [46] and [49]). Again, there is a "due diligence" defence contained in s.50 of the 1999 Act. The Criminal Procedure Rules 2015 set out, at r.6.4(3)(f), the procedure for applying for a s.45A order.

In *Aitken v DPP* [2015] EWHC 1079 (Admin); (2015) 179 J.P. 223 at [70]–[73], [75] the Divisional Court took the view that the "scheme of statutory reporting restrictions remains incoherent and is in need of further review". In his judgment, Warby J identified three remaining discrepancies which seem "undesirable, and liable to generate needless and problematic uncertainty". First, the new regime had not removed the discrepancy between provisions for criminal and civil proceedings; namely that "criminal liability for newspaper publications in breach of a reporting restriction in respect of criminal proceedings is now expressly limited by ss.45, 45A of the Youth Justice and Criminal Evidence Act 1999 and s.49 of the 1933 Act to proprietors, editors, and publishers, but the same is not true of liability for breach of s.39 orders". While the phrase "any person who publishes" in s.39(2) had been amended, the amendment attributed liability to "any person who includes in a publication" material prohibited by a s.39 order. Secondly, there is no "due diligence" defence to a charge of breaching a s.39 order. Thirdly, the wording of s.39 does not confer any power to grant anonymity into adulthood remained and, therefore, "there is no counterpart in civil proceedings of the power to grant lifelong anonymity that is conferred on criminal courts by s.45A of the Youth Justice and Criminal Evidence Act 1999".

C. The reporting restrictions: the current terms of s.49

8–28 [*Add to end of paragraph*]

The offence of breaching such a restriction is subject to a defence (known as a "due diligence" defence), under s.49(9A) of the 1933 Act (as amended by Sch 2 para 3(7) of the Youth Justice and Criminal Evidence Act 1999), that at the time of the alleged offence the defendant was not aware, and neither suspected nor had reason to suspect, that the publication included the material in question.

[*Add to note 72*] **8–30**

At the time of writing there are no current plans to bring s.44 of the Youth Justice and Criminal Evidence Act 1999 into force.

[*Add to end of paragraph*] **8–31**

It was confirmed in *R (JC and RT) v Central Criminal Court* [2014] EWCA Civ 1777, [2015] 1 W.L.R. 2865, that an order under s.39 of the Children and Young Persons Act 1933 expires automatically once the person concerned attains the age of 18: see also 8–25 above. By contrast, there is now a power granted to the adult criminal courts and Youth Courts, by s.45A of the Youth Justice and Criminal Evidence Act 1999 (inserted by the Criminal Justice and Courts Act 2015), to make a lifelong reporting restriction in respect of a victim or witness who is under 18 during the proceedings.

F. The statutory changes in the context of anti-social behaviour orders

[*Add to end of paragraph*] **8–42**

From 20 October 2014, the new scheme of Criminal Behaviour Orders and Crime Prevention Injunctions has come into effect, replacing a range of tools formerly available for dealing with anti-social behaviour, including the Anti-Social Behaviour Order (ASBO). The Crime Prevention Injunction under Part 1 of the Anti-social Behaviour, Crime and Policing Act 2014 is a purely civil order available in the County Court for adults, and in the Youth Court for those aged 10 or over but under the age of 18. A Criminal Behaviour Order ("CBO") under Part 2 is an order available following a conviction for any criminal offence in the Crown Court, Magistrates' Court or Youth Court.

The automatic restriction on reporting legal proceedings in relation to someone aged under 18 (s.49 of the Children and Young Persons Act 1933) does not apply to proceedings for the making of a Crime Prevention Injunction under s.1 (Anti-social Behaviour, Crime and Policing Act 2014, s.17) or a Criminal Behaviour Order under s.22 (Anti-social Behaviour, Crime and Policing Act 2014 s.23(8)(a)). However, s.39 of the Act does apply to these proceeding and gives the court the discretion to restrict the publication of matters likely to lead to the identification of the child or young person (s.23(8)(b)). (See the discussion at 8–25A above.)

Where a child or young person is prosecuted for a breach of a Criminal Behaviour Order under s.30 of the Anti-social Behaviour, Crime and Policing Act 2014, there are no automatic reporting restrictions on the proceedings in respect of the breach (Anti-social Behaviour, Crime and Policing Act 2014 s.30(5)), although any other charges heard at the same time will still be subject to s.49 of the Children and Young Persons act 1933. However, s.45 of the Youth Justice and Criminal Evidence Act 1999 applies to Criminal Behaviour Order breach proceedings against someone aged under 18 and gives the court the discretion to restrict the publication of certain information in criminal proceedings in order to protect the identity of the child or young person (Anti-social Behaviour, Crime and Policing Act 2014 s.30(5)(b)).

8–43 [*Add to note 98 and 99]*

With effect from 20 October 2014, s.1C of the Crime and Disorder Act 1998 was repealed by the Anti-social Behaviour, Crime and Policing Act 2014, Sch.11(1) para.24(a), and is replaced by the new scheme of anti-social behaviour injunctions (known as Crime Prevention Injunctions) and Criminal Behaviour Orders in the Anti-social Behaviour, Crime and Policing Act 2014, Parts 1 and 2. (See generally at 8–42 above.)

8–43 [*Add to note 100*]

With effect from 20 October 2014, ss.1 to 1K of the Crime and Disorder Act 1998 were repealed by the Anti-social Behaviour, Crime and Policing Act 2014, Sch.11(1) para.24(a), and were replaced by the new scheme of anti-social behaviour injunctions (known as Crime Prevention Injunctions) and Criminal Behaviour Orders in the Anti-social Behaviour, Crime and Policing Act 2014, Parts 1 and 2. (See generally at 8–42 above.)

8–43 [*Add to note 101*]

From 13 April 2015, the regime for discretionary reporting restrictions provided for by s.45 of the Youth Justice and Criminal Evidence Act 1999 has been brought into effect. (See generally at 8–25 above.)

I. Protection for children or young persons in adult proceedings: s.39 of the 1933 Act

8–50 [*Add to text at end of paragraph*]

With effect from 13 April 2015, s.39 of the Children and Young Persons Act 1933 ceases to apply to cases in the criminal courts, except those involving Crime Prevention Injunctions and Criminal Behaviour Orders (see at 8.42 above). Section 39 of the 1933 Act continues to apply in relation to civil and family proceedings, but it has been amended by s.79(7) of the Criminal Justice and Courts Act 2015 to widen the definition of publication, thereby ending the anomaly that it did not apply to material published on the internet or social media, as pointed out in *MXB v East Sussex Hospitals NHS Trust* [2012] EWHC 3279 (QB). (See above generally at 8–25.) The discretionary reporting restrictions for children and young persons involved in adult criminal proceedings can now be found in ss.45 and 45A of the Youth Justice and Criminal Evidence Act 1999. (See *Aitken v DPP* [2015] EWHC 1079 (Admin); (2015) 179 J.P. 223 at [70]–[73] for a review of these changes and the Divisional Court's criticisms of the remaining discrepancies in this area.)

[*Add to note 118*]

Where a newspaper had published material in breach of a reporting restriction imposed under s.39(1) of the Children and Young Persons Act 1933, it was held that the newspaper's editor did not fall outside the scope of the expression "any person who published" under s.39(2): *Aitken v DPP* [2015] EWHC 1079 (Admin); (2015) 179 J.P. 223 **8–51**

J. The anomalies and the residual role of the inherent jurisdiction

[Add to note 127] **8–53**

See now also *X Children, Re* [2007] EWHC 1719 (Fam); [2008] 1 F.L.R. 589; *A (A Child) (Application for Reporting Restrictions)* [2011] EWHC 1764 (Fam); [2012] 1 F.L.R. 239; *A (Council v B (Children) (Reporting Restrictions)* [2012] EWHC 2038 (Fam); *Z v News Group Newspapers Ltd* [2013] EWHC 1371 (Fam), *A Council v M (Children) (Reporting Restriction Order)* [2012] EWHC 2038 (Fam); [2013] 2 F.L.R. 1270; [2013] Fam. Law 970; Swansea v XZ & Anor [2014] EWHC 212 (Fam), discussed at para.6–119B and following. The decision in *A (A Child) (Application for Reporting Restrictions), Re* [2011] EWHC 1764 (Fam); [2012] 1 F.L.R. 239; [2011] 3 F.C.R. 176; [2011] Fam. Law 1076 is a recent example of the balance falling in the other, and more common, direction. Baker J. declined to make an order restricting the identification of a very vulnerable mother who had been arrested on suspicion of the murder of two of her children. An order protecting her surviving child was made by agreement. In *Surrey County Council v ME* [2014] EWHC 489 Fam; [2014] 2 F.L.R. 1267; [2014] Fam. Law 815. At [21], Keehan J distinguished *A Local Authority v W* [2005] EWHC 1564 (Fam) and *A Council v M (supra)* on the grounds that the facts in those cases were wholly exceptional and refused to grant a reporting restrictions order restraining the media from identifying a 14-year-old defendant to a murder charge, his parents and siblings. The trial judge had lifted the order made pursuant to s.39 of the Children and Young Persons Act 1933 prohibiting his identification, following his indication that he would plead guilty to a manslaughter charge, and the media having indicated that they did not intend to name the siblings. See para.6–114 of the main text and 6119C above.

[*Add new paragraph*] **8–53A**

The meaning of a child or young person "concerned in the proceedings" was considered by the Divisional Court in *R (on the application of A) v Lowestoft Magistrates Court* [2013] EWHC 659 and also by the Court of Appeal in *R v Jolleys, Ex p. Press Association* [2013] EWCA Crim 1135. Under s.39, protection exists only in respect of children and young persons

> "concerned in the proceedings, either as being the person by or against or in respect of whom the proceedings are taken, or as being a witness therein."

In *R. v Jolleys, Ex p. Press Association*, the Court of Appeal overturned an order made in respect of the teenage son of a defendant charged with fraud. The defendant was a former army officer charged with defrauding taxpayers by claiming a military education allowance to which he had not been entitled. At the time of the trial, only his youngest son, then aged 15, was still of school age. The court stated that the phrase "concerned in the proceedings" was defined and limited by the words which followed (as cited above) and "does not extend to children or young persons simply on the basis that they may be concerned in the more general sense".

8–53B *[Add new paragraph]*

On the other hand, in *R. (on the application of A) v Lowestoft Magistrates' Court*, the Divisional Court was prepared in principle to extend the protection to a child whose mother had been charged with "being drunk in a public place while having the charge of a child under the age of 7 years" contrary to s.2(1) of the Licensing Act 1902. The court concluded that it was plain that the legislature in enacting s.39 sought to capture, in wide language, at least the central participants in proceedings, whether civil or criminal, who would for that very reason be likely to be the focus of any report of the proceedings: a narrow interpretation of s.39 would tend to defeat the main objective of protecting, where appropriate, the identity of a child or young person in that position. The court was prepared to interpret the provision in the Licensing Act as intended, among other things, to promote the welfare of small children who could be at risk of physical or psychological harm if a person responsible for that welfare is intoxicated. Accordingly, the Licensing Act proceedings, on any sensible construction of s.39, had been taken "in respect of", and thus "concerned", that child. Although an order could thus have been made, the balancing of the competing considerations in that case led the court to conclude that the magistrates' refusal had been correct.

8–53C *[Add new paragraph]*

The facts of *Z v News Group Newspapers Ltd* [2013] EWHC 1150 (Fam) and [2013] EWHC 1371 (Fam) provide a further illustration of the anomalous effect of confining protection under s.39 to a defendant, witness or victim. A mother was charged with making false claims for disability allowance in respect of her children. A s.39 order was discharged by the trial judge in the Crown Court on the ground that the children did not fall within the terms of that section. Although the children's medical histories, which were said to have justified the claim of benefits, were potentially to be the focus of scrutiny at trial, none of the children would be called as witnesses. Nor could they properly be described as persons by or against or in respect of whom the criminal proceedings were taken. In consequence, an order was made in the Family Division preventing the publication of any matter likely to lead to the identification of the children, including the name of the defendant mother. On her conviction, restrictions were relaxed to permit the mother to be named. There was a prohibition, however, on the publication of the forenames or of any photographs of the children which would connect them to the trial. The court drew a careful distinction between the child in *S, Re*, who was not involved in the trial and would not need to be referred to, and the children in this case. Many of the same considerations applicable to children as witnesses or victims were held to apply with force to the circumstances of those children. The children were not incidental to the alleged offending; they were central to it. Given their integral roles in the alleged fraud, a detailed review of their lives (and more pertinently their medical records) in the press would represent an exceptional intrusion into their private lives: see [2013] EWHC 1150 (Fam) at [70]–[72].

K. The amendments contained in the Youth Justice and Criminal Evidence Act 1999

[*Add to note 128*] **8–54**

Since 13 April 2015, see s.45 and s.45A of the Youth Justice and Criminal Evidence Act 1999 and the changes to s.39 and s.49 of the Children and Young Persons Act 1933, as reviewed by the Divisional Court in *Aitken v DPP* [2015] EWHC 1079 (Admin); (2015) 179 J.P. 223 at [70]. See also 8–25 and 8–50 above.

[*Add to note 129*] **8–54**

The proposals for reform, including the proposed amendment to s.39 of the 1933 Act, in the Children, Schools and Families Act 2010, have now been abandoned and the provisions are repealed by the Crime and Courts Act 2013 Pt 2 s.17(4), with effect from 4 September 2013 (SI 2013/2200).

[*Add new paragraph*] **8–54A**

With effect from 13 April 2015, the regime for discretionary reporting restrictions in criminal proceedings provided for by s.45 of the Youth Justice and Criminal Evidence Act 1999 was finally brought into force. Section 39 of the Children and Young Persons Act 1933 (as amended by s.79 of the Criminal Justice and Courts Act 2015) now applies, as was the intention in 1999, to proceedings other than criminal proceedings, namely civil matters and certain hybrid proceedings. (For the new regime of reporting restrictions aimed at the protection of children and young persons involved in court proceedings, see generally at 8–25 above.) At the time of writing there are no current plans to bring s.44 of the 1999 Act into force, the provisions of which would automatically prevent reporting of any matter which might lead the public to identify a person under 18 as a potential defendant, victim or witness as soon as a criminal investigation has begun.

8–55 [*Add to note 131*]

The Youth Justice and Criminal Evidence Act 1999 ss.49 and 50 (as amended by the Criminal Justice and and Courts Act 2015, s.78) were brought into force on 13 April 2015: see 8–25 and 8–50 above. Section 44 of the Youth Justice and Criminal Evidence Act 1999 has not been brought into force at the time of writing.

8–55 [*Add to note 133*]

The Youth Justice and Criminal Evidence Act 1999 ss.49 and 50 (as amended by the Criminal Justice and and Courts Act 2015, s.78) were brought into force on 13 April 2015: see 8–25 and 8–50 above.

8–55 [*Add to note 134*]

For the meaning of a child or young person "concerned in the proceedings', see the cases cited at 8–53A above.

L. Guidance from the courts on the exercise of the s.39 discretion

8–56A [*Insert new paragraph*]

With effect from 13 April 2015, s.39 of the Children and Young Persons Act 1933 ceases to apply to cases in the criminal courts, except those involving Criminal Behaviour Orders (see 8–43 above). It now applies (as amended by s.79 of the Criminal Justice and Courts Act 2015), as was the intention in 1999, to proceedings other than criminal proceedings: namely civil matters and certain hybrid proceedings: see generally at 8–25 above. The following guidance (i.e. in the main text at 8–57 *et seq*) will continue to apply to the making of orders under s.39 in proceedings other than criminal proceedings and, it is submitted, may also be cited in respect of the new power to make discretionary reporting restrictions under s.45 of the 1999 Act.

8–62 [*Add to end of paragraph*]

In *X v Dartford & Gravesham NHS Trust* [2015] EWCA Civ 96; [2015] 1 W.L.R. 3647; [2015] C.P. Rep 22; [2015] E.M.L.R 14; [2015] P.I.Q.R P14 the Court of Appeal held, in relation to settlement hearings for personal injury claims in the case of a child, that the judge should make an anonymity order rather than an order under s.39 of the Children and Young Persons Act 1933 both for the reasons articulated by Tugendhat J in *MXB v East Sussex Hospitals NHS Trust* [2012] EWHC 3279 (QB); (2013) 177 J.P. 31; [2013] 1 F.L.R. 1152 and because such an order ceases to have effect when the child reaches the age of majority: see *R (JC and RT) v Central Criminal Court* ([2014] EWCA Civ 1777; [2014] 1 WLR 3697. For anonymity orders generally, see 6–120 *et seq* and 7–124 *et seq* in the main text and above.

[*Add to note 156*] **8–64**

The Youth Justice and Criminal Evidence Act 1999 s.45(5) was brought into force on 13 April 2015: see 8–25 and 8–50 above

[*Add to text at end of paragraph*] **8–67**

In *R. (on the application of A) v Lowestoft Magistrates Court* [2013] EWHC 659, the Divisional Court dismissed an application for judicial review of the magistrates' refusal to make a s.39 order. The court held that the following factors weighed in favour of refusing a s.39 order: (i) the defendant was an elected councillor, and her conduct in public had fallen below the standard that could reasonably be expected by the public, who had a legitimate interest in learning of how she had behaved; (ii) the practical effect of a s.39 order would be to prohibit the media from naming the defendant, and the public would simply not know what the defendant had done; (iii) the three-year-old child would have little or no present understanding of what had occurred, and any press report of the criminal proceedings could have no direct impact on her; (iv) the notion that responsible adults would behave in a manner adverse to her welfare was far-fetched and not based upon any solid empirical foundation and the child's best interests did not lie unambiguously in concealment; (v) the child was too young to be exposed to, or affected by, the kind of behaviour of other children that concerned the court in *K v News Group Newspapers Ltd* [2011] 1 W.L.R. 1827. Concerns about possible bullying in the future were, in the instant case, highly speculative. See also the review of the authorities in *R. (on the application of Y) v Aylesbury Crown Court* [2012] EWHC 1140 (Admin); [2012] E.M.L.R. 26; [2012] Crim L.R. 893, which led to the conclusion that an order should have been made in respect of a 16-year-old defendant convicted of a single offence of simple arson. It was recognised that it might not have been appropriate if he had been convicted of (say) a serious campaign of revenge arson.

[Add new paragraph] **8–67A**

In *MXB v East Sussex Hospitals NHS Trust* [2012] EWHC 3279 (QB); (2013) 177 J.P. 31; [2013] 1 F.L.R. 1152, Tugendhat J. took the view, in the context of an application for anonymity in relation to an infant settlement, that there was "force" in the submission that s.39 might not be sufficient to provide the court with jurisdiction to prohibit the publication of reports on the internet or via social media. The scope of s.39 was extended by the Children and Young Persons Act 1963 s. 57(4) to include sound and television broadcasts. But no extension has been made to embrace any other form of report, such as one made in the social media or the internet. Whereas reports in newspapers and broadcasts are ephemeral and relatively difficult to find after the original publication, reports on the internet are easy to find with a search engine, and difficult to remove. The confinement of s.39 of the 1933 Act to newspaper reports could thus be regarded as anomalous, in failing to provide for forms of reports to the public that had become technically possible, and now common, in addition to newspapers and broadcasts. In consequence of his concern that s.39 would not provide sufficient protection, Tugendhat J. made an anonymity order under CPR r.39.2(4). The point was briefly revisited by the Court of Appeal in *R. v Jolleys, Ex p. Press Association* [2013] EWCA Crim 1135 at [18]–[19]. A recorder sitting in the Crown Court had made an order under s.39 (which was defective for the reason that the subjects of the order were not within the wording of the section, as discussed at 8–53A above) purporting to extend to any "media report". It was acknowledged in the Court of Appeal that s.39 restrictions might not extend to reports appearing on web-based social media, such as Facebook and Twitter. Section 39 has subsequently been amended by s.79(7) of the Criminal Justice and Courts Act 2015 to widen the definition of publication so as to include online publications: see 8–25 and 8–50 above. See *Aitken v DPP* [2015] EWHC 1079 (Admin); (2015) 179 J.P. 223 for an analysis of the ongoing anomalies (at para.8–25A, 8–50 and 8–54 above)

Procedure for making orders under the Children and Young Persons Act

8–68 [*Add to note 163*]

Part 16 of the Criminal Procedure Rules 2011 has now been superseded by Part 6 of the Criminal Procedure Rules 2015 (SI 2015/1490) in force with effect from 5 October 2015, which is expressed in like terms.

8–70 [*Add to text at end of paragraph*]

In *R. v Jolleys, Ex p. Press Association* [2013] EWCA Crim 1135, the Court of Appeal criticised a decision made in the Swindon Crown Court refusing to allow representations from the press as to whether a s.39 order ought to have been made. Rule 16.2 of the Criminal Procedure Rules required that those affected by the order should be given such an opportunity. As to whether notice of the order should have been given to the press, Leveson L.J. stated that, ordinarily, notification via the court list of the fact that an order either has been or may be made under s.39 is more than enough notice. In an unusual case, however, the press should be alerted in good time and given notice, for example where there was any doubt as to the application of the law. Part 16 of the Criminal Procedure Rules 2011 has now been superseded by Part 6 of the Criminal Procedure Rules 2015 (2015/1490) (in force from 5 October 2015).

8–71 [*Add to text at end of paragraph*]

See now *X v Dartford & Gravesham NHS Trust* [2015] EWCA Civ 96; [2015] C.P. Rep 22; [2015] E.M.L.R 14; [2015] P.I.Q.R P14, discussed at 8–62 above.

M. Judicial review of decisions under s.39 of the 1933 Act

[Add to note 169] **8–72**

See now the Criminal Procedure Rules 2015 (SI 2015/1490) in force with effect from 5 October 2015, r.36 and 40.

[*Add to end of paragraph*] **8–74**

In *R (JC and RT) v Central Criminal Court* [2014] EWHC 1041 (QB); [2014] 1 W.L.R. 3697; [2014] 4 All E.R. 319; [2014] 2 Cr. App. R. 13; [2014] E.M.L.R. 20; [2014] 2 F.C.R. 571; [2014] Crim. L.R. 902, [40]–[42], in an addendum to its judgment, the Divisional Court referred to the line of authority raising doubt as to whether, in England and Wales, it is open to claimants aggrieved by a failure to restrain publication to commence proceedings for judicial review. Attention was drawn to the inconsistent approaches, as between Northern Ireland (see *R v McGreechan* [2014] NICA 5) and England and Wales, in respect of the meaning of s.159 and the appropriate route for challenging the withholding or discharge of a reporting restriction order. The Divisional Court stated that there was a need for "urgent legislative intervention" to remedy this disparity of approach. (See also at 7–300 *et seq* above.)

V. ANONYMITY FOR WITNESSES: SECTION 46 OF THE YOUTH JUSTICE AND CRIMINAL EVIDENCE ACT 1999

A. Protection and special measures for witnesses: ss.46 and 47 of the Youth Justice and Criminal Evidence Act 1999

[*Add to note 186*] **8–78**

Part 16 of the Criminal Procedure Rules 2011 has now been superseded by Part 6 of the Criminal Procedure Rules 2015 (SI 2015/1490) in force with effect from 5 October 2015. The terms of r.16.4(3) are unchanged. The requirements for an application for an order under s.46 of the Youth Justice and Criminal Evidence Act 1999 are set out in CrimPR r.6.4(3)(f).

[*Add to end of paragraph*] **8–78**

Under the new regime in force from 13 April 2015, discussed at 8–25 and 8–50 above, a new s.45A of the Youth Justice and Criminal Evidence Act 1999, inserted by the Criminal Justice and Courts Act 2015, gives adult criminal courts and Youth Courts the same discretionary powers to grant lifelong anonymity to victims and witnesses aged under 18 as they have in relation to adults under s.46 of the 1999 Act. This last change was evidently prompted by *R (JC and RT) v Central Criminal Court* [2014] EWHC 1041 (QB), [2014] 1 WLR 3697 in which the court identified as "a lacuna in the law" the fact that, under the law as it stood, anonymity could only last for as long as a person remained under 18. The Divisional Court suggested, at [36]-[38], that this "requires to be addressed as a matter of real urgency": The Court of Appeal agreed: see at [2014] EWCA Civ 1777, [2015] 1 WLR 2865 at [46] and [49] see 8–25A and 8–31 above.

8–79 [*Add to end of paragraph*]

In *R. v ITN News* [2013] EWCA Crim 773 , the media appealed under s.159 of the Criminal Justice Act 1988 against a reporting restriction order made in respect of a witness in the trial of a father accused of causing the death of his six children in a fire. The witness, who was the former girlfriend of the defendant and mother of his surviving children, was fearful of the defendant and his friends and, having changed her appearance and their surnames, was allowed to give evidence from behind screens under special measures. The judge made an order under the Youth Justice and Criminal Evidence Act 1999 s.46, prohibiting publication of any pictures of the witness or her children in any way which connected them with the criminal proceedings. The media appealed on the grounds that: (i) pictures of the witness had already been widely published; and (ii) the protection of the children of an adult witness had not been in contention and such issues were better addressed in the family court. In dismissing the appeal, the Court of Appeal held that the effect of the argument would be to confine s.46 to those cases where the witness was anonymous, which could not be the intention as this was an entirely separate and specific form of special measure. Pictures of a witness may be prohibited under s.46(7) if the "eligibility" test is satisfied, whether or not the name and identity of the witness is otherwise known. In relation to the identification of children, taken separately from their parent, the Family Division was normally the appropriate venue. Nevertheless, the criminal courts must control their own processes and the protection of the family court was not sufficient to deprive the Crown Court of jurisdiction under s.46. Publication of photographs of the children would have been likely to lead to identification of the mother, and the risk would be likely to affect the quality of her evidence.

B. Power to hear evidence in private: s.25 of the Youth Justice and Criminal Evidence Act 1999

8–81 [*Add to note 190*]

The power to exclude has been extended to offences for trafficking people for exploitation under Asylum and Immigration (Treatment of Claimants, etc.) Act 2004, s.4. (inserted by the Trafficking People for Exploitation Regulations 2013/554 Sch.1 para.3 (in force from 6 April 2013).

VI. PROTECTION FOR FAMILY PROCEEDINGS

[*Add to note 192*] **8–83**

FPR PD 27C (Attendance of Media Representatives at Hearings in Family Proceedings (Family Proceedings Court)) has been withdrawn. The Family Proceedings Court no longer exists and all family work is dealt with by the single Family Court: see generally at 8–85 below. PD 27B provides guidance on the right of media representatives to attend hearings of family proceedings in the Family Court, which take place in private subject to the discretion of the court to exclude such representatives under FPR 27.11 from the whole or part of any hearing on specified grounds.

[*Add to note 193*] **8–83**

FPR PD 27C (Attendance of Media Representatives at Hearings in Family Proceedings (Family Proceedings Court)) has been withdrawn. The Family Proceedings Court no longer exists and all family work is dealt with by the single Family Court: see generally at 8–85 below.

[*Add new paragraph*] **8–83A**

The President of the Family Division, Sir James Munby, issued important new guidance on *Transparency in the Family Courts: Publication of Judgments* and *Transparency in the Court of Protection: Publication of Judgments* on 16 January 2014 intended "to bring about an immediate and significant change in practice in relation to the publication of judgments in family courts and the Court of Protection". (The guidance is discussed at 2–63A above and 8–97 below.) For an authoritative summary of the continuing debate and the efficacy of the new rules relating to media reporting of, and access to, the family courts, see *Privacy and Publicity in Family Law: their eternal tension*, Sir Nicholas Wall P, Fam. Law 2012 42 (Dec) 1463-1477; *Lost opportunities: law reform and transparency in the family courts*, Sir James Munby P [2010] CFLO 273; *View from the President's Chambers: The Process of Reform* (1) [2013] Fam. Law 548 and (4) July 16, 2013 and *Freedom to Inform*, a speech by Sir James Munby P at the Annual Conference of the Society of Editors, 11 November 2013. In his judgment in *J (A Child), Re* [2013] EWHC 2694 (Fam). [25]–[65], the President had addressed the pressing need for more transparency in the family justice system in order to maintain public confidence in the system and also, more widely, the need for the courts to adapt to the realities of the internet and social media. Referring to his comments in *Re Roddy (A child) (Identification: Restriction on Publication)* [2003] EWHC 2927 (Fam); [2004] 2 F.L.R. 949, [89], he further stated at [37]–[40], [80] that "it is not the role of the judge to seek to exercise any kind of editorial control over the manner in which the media reports information which it is entitled to publish" and that "an injunction which cannot otherwise be justified is not to be granted because of the manner or style in which the material is being presented on the internet, nor to spare the blushes of those being attacked, however abusive and unjustified those attacks may be. The only justification is if restraint is necessary in order to protect the [applicant's] art.8 rights".

8–84 *[Add to note 195]*

The provisions for reform in the Children, Schools and Families Act 2010 have now been abandoned and are repealed by the Crime and Courts Act 2013 Pt 2 s.17(4) with effect from September 4, 2013 (SI 2013/2200). For the reasoning behind the decision not to implement the measures, see the Family Justice Review Final Report, November 2011, paras 2.234–235; *Operation of the Family Courts*, Sixth Report of Session 2010–12, *Volume I* (2011), House of Commons Justice Committee, para 281; and the *Government Response to Justice Committee's Sixth Report of Session 2010–12: Operation of the Family Courts* (October 2011), at paras 73–74.

A. The abolition of the Family Proceedings Court

8–85 *[Substitute new paragraph]*

Since the coming into effect, from 22 April 2014, of Pt 2 s.17(3) of the Crime and Courts Act 2013, the Family Proceedings Court no longer exists and all family work is dealt with by the single Family Court (subject to transitional provision specified in SI 2014/954 art.3). Section 65(1) of the Magistrates' Court Act 1980 is repealed by the Crime and Courts Act 2013, Sch.10(2), para. 48. The key features of the Family Court are: (1) The Family Court will deal with all family cases with the exception of two classes of case that are reserved for the Family Division (reserved work): (a) cases invoking the inherent jurisdiction of the High Court, whether in relation to children (wardship) or incapacitated or vulnerable adults; (b) international cases (including cases involving applications for relief under either the Hague Convention or Brussels IIR); (2) The Family Proceedings Court will no longer exist. All family work currently dealt with in the County Court will be dealt with in the Family Court. The Family Division will deal only with reserved work. Except for reserved work, cases that require to be heard by a High Court Judge will be heard in the Family Court by a High Court Judge (or a section 9 judge). Cases will accordingly no longer be transferred to the High Court on the grounds of complexity. No transfer of a case from the Family Court to the High Court will be permitted unless ordered by the President of the Family Division or a High Court Judge (not a section 9 judge): see *The Single Family Court: A Joint Statement by the President of the Family Division and the HMCTS Family Business Authority* (April 2013) [2013] Fam. Law 600.

B. The hybrid status of family proceedings: restrictions on attendance

Attendance at family hearings held "in private"

[*Add to end of paragraph*] **8–88**

With the coming into force, from 22 April 2014, of Pt 2 s.17(3) of the Crime and Courts Act 2013, the Family Proceedings Court no longer exists and all family work is dealt with by the single Family Court (subject to transitional provision specified in SI 2014/954 art.3). (See generally at 8–85 above.)

[*Add to note 229*] **8–88**

FPR PD 27C (Attendance of Media Representatives at Hearings in Family Proceedings (Family Proceedings Court)) has been withdrawn. The Family Proceedings Court no longer exists and all family work is dealt with by the single Family Court: see generally at 8–85 above. PD 27B provides guidance on the right of media representatives to attend at hearings of any family proceedings which take place in private subject to the discretion of the court to exclude such representatives under FPR 27.11 from the whole or part of any hearing on specified grounds.

[*Substitute new paragraph*] **8–89**

Section 69 of the Magistrates' Court Act 1980 is repealed by the Crime and Courts Act 2013, Sch.10(2), para 48. (See generally at 8–85 above.)

[*Add to note 240*] **8–90**

Section 69 of the Magistrates' Court Act 1980 is repealed by the Crime and Courts Act 2013, Sch.10(2), para. 48. (See generally at 8–85 above.)

[*Add to note 243*] **8–91**

FPR PD 27C (Attendance of Media Representatives at Hearings in Family Proceedings (Family Proceedings Court)) has been withdrawn. The Family Proceedings Court no longer exists and all family work is dealt with by the single Family Court: see generally at 8–85 above.

Statutory exclusion of the media

[*Add to notes 247, 248, 249, 254 and 258*] **8–92**

FPR PD 27C (Attendance of Media Representatives at Hearings in Family Proceedings (Family Proceedings Court)) has been withdrawn. The Family Proceedings Court no longer exists and all family work is dealt with by the single Family Court: see generally at 8–85 above.

8–95 *[Add to note 260]*

Para 6.4 of FPR PD 27B *Attendance of Media Representatives at Hearings in Family Proceedings (High Court and County Courts)* has been amended to take account of the criticism made by Baker J in *Al-Hilli (Children), Re* [2013] EWHC 2190 (Fam), Baker J. at [73]. In that case the issue arose as to whether an applicant for an order to exclude the media was required by para 6.4 to file evidence in support of the application. Baker J held that the wording of para 6.4 was only intended to import the provisions regarding service, as opposed to setting down any requirement as to evidence in support of such an application. In his view, unless the judge specifies that evidence should be served, the applicant is not under an obligation to provide evidence to the media, although when giving notice he should outline the reasons for the application. Para 6.4 of FPR PD 27B has accordingly been amended.

8–95 [*Add to note 263*]

FPR PD 27C (Attendance of Media Representatives at Hearings in Family Proceedings (Family Proceedings Court)) has been withdrawn. The Family Proceedings Court no longer exists and all family work is dealt with by the single Family Court: see generally at 8–85 above.

8–96 *[Add to note 264]*

See notes 260 and 263 above. Also, in *P (A child)* [2013] EWHC 4048 (Fam), in an addendum to his judgment, the President noted the limitations of the CopyDirect service and that the system does not serve all media organisations. For guidance on applications for *contra mundum* Reporting Restriction Orders against defendants based outside the jurisdiction, and service out of the jurisdiction under the FPR, see *J (A Child), Re* [2013] EWHC 2694 (Fam), [44]–[65], per Sir James Munby P, discussed at 2–63A and 6–53 above.

C. Media reporting of family proceedings

8–97 *[Add to Note 269]*

In *X (Children) (Expert Witness), Re* [2011] EWHC 1157 (Fam); [2012] 1 W.L.R. 182; [2011] E.M.L.R. 26; [2011] 2 F.L.R. 1437 at [102] Sir Nicholas Wall, then President, approved earlier judicial statements concerning the importance of responsible media reporting of family cases in *L (A Child) (Media Reporting), Re* [2011] EWHC 1285 (Fam) at [185]–[193], and as to the problems posed by tendentious and inaccurate accounts, which had been exemplified in that case.

[Add to note 271] **8–97**

But no restriction would, for example, apply to cases in the Family Division under the inherent jurisdiction in respect of adults where neither s.12(1)(a) of the Administration of Justice Act 1960 (cases involving children), nor s.12(1)(b) (cases in the Court of Protection), applied and the case did not engage the restrictions applicable to proceedings for ancillary relief (see 8–3 above): *RB (An Adult), Re* [2011] EWHC 3017 (Fam). In the absence of any relevant statutory restriction, it is not a contempt of court to publish or report a judgment (whether in whole or in part) merely because it was given or handed down in private and not in open court: *Forbes v Smith* [1998] 1 All E.R. 973 and *Hodgson v Imperial Tobacco Ltd* [1998] 1 W.L.R. 1056. Exactly the same principle applies in the Family Division: *Clibbery v Allan* [2002] EWCA Civ 45; [2002] Fam. 261. For judgments involving children and incapacitated adults, see now the guidance on *Transparency in the Family Courts: Publication of Judgments* and *Transparency in the Court of Protection: Publication of Judgments*, discussed at 2–63B and 8–97 above.

[Add to end of paragraph] **8–97**

With effect from 22 April 2014, the Family Proceedings Court ceased to exist: Pt 2 s.17(3) of the Crime and Courts Act 2013. All family work is dealt with by the single Family Court (subject to transitional provision specified in SI 2014/954 art.3). Section 71 of the Magistrates' Court Act 1980 was repealed by the Crime and Courts Act 2013, Sch.10(2), para 48. (See generally at 8–85 above.)

[Add new paragraph] **8–97A**

Sir James Munby P issued important new guidance on *Transparency in the Family Courts: Publication of Judgments* and *Transparency in the Court of Protection: Publication of Judgments* (with effect from 3 February 2014) intended "to bring about an immediate and significant change in practice in relation to the publication of judgments in family courts and the Court of Protection". The President noted that very similar issues arise in both courts "in relation to the need to protect the personal privacy of children and vulnerable adults" and adopted an incremental approach. The President anticipated issuing further Guidance, more formal Practice Directions and changes to the Family Procedure Rules and the Court of Protection Rules. On 15 August 2014 he launched a Consultation Paper *'Transparency — the next steps'*, about the possibility of making documents used in Family Court proceedings available to the media. Following the introduction of the Practice Guidance, 255 judgments of the Family Court had been published on BAILII between February and July 2014, compared to 115 judgments in the corresponding period for 2013.

8–97B *[Add new paragraph]*

The guidance provides that permission to publish should always be given "whenever the judge concludes that publication would be in the public interest" whether or not a request has been made. The guidance set out certain categories of case in the Family Court and the Court of Protection in which there is a presumption of publication. In such cases where "a written judgment already exists in a publishable form or the judge has already ordered that the judgment be transcribed, the starting point is that permission should be given for the judgment to be published unless there are compelling reasons why the judgment should not be published" (para 17). In all other cases, the starting point is that permission may be given for publication of a judgment whenever a party or an accredited member of the media applies for an order permitting publication (para 18).

The guidance provides that in all cases where a judge gives permission for a judgment to be published: (i) public authorities and expert witnesses should be named in the judgment approved for publication, unless there are compelling reasons why they should not be so named; (ii) the children who are the subject of the proceedings in the family courts, and other members of their family, and the person who is the subject of proceedings under the inherent jurisdiction of the High Court relating to incapacitated or vulnerable adults, and other members of their family, should not normally be named in the judgment approved for publication unless the judge otherwise orders; (iii) anonymity in the judgment as published should not normally extend beyond protecting the privacy of the children and adults who are the subject of the proceedings and other members of their families, unless there are compelling reasons to do so". Unless the judge orders otherwise, all judgments will be deemed to include the following rubric: "This judgment was delivered in private. The judge has given leave for this version of the judgment to be published on condition that (irrespective of what is contained in the judgment) in any published version of the judgment the anonymity of the incapacitated person and members of their family must be strictly preserved. All persons, including representatives of the media, must ensure that this condition is strictly complied with. Failure to do so will be a contempt of court". A copy of the guidance is available at *https://www.judiciary.gov.uk*.

8–97C *[Add new paragraph]*

There is considerable guidance available in earlier case law as to when it might be appropriate for the court to relax or add to the automatic restraints on media reporting contained in s.97 of the Children Act 1989 and s.12 of the Administration of Justice Act 1960. In what circumstances, for example, it will be appropriate to extend by means of a *contra mundum* Reporting Restriction Order the anonymity of the child beyond the point at which s.97 of the 1989 Act ceases to have effect? This is discussed at 6–46 *et seq* and 8–104 of the main text and in *J (A Child), Re* [2013] EWHC 2694 (Fam). The court may likewise, by an appropriate injunction, afford anonymity to other participants in the process, for example, an expert, a local authority, or a social worker: see generally at 8–50 of the main text and below.

For recent cases in which a Reporting Restriction Order has been made, see e.g. *Z v News Group Newspapers Ltd* [2013] EWHC 1371 (Fam); *A Council v M (Children) (Reporting Restriction Order)* [2012] EWHC 2038 (Fam), [2013] 2 F.L.R. 1270, [2013] Fam. Law 970; *Swansea v XZ & Anor* [2014] EWHC 212 (Fam), *J (A Child), Re* [2013] EWHC 2694 (Fam), discussed at 6–119B and 8–104. On the other hand, the decisions in *A (A Child) (Application for Reporting Restrictions), Re* [2011] EWHC 1764 (Fam), [2012] 1 F.L.R. 239, [2011] 3 F.C.R. 176, [2011] Fam. Law 1076 and *Surrey County Council v ME and others* [2014] EWHC 489 Fam, [2014] 2 F.L.R. 1267, [2014] Fam. Law 815, provide recent instances where the balance lay in the opposite (and more common) direction. FPR PD 12I provides guidance in relation to any application founded on Convention rights for an order restricting publication of information about children or incapacitated adults. The power of the Court of Appeal to anonymise parties in appeals from the Family Court was considered in *DE v AB* [2014] EWCA Civ 1064; [2015] 1 F.L.R. 1119; [2014] Fam. Law 1530 see 6–131C above.

[*Add to end of paragraph*] **8–98**

Section 71 of the Magistrates' Court Act 1980 was repealed by the Crime and Courts Act 2013, Sch.10(2), para 48 (in force from 22 April 2014). (See generally at 8–85 above.)

[*Substitute new paragraph*] **8–99 to 8–101**

With the coming into force, from 22 April 2014, of Pt 2 s.17(3) of the Crime and Courts Act 2013, the Family Proceedings Court no longer exists and all family work is dealt with by the single Family Court (subject to transitional provision specified in SI 2014/954 art.3). Section 71 of the Magistrates' Court Act 1980 was repealed by the Crime and Courts Act 2013, Sch.10(2), para 48. (See generally at 8–85 above.)

D. Privacy under s.97(2) of the Children Act 1989

[*Add to note 294*] **8–104**

FPR PD 27C (Attendance of Media Representatives at Hearings in Family Proceedings (Family Proceedings Court)) has been withdrawn. The Family Proceedings Court no longer exists and all family work is dealt with by the single Family Court: see generally at 8–85 above.

[*Add to end of paragraph*] **8–104**

Despite the scepticism expressed by Sir Mark Potter, then President, and Wall L.J., as he then was, in *Clayton v Clayton* [2006] EWCA Civ 878, [2006]

Fam. 83, [2007] 1 F.L.R. 11, as to the likely need for specific orders protecting a child's identity beyond the conclusion of the proceedings, Sir James Munby P was prepared to find that continuing restraint was required after the proceedings had come to an end in *J (A Child), Re* [2013] EWHC 2694 (Fam), at [77]. This related to the name of the child, essentially because of the fact that identifying information, damaging to the child, would remain indefinitely and easily accessible on the internet.

8–105 *[Add to note 295]*

See also *DE v AB* [2014] EWCA Civ 1064, [2015] 1 FLR 1119.

8–107 *[Add to note 300]*

The case of *Doncaster MBC v Haigh* [2011] EWHC 2412 (Fam); [2012] 1 F.L.R. 577 had been described by Sir Nicholas Wall, then President, as being an unprecedented case. He granted an application by a local authority to put into the public domain the correct version of facts concerning care proceedings, subject to restrictions as to the child's identity (although the parents could be named). See the discussion in *Confidentiality in Children Cases after Doncaster MBC v Haigh,* Kevin Skinner, Fam. Law 2011, 41(Dec), 1348-1351. See also *Al-Hilli (Children), Re* [2013] EWHC 2190 (Fam), Baker J. and *J (A Child), Re* [2013] EWHC 2694 (Fam). This was a reserved judgment of Sir James Munby P in which he considered the right of "disgruntled parents" to speak out about the justice and care systems and also, more generally, the need for the courts to adapt to the realities of the internet and social media.

A rare example was provided by the decision of Macur J., on October 19, 2012, in *Hunt v Hunt* [2012] All E.R. (D) 217 (Oct). The dispute concerned a child called Lydia whose welfare and residence had formed the subject-matter of long running litigation both in England and in Mexico. There had already been much publicity given to the circumstances of the case in Parliament, the media and online. A balancing exercise was carried out in accordance with *S (A Child), Re* [2005] 1 A.C. 593. Although the judge weighed the rights of the child and her family under art.8 of the ECHR, she came down in favour of giving the newspaper permission

> "to use the case as an anchor story upon which to base an article, or series of articles, relating to increasing numbers of child abduction cases coming before the courts and difficulties experienced in pursuing 'Hague Convention' remedies."

E. The Court of Protection

8–108 [*Add to note 304*]

In his speech *Freedom to Inform* to the Annual Conference of the Society of Editors on 11 November 2013, Sir James Munby P expressed the view that he was inclined to think that the arguments in favour of allowing accredited journalists a right to attend proceedings in the Court of Protection, unless there are proper grounds for excluding them, and thereby aligning the Court of Protection with the practice in the Family Court were compelling. A copy of the speech is available at *https://www.judiciary.gov.uk*.

[*Add to note 307*] **8–108**

For a recent example of the court authorising the publication of such information, see *Westminister City Council v Sykes* [2014] EWHC B9 (COP), (2014) 17 C.C.L. Rep. 139.

[Add to end of paragraph] **8–108**

The President of the Family Division, Sir James Munby, issued important new guidance on "Transparency in the Family Courts: Publication of Judgments" and "Transparency in the Court of Protection: Publication of Judgments" on 16 January 2014 intended "to bring about an immediate and significant change in practice in relation to the publication of judgments in family courts and the Court of Protection" see 8–97 and 2–63B above.

The Court of Protection Guidance took effect from 3 February 2014 and applies to all judgments in the Court of Protection delivered by the Senior Judge, nominated circuit judges and High Court judges. The guidance in respect of the family courts also took effect on 3 February 2014 and expressly applied to all judgments delivered by High Court judges exercising the inherent jurisdiction to make orders in respect of incapacitated or vulnerable adults. Both sets of guidance distinguish between two classes of judgments: (a) those that the judge must ordinarily allow to be published; and (b) those that *may* be published. Permission to publish a judgment should always be given when the judge concludes that the publication would be in the public interest, and whether or not a request to publish has been made.

The starting point is that where a written judgment already exists in publishable form, or the judge has already ordered that the judgment be transcribed, permission should be given to publish judgments arising from a wide range of specified proceedings in the Court of Protection or under the inherent jurisdiction of the High Court, including: (a) applications for an order involving the giving or withholding of serious medical treatment; (b) any application for a declaration or order involving a deprivation, or possible deprivation, of liberty; (c) a dispute as to who should act as an attorney or deputy; (d) any application for an order that the incapacitated or vulnerable adult should be moved into or out of a residential establishment or other institution;(e) any case where the sale of the incapacitated or vulnerable adult's home is in issue; (f) any application for a declaration regarding capacity to marry or consent to sexual relations, unless there are compelling reasons why the judgment should not be published. In all other cases, the starting point is that permission for publication may be given by the judge at his discretion, on an application by a party or an accredited member of the media. In both sets of guidance, the President makes clear that the person who is the subject of proceedings, and that person's family members, should not normally be named. Regarding local authorities and expert witnesses, the guidance provides that they should be named in the published judgments *unless* there are compelling reasons why they should not be. A copy of the guidance is available at *https://www.judiciary.gov.uk*.

8–109 *[Add to note 309]*

This was confirmed by Baker J. in *In M (Adult Patient) (Minimally Conscious State: Withdrawal of Treatment)* [2011] EWHC 1197 (COP); [2012] 1 W.L.R. 287 at [25]–[26].

8–109 [*Add to note 310*]

Where the incapacitated adult whose case is before the Court of Protection has died before the conclusion of the case, it does not necessarily follow that a restriction should be lifted: see *The Press Association v Newcastle Upon Tyne Hospitals Foundation Trust* [2014] EWCOP 6.

8–109 *[Add to end of paragraph]*

In relation to the reporting of private proceedings in the Court of Protection, Baker J stated in *In Re M (A Patient) (Court of Protection: Reporting Restrictions)* [2011] EWHC 1197 (COP); [2012] 1 WLR 287 at [61] that the court should recognise "that the reporting of such cases is difficult if the restrictions imposed on the media are too onerous. The issues raised are invariably given sharper focus if the media are free to report the human stories behind the legal issues". At [62], he went on to endorse the observation of Peter Jackson J in *Hillingdon London Borough Council v Neary* [2011] EWHC 413 (Fam), at [15(4)], to the effect that it is particularly important that the public should have confidence in the way in which the Court of Protection is working:

> "All judges are aware of the unease expressed in some quarters about the so-called 'secrecy' of proceedings in the family courts and the Court of Protection. Where a case warrants an exception to the general rule that the Court of Protection proceedings should be held in private, the court should ensure that reporters are free to give as full a picture as possible of the court proceedings".

On 16 January 2014, the President of the Family Division, Sir James Munby, issued important new guidance on the "Transparency in the Court of Protection: Publication of Judgments" see 8–97 and 2–63B above.

VII. PRE-TRIAL HEARINGS IN CRIMINAL PROCEEDINGS

A. Committal proceedings: Magistrates' Courts Act 1980 s.8

[Add new paragraph] **8–110A**

With the coming into force of Sch.3 to the Criminal Justice Act 2003, the government has altered the procedure to be followed by magistrates' courts in determining whether cases triable either way should be tried summarily or on indictment. There is to be a new "allocation and sending" procedure to the Crown Court for suitable cases. Under the new procedure, the magistrates will not have to consider whether the evidence is sufficient. The amendments to the Magistrates' Courts Act 1980 and the Crime and Disorder Act 1998 are set out in Sch.3 to the Criminal Justice Act 2003, as amended. These provisions are intended to bring closer alignment between the Crown Court and the magistrates' courts, as proposed in the government paper "*Justice for All*" (2002), and to give effect to a number of recommendations from Lord Justice Auld's *Review of the Criminal Courts* (2001*)*. Magistrates are to be made aware, when they determine allocation, of any previous convictions of the defendant. Committal proceedings and transfers in serious fraud and child witness cases are replaced by a common system for sending cases to the Crown Court, based on the present arrangements for indictable-only cases. The phasing out of committal proceedings started in April 2012, but they can still take place where defendants first appeared for the relevant offence on or after the 5 November 2012 (Criminal Justice Act (Commencement No 29 and Saving Provisions) Order 2012 (2012/2574)).

[Add new paragraph] **8–110B**

Section 51 of the Crime and Disorder Act 1998 applies not only to indictable-only offences (and cases related to such offences), but also where an either-way case involving an adult defendant is allocated for trial on indictment. Section 51A of this Act replaces the existing provisions for moving cases where the principal defendant is under 18 to the Crown Court for trial. Sections 51B and 51C subsume, respectively, the transfer provisions now in s.4 of the Criminal Justice Act 1987 (serious fraud cases) and s.53 of the Criminal Justice Act 1991 (child witness cases) respectively. Section 8C of the Magistrates' Courts Act 1980 provides reporting restrictions in respect of pre-trial rulings in magistrates' courts This was inserted by s.45 of, and Sch.3 to, the Courts Act 2003.

[Add new paragraph] **8–110C**

Sections 52A and 52B of the 1998 Act and s.8C of the Magistrates' Courts Act 1980 (inserted by s.45 of, and Sch.3 to, the Courts Act 2003) impose broadly similar reporting restrictions in respect of allocation and sending proceedings to those which had applied under the old committal proceedings. They also create corresponding criminal offences in respect of breaches. For the relevant procedural rules, see Pts 9 and 16 of the Criminal Procedure Rules 2015 (SI 2015/1490) in force with effect from 5 October 2015. Once the case is at the Crown Court, the defendant may apply for the dismissal of any charge under para.2, Sch.3 to the 1998 Act. Paragraph 3 of Sch.3 imposes reporting restrictions in respect of dismissal applications: see also at 8–120 below.

In April 2013, News Group Newspapers Limited pleaded guilty to one offence under s.52B(1)(a) and (2) of the Crime and Disorder Act 1998 relating to the reporting in *The Sun* newspaper in September 2012 of the sending of Andrew Partington for trial after a preliminary hearing at Oldham Magistrates' court. The court concluded that the reporting "clearly went way beyond what was permitted" and imposed a fine of £3,350, together with a victim surcharge of £120.00 and prosecution costs of £500.00. See the sentencing remarks by DJ Jonathan Taafe in Manchester Magistrates' Court, April 5, 2013, available at *https://www.judiciary.gov.uk/wp-content/uploads/JCO/Documents/Judgments/sentencing-remarks-dj-taaffe-r-v-news-grp-newspapers-ltd.pdf* (accessed 5 August 2015) on *http://www.judiciary.gov.uk* [Accessed August 5, 2015].

8–111 *[Add to note 315]*

Section 52A of the 1998 Act has now been brought into force in relation to certain local justice areas (see SI 2012/1320; 2012/2573; 2013/1103) and otherwise with effect from a date to be appointed.

8–112 *[Add to note 317]*

Under Part 9 of the Criminal Procedure Rules 2015 (SI 2015/1490) in force with effect from 5 October 2015, the court must explain to the defendant that restrictions apply to the allocation and sending procedure, which the defendant may ask the court to vary or remove: see Parts 9 and 6 of the 2015 Rules (procedure to be followed in any application to vary or remove reporting restrictions).

8–112 *[Add at end of paragraph]*

Section 8 of the 1980 Act is repealed by paragraph 51 of Schedule 3, and Part 4 of Schedule 37, to the Criminal Justice Act 2003 in relation to certain local justice areas (see S.I. 2012/1320; 2012/2574; 2013/1103; and otherwise with effect from a date to be appointed).

8–112A *[Add new paragraph]*

With effect from 1 October 2012, new automatic reporting restrictions have been introduced to restrict publication of any information to the public at large, or any section of the public, that would identify a teacher who is the subject of an allegation of criminal misconduct where the alleged victim of the offence is a registered pupil at the relevant school. Such restrictions remain in place unless or until the Secretary of State or the General Teaching Council for Wales, as the case may be, publishes information about an investigation or decision in a disciplinary case arising from the allegation, or proceedings for the offence have been instituted or the teacher concerned includes a matter in a publication, or otherwise consents to publication. It is a defence to show that, at the time of the alleged offence, the person was not aware, and neither suspected nor had reason to suspect, that the publication included the matter in question or that the allegation in question had been made: s.141F–H inserted in Part 8 of the Education Act 2002 by the Education Act 2011, Pt 3 s.13(1). The Criminal Procedure Rules 2015 r.6.5(4) sets out the procedure for applying to the Crown Court to appeal a refusal by a magistrates' court to remove the restrictions.

C. The comparable restrictions under the Criminal Justice Act 1987 s.11 and Criminal Procedure and Investigations Act 1996 s.37 (transfers for trial and preparatory hearings)

[Add to note 326] **8–115**

In *R. v Chaytor* [2010] EWCA Crim 1910; [2010] 2 Cr. App. R. 34, on an appeal arising from the decision in a preparatory hearing, the Court of Appeal held, reflecting the provisions of s.37 of the Criminal Procedure and Investigations Act 1996, that the appeal should not be subject to reporting restrictions, including the arguments and submissions advanced on each side. The appeal involved purely legal questions, which were "confined to a narrow but important issue of constitutional law". The allegations of dishonesty made against the defendants were not canvassed on the appeal, which was mainly concerned with the matter of parliamentary privilege. (The issues were subsequently addressed by the Supreme Court: [2010] UKSC 52.)

[Add at end of paragraph] **8–115**

The notice of transfer procedure has now been repealed by the Criminal Justice Act 2003 Sch.37(4) para.1 (with associated saving provisions, as to which see SI 2012/1320; 2012/2574; 2013/1103). It has been replaced by the sending procedure contained in s.51B of the Crime and Disorder Act 1998 (as amended by Criminal Justice Act 2003 Sch.3(1) para.18), discussed at 8–110A *et seq* above.

[Add at end of paragraph] **8–116**

The provisions in para.6 of Sch.6, relating to transfers in child witness cases, have now been repealed by the Criminal Justice Act 2003 (with associated saving provisions, as to which see SI 2012/1320; 2012/2574; 2013/1103). They are replaced by the sending procedure contained in s.51C of the Crime and Disorder Act 1998 (as amended by Criminal Justice Act 2003 Sch.3(1) para.18), discussed at 8–110A *et seq* above.

E. Rulings at pre-trial hearings: Criminal Procedure and Investigations Act 1996 s.41 and the Magistrates' Courts Act 1980 s.8C

8–119 *[Add to note 334]*

See now the Criminal Procedure Rules 2015 (SI 2015/1490) in force with effect from 5 October 2015 Part 6.

F. Application for dismissal: Crime and Disorder Act 1998 Sch 3, para 3

8–120 *[Add to note 336]*

With the coming into force of Sch.3 to the Criminal Justice Act 2003, prosecutors' powers to transfer cases under the Criminal Justice Acts 1987 and 1991 have been repealed and replaced by a sending procedure, discussed at 8–110A *et seq* above. Part 6 of the Criminal Procedure Rules 2015 (SI 2015/1490) in force with effect from 5 October 2015 has superseded Pt 16 of the Criminal Procedure Rules 2011.

8–120 *[Add at end of paragraph]*

Dismissal applications may now also be made where an either-way case is allocated for trial on indictment: s.51 of the Crime and Disorder Act 1998 (as amended by Criminal Justice Act 2003 Sch.3(1) para.18), discussed at 8–110A *et seq* above.

IX. DISCLOSURES RELATING TO PROCEEDINGS IN PRIVATE

D. Disclosure of information from proceedings relating to children

8–136 *[Delete the words Add to new paragraph]*

8–138 *[Add to note 372]*

See also *Doncaster MBC v Watson* [2012] 1 F.L.R. 599; [2011] 3 F.C.R. 422; [2011] Fam. Law 1194W, discussed at 12–25A below. The case concerned a "private case investigator" who had campaigned on behalf of a mother whose child was the subject of care proceedings instituted by the local authority. Sir Nicholas Wall, then President, held with regard to committal for contempt that the fact that some of the communications had been made to those in authority might go to mitigation, but not to the substance of the alleged contempt.

8–139 *[Add to text at end of paragraph]*

There is now considerable case law offering guidance as to when it may be appropriate for the court to relax or add to the automatic restraints on media reporting imposed by s.12 of the Administration of Justice Act 1960 (and s.97 of the Children Act 1989) by e.g granting a *contra mundum* injunction: see 6–46 *et seq* above, 8–150 *et seq*.

F. What can be published about proceedings in private?

[Add to note 396] **8–149**

Injunctions affording anonymity to other participants in the process, for example, an expert, a local authority, or a social worker, will not readily be granted and should not be made unless there are compelling reasons: see the discussions in *A v Ward* (also known as *Ward, Re*) [2010] EWHC 16 (Fam); [2010] 1 F.L.R. 1497 and *X (Children) (Expert Witnesses), Re* (also known as *In re X and others (Children) (Morgan and others intervening))* [2011] EWHC 1157 (Fam); [2012] 1 W.L.R. 182; [2011] E.M.L.R. 26; [2011] 2 F.L.R. 1437. For an example of a case in which the anonymity of the expert was preserved, see the decision of Sir Mark Potter, then President, in *X (A Child) (Residence and Contact: Rights of Media Attendance), Re* [2009] EWHC 1728 (Fam); [2009] 3 FCR 370, discussed at para.8–94 of the main text.

[Add at end of paragraph] **8–150**

In *X (Children) (Expert Witnesses), Re* (also known as *In re X and others (Children) (Morgan and others intervening)* [2011] EWHC 1157 (Fam); [2012] 1 W.L.R. 182; [2011] E.M.L.R. 26; [2011] 2 F.L.R. 1437 the court relaxed the s.12 restrictions to permit the disclosure of an expert paediatrician's report prepared for the purpose of care proceedings, suitably redacted to preserve the children's anonymity. Sir Nicholas Wall, then President, said at [93]-[97] that he would like to see a practice develop in which expert reports would be routinely disclosed to the media, and the media able to comment both on the reports and on the use to which they were put in the proceedings, provided (a) that the child's anonymity was preserved and (b) that the child would not refuse to engage in the forensic process if the expert was identified. In *BBC (Care Proceedings: Costs: Identification of Local Authority), Re* [2011] 1 F.L.R. 977 District Judge Bellamy held it was not a proportionate restriction on the art.10 rights of the media to prevent them from naming a local authority, whom he had ordered to pay a substantial contribution to the parents' costs in care proceedings, notwithstanding the risk that such disclosure might lead to the children being identified. In *Doncaster MBC v Haigh* [2011] EWHC 2412 (Fam); [2012] 1 F.L.R. 577 the court granted an unprecedented application by the local authority to put into the public domain the correct version of facts concerning care proceedings, subject to restrictions as to the child's identity (although the parents could be named). In *J (A Child), Re* [2013] EWHC 2694 (Fam), [69]-[70], the President declined to make the extensive reporting restriction order sought, pointing out that the naming of social workers or the children's guardian or the local authority, or even all of them, would not necessarily make it likely that the child would be identified.

8–151A *[Add new paragraph]*

A person who publishes or reports a judgment in a way which does not comply with the rubric on the front sheet of the judgment will, in principle, be guilty of a contempt of court in accordance with s.12. The remedy for someone who wishes to publish material prohibited by the rubric is to apply for a suitable modification: see, for example, in *B, Re* [2007] EWHC 1622 (Fam), [2008] 1 F.L.R. 482; *X Council v B* [2008] EWHC 270 (Fam), [2008] 1 F.L.R. 1460; *RB (An Adult), Re* [2011] EWHC 3017 (Fam), [2012] 1 F.L.R. 466. See too para. 18 of the new guidance on *Transparency in the Family Courts: Publication of Judgments* and *Transparency in the Court of Protection: Publication of Judgments*, referred to at 8–83A above.

X. EMPLOYMENT AND OTHER TRIBUNALS

A. Employment Tribunals: restrictions on reporting

8–169 [*Add to note 444*]

The procedure for bringing and responding to claims in the employment tribunal was substantially reformed with effect from 29 July 2013. The Employment Tribunals (Constitution and Rules of Procedure) Regulations 2004 (SI2004/1861) have been replaced by the Employment Tribunals (Constitution and Rules of Procedure) Regulations 2013/1237 (in force from 29 July 2013). The rules of procedure in Schedules 1 to 3 replace the former rules of procedure in employment tribunals set out in Schedules 1 to 6 to the 2004 Regulations.

8–169 [*Add to note 445*]

The Employment Tribunals (Constitution and Rules of Procedure) Regulations 2004 (SI2004/1861) have been replaced by the Employment Tribunals (Constitution and Rules of Procedure) Regulations 2013/1237 (in force from 29 July 2013).

8–169 [*Add to note 447*]

The Employment Tribunals (Constitution and Rules of Procedure) Regulations 2004 (SI 2004/1861), Sch. 1 para. 50, have been replaced by the Employment Tribunals (Constitution and Rules of Procedure) Regulations 2013/1237, r. 50 (in force from 29 July 2013).

[Add new paragraph] **8–169A**

The rules of procedure in employment tribunals were substantially reformed with effect from 29 July 2013. Rule 50 of the Employment Tribunals (Constitution and Rules of Procedure) Regulations (SI 2013/1237) introduced a new regime for privacy and restrictions on disclosure in employment tribunals, which widens the scope under which an application can be made and expressly includes a tribunal's right to make orders that protect the Convention rights of any individual. The new rules are intended to unify the approach of tribunals and the High Court.

[Add new paragraph] **8–169B**

Under r. 50 a tribunal may at any stage of the proceedings, on its own initiative or on application, make an order with a view to preventing or restricting the public disclosure of any aspect of those proceedings so far as it considers necessary in the interests of justice, or in order to protect the Convention rights of any person, or to prevent the disclosure of confidential information (as defined in the Employment Tribunals Act 1996, s.10A). In considering whether to make an order under r.50, the tribunal shall give full weight to the principle of open justice and to the Convention right to freedom of expression. Such orders may include (a) an order that a hearing that would otherwise be in public be conducted, in whole or in part, in private; (b) an order that the identities of specified parties, witnesses or other persons referred to in the proceedings should not be disclosed to the public; (c) an order for special measures preventing witnesses at a public hearing being identifiable by members of the public; (d) a restricted reporting order in cases involving sexual misconduct or disability.

[Add new paragraph] **8–169C**

In his review of the Employment Tribunal Rules of Procedure published in 2012, Underhill J, the former President of the Employment Appeal Tribunal, stated that the previous regime was "poorly conceived and drafted" and "provide[d] a limited and sharply-defined regime governing where anonymity and restricted reporting orders can be made, deriving from the prescriptive terms of ss.11 and 12 of the Employment Tribunals Act 1996. These have been held by recent case-law to be out of step with the requirements both of the Human Rights Act and of EU jurisprudence. Our proposed new rule provides for a more flexible regime which allows Tribunals to take appropriate steps to balance the important principles of open justice and freedom of expression on the one hand and of privacy and effective justice on the other".

[Add new paragraph] **8–169D**

In reply to media complaints that the new proposed rules represented a move to a more restrictive regime, the government stated: "The old rules on privacy and restricted reporting were designed to deal with specific instances where hearings should be held in private, and covered proceedings that involved, for the main part, allegations of sexual misconduct or disability discrimination. Mr Justice Underhill felt that it was important that his review brought the provisions on privacy in Employment Tribunals more into line with the requirements of the Human Rights Act 1998 and jurisprudence of the European Court of Human Rights and new rule is therefore less prescriptive. Whilst the suggested changes to the rules widen the existing legislative provisions in this area, and give judges more discretion and flexibility in the rules for deciding whether anonymity or restricted reporting orders are required, such power already exists (see the case of *F v G* [2012] ICR 246). ... [The government] agrees that it should not become the normal practice of tribunals to hold proceedings in private. As it is now, reporting should only be restricted where it is in the interests of justice to do so. To address these concerns the new draft of the rules makes clear that in making a decision on privacy, the tribunal shall give full weight to the principle of open justice and to the Convention right to freedom of expression". In *F v G* [2012] ICR 246, decided under the old rules, the Employment Appeal Tribunal had held that where anonymisation or reporting restrictions are needed to protect a party's rights under article 8, an employment tribunal can use its general powers under old r.10 to take such measures.

8–169E *[Add new paragraph]*

For an explanation and analysis of the modern principles relating to anonymity, and of the need to carry out a proper balancing exercise when orders are sought which would derogate from the principle of open justice, see *BBC v Roden* [2015] UKEAT 0385 14 1205 (Simler J).

C. Tribunals under the Tribunals, Courts and Enforcement Act 2007: The First-tier and Upper Tribunal

8–189 *[Add to note 477]*

The Asylum and Immigration Tribunal (Procedure) Rules 2005 (SI 2005/230) have been replaced by the Tribunal Procedure (First-tier Tribunal) (Immigration and Asylum Chamber) Rules 2014/2604 (in force from 20 October 2014). Rule 27 permits the Tribunal to give a direction that a hearing, or part of it, is to be held in private. No further indication of when this might be appropriate is provided. This is in contrast with old r. 54 which limited the Tribunal to exclude the public if necessary in the interests of public order or national security, to protect the private life of a party or the interests of a minor, or, in exceptional circumstances, to ensure that publicity does not prejudice the interests of justice.

[*Add to note 478*] **8–189**

The Asylum and Immigration Tribunal (Procedure) Rules 2005 (SI 2005/230) have been replaced by the Tribunal Procedure (First-tier Tribunal) (Immigration and Asylum Chamber) Rules 2014/2604 (in force from 20 October 2014). Under r.13 of the new rules the tribunal has power to prohibit the disclosure or publication of specified documents or information relating to the proceedings, or any matter likely to lead members of the public to identify any person whom the Tribunal considers should not be identified. The rule appears to be directed towards cases where serious harm could result from disclosure, or cases of national security, but it could potentially have much wider application. The general discretion in r.13(1) to prohibit disclosure or publication is not expressly limited by any particular or mandatory considerations, although it is reasonable to suppose that a tribunal will be guided by the many authoritative statements now available on the principle of open justice: see e.g. *A v BBC* [2015] AC 588; *Re Guardian News and Media Ltd* [2014] EWCA Crim 1861, [2015] 1 Cr. App. R.4, [2015] E.M.L.R. 2, [2014] H.R.L.R. 28 at [15]–[19]; and *BBC v Roden* [2015] UKEAT 0385 14 1205 (Simler J), cited above.

XI. RESTRICTIONS ON ATTENDANCE UNDER THE OFFICIAL SECRETS ACT 1920

[Add to note 481] **8–191**

Rule 16.6 of the Criminal Procedure Rules 2011 is now replaced by r.6.6 of the Criminal Procedure Rules 2015 (SI 2015/1490) in force with effect from 5 October 2015, the terms of which are unchanged.

XII. ANONYMITY UNDER THE PREVENTION OF TERRORISM ACT 2005

[Add at end of paragraph] **8–192**

The Terrorism Prevention and Investigation Measures Act 2011 repealed the Prevention of Terrorism Act 2005. In place of the control orders regime, a new system of terrorism prevention and investigation measures (TPIM) has come into effect (with effect from December 15, 2011 subject to transitional and saving provisions). The TPIM regime is intended to impose less intrusive restrictions than those which had been available under control orders, and to increase the safeguards for the civil liberties of those subject to the measures. Part 80 was added to the CPR by the Civil Procedure (Amendment No.3) Rules 2011 (SI 2011/2970) for the purpose of providing rules of court about proceedings under the 2011 Act. CPR Pt 76, which contains rules about proceedings under the 2005 Act, was not revoked by that statutory instrument, because those rules will remain necessary for as long as proceedings may arise in the High Court and the Court of Appeal under the earlier statute. In structure, and in much of its detail, Pt 80 is modelled on Pt 76. Paragraph 6(3) of Sch.4 to the TPIM Act empowers the court to impose

> "such prohibition or restriction as it thinks fit on the disclosure (a) by such persons as the court specifies or describes, or (b) by persons generally, of the identity of the relevant individual or of any information that would tend to identify the relevant individual."

CPR r.80.15 is similar in effect to r.76.19. In relation to the tensions between the principle of open justice and the needs of national security, see the discussion in *Re Guardian News and Media Ltd* [2014] EWCA Crim 1861, [2015] 1 Cr. App. R.4, [2015] E.M.L.R. 2, [2014] H.R.L.R. 28 at [15]–[19]. The TPIM regime was described by the Joint Committee of Human Rights as "withering on the vine" (*Post-Legislative Scrutiny: Terrorism Prevention and Investigation Measures Act 2011*, 10th Report of 201–2014, Conclusions para 15). In 2014, only one person was subject to a TPIM (David Anderson QC *Terrorism Prevention and Investigation Measures in 2014*, March 2015). In relation to the tensions between the principle of open justice and the needs of national security, see the discussion in *Re Guardian News and Media Ltd* [2014] EWCA Crim 1861, [2015] 1 Cr. App. R.4, [2015] E.M.L.R. 2, [2014] H.R.L.R. 28 at [15]–[19].

CHAPTER 9

PROTECTION OF SOURCES

I. THE COMMON LAW CONTEXT

A. Introduction: the significance of journalists' sources

[Add to note 3] **9–1**

See also the Guidelines of the Committee of Ministers of the Council of Europe on Protecting Freedom of Expression and Information in Times of Crisis, adopted by the Committee of Ministers on September 26, 2007 at the 1005th meeting of the Ministers' Deputies.

[Add to note 4] **9–1**

The reference to *R v The National Post* (2004) 236 DLR (4th) 551 should be (2004) 69 OR (3d) 427 (Benotto J). This decision was overturned by the Ontario Court of Appeal in 2008 and the newspaper's appeal to the Supreme Court of Canada in 2010 was dismissed [2010] SCC 16; [2010] 1 SCR 477.

[Add to note 7] **9–2**

See also *Sunday Times v UK (No.2)* (1991) 14 E.H.R.R. 229, *Roemen and Schmit v Luxembourg* [2003] ECHR 102, *Ernst v Belgium* (2004) 39 E.H.R.R. 35 at [103], *Sanoma Uitgevers BV v The Netherlands* (2010) 51 E.H.R.R. 31, *Financial Times Ltd v United Kingdom* (2010) 50 E.H.R.R. 46 at [60], *Nagla v Latvia* 16 July 2013, Application No (73469/10, [2013] ECHR 688 at [95]. The question of who can be considered as a journalist's "source" is discussed at para 9–55A below.

9–2 *[Add to note 8]*

Financial Times Ltd v United Kingdom (2010) 50 EHRR 46 is discussed at para 9–183.

9–2 *[Add to note 9]*

See also *Telegraaf Media Nederland Landelijke Media B.V. v The Netherlands* (2012) 34 B.H.R.C. 193. *Samona Uitgevers BV v The Netherlands* (2010) 51 EHRR 31 is discussed at para.9–202.

B. The common law background

9–4 *[Add to note 14]*

See now *Gatley on Libel and Slander*, 12th edn (2014) paras 31.32 to 31.37.

9–4 *[Add to note 15]*

See now *Gatley on Libel & Slander*, 12th edn (2014) paras 31.32 to 31.37.

Hesitant recognition of the "chilling effect"

9–7 *[Add to note 22]*

It has been recognised that an order directed to the handing over of journalistic materials may have a chilling effect on the exercise of journalistic freedom of expression even where "source protection" is not in issue; for example, because the individual from whom the journalist has received information is not a "source" (on which, see the discussion at para 9–55A below) or because the identity of the source is no secret (as in *R (Miranda) v Secretary of State for the Home Department* [2014] EWHC 255 (Admin); [2014] 1 W.L.R. 3140): see e.g. *Nordisk Film & TV A/S v Denmark* (App No 40485/02, 8 December 2005), at p.10, *Stichting Ostade Blade v Netherlands* (2014) 59 E.H.R.R. SE9 at [64] and *Miranda*, cited above, at [48] and [72].

9–12 *[Add to note 28]*

See also *Voskuil v Netherlands* (2010) 50 E.H.R.R. 9 at [65]; *Sanoma Uitgevers BV v The Netherlands* (2010) 51 E.H.R.R. 31, at [54]; *Financial Times Ltd v United Kingdom* (2010) 50 E.H.R.R. 46, at [59]; and *Telegraaf Media Nederland Landelikje Media BV v The Netherlands* (2012) 34 B.H.R.C. 193, at [127].

C. The discretionary or "balancing" approach of the common law

[Add to note 30] 9–13

Nonetheless, the privilege retains its importance and is expressly highlighted, for example, in the current precedents for freezing orders (although some qualification is required so far as intellectual property cases are concerned: see para 7.9 of PD 25A and the discussion at para 3–201).

D. Competing policy considerations: the role of the media

[Add new paragraph] 9–18A

Further guidance was given in *R (Miranda) v Secretary of State for the Home Department* [2014] EWHC 255 (Admin), [2014] 1 W.L.R. 3140, at [46], by Laws LJ (with whom Ouseley and Openshaw JJ agreed). In considering whether a measure constitutes a proportionate interference with *journalistic* expression (said to be a distinct sub-class of the general right to free expression which belongs to every individual for his own sake), the court is not merely conducting a balancing exercise between, on the one hand, the private right of an individual journalist to freedom of expression and, on the other, the interests of the community (in that case, in respect of national security). Because journalistic freedom of expression serves "the public at large", the balancing is rather between two aspects of the public interest. Accordingly, the fourth limb of the proportionality principle recently restated by Lord Sumption JSC in *Bank Mellat v HM Treasury (Liberty intervening) (No 2)* [2014] AC 700, at [20], ("whether ... a fair balance has been struck between the rights of the individual and the interests of the community") would need to be modified to that extent.

[Add to note 50] 9–19

See the discussion at 2–50 *et seq.* and the observations of Thomas LJ (as he then was) in *R (on the application of Mohamed) v Secretary of State for Foreign and Commonwealth Affairs* [2009] EWHC 152 (Admin), [2009] 1 WLR 2653 at [53]. In *R (Miranda) v Secretary of State for the Home Department* [2014] EWHC 255 (Admin); [2014] 1 W.L.R. 3140 at [70]-[71], however, Laws LJ made clear that the "constitutional" role of the press does not extend to responsibility for the protection of national security, which lies only with elected government.

[Add new paragraph] 9–24A

In his report on the Culture, Practices and Ethics of the Press, published in November 2012, Sir Brian Leveson referred to protection of sources as one of a number of "privileges" afforded to the press "going beyond those protected by freedom of speech": Part B, Chapter 2, 6, Section 6 and Chapter 4, Section 4. He added that

> "these privileges afforded to the press are important precisely because they enable the press to serve the public interest in carrying out investigative journalism and disseminating information: they are not afforded for any other reason."

In response to an invitation made during the Leveson inquiry, The Director of Public Prosecutions issued Guidelines for prosecutors assessing the public interest in cases affecting the media (which is available on the CPS website). These recognise the sensitivity of cases which may involve the possibility of a journalist having to reveal a confidential source: see paras 38–40. "Special care" is necessary and weight needs to be given to the public interest in protecting sources: see also A.T.H. Smith, *"Assessing the Public Interest in Cases Affecting the Media — The Prosecution Guidelines"* [2013] Crim. L.R. 448.

E. Whistleblowing

9–27 *[Add to note 65]*

See also *Telegraaf Media Nederland Landelikje Media BV v The Netherlands* (2012) 34 B.H.R.C. 193, at [128], and *Nagla v Latvia* (73469/10, [2013] ECHR 688, 16 July 2013), at [97], and the statements by the European Court of Human Rights that the right of a journalist not to disclose his or her sources cannot be considered a privilege, dependent on the lawful or unlawful actions of their sources but is rather an intrinsic part of the right to information, which should be treated with the utmost caution (see *Nagla v Latvia* at [97], *Tillack v Belgium* (2012) 55 E.H.R.R. 25 at [65], and *Ressiot and Ors v France* (15054/07, 28 June 2012)).

9–27A *[Add new paragraph]*

It should also be noted that, in light of the European Court of Human Rights case of *Stichting Ostade Blade v Netherlands* (2014) 59 E.H.R.R. SE9, discussed at para 9–55A below, there may be circumstances in which an individual's conduct means that he or she may not properly be considered a "source" at all.

9–32 *[Add to note 75]*

Replace citation for *R v The National Post* (2004) D.L.R. (4th) 551 with (2004) 69 O.R. (3d) 427. In Canada, the privilege of source protection can only be claimed where the source has been given an express promise of confidentiality (this is the first of the four Wigmore criteria which must be satisfied in order for the journalist-source privilege to arise). See, for example, *R v The National Post* [2010] S.C.C. 16, [2010] 1 S.C.R. 477 at [56].

F. Reconciling source protection with the rule of law

[Add to note 77] 9–34

See also the Irish Supreme Court case of *Mahon Tribunal v Keena & Anor* [2009] IESC 78 and *Keena v Ireland* (29804/10, 30 September 2014). *Cf* the reasoning of Elias CJ (dissenting) in *Siemer v Solicitor-General* [2014] 2 LRC 186, discussed at 6–154 and 6–166 above, who expressed the view that it would be open to a respondent in contempt proceedings to make a "collateral challenge" to the original order alleged to have been breached.

[Add to note 87] 9–37

Following the closure of the Press Complaints Commission on 8 September 2014, and its replacement by the Independent Press Standards Organisation (IPSO), see now the IPSO Editors' Code of Practice, para 14.

[Add new paragraph] 9–42A

Where steps have been taken with the positive intention of depriving the court of its jurisdiction to strike the balance between the rights and interests at issue, this will be seen as defiance to the rule of law. In *Judge Mahon v Keena & Anor* [2007] IEHC 348, the editor and a journalist of *The Irish Times* decided to destroy documents relevant to an article regarding the work of the Mahon Tribunal, a public inquiry established in Ireland in 1997 to investigate corrupt payments by politicians in relation to planning permission and rezoning issues in the Dublin area. The Tribunal had ordered these documents be handed over and the journalists destroyed them upon-receipt of the Tribunal's order. This was described by the High Court of Ireland as "anathema to the rule of law and an affront to democratic order". The Court stated that when considering a journalist's rights under Article 10, the rights and interests of other persons and institutions also had to be taken into account. In a democratic society based on the rule of law, that was a task reserved for the courts. There was no basis for the applicants to fear that their right not to reveal sources would not have been given just consideration and vindicated as appropriate; their decision instead to destroy the documents after they had received a summons from the Tribunal, and after having taken legal advice, was "an astounding and flagrant disregard of the rule of law" in which the journalists "cast themselves as the adjudicators of the proper balance to be struck between the rights and interests of all concerned" and in so doing "usurped the function of this Court".

[Add new paragraph] 9–42B

In due course, the Supreme Court of Ireland approved the High Court's view and confirmed that the unilateral decision of a journalist to destroy evidence, with the intention to deprive the courts of their jurisdiction, was designed to subvert the rule of law: *Mahon Tribunal v Keena & Anor* [2009]

IESC 78. At [61], Fennelly J (delivering the unanimous judgment of the court) asked, rhetorically, whether it could truly be said to be in accord with the interests of a democratic society based on the rule of law that journalists, as a unique class, have the right to decide for themselves to withhold information from any and every public institution or court regardless of the existence of a compelling need.

9–42C *[Add new paragraph]*

The Supreme Court held, however, that the High Court had erred in reaching the conclusion that the destruction of the documents was a relevant consideration, to which "great weight" had to be given, in deciding whether to order the journalists to appear before the Tribunal to answer any question about the source and the present whereabouts of the documents in question. Any such order had to be justified "by the situation as it now exists" and not by the need to mark disapproval of the "unquestionably reprehensible conduct" of the applicants. The journalists' appeal from the decision of the High Court was therefore allowed, and the court's disapproval of their conduct was reflected in the order that they should pay the unsuccessful party's costs.

9–42D *[Add new paragraph]*

At the next stage, in *Keena v Ireland* (29804/10, 30 September 2014), the European Court of Human Rights, at [46]–[48], agreed that the journalists' actions had been contrary to the rule of law. It had not been a legitimate exercise of their rights under Article 10 to refuse to disclose their source. The court dismissed the journalists' complaint that the costs order would have a chilling effect on freedom of expression, holding, at [50], that "the order for costs in the circumstances of this case can have no impact on public interest journalists who vehemently protect their sources yet recognise and respect the rule of law".

G. Judicial discretion at common law

9–43 *[Add to note 98]*

As to the meaning of "court" in this context, see paras 4–18, 13–3 and 13–46.

H. Experience in other common law jurisdictions

9–51 *[Add to end of paragraph]*

In New Zealand, the matter is now governed by s.68 of the Evidence Act 2006, which in certain circumstances prevents a journalist, or his or her employer, from being compelled in civil or criminal proceedings to answer any question or produce any document that would disclose the identity of the journalist's source or enable that identity to be discovered. The presumption of non-disclosure will be displaced if the party seeking disclosure satisfies the court that a competing public interest is paramount in the particular case. Separate protection, which is not limited to journalists, is provided by Rule 8.46 of the High Court Rules. This provides that, in defamation proceedings in which the defendant pleads a defence of honest opinion or privilege, no interrogatories as to the defendant's sources of information or grounds of belief may be allowed unless the interrogatories are necessary in the interests of justice. In Australia, until recently the principles applied were essentially those of the common law, see cases cited at note 108.

The Commonwealth Evidence Amendment (Journalists' Privilege) Act 2011, however, replaced the discretionary protection in the Evidence Act 1995 with a stronger privilege, which is in substantially the same terms as New Zealand's Evidence Act 2006, s.68. See now Evidence Act 1995 (Cth) s.126H. A number of Australian states have followed the Commonwealth's lead, including Western Australia where the 2012 amendment to the Evidence Act 1906 (WA), introducing ss. 20A-20M, was successfully relied on by the journalists in the Supreme Court of Western Australia cases of *Hancock Prospecting Pty Ltd v Hancock* [2013] WASC 290 and *Hancock Prospecting Pty Ltd v Hancock (No. 2)* [2014] WASC 85. However, South Australia, Queensland and the Northern Territory still rely on the Australian common law, and Tasmania has only a discretionary confidential professional relationships privilege, set out in Evidence Act 2001 (Tas) div 1A. See also *Liu v The Age Co Ltd* [2012] NSWC 12 and [2013] NSWCA 26 and H. Ryan *"The half-hearted protection of journalists' sources: Judicial interpretation of Australia's shield laws"* (2014) 19 Media and Arts Law Review 325.

[Add to note 107] **9–51**

See now s 68 (2) of the Evidence Act 2006. See also the report of the New Zealand Law Commission *The News Media Meets 'New Media': Rights, Responsibilities and Regulation in the Digital* Age, NZLC R128, 2013, Chapter 2. See now also *Slater v Blomfield* [2014] NZHC 2221 on the interpretation of the Evidence Act 2006, s.68 and Rule 8.46 of the High Court Rules.

[Add to note 109] **9–52**

For the position in Scotland, see *HM Advocate v Airs* 1975 S.L.T. 117, discussed in para 16–39 and para 16–393.

[Add to note 110] **9–52**

Replace citation for *R v The National Post* (2004) D.L.R. (4th) 551 with (2004) 69 O.R. (3d) 427 See also *R v The National Post* [2010] S.C.C. 16; [2010] 1 SCR 477.

II. THE GENERAL SCOPE OF SECTION 10

[Add new sub-section]

AA. — The Meaning of "... the source of information"

9–55A *[Add new paragraph]*

Although the question of who can qualify as a "source" for the purposes of s.10 has not so far come before the courts in this jurisdiction, the concept of a "journalistic source" has been considered on a number of occasions by the European Court of Human Rights. In *Nordisk Film & TV A/S v Denmark* (App No 40485/02, 8 December 2005), *Telegraaf Media Nederland Landelikje Media BV v The Netherlands* (2012) 34 B.H.R.C. 193, at [86], and *Nagla v Latvia* (App No 73469/10, [2013] ECHR 688, 16 July 2013) at [81], the European Court stated that its understanding of the concept of a journalistic "source" corresponds to the broad definition set out in the Committee of Ministers' *Recommendation No. R (2000) 7 on the right of journalists not to disclose their sources of information*. This includes "any person who provides information to a journalist". As to "information identifying a source", this would include both "the factual circumstances of acquiring information from a source by a journalist" and "the unpublished content of the information provided by a source to a journalist", in so far as they are likely to lead to the identification of a source.

9–55B *[Add new paragraph]*

The cases of *Nordisk Film*, cited above, and *Stichting Ostade Blade* (2014) 59 E.H.R.R. SE9, however, illustrate the limits of this broad Convention concept of a "journalistic source". In *Nordisk*, the European Court declared inadmissible a television producer's complaint about an order to hand over to the police film recordings covertly made as part of a programme investigating paedophilia in Denmark (and notes made in connection with them). These were capable of identifying individuals suspected of criminal activity. The domestic Supreme Court had held that footage and notes which might lead to the identification of three specific participants in the programme who were journalistic sources "in the traditional sense" could be withheld. But the same could not be said for those who were the subject of the covert recordings. The European Court held, at p.10, that the three "traditional" sources had known before their participation that they were talking to a journalist about a matter of public interest, and been promised that they could participate in the programme without the possibility of being identified. By contrast, the individuals covertly filmed "were not freely assisting the press to inform the public about matters of public interest or matters concerning others ... nor did they consent to being filmed or recorded and thus providing information in that way. Consequently, those participants cannot be regarded as sources of journalistic information in the traditional sense."

[Add new paragraph] **9–55C**

In *Stichting Ostade Blade,* the European Court held that an article 10 application by a Dutch magazine concerning a police raid was inadmissible. The purpose of the court-sanctioned raid had been to obtain a letter, referred to in a press release from the magazine, which claimed responsibility for a bomb attack. The European Court accepted that the order to hand over the letter, followed by a search of the magazine's offices when there was no compliance, interfered with the magazine's right to receive and impart information. As to "the nature of the interference", however, the Court rejected the magazine's argument that the case concerned the protection of journalistic sources. It was found that the author of the letter was not a journalistic source: "not every individual who is used by a journalist for information is a source" (at [62]). It was found that he was not motivated by a desire to provide information which the public was entitled to know. Rather, "his purpose in seeking publicity through the magazine *Ravage* was to don the veil of anonymity with a view to evading his own accountability" (at [65]). For this reason, the Court took the view that the author was not, in principle, entitled to the same protection as the "sources" in cases such as *Goodwin, Roemen, Ernst, Voskuil, Tillack, Financial Times, Sanoma,* and *Telegraaf.* The state's interference was, therefore, in accordance with law and pursued the legitimate aim of preventing crime. Having regard to the inherent dangerousness of the bombings, the investigative measures were sufficiently justified so as to meet the requirement of necessity in a democratic society. The approach of the European Court in *Stichting* has been criticised for considering the informant's motivation in determining the initial availability of protection under Article 10, rather than affirming the principled need to protect journalistic sources and resolving the disclosure question as a matter of justification on the facts ((2014) E.H.R.L.R 537). Court's approach in *Stichting Ostade Blade* was characterised as a retreat from its position in the earlier case of *Financial Times Ltd v United Kingdom* (2010) 50 E.H.R.R. 46, discussed at para 9–183 below. In the latter case, the Court had held that the applicant's Article 10 rights were violated when they were ordered to disclose confidential documents provided to a journalist on the basis of the source's "evident purpose" to do harm.

[Add new paragraph] **9–55D**

In both *Nordisk Film* (at pp. 10–11) and *Stichting Ostade Blade* at [64], however, the European Court held that even where "source protection" is not in issue, an order directed to a journalist to hand over original materials may nonetheless have a chilling effect on the exercise of journalistic freedom of expression. On the other hand, the degree of protection under Article 10 to be applied in such a situation does not necessarily reach the same level as that afforded to journalists when it comes to their right to keep their sources confidential. According to the Court, "the distinction lies in that the latter protection is twofold, relating not only to the journalist, but also and in particular to the 'source' who volunteers to assist the press in informing the public about matters of public interest."

B. The meaning of "... for which he is responsible"

9–56A *[Add new paragraph]*

The case of *R (Miranda) v Secretary of State for the Home Department* [2014] EWHC 255 (Admin), [2014] 1 W.L.R. 3140, however, suggests the courts may be likely to give a broad interpretation to this element of s.10. In *Miranda* (not itself a s.10 case), the court considered the exercise of police powers under Schedule 7 of the Terrorism Act 2000 (i.e. to stop, question and detain an individual in order to determine whether they appeared to be a person concerned in the commission, preparation or instigation of acts terrorism). Had there been a disproportionate interference with the right to journalistic expression when these powers were deployed against an individual travelling on behalf of and assisting a journalist? The Claimant, David Miranda, was not a journalist himself but was the partner of an American journalist, Glenn Greenwald, who had written a series of stories for the *Guardian* and the *New York Times* relating to mass surveillance programmes by the agencies of the United States and United Kingdom governments. When detained at Heathrow Airport, the Claimant was travelling in order to meet another journalist, and was carrying encrypted material derived from data stolen from the National Security Agency of the United States in order to assist in his partner's journalistic activity. The Court, at [50], accepted that "the protection of journalistic material is not in principle limited to cases where the complainant works as a journalist". It was recognised that journalism is a "collaborative activity", involving multiple individuals including non-journalists such as cameramen, interpreters and administrative assistants. In the light of this, and of the fact that Principle 2 of the Committee of Ministers' *Recommendation No. R (2000) 7 on the right of journalists not to disclose their sources of information* makes clear that the principle of source protection extends to persons other than journalists, who by reason of their professional relations with journalists acquire information about the identity of a journalist's source, "responsibility for publication" may be widely interpreted by the courts.

E. The Meaning of "Publication"

9–61 *[Amendment to note 120]*

See Gatley on Libel & Slander, 12th edn (2014) ch.6

F. Information "contained in a publication"

9–62 *[Add to note 121]*

This would seem to accord with the characterisation of the European case law on the protection of journalists' sources as proceeding on a "functional" theory, asking in each case whether there is a pressing social need for the imposition of the restriction (*Mahon Tribunal v Keena & Anor* [2009] IESC 78 at [67]; *Keena v Ireland* (29804/10, 30 September 2014) at [26]).

I. Does the Act supplement or supersede the common law?

[Add to note 134] **9–68**

On the scope of "journalistic material" in the context of the Police and Criminal Evidence Act 1984 s.13, see *R (Miranda) v Secretary of State for the Home Department* [2014] EWHC 255 (Admin); [2014] 1 W.L.R. 3140 at [64] and [72] in which, although the exact categorisation of documentation carried by the Claimant was not directly in issue, the court doubted whether the 58,000 highly classified intelligence documents stolen from GCHQ, as distinct from documentation in his possession "created or worked on for journalistic purposes", were "journalistic material" within the scope of s.13.

J. The elusive concept of "necessary"

[Add to Note 160] **9–88**

See, for example, *Saint-Paul Luxembourg S.A. v Luxembourg* (26419/10, 18 April 2013), where the carrying out of a search and seizure operation against the publisher of a newspaper in order to confirm the identity of an article's author was held to be unnecessary as the identity could easily have been established by other means.

L. The onus of proof

[Add to Note 170] **9–95**

See also *Saint-Paul Luxembourg S.A. v Luxembourg* (26419/10, 18 April 2013) and *Nagla v Latvia* (73469/10, [2013] ECHR 688, 16 July 2013) at [82]-[83].

M. Factors to be considered in determining "necessity"

[Add to Note 178] **9–100**

Cf. Slater v Blomfield [2014] NZHC 2221 at [134] and [138], where the likelihood that the information was obtained illegally by the sources was a factor weighing in favour of disclosure. Note also the emphasis by the European Court of Human Rights that the right of a journalist not to disclose his or her sources cannot be considered a privilege, dependent on the lawfulness or unlawfulness of the sources actions, but is rather an intrinsic part of the right to information which should be treated with the utmost caution (see *Nagla v Latvia* (73469/10, [2013] ECHR 688, 16 July

2013), at [97], *Tillack v Belgium* (2012) 55 E.H.R.R. 25, at [65], and *Ressiot and Ors v France* (15054/07, 28 June 2012).

9–100 *[Add to Note 179]*

Replace reference for *R v The National Post* (2004) D.L.R. (4th) 551 with (2004) 69 O.R. (3d) 427. See also *R v The National Post* [2010] S.C.C. 16; [2010] 1 SCR 477.

N. Necessity and proportionality

9–111 *[Add to note 196]*

See now also *R. (on the application of British Sky Broadcasting Ltd) v Chelmsford Crown Court* [2012] EWHC 1295 (Admin); [2012] E.M.L.R. 30 in the context of the Police and Criminal Evidence Act 1984.

III. THE FOUR STATUTORY EXCEPTIONS FURTHER ANALYSED

C. "Interests of justice" considered by the European Court of Human Rights

9–153 *[Add to note 262]*

See now C. Hollander, *Documentary Evidence*, 12th edn (2015), Ch.5.

E. Later judicial developments

4. *Financial Times Ltd v United Kingdom*

9–184 [*Add new paragraph]*

As to the relevance of the source's purpose, see para 9–55C above.

F. National security

9–187 *[Add to note 307]*

See also the Irish Supreme Court case of *Mahon Tribunal v Keena & Anor* [2009] IESC 78 and *Keena v Ireland* (29804/10, 30 September 2014), discussed at 9–42A above.

9–189 *[Add to note 310]*

See now *Archbold 2015* para 12–24 *et seq*. See also *R (Miranda) v Secretary of State for the Home Department* [2014] EWHC 255 (Admin); [2014] 1 W.L.R. 3140 at 3166E–F.

G. "Prevention of crime"

3. *Voskuil v Netherlands*

[Add to note 319] 9–201

The case is now reported at [2008] E.M.L.R. 14; (2010) 50 E.H.R.R. 9.

4. *Sanoma Uitgevers BV v Netherlands*

[Add to note 322] 9–203

See paras 9–251A *et seq* for discussion of the provisions for judicial oversight in Part I, Chapter II of the Regulation of Investigatory Powers Act 2000. In *R (Miranda) v Secretary of State for the Home Department* [2014] EWHC 255 (Admin); [2014] 1 W.L.R. 3140, at [88], the court accepted the submission that, despite the fact that the European Court's reasoning is sometimes expressed in very general terms (as in paras 90 and 92 of *Sanoma*), the Strasbourg court has not developed an absolute rule of prior judicial scrutiny for cases involving state interference with journalistic freedom.

[Add new section]

5. *Nagla v Latvia*

[Add new paragraph] 9–203A

The question whether a *prima facie* interference with a journalist's Article 10 rights were "prescribed by law" was also considered in *Nagla v Latvia* (73469/10, [2013] ECHR 688, 16 July 2013). The case concerned the search by the police of a well-known broadcast journalist's home, and their seizure of data storage devices. Her home was searched following a broadcast she had aired in February 2010 informing the public of an information leak from the State Revenue Service database. One week after the broadcast, her source, identifying himself as "Neo", began to use Twitter to publish information concerning the salaries of state officials in various public institutions. A search was subsequently carried out pursuant to a warrant granted by a public prosecutor using an urgent procedure. The European Court held that because under domestic law such warrants had to be submitted on the following day to the investigating judge, for examination of the lawfulness of and grounds for the search, there were procedural safeguards which rendered the provision enforceable. Unlike in *Sanoma Uitgevers*, the investigating judge had the authority under Latvian law to revoke the search warrant and to declare such evidence inadmissible, as well as to withhold the disclosure of the identity of journalistic sources. These factors were sufficient to distinguish the case from *Sanoma Uitgevers* In *R (Miranda) v Secretary of State for the Home Department* [2014] EWHC 255 (Admin); [2014] 1 W.L.R. 3140, the court accepted the submission that, despite the fact that the European Court's reasoning is sometimes expressed in very general terms (as in paras 90 and 92 of *Sanoma*), the Strasbourg court has not developed an absolute rule of prior judicial scrutiny for cases involving state interference with journalistic freedom. See also *Telegraaf Media Nederland Landelikje Media BV v The Netherlands* (2012) 34 B.H.R.C. 193.

9–203B *[Add new paragraph]*

Having found that the search and seizure had been "prescribed by law", the European Court also found that the interference was intended to prevent disorder or crime and to protect the rights of others, both of which were legitimate aims. However, the Court found that the reasons given by the domestic authorities for the search had not been "relevant" and "sufficient", nor did they constitute a "pressing social need", and there had therefore been a violation of Article 10. When the investigating authorities, almost three months after the broadcast and after the applicant had agreed to testify, decided that a search at her home was necessary, they proceeded under the urgent procedure without any judicial authority having properly examined the relationship of proportionality between the public interest of the investigation in securing evidence, on the one hand, and the protection of the journalist's freedom of expression on the other. Taking into account that there was no information linking the applicant to the suspect in any way other than in her capacity as a journalist, and that their communication had stopped on the day of the broadcast, only weighty reasons could have justified the urgency of the search. The investigating authorities' delay in carrying out the search and the lack of any indication of impending destruction of evidence were further factors weighing against the state. The Court, citing *Tillack v Belgium* (2012) 55 E.H.R.R. 25, at [65], emphasised that although the actions of the applicant's source were subject to a pending criminal investigation, the right of journalists not to disclose their sources cannot be considered a mere privilege to be granted or taken away depending on the lawfulness or unlawful actions of their sources , but part and parcel of the right to information which should be treated with the utmost caution.

[Add new section]

6. *Stichting Ostade Blade v Netherlands*

9–203C *[Add new paragraph]*

The "necessity" test was, however, satisfied in *Stichting Ostade Blade v Netherlands* (2014) 59 E.H.R.R. SE9. The search of a magazine's premises to obtain a letter, which had been referred to in a press release from the magazine claiming responsibility for a bomb attack, was held to comply with the requirements of Article 10. The original document was sought as a possible lead towards identifying a person or persons unknown suspected of having carried out a plurality of bomb attacks, and the inherent dangerousness of the crimes committed constituted sufficient justification for the search. The Court held that even if (as the magazine alleged) the letter had been quoted literally and in its entirety, and other investigatory leads were available, the search would still have been justified: "even assuming such to be the case, the Court cannot find that the original document, whether on its own or in conjunction with other evidence, was incapable of yielding useful information. Indeed, if that be so then it cannot be seen what prevented the editors of the magazine from handing it over of their own accord" (at [71]). As discussed at para 9–55A above, however, the Court also held that "source protection" was not in issue: the magazine was thus entitled to a lower degree of protection under Article 10 than in such cases.

IV. WHEN DOES A JOURNALIST'S REFUSAL BECOME CONTEMPT?

B. The need to reconcile two lines of authority

[Add to note 332] 9–211

See also, in the family law context, the Court of Appeal decision of *In re W (A Child) (Care Proceedings: Court's Function)* [2014] 1 WLR 1611, at [74] ("The court is not dependent on a willing party. Indeed an unwilling party who flouts the court's orders may find itself in contempt, even if it is an agency of the state such as a local authority. It is necessary to point out for the discussion which follows that the court's orders are to be complied with. They are not preferences, requests or mere indications: they are orders and non-compliance with orders should be expected to and will usually have a consequence") and *Re W (A Child) (Adoption Order: Leave to Oppose)* [2014] 1 WLR 1993, at [50]–[54]. *Cf.* the reasoning of Elias CJ (dissenting) in *Siemer v Solicitor-General* [2014] 2 LRC 186, at [33]–[34] and [37], discussed at 6–154 and 6–166 above, who expressed the view that it would be open to a respondent in contempt proceedings to make a "collateral challenge" to the original order alleged to have been breached.

E. The rule that court orders must be implicitly obeyed

[Add to end of paragraph] 9–216

Where an order has become final, principles of finality and legal certainty require that it should continue to be obeyed even in circumstances where a later decision has given the law a different interpretation such that an order would no longer be made in similar terms. That would not of itself justify re-opening or overturning such an order: see the decision of the Court of Appeal in *SOCA v O'Docherty* [2013] EWCA Civ 518, addressing the consequences for pre-existing orders in the light of the Supreme Court's (majority) decision in *SOCA v Perry (Nos 1&2)* [2012] UKSC 35; [2013] 1 AC 182.

9–226 *[Add to end of paragraph]*

The court's jurisdiction pursuant to s.37(1) of the Senior Courts Act 1981 to grant publicity orders and website-blocking injunctions in intellectual property cases was considered in *Cartier International AG v British Sky Broadcasting Ltd* [2015] 1 All ER 949 and *Samsung Electronics (UK) Ltd v Apple Inc* [2013] EMLR 10.

9–230A *[Add new paragraph]*

Further, in *PricewaterhouseCoopers v Saad Investments Co Ltd* [2014] 1 W.L.R. 4482 the Privy Council held that although the Supreme Court of Bermuda had not had jurisdiction to make a winding up order in respect of an overseas company which did not trade or carry on business in Bermuda, the winding up order, having been made by a court of unlimited jurisdiction, had to be treated as effective in law until set aside. The Board said (at [25]) that this was because of "the short and well established ground that an order made by a court of unlimited jurisdiction ... must be obeyed unless and until it has been set aside by the court" (*per* Lord Diplock in *Isaacs v Robertson* [1985] A.C. 97 at 101F). *Cf.* the reasoning of Elias CJ (dissenting) in *Siemer v Solicitor-General* [2014] 2 LRC 186, at[33]-[34] and [37], discussed at 6–154, 6–166, 9–34 and 9– 211 above.

VI. A General Summary of the Principles

9–252 *[Add to note 387]*

The question of who can be considered as a journalist's "source" is discussed at para 9–55A above.

9–252 *[Add to note 405]*

See now CPR Pt 81.

[Add new section]

VII. Similar Policy Considerations Considered in the Context of RIPA

9–251A *[Add new paragraph]*

This chapter addresses primarily the issue of when a court may compel the disclosure of a journalistic source in the context of s.10 of the Contempt of Court Act 1981. It is probably convenient, however, that the provisions in Part I, Chapter II of the Regulation of Investigatory Powers Act 2000 (RIPA) should also be considered, since the relevant policy considerations are closely linked. These statutory provisions permit a number of public authorities, including police forces, to acquire and disclose communications data from a communications service provider without judicial approval. The term "communications data" embraces the metadata or, colloquially, the "who", "when" and "where" of a communication, but not its content. Such data can also reveal the time and duration of a communication, the number or email address of the originator and recipient, and sometimes the location of the device from which the communication was made. RIPA provides for a "designated person", within the public authority, to authorise the obtaining of communications data where that person believes (a) that it is necessary for one or more of the statutory purposes set out in s.22(2) and (b) that obtaining the data in question, by the conduct authorised or required, is proportionate to the purpose sought to be achieved by obtaining the data: see s.22(5). A person exercising these powers must have regard to any relevant Code of Practice issued by the Secretary of State under s.71 of RIPA.

[Add new paragraph] **9–251B**

In late 2014, it emerged that the provisions in Part I, Chapter II of RIPA had been used by a number of police forces to identify journalistic sources. The subsequent inquiry by the Interception of Communications Commissioners' Office found, in a report published on 4 February 2015, that in the three-year period covered by the inquiry, some 82 journalists had had their communications data obtained by police under these provisions. The Commissioner concluded that, generally speaking, the police forces did not give the questions of necessity, proportionality and "collateral intrusion" sufficient consideration (whilst collateral intrusion is not defined, it appears to refer to the potential identification of other journalistic sources not the subject of the investigation in question.) Rather, "they focused on privacy considerations (Article 8 of the European Convention on Human Rights) and did not give due consideration to freedom of speech (Article 10)": see para 8.6 of the report. In the Commissioner's view, the current Home Office Code of Practice (and the recently revised draft Code said to provide protection for "sensitive professions") did not contain adequate safeguards to protect journalistic sources or to prevent unnecessary or disproportionate intrusions. It was recommended that judicial authorisation should be obtained in cases where communications data are sought to determine the source of journalistic information.

[Add new paragraph] **9–251C**

In light of this, in March 2015 amendments were made to s.71 of RIPA so as to require Codes of Practice to include provisions designed to protect the public interest in the confidentiality of journalistic sources: see now s.71(2A). On 25 March 2015, therefore, a new *Code of Practice on the Acquisition and Disclosure of Communications Data* came into force. Its provisions are intended as a temporary measure until such time as there is primary legislation to provide for judicial authorisation of such disclosures. The new Code requires that, where it is desired to obtain communications data in order to identify a journalist's source, those law enforcement agencies (including the police, National Crime Agency and Her Majesty's Revenue and Customs) in England and Wales with powers under the Police and Criminal Evidence Act 1984 (PACE) must apply to a court for a production order pursuant to s.9 and schedule 1 of PACE to obtain this data: see para 3.78. Similar provisions apply to law enforcement agencies in Northern Ireland and Scotland. Only where there is believed to be "an immediate threat of loss of human life, such that a person's life might be endangered by the delay inherent in the process of judicial authorisation" may law enforcement agencies continue to use the existing internal authorisation process under RIPA: see para 3.83. In his subsequent report in July 2015 the Interception of Communications Commissioner commented that the wording of paragraphs 3.78 and 3.79 of the new Code could have been clearer as to when the requirement to apply for a production order under PACE applies. In the Commissioner's view, such an order must be applied for even if the identity of the source is already known or suspected by the law enforcement agency. The agency should seek judicial approval whenever it is seeking to determine journalistic sources, including when seeking to "confirm or corroborate other evidence of the identity of a journalist's source": see paras 3.10–3.26 of the July 2015 Report. See also *"A Question of Trust: Report of the Investigatory Powers Review"* by David Anderson QC, published in June 2015. This Report proposes that when a public authority seeks communications data for the purposes of determining matters that are privileged or confidential, such as the identity of a journalist's confidential source, the request should either be refused or referred to an independent Judicial Commissioner working for a proposed new regulator called the Independent Surveillance and Intelligence Commission who would decide whether to authorise the request.

CHAPTER 10

CONTEMPT IN THE FACE OF THE COURT

I. INTRODUCTION

A. The common thread

[Add to note 4] **10–3**

And see *Robertson (Stewart) v HM Advocate* [2007] HCJAC 63; 2008 J.C. 146 at [66]–[69] and [112], drawing attention to the importance of the summary jurisdiction in cases of witness prevarication. The case is also referred to at 5–240, 10–52, 16–6, 16–39, 16–46 and 16–120 of the main text.

B. The significance of the contempt "in the face"

2. *The scope of the jurisdiction of the Divisional Court*

[Add to note 15] **10–7**

See now CPR rr.81.12(e) and 81.13(e).

[Add to note 18] **10–7**

See now CPR Pt 81.

[Add to note 19] **10–7**

See now the Practice Direction to CPR Pt 81 at para 4.1: "Normally, it will be appropriate to defer consideration of the respondent's actions and behaviour to allow reflection on what has occurred".

4. *Public funding for legal advice and representation*

10–10 *[Add to note 23]*

See now the Legal Aid, Sentencing and Punishment of Offenders Act 2012, in force from April 1, 2013. Section 14(g) extends legal aid to proceedings for contempt "in the face of the court". See also ss.15 and 16.

C. What constitutes "the face of the court"?

10–13 *[Add to note 27]*

Compare the Canadian Judicial Council's "*Some Guidelines on the Use of Contempt Powers*", dated 2001, which recommends that: "the safer course is to treat any conduct not actually witnessed by the judge as a contempt out of the face of the court", as was done in *R v Vermette* [1987] 1 S.C.R. 577. The guidelines have not been fully updated or superseded, but they carry a warning that the law has been changing since 2001 and emphasise that they are intended only to offer some guidance.

10–13 *[Add to note 37]*

In *British Columbia Government Employee Union v Att Gen of British Columbia* [1988] 2 S.C.R. 214, where picketing outside the court house, actually observed by the Chief Justice, was treated as contempt in the face.

10–26 *[Add to note 48]*

In *R. v Curtis* [2012] EWCA Crim 945; [2013] 1 Cr. App. R. (S) 28, a trial judge effectively treated as contempt "in the face" the conduct of two women who had followed jurors on to a bus, sat next to them, and unsettled them by the content of a mobile telephone conversation about the trial in which they were engaged. That approach was endorsed on appeal.

10–27 *[Add to end of paragraph]*

See now CPR r.81.13(1)(e).

D. Procedure to be used sparingly

10–29 *[Add to end of paragraph]*

See now the Criminal Procedure Rules 2015 (SI 2015/1490) in force with effect from 5 October 2015, Part 48.

[Add to note 56] **10–31**

But see *Robertson (Stewart) v HM Advocate* [2007] HCJAC 63; 2008 J.C. 146 at [66]–[69] and [112], drawing attention to the importance of the summary jurisdiction in cases of witness prevarication.

[Add to note 59] **10–33**

And see CPR PD 81 paras 4.1–4.5, which sets out the matters to which a judge should have particular regard when adopting the summary procedure. See also *National Farmers' Union v Tiernan* [2015] CA, unreported where it was suggested that any litigant should be clearly informed of the right to remain silent but also of the possibility that it could lead to an adverse inference being drawn.

II. THE REQUIREMENTS OF NATURAL JUSTICE: ARTICLE 6

A. The contempt jurisdiction as "rough justice"

[Add to note 71] **10–40**

See also *Pecnik v Slovakia* (App No 44901/05), 27 September 2012, and *Lewandowski v Poland* (App No 66484/09), 3 July 2012, where the Court found breaches of the requirement under Article 6 for an independent and impartial tribunal.

B. The need for safeguards

[Add to note 77] **10–42**

See now the Criminal Procedure Rules 2015 [2015] EWCA Crim 1567 Part 48.

[Add to end of paragraph] **10–42**

Contempt in the face of the High Court and the County Court is governed by CPR 81.16. In the Crown Court and Magistrates' Court, the procedure is governed by Part 48 of the Criminal Procedure Rules 2015 and CPD XI, 48A.

[Add to note 78] **10–43**

Add citation: [1996] C.L.Y. 1564.

[Add to note 80] **10–44**

See now *Archbold 2015* para.28–92.

2. *Should a judge refer proceedings to another tribunal?*

10–52 *[Add to note 93]*

See *Petition of Leanne Martin to the Nobile Officium of the High Court of Justiciary* [2014] ScotHC HCJAC 15, where the Sheriff's finding of contempt was set aside for undue haste and a failure to comply with the safeguards recommended in *Robertson & Gough v HMA* 2008 SCCR 20, at [90]-[95], as summarised at 16–130A below. See also *Pecnik v Slovakia* (App No 44901/05), 27 September 2012, and *Lewandowski v Poland* (App No 66484/09), 3 July 2012, where the Court found breaches of the requirement under Article 6 for an independent and impartial tribunal.

10–53 *[Add to note 96]*

See now CPR Part 81 and the Practice Direction at 81 PD5. Para 4.4 provides: "If there is a risk of the appearance of bias, the judge should ask another judge to hear the committal application".

10–53 *[Add to note 96]*

See now CPR Pt 81 and the Practice Direction at PD 81 paras 4.1–4.5. Paragraph 4.4 provides: "If there is a risk of the appearance of bias, the judge should ask another judge to hear the committal application".

10–53 *[Add to note 97]*

See also *JSC BTA Bank v Ablyazov* [2012] EWCA Civ 1551; [2013] 1 W.L.R. 1845 at [67]–[70] and *O'Neill v HMA No2 (Scotland)* [2013] UKSC 36 at [50]–[51].

3. *The need for the charge to be formulated with precision*

10–56 *[Add to end of paragraph]*

See now the Criminal Procedure Rules 2015 (SI 2015/1490) in force with effect from 5 October 2015, 48.5(2), 48.7 (2) and (3).

10–57 *[Add to note 105]*

See also *Pecnik v Slovakia* (App No 44901/05), 27 September 2012, and *Lewandowski v Poland* (App No 66484/09), 3 July 2012, where the Court found breaches of the requirement under Article 6 for an independent and impartial tribunal.

4. *Time to prepare a defence and take legal advice*

[Add to note 124] **10–68**

Section 83(6) provides that "sentence of imprisonment" does not include a committal for contempt or any kindred offence.

6. *General guidance given in R. v Schot and Barclay*

[Add to note 136] **10–87**

See now the Criminal Practice Directions 2015 [2015] EWCA Crim 1567, CPD 26.B2.

[Add to note 139] **10–87**

See now *Archbold 2015*, paras 28.99 and 28.100.

[Add to note 140] **10–88**

See now *Archbold 2015*, paras 4.492 and 4.518.

[Add to end of sub-paragraph 7] **10–88**

See now CPR Pt 81 and the Practice Direction at PD 81 paras 4.1–4.5. Paragraph 4.4 provides: "If there is a risk of the appearance of bias, the judge should ask another judge to hear the committal application".

IV. STATUTORY CONTEMPTS IN THE FACE

A. Contempt in the face of the magistrates' court: s.12

[Add to note 201] **10–119**

See now Criminal Procedure Rules 2015 [2015] EWCA Crim 1567 in force with effect from 5 October 2015, Part 48.

[Add to note 204] **10–119**

The Law Commission in its Consultation Paper No.209 has proposed that magistrates' courts should have the power to suspend an order of committal made under s.12, but no other relevant proposals are made. Section 12 has not been amended. The Law Commission has yet to report on Contempt in the Face. Its report is expected late in 2015.

V. IMPROPER CONDUCT OF A CASE

B. Professional advocates

10–139 *[Add to note 242]*

See now CPR r.81.12(1)(d).

10–144 *[Add to end of paragraph]*

The conduct of lawyers was considered in *R. (on the application of B) v SSHD* [2012] EWHC 3770 (Admin); [2013] A.C.D. 28. Applications for judicial review of immigration and asylum decisions were held to be hopeless and the court addressed issues of professional conduct that arose in that context. It was concluded that there had been incompetence and a breach of the advocate's duty to the court, but apologies were accepted together with undertakings for the future. There was warning that representatives behaving in a similar way could in the future find themselves referred to the relevant regulatory authorities.

VI. CONTEMPT COMMITTED BY WITNESSES

A. Examples of contempt by witnesses

10–163 *[Add to note 295]*

Section 55 of the County Courts Act 1984 has been amended by Schedule 9 of the Crime and Courts Act 2013 with effect from 22 April 2014 substituting the word 'court' for 'judge' in subss.(1), (2) and (4) and repealing s.55(4A).

C. Refusing to answer questions or prevarication

10–169 *[Add to note 308]*

Section 55 of the County Courts Act 1984 has been amended by Sch.9 to the Crime and Courts Act 2013 with effect from 22 April 2014, substituting the word "court" for "judge" in subss.(1), (2) and (4) and repealing s.55(4A). But see *Robertson (Stewart) v HM Advocate* [2007] HCJAC 63; 2008 J.C. 146 at [66]–[69] and [112], drawing attention to the potential importance of the summary jurisdiction in cases of witness prevarication. The case is also cited at 10–3 above and 16–6, at note 10.

D. Witnesses and duress

[Add to note 313] **10–170**

See now the Criminal Procedure Rules 2015 (SI 2015/1490) in force with effect from 5 October 2015 and the Ministry of Justice guidelines *Achieving Best Evidence in Criminal Proceedings: Guidance on intervewing victims and witnesses, and guidance on using special measures* (March 2011) available at *http://www.cps.gov.uk/publications/docs/best_evidence_in_criminal_proceedings.pdf* (accessed on August 17, 2015).

[Add to note 317] **10–171**

See now *Archbold* 2015, para.17–122.

[Add to end of paragraph] **10–173**

Nevertheless, it is of relevance to consider the decision of the Court of Appeal in a case concerning a conviction for perverting the course of justice. In *R. v A* [2012] EWCA Crim 434; [2012] 2 Cr. App. R. 8, the defendant had withdrawn a true complaint of rape against her husband. It was pointed out that the limitations on the defence of duress should not be further eroded, and that her guilt and distress over the consequences of maintaining the complaint against him could not be said to amount to duress.

[Add to note 323] **10–175**

See now the publication of the same title at *http://www.cps.gov.uk/publications/prosecution/domestic/domv.html* (accessed August 17, 2015).

[Add to note 324] **10–175**

The regime for dealing with vulnerable witnesses is described now in *Archbold 2015* at paras 8–71 and following.

VII. CONTEMPT COMMITTED BY JURORS

A. The importance of jury service

[Add to end of paragraph] **10–181**

In the light of increased concern about the possibility of juror misconduct, the Law Commission canvassed the introduction of a new offence of intentionally seeking information relating to a case that a juror is trying: see Consultation Paper No 209, paras 4.33 to 4.40. This was implemented in the Criminal Justice and Courts Act which introduced an amendment to the Juries Act 1974 creating new offences prohibiting research by jurors (20A of the 1974 Act as amended by s 71 of the 2015 Act); sharing the fruits of such research (s 20B of the 1974 Act as amended by s 72 of the 2015 Act); engaging in other 'prohibited conduct' (s 20 C of the 1974 Act as amended by s 73 of the 2015 Act and disclosing jury deliberations (s 20D of the 1974 Act as amended by s 74 of the 2015 Act). See further the discussion at 1–183B, 11–396 and the discussion below at 10–188B *et seq.*

D. Misconduct in relation to deliberations or verdict

10–187 *[Add to note 361]*

See *R. v Connors (Josie)* [2013] EWCA Crim 368, where a juror alleged that some of her fellows were racially prejudiced and were attempting to bully other jurors in order to secure a conviction. The trial judge declined to question the jury or to discharge them, since they appeared to him to be attentive and careful. His approach was approved by the Court of Court of Appeal. See also the case of *Att Gen v Dallas* [2012] EWHC 156 (Admin); [2012] 1 W.L.R. 991; [2012] Crim. L.R. 696 (mentioned at 3–67, 3–91 and 3–144 above).

10–188 *[Add to note 365]*

And see J Brannan, *Crime and social networking sites*, (2013) 1 Juridical Review 41; C Thomas, *Avoiding the perfect storm of juror contempt*, [2013] Crim LR 483, N Taylor and R Denyer 'Judicial Management of Juror Impropriety' [2014] Journal of Criminal Law 43; J Spencer 'Contempt of Court and Misbehaving Jurors' [2014] Criminal Law Review 245; A Ashworth 'Contempt of Court: Juror Misconduct and Internet Publications' [2014] Criminal Law Review 169.

10–188A *[Add new paragraph]*

The court considered another case of juror misconduct in *Att Gen v Dallas* [2012] EWHC 156 (Admin); [2012] 1 W.L.R. 991; [2012] Crim. L.R. 696. She was found to have researched the defendant on the internet, contrary to judicial instructions, in a case she was trying in which he had been charged with grievous bodily harm. She also informed her fellow jurors that he had been involved in earlier proceedings concerning an allegation of rape (of which he had been acquitted). That information had been excluded by the judge, although the jury had been told of an admission to the effect that he had been guilty of an assault. Her evidence as to how she had found the material was disbelieved and she was sentenced to six months' imprisonment.

10–188B *[Add new paragraph]*

One of the proposals canvassed by the Law Commission in its Consultation Paper No.209 was that a specific statutory offence for jurors intentionally undertaking research into the case they are trying, with a view to informing their deliberations, should be created. Further, the proposal was that such offences should be triable on indictment and not in the Divisional Court, where civil procedure rules are applied in accordance with CPR Pt 81. It was thought that this would be more compatible with the relevant juror's rights under arts 5 and 6. In order to bring such misconduct further into line with general criminal law and practice, there should also be made available the usual range of sentencing options including community sentences. Similar offences have been introduced in Queensland, New South Wales and Victoria. So far, however, only one prosecution has taken place (in Victoria): see "Juror in Hot Water for Online Search", *Herald Sun* (Melbourne), June 19, 2011. See too *Juries and Social Media*, a Report prepared for the Victorian Department of Justice and published on April 16, 2013. Some have suggested that the creation of a new criminal offence is unnecessary, given the existing law and procedure relating to contempt of court: see e.g. J.R. Spencer, "*The Law Commission's consultation paper on contempt of court*" [2013] Crim. L.R. 1. The reaction of the Law Commission was broadly that it would nonetheless bring greater clarity and consistency to the law, without leading to any confusion or duplication. Furthermore, the position would be clearer in relation to the availability of public funding. In the Legal Aid, Sentencing and Punishment of Offenders Act 2012 "criminal proceedings" are defined to cover only contempts in the face of the court: s.14(g). Juror research would almost certainly not fall within that category. Also, the current practice of hearing such cases in the Divisional Court means that the only route of appeal is to the Supreme Court: s.13 of the Administration of Justice Act 1960. The implementation of the proposals is summarised at 10–181 above.

[Add new paragraph] **10–188C**

It may be that Parliament, or perhaps the Judicial College, will make provision for greater clarity and consistency in the information, and as to the instructions, jurors are given as to not conducting research, but in the meantime the words of Sir John Thomas in *Att.-Gen. v Davey; Att.-Gen. v Beard* [2013] EWHC 2317 (Admin), at [59]–[61], should be borne in mind:

> "Many judges have adopted the practice not only of warning the jury in terms similar to what the judges in these two cases did, but also handing the jury a notice setting out what they must and must not do and the penal consequences of any breach. They have done this so that no juror can subsequently claim that he or she did not understand what they should not do and what the consequences might be. It is to be noted that in civil proceedings committal for contempt for breach of an injunction ordinarily requires not only proof of the breach of the terms of an injunction, but that the injunction contained a penal notice...
>
> We propose to invite the Criminal Procedure Rules Committee in consultation with the Judicial College to review the terminology used in the material given to the jury and to consider whether to recommend that the practice to which we have referred ... should be universally followed".

The *Practice Direction (Crown Court: Jury Irregularities)* [2013] 1 WLR 486 has been replaced by the Criminal Practice Directions 2015 [EWCA] 1567 CPD VI 26.M. There is set out the procedure to deal with jury irregularities in light of the new regime pertaining to jury misconduct set out in the 2015 Act both during the trial and after the jury has been discharged.

10–188D *[Add to end of paragraph]*

The practical difficulties as to directing jurors as to the internet are discussed also in *Fraser v HMA* [2013] ScotHC HCJAC 117. See too the Scottish Jury Manual (most recently amended in January 2015]).

10–188E *[Add new paragraph]*

In *R v Mahil* [2013] EWCA Crim 673, a juror in a manslaughter trial visited a memorial page for the victim on a social media site following the verdict. She then made a series of postings strongly hostile to one defendant and challenging her claim to have been sexually assaulted by another defendant (which had been common ground at the trial). The Court of Appeal described her comments as "ill-advised and reprehensible", but refused to allow an appeal and did not consider her conduct called into question the validity of the verdicts: see especially at [63]-[70]. There was no evidence that the juror had accessed the site during the trial and it was said to be clear that she had taken against the defendant on the basis of the evidence she had heard. The court's view might appear to be a generous one, given the tenor of the juror's remarks. A similarly sanguine view was expressed in *R v Lewis (Ian)* [2013] EWCA Crim 776. In that case, a juror approached a defendant to inform him that there had been jury misconduct at his trial for conspiracy to steal, because a fellow juror had looked at extraneous material on the internet, others had discussed it, and a female juror had been bullied into changing her mind about the verdicts. These claims were not supported by any other juror. The juror was sentenced to four months' imprisonment for his contempt in speaking to the defendant. The Court of Appeal characterised him as a "dissentient" who was not prepared to accept the jury's decision and dismissed the defendant's appeal. See the discussion at 4–187A above.

VIII. UNAUTHORISED RECORDING OF COURT PROCEEDINGS

A. Use of tape recorders in court: s.9

10–196 *[Add to note 382]*

The *Practice Guidance (Court Proceedings: Live Text-based Communications) (No 2)* [2012] 1 WLR 12; [2012] 1 Cr App R 21; (2012) 109(3) LSG 16 has been revoked and is replaced by the Criminal Practice Directions 2015 [2015] EWCA Crim 1567 in force with effect from 5 October 2015. CPR I,

6C deals with the use of live text-based forms of communication (including *Twitter*) from court for the purposes of fair and accurate reporting.

[Add to end of paragraph] **10–196**

Of the means that might be used to record court proceedings, only tape recorders and photography are specifically dealt with by legislation. The current practice guidance on the use of live text-based communications stated there was "no statutory prohibition" on the use of live text-based communications (such as Twitter) in open court. It presumes that a representative of the media or a legal commentator using live, text-based communications from court does not pose a danger of interference to the proper administration of justice in the individual case. This is because the most obvious purpose of permitting the use of live, text-based communications would be to enable the media to produce fair and accurate reports of the proceedings. As such, a representative of the media or a legal commentator who wishes to use such communications from court may do so without making an application to the court. Other members of the public, however, are required to apply for permission before using such communications and the paramount question for the judge will be whether the application might interfere with the proper administration of justice. The *Practice Guidance (Court Proceedings: Live Text-based Communications) (No 2)* [2012] 1 WLR 12; [2012] 1 Cr App R 21; (2012) 109(3) LSG 16 has been revoked and is replaced by the Criminal Practice Directions 2015 [2015] EWCA Crim 1567 in force with effect from 5 October 2015. CPR I, Preliminary Proceedings 6C deals with the use of live text-based forms of communication (including *Twitter*) from court for the purposes of fair and accurate reporting.

[Add to end of paragraph] **10–197**

Section 9 of the Contempt of Court Act 1981 has been amended by s.31 of the Crime and Courts Act 2013, as follows:

"... (2) After subs.(1) insert —

'(1A) In the case of a recording of Supreme Court proceedings, subs.(1)(b) does not apply to its publication or disposal with the leave of the Court'.

(3) In subs.(2) (leave under subs.(1)(a): grant, refusal, conditions, withdrawal and amendment) —

(a) after 'paragraph (a) of subs.(1)' insert ', or under subs.(1A),',
(b) for 'if granted may' substitute 'if granted —
  (a) may, in the case of leave under subs.(1)(a),', and
(c) after 'leave; and' insert —
  '(b) may, in the case of leave under subs.(1A), be granted subject to such conditions as the Supreme Court thinks proper with respect to publication or disposal of any recording to which the leave relates; and'.

(4) In subs.(1) (activities which are contempt of court) after paragraph (c) insert —

'(d) to publish or dispose of any recording in contravention of any conditions of leave granted under subs.(1A).' "

10–199 *[Add to end of paragraph]*

See now CPR rr.81.12 and 81.13.

10–201 *[Add to end of paragraph]*

See now CPR r.81.13(1)(e).

F. Televising court proceedings

10–212 *[Add to end of paragraph]*

Section 31 of the Crime and Courts Act 2013 (in force from July 15, 2013) has also amended s.9 of the Contempt of Court Act 1981 so as to permit the recording of Supreme Court proceedings (see para.10–197 above). Visual broadcasts of such proceedings have now taken place. Leave for such broadcasts may be subject to such conditions as to publication or disposal as the Supreme Court thinks proper. Section 32 of that Act now enables the Lord Chancellor to disapply s.41 of the Criminal Justice Act 1925 and s.9 of the Contempt of Court Act 1981 to permit the making and use of visual and sound recordings of other court proceedings, as follows:

2 Enabling the making, and use, of films and other recordings of proceedings

(1) The Lord Chancellor may, by order made with the concurrence of the Lord Chief Justice, provide that a section mentioned in subs.(2) or any provision of either of those sections —

(a) does not apply in relation to the making of a recording or the making of a prescribed recording;
(b) does not apply in relation to the making of a recording, or the making of a prescribed recording, if prescribed conditions are met, including conditions as to a court or tribunal or any other person being satisfied as to anything or agreeing;
(c) does not apply in relation to prescribed use of a prescribed recording.

(2) Those sections are —

(a) section 41 of the Criminal Justice Act 1925 (no photography or drawing in court of persons involved in proceedings, and no publication of contravening images);
(b) section 9 of the Contempt of Court Act 1981 (no sound recording in court without permission, and no public playing of recordings).

(3) In the case of any particular proceedings of a court or tribunal, the court or tribunal may in the interests of justice or in order that a person is not unduly prejudiced —

(a) direct that a provision disapplied in relation to the proceedings by an order under subs.(1) is, despite the order, to apply in relation to the proceedings, or
(b) direct that a provision disapplied in relation to the proceedings by an order under subs.(1) is, despite the order, disapplied in relation to the proceedings only if conditions specified in the direction are met.

(4) No appeal may be made against —

(a) a direction given under subs.(3), or
(b) a decision not to give a direction under that subsection.

(5) In this section —

"recording" means a visual or sound recording on any medium, including (in particular) —
(a) films and other video-recordings, with or without sound,
(b) other photographs, and
(c) sketches and portraits;
"prescribed" means prescribed by an order under subs.(1).

(6) The preceding provisions of this section do not apply in relation to Supreme Court proceedings.

(7) In s.41 of the Criminal Justice Act 1925 after subs.(1) insert —

"(1A) See s.32 of the Crime and Courts Act 2013 for power to provide for exceptions."

(8) In s.9 of the Contempt of Court Act 1981 after subs.(4) insert —

"(5) See s.32 of the Crime and Courts Act 2013 for power to provide for further exceptions."

[Add to end of paragraph] **10–213**

The Lord President, Lord Gill, announced that it was in his view time for an extended review of the existing practice in Scotland the light of the many technological developments since the first practice note had been promulgated in August 1992. No further applications for filming in the courts would be considered until the outcome of that review was known. (See 16–430A below.) On 28 January 2015, Lord Gill announced the outcome of his committee's investigation (chaired by Lady Dorrian). It was recommended that there should be opportunities for live and documentary television coverage of appellate and most first instance civil proceedings (subject to clear and robust guidelines). As for criminal trials, the recommendation was more restricted (and again subject to guidelines). There was concern to limit coverage of sensitive cases, such as those relating to sexual offences, and to protect vulnerable witnesses. Sentencing remarks could be shown, provided the focus remained on the judge. See *http://www.scotland-judiciary.org.uk/25/1369/Report-of-the-Review-of-Policy-on-Recording-and-Broadcasting-of-Proceedings-in-Court–and-Use-of-Live-Text-Based-Communications* (accessed August 2015).

The experience of television in court rooms in New Zealand, over some years, has not been widely acknowledged as a success: see e.g. *Law Talk*, 26

October 2012 (a journal published by the New Zealand Law Society). The Chief Justice, on 9 August 2013, instituted a review by a panel of judges of "in-court television coverage, photography and sound recording by mainstream media". It addressed current guidelines, any changes that may be required in the light of continuing developments in the available technology, and whether appropriate safeguards were in place to protect the fair trial process. On 20 July 2015, a final Report to the Chief Justice on In-Court Media Coverage was published. The Report concluded that it did not recommend any fundamental changes to the existing system, saying at [6] that "We consider it better to have the present coverage than none at all. There is room for improvement, particularly in the procedures, and the quality and detail of the publications. Lawyers and judges want more accuracy and balance in reporting". New "In-Court Media Coverage Guidelines 2015" have been produced to reflect these aspirations, aiming principally at greater liaison between the press and the courts, and an increased role for the Media and Courts Committee in monitoring compliance with existing guidelines.

Chapter 11

DIRECT INTERFERENCE WITH THE ADMINISTRATION OF JUSTICE

I. General Considerations

A. The diminished role for the summary process

[Add to note 2] **11–1**

Section 3 of the new CPR Pt 81 now deals with committal for interference with the due administration of justice, except where the contempt is committed in the face of the court or consists of disobedience to a court order or breach of an undertaking to the court. Committal applications falling under Section 3 may only be made with the permission of the High Court and the application for permission is made on notice to the respondent: CPR rr.81.12(3), 81.13 & 81.14. Where the Crown Court or a magistrates' court has power to deal with the forms of contempt discussed in this chapter, it is required, unless the respondent's behaviour makes it impracticable to do so, to allow the respondent a reasonable opportunity to reflect, take advice, explain and, if he or she so wishes, apologise. The court may postpone any enquiry it decides to hold into the respondent's conduct (though a magistrates' court may only postpone the enquiry until later the same day): Criminal Procedure Rules 2015 (SI 2015/1490) in force with effect from 5 October 2015, r.48.5 (3).

11–1 *[Add to note 6]*

In *R. v Kenny (Mark)* [2013] 3 W.L.R. 59, the Court of Appeal considered the relationship between contempt and the offence of perverting the course of justice. The defendant had participated in a transaction which led to the breach of a restraint order under the Proceeds of Crime Act 2002. While it was recognised that the breach of a restraint order may properly be treated as an offence of perverting the course of justice, the Court of Appeal indicated that it should only be charged as such where there were serious aggravating features such that that the maximum sentence for contempt could be insufficient.

There is no maximum penalty or sentencing guidelines for perverting the course of justice. Custodial sentences should be imposed in all but the most exceptional cases (*Attorney General's Reference (No 17 of 2008)* [2008] RTR 20; *Archbold* 2015 para 28–25). Custodial sentences where Defendants have been convicted of conduct involving the intimidation of witnesses have tended to involve terms of between 4 and 24 months imprisonment although longer sentences have been upheld in cases where attempts to intimidate witnesses were sustained (Archbold 2015 para 28–25). Similarly, making false allegations have tended to involve sentences of between 4 and 12 months and concealing evidence sentences between 4 to 18 months although in both types of case, longer sentences have been handed down where the evidence or allegation related to a serious crime (ibid).

11–2 *[Add to note 8]*

The Supreme Court, however, in *Summers v Fairclough Homes Ltd* [2012] 1 W.L.R. 2004 at [56]–[59], endorsed the contempt jurisdiction as an effective sanction for dishonest conduct in the course of proceedings.

C. Omissions

11–4 *[Add to end of paragraph]*

In *R. v Rochford* [2011] EWCA Crim 1928; [2011] 1 W.L.R. 534, it was held that the failure to submit a defence statement in criminal proceedings, such as to comply with ss.5(5) and 6A of the Criminal Procedure and Investigations Act 1996, did not in itself constitute a contempt of court. The only legal sanctions were those available under s.11 of that statute.

E. Is it possible to be guilty of attempted contempt?

11–15 *[Add to end of paragraph]*

See now CPR Pt 81.

[Note 37] **11–20**

See paras 3–83 to 3–89.

II. The Mental Element in Non-Publication Contempts

B. Differing strands of modern authority

[Add to end of paragraph] **11–30**

In *Nield v Loveday* [2011] EWHC 2324 at [9], Keith J. was concerned with a committal application in respect of a false statement of truth and concluded that "in addition to knowing that what you were saying was false, you had to have known that what you were saying was likely to interfere with the course of justice": see *Malgar Ltd v R E Leach (Engineering) Ltd* [2000] F.S.R. 393 and *Stobart Group Ltd v Howarth and Elliott* [2013] EWHC 797 at [23] where the words of Keith J were restated as the legal test that needed to be met in order for an allegation of contempt to succeed (HHJ Pelling QC).

III. Subverting the Orders or Procedures of the Court

D. The principle applicable even in the absence of an order

[Add note 65A] **11–43**

See however *MASM v MMAM* [2015] EWCOP 3. The Court of Protection had made a declaration under the Mental Capacity Act 2005 that it was in the First Respondent's best interest to reside and receive care in a specified residential home. The Court did not however make any order prohibiting her removal. The First Respondent's son then arranged for her to be removed her from the home and transported to Saudi Arabia. Hayden J acknowledged that when a court is exercising the *parens patriae* or wardship jurisdiction in relation to children, any action hampering the objectives of the court may be a contempt. However, he did not consider that the Court of Protection was in an analogous position when dealing with vulnerable adults, and appears to have considered the existence of a relevant order to be an essential element, holding that the son "has frustrated the objectives of the litigation but he is not, as I ultimately find, acting in defiance of an order and therefore is not exposed to contempt proceedings": [46]–[49]. Sections 15 and 16 of the Mental Capacity Act would permit a judge in future to make it clear that the declaration is an "order" as specified in s.16(2)(a). It would then carry a penal notice and all that is entailed thereby and that would then fall within the scope of contempt under the well established principles as modified by the more recent recognition of the principles surrounding the liberty of the subject in contempt proceedings.

In *Re MN (Adult)* [2015] EWCA Civ 411, Sir James Munby P acknowledged, at [90], that a declaration is in itself unenforceable by process of contempt, citing *MASM v MMAM* and *A v A Health Authority* [2002] EWHC 18 (Fam/Admin), [2002] Fam 213 by way of illustration: see also *Webster v Southwark LBC* [1983] QB 698 and paragraphs 12–1 and 14–124 of the main text. He also referred to what appeared to be a settled practice in the Court of Protection whereby judges had regularly been making declarations, and in particular as to a person's "best interests": see s.4 of the Mental Incapacity Act 2005, where that phrase is explained, and s.15 which refers expressly to the court's power to grant a declaration. He recommended, for the future, that judges should be readier to consider accepting undertakings or, where appropriate, granting an injunction, as contemplated by s.16 of the 2005 Act. In such circumstances, the possibility of invoking the (civil) contempt jurisdiction may give more support for the court's intentions. It is necessary, however, to bear in mind the further possibility, depending on the facts, that someone who has set out deliberately to subvert or undermine the court's objective in litigation, and can be proved to have done so, could be found to be in (criminal) contempt even if not directly in breach of an order: see *Att.-Gen v Times Newspapers Ltd.* [1992] 1 AC 191 and the discussion at 6–140 *et seq.*in the main text.

IV. ABUSING THE COURT'S PROCEDURES

A. Forging a court document

11–51 *[Add to note 75]*

In *Dryer v HSBC Bank Plc* [2014] EWHC 3949 (Ch) Morgan J declined to deal summarily with an allegation that a court order had been forged but gave directions permitting two of the parties to make an application for committal and providing for the matter to be referred to the Attorney General if no such application were made.

B. Putting forward a false case

11–56 *[Add to note 85]*

See now Criminal Procedure Rules 2015 (SI 2015/1490) in force with effect from 5 October 2015, r.45.9 and Practice Direction: (Costs in Criminal Proceedings) [2015] EWCA Crim 1568.

11–57 *[Add to end of paragraph]*

The Supreme Court has stressed the seriousness with which the court regards dishonest claims. It was made clear that a custodial penalty should be usually be imposed: see *Summers v Fairclough Homes Ltd* [2012] 1 W.L.R. 2004 at [57]–[58], and *South Wales Fire and Rescue Service v Smith*

[2011] EWHC 1749 (Admin). In the field of personal injury litigation, legislation has been enacted to address the problem of dishonest claims. Where the court has found that a claimant is entitled to damages for personal injury, s.57 of the Criminal Justice and Courts Act 2015 requires the court, on the application of the defendant, to dismiss the claim if satisfied on the balance of probabilities that the claimant has been fundamentally dishonest in relation to that claim or any related claim, unless satisfied that the claimant would suffer substantial injustice if the claim were dismissed. If criminal proceedings, or proceedings for contempt of court ensue, the court dealing with those proceedings must have regard to the dismissal of the civil claim when sentencing the claimant or otherwise disposing of the proceedings.

C. A false statement of truth: CPR 32.14

[Add to note 88] 11–58

See now CPR rr.81.17 to 81.18 and CPR PD 81 paras 4.1–4.5, which have replaced CPR r.32.14 and parts of CPR PD 32. It was emphasised by Moses L.J. in the Divisional Court in *South Wales Fire and Rescue Service v Smith* [2011] EWHC 1749 (Admin) at [5]–[6], that anyone committing this form of contempt can ordinarily expect to receive an immediate custodial penalty, by way of marking the gravity of such misconduct and also for the purpose of deterring others. The only reason why the culprit in that case was not sent to prison was the significant delay. The conduct itself dated back to 2007 and his admission of contempt to 2009. See also *Fairclough Homes v Summers* [2012] UKSC 26; *Airbus Operations Ltd v Roberts* [2012] EWHC 3631 (Admin); and *Havering LBC v Bowyer* [2012] EWHC 2798 and 2237 (Admin). A statement of truth made recklessly will satisfy the requirement for lack of honest belief ("saying something which it can be proved beyond reasonable doubt that [the maker of the statement] consciously has no idea whether it is right or wrong"): *Berry Piling Systems Ltd v Sheer Projects Ltd* [2013] EWHC 347 at [28]. See also at 11–30 above. In *Montgomery v Brown* [2011] EWHC 875 (QB), having given detailed consideration to each of the "counts" of alleged contempt, the Judge concluded that she was not satisfied to the criminal standard in respect of any of them.

[Add to note 90] 11–59

See also *Cavendish Square Holdings BV v Makdessi* [2013] EWCA Civ 1540. Christopher Clarke LJ said, at [73], "The extent to which a statement has been persisted in is plainly a relevant consideration. I do not, however, accept that an application to commit should be regarded as inappropriate simply because the maker of it recants before trial. Any such principle would risk becoming a licence to lie until the penultimate moment. Nor is there any rule that permission to apply to commit should be refused unless the statement in question has affected the outcome of a trial." A person seeking permission to bring contempt proceedings in respect of a false statement of truth must state precisely what is asserted to be untrue, and in which respect it is said not to be true: *Royal & Sun Alliance Insurance Plc v Kosky* [2013] EWHC 835 (QB), at [14].

11–59 [*Add to note 91]*

See now too the emphasis on the overriding objective at CPR 81 PD 5.2(3), 5.5(3) and 5.7. The fact that the police or the CPS may have decided that there is insufficient evidence to bring criminal proceedings does not necessarily mean that permission should be refused to make an application for committal, or that such an application should be dismissed, or that it is not in the public interest to allow such an application to proceed. The court and the prosecuting authorities are concerned with different, though no doubt overlapping, aspects of the public interest. The specific duty of the court under the contempt jurisdiction is to protect the integrity of the justice process, whereas the police and CPS are concerned to investigate crime and bring criminals to justice. Moreover, the evidential test under the Code for Crown Prosecutors has no application to contempt proceedings. See *Accident Exchange Ltd v George-Broom* [2015] EWHC 2205 (Admin), *per* Laws LJ.

11–60 *[Add to end of paragraph]*

It seems clear that a strong prima facie case of recklessness will suffice: *Berry Piling Systems Ltd v Sheer Projects Ltd* [2013] EWHC 347 at [28]–[30].

11–60A *[Add new paragraph]*

Where the substantive proceedings have not yet been tried, it may be appropriate for the court to grant permission to bring contempt proceedings but to direct that they should be tried at or after the main trial: *GB Minerals Holdings Ltd v Short* [2015] EWHC 1387 (TCC) at [54]–[58].

11–61 *[Add to note 92]*

See now CPR r.81.2.

11–61 *[Add to note 94]*

It was held in *R. v Rochford* [2011] EWCA Crim 1928; [2011] 1 W.L.R. 534 that the mere failure to submit a defence statement complying with ss.5(5) and 6A of the Criminal Procedure and Investigations Act 1996 did not constitute a contempt of court.

And see CPR PD 81 para.5.7.

[Add to end of paragraph] **11–62**

The position has changed significantly. CPR r.81.18 provides that a committal application in relation to a false statement of truth may be brought only with the permission of the court or by the Attorney General. A separate procedure is prescribed where the application is based both on a false statement of truth, or false disclosure statement, and some other form of contempt: CPR r.81.17(3)–(6). Where the false statement is made in connection with proceedings in the High Court, a Divisional Court or the Court of Appeal, permission must be sought from the court dealing with the relevant proceedings. As was pointed out in the text above, there had been some confusion as to the correct procedure in the case of proceedings commenced in the county court: see *Tariq Ali v Kayne* [2011] EWCA Civ 1582, [2012] 1 W.L.R. 1868, in which the earlier decision in *Brighton & Hove Bus and Coach Co Ltd v Brooks* [2011] EWHC 806 (Admin) was not followed. It is now clear from CPR r.81.18(3) that permission is to be sought from a single judge of the Queen's Bench Division. It is also provided that a court hearing such an application may direct that the matter be referred to the Attorney General with a request that he consider whether to bring proceedings for contempt himself: CPR r.81.18(5). See also CPR r.81.17(4)(b) and (c). It is also recorded in CPR PD 81 para.5.1 that the Attorney General prefers that a request should come from the court rather than directly from a party. (Yet a direct request is not to be seen as a means of appealing the judge's decision.) An application by the Attorney may be made to a single judge or to a Divisional Court: CPR r.81.18(6). For the importance of complying, in an application under CPR 81.18, with the strict procedural requirements of CPR 81.14, see *Cavendish Square Holdings BV v Makdessi* [2013] EWCA Civ 1540 at [50].

It became necessary in *International Sports Tours Ltd v Shorley* [2015] EWHC 2040 for the judge to determine whether the application to commit before him related to an allegation of false evidence contained in an affidavit, or to other matters. He came to the conclusion, at [43], that it did and thus permission was not required.

[Add to note 101] **11–62**

See now *South Wales Fire and Rescue Service v Smith* [2011] EWHC 1749 (Admin) at [20].

D. A false disclosure statement: CPR 31.23

[Add to note 102] **11–63**

But see now CPR rr.81.17 to 81.18 and CPR PD 81 PD 5.

E. Treatment of vexatious claims

11–64 *[Add to note 105]*

See also the jurisdiction to make "civil restraint orders" to control vexatious litigants: CPR 2.3(1), CPR 3.11, CPR PD 3C.

H. Misconduct by solicitors

11–72 *[Add to note 117]*

See now CPR 81.11. The work of solicitors includes "reserved legal activities", which a person is only entitled to carry on if approved for that purpose by the relevant regulator (in the case of solicitors, the Law Society). Carrying on a reserved legal activity when not entitled is an offence: see Legal Services Act 2007, Part III.

11–72 *[Note 121]*

For CPR 48.7, substitute CPR 46.8

11–76 *[Add to note 131]*

The Bar Standards Board Guidance is no longer in force. Rule C9 in the Bar Standards Board Handbook (2nd Ed, April 2015) deals with barristers' contact with witnesses.

I. Gaining improper access to court documents

11–83 *[Add to note 153]*

The matter is now governed by the principles identified in: *R (Guardian News & Media Ltd) v Westminster Magistrates' Court* [2013] QB 618, [69]-[88]. It is clear that the power to allow access to court documents derives from the common law principle of open justice, which applies to all tribunals exercising the power of the state. Parliament should not be taken to have legislated so as to control or limit a court's power to determine the requirements of the open justice principle unless the language of a statute makes it plain beyond possible doubt that this was Parliament's intention. If no such statutory limitation applies then, in a case where documents have been placed before a judge and referred to in the course of proceedings, access should be permitted on the open justice principle unless there are sufficiently strong countervailing reasons. The court must carry out a fact-specific proportionality exercise. Central to the court's evaluation will be the purpose of the open justice principle, the potential value of the material in advancing that purpose and, conversely, any risk of harm which access to the documents may cause to the legitimate interests of others.

[Add to note 159] **11–85**

See also the *Master of the Rolls' Practice Guidance: Interim Non-Disclosure Orders* [2012] E.M.L.R. 5 at [9]–[14] and [42]–[45].

J. The statutory duty of confidentiality for defendants in criminal proceedings

[Add to end of paragraph] **11–88**

Where a breach of s.17 of the 1996 Act is alleged, the procedure is prescribed by r.15.8 and Part 48 of the Criminal Procedure Rules 2015 (SI 2015/1490) in force with effect from 5 October 2015.

V. Failure to Attend Court

A. Advocates

[Add to note 183] **11–93**

In *Re West* [2015] 1 W.L.R. 109 a barrister had been found in contempt for his "conscious and deliberate act of defiance in failing to attend court" when directed to attend by the judge. The Court of Appeal allowed the barrister's appeal for want of procedural regularity, but confirmed, at [50], that, in principle, an advocate's failure to co-operate with, or refusal to attend, court may amount to contempt.

B. Witnesses: compelling attendance

[Add to note 187] **11–95**

For a recent example in Scotland, see *Haney (Catherine) v HMA* 2013 SCL 54. The initial failure of a witness to attend a trial, together with her behaviour when she did attend, was treated as contempt of court. And see 16–84 below.

C. The High Court and county court procedure

[Add to note 189] **11–96**

See now *Civil Procedure 2015* Vol.2 Section 2C.

[Add to end of paragraph] **11–97**

Disobedience to a witness summons would now fall to be addressed by the court under CPR Pt 81 and the earlier case law governing subpoenas. Although Pt 34 governs witness summonses for High Court and county court proceedings, penalties for non-compliance with regard to the county court will still be covered by s.55 of the County Courts Act 1984 and now also by CPR r.81.36.

11–100 *[Add to note 196]*

Note that the correct reference is to CPR r.71.8.

5. *Disobedience to a witness summons: necessary procedural steps*

11–105 *[Add to note 205]*

See *Civil Procedure 2015* Vol.1 at 34.0.3.

11–105 *[Add to note 209]*

See now *Civil Procedure 2015* Vol 1, at 34.6.1 and 34.6.2.

7. *Materiality of the witness' potential evidence*

11–113 *[Add to note 226]*

See now the notes in *Civil Procedure 2015* Vol 1, 34.3.5.

D. Crown Court: compelling attendance under the 1965 Act

11–121 *[Add to note 248]*

See now *Archbold 2015* 8–14 and Criminal Procedure Rules 2015, r.17.7.

11–122 Delete note 251.

11–123 *[Add to note 252]*

See now *Archbold 2015* 8–24.

11–125 *[Add to end of paragraph]*

The procedure is now governed by Section 2 of Pt 48 of the Criminal Procedure Rules 2015 which provides, among other things, that, unless the respondent's behaviour makes it impracticable to do so, the court must allow him or her a reasonable opportunity to reflect, take advice, explain and, if he or she wishes, apologise: r.48.5(2). If the Crown Court decides to postpone its enquiry into the conduct, it must arrange for a written statement to be prepared giving particulars of the conduct in question: r.48.7.

[Add to end of paragraph] **11–127**

The Criminal Procedure Rules 2012 would appear to have changed this practice. Under the current Rules (2015), where the Crown Court has postponed its enquiry, the court is required to serve on the respondent the written statement particularising the conduct complained of, together with a notice of the postponed enquiry, the possible sanctions, and the possibility that the court will proceed in the respondent's absence if the respondent does not attend: see r.48.7(3).

"Without just excuse"

[Add to note 268] **11–132**

See now *Archbold 2015* at 8–24.

E. Crown Court: breach of bail

[Add to note 274] **11–134**

Part 48 of the Criminal Procedure Rules 2015 is expressly stated not to apply to a failure to surrender to bail under s.6 of the Bail Act 1976: see r.48.5(1)(e).

G. Production of "documents or things" in criminal proceedings

As further amended, s.97(1) of the Magistrates' Courts Act 1980 presently provides: **11–139**

"(1) Where a justice of the peace is satisfied that—

(a) any person in England or Wales is likely to be able to give material evidence, or produce any document or thing likely to be material evidence, at the summary trial of an information or hearing of a complaint by a magistrates' court, and

(b) it is in the interests of justice to issue a summons under this subsection to secure the attendance of that person to give evidence or produce the document or thing,

the justice shall issue a summons directed to that person requiring him to attend before the court at the time and place appointed in the summons to give evidence or to produce the document or thing."

H. Attendance by jurors: s.20 of the Jurors Act 1974

[Add to note 307] **11–147**

See now Criminal Procedure Rules 2015, r.26.1 and Criminal Practice Directions 2015 CPD VI 26B and C. The procedural safeguards afforded by s.2 of Part 48 of the Criminal Procedure Rules apply to contraventions of s.20 of the Juries Act 1974: see r. 48.5(1)(b)(ii). In *R v Knight (Stephen)* [2011] EWCA Crim 1484 a finding of contempt was overturned where the summons had been sent to the wrong address and the appellant had never received it.

11–147 *[Add to note 308]*

See now Criminal Practice Direction 26C.5

11–147 *[Add to note 310]*

And see Criminal Procedure Rules 2015, r.26.2

11–147 *[Add to note 311]*

See now Criminal Procedure Rules 2015, r.26.1

11–147 *[Add to note 312]*

See now Criminal Practice Direction 26C.5

I. Coroner's court

11–150 *[Add to note 319]*

See now *Jervis on Coroners*, 13th edn (2014).

VI. The Statutory Provisions against Intimidation

A. Criminal Justice and Public Order Act 1994 s.51

2. *The wording of the section*

11–152 *[Replace s51 with the current version, as amended:]*

51.—Intimidation, etc., of witnesses, jurors and others.

(1) A person commits an offence if—

(a) he does an act which intimidates, and is intended to intimidate, another person ("the victim"),
(b) he does the act knowing or believing that the victim is assisting in the investigation of an offence or is a witness or potential witness or a juror or potential juror in proceedings for an offence, and
(c) he does it intending thereby to cause the investigation or the course of justice to be obstructed, perverted or interfered with.

(2) A person commits an offence if—

(a) he does an act which harms, and is intended to harm, another person or, intending to cause another person to fear harm, he threatens to do an act which would harm that other person,

(b) he does or threatens to do the act knowing or believing that the person harmed or threatened to be harmed ("the victim"), or some other person, has assisted in an investigation into an offence or has given evidence or particular evidence in proceedings for an offence, or has acted as a juror or concurred in a particular verdict in proceedings for an offence, and

(c) he does or threatens to do it because of that knowledge or belief.

(3) For the purposes of subss.(1) and (2) it is immaterial that the act is or would be done, or that the threat is made—

(a) otherwise than in the presence of the victim, or

(b) to a person other than the victim.

(4) The harm that may be done or threatened may be financial as well as physical (whether to the person or a person's property) and similarly as respects an intimidatory act which consists of threats.

(5) The intention required by subs.(1)(c) and the motive required by subs.(2)(c) above need not be the only or the predominating intention or motive with which the act is done or, in the case of subs.(2), threatened.

(6) A person guilty of an offence under this section shall be liable—

(a) on conviction on indictment, to imprisonment for a term not exceeding five years or a fine or both;

(b) on summary conviction, to imprisonment for a term not exceeding six months or a fine not exceeding the statutory maximum or both.

(7) If, in proceedings against a person for an offence under subs.(1) above, it is proved that he did an act falling within paragraph (a) with the knowledge or belief required by paragraph (b), he shall be presumed, unless the contrary is proved, to have done the act with the intention required by paragraph (c) of that subsection.

(8) If, in proceedings against a person for an offence under subs.(2) above, it is proved that he did or threatened to do an act falling within paragraph (a) within the relevant period—

(a) he did an act which harmed, and was intended to harm, another person, or

(b) intending to cause another person fear of harm, he threatened to do an act which would harm that other person,

and that he did the act, or (as the case may be) threatened to do the act with the knowledge or belief required by paragraph (b), he shall be presumed, unless the contrary is proved, to have done the act or (as the case may be) threatened to do the act with the motive required by paragraph (c) of that subsection.

(9) In this section—

"investigation into an offence" means such an investigation by the police or other person charged with the duty of investigating offences or charging offenders;

"offence" includes an alleged or suspected offence;

"potential", in relation to a juror, means a person who has been summoned for jury service at the court at which proceedings for the offence are pending; and

"the relevant period"—

(a) in relation to a witness or juror in any proceedings for an offence, means the period beginning with the institution of the proceedings and ending with the first anniversary of the conclusion of the trial or, if there is an appeal or a reference under s.9 or 11 of the Criminal Appeal Act 1995, of the conclusion of the appeal;

(b) in relation to a person who has, or is believed by the accused to have, assisted in an investigation into an offence, but was not also a witness in proceedings for an offence, means the period of one year beginning with any act of his, or any act believed by the accused to be an act of his, assisting in the investigation; and

(c) in relation to a person who both has, or is believed by the accused to have, assisted in the investigation into an offence and was a witness in proceedings for the offence, means the period beginning with any act of his, or any act believed by the accused to be an act of his, assisting in the investigation and ending with the anniversary mentioned in paragraph (a) above.

(10) For the purposes of the definition of the relevant period in subs.(9) above—

(a) proceedings for an offence are instituted at the earliest of the following times—

(i) when a justice of the peace issues a summons or warrant under s.1 of the Magistrates' Courts Act 1980 in respect of the offence;

(ii) when a person is charged with the offence after being taken into custody without a warrant;

(iii) when a bill of indictment is preferred by virtue of s.2(2)(b) or (ba) of the Administration of Justice (Miscellaneous Provisions) Act 1933;

(b) proceedings at a trial of an offence are concluded with the occurrence of any of the following, the discontinuance of the prosecution, the discharge of the jury without a finding otherwise than in circumstances where the proceedings are continued without a jury, the acquittal of the accused or the sentencing of or other dealing with the accused for the offence of which he was convicted; and

(c) proceedings on an appeal are concluded on the determination of the appeal or the abandonment of the appeal.

(11) This section is in addition to, and not in derogation of, any offence subsisting at common law.

11–153 *[Add to end of paragraph]*

In *R. v ZN* [2013] EWCA Crim 989, the Court of Appeal held that, where a victim is not in fact intimidated, but the other ingredients are proved, the accused may indeed be guilty of attempted intimidation. A conviction for that offence was accordingly substituted. The obiter suggestion in *Patrascu*, to the effect that it was possible to be guilty of intimidation when the alleged "victim" was *not* in fact intimidated, was disapproved.

E. Mens rea under the Act

Omit quotation marks around "what he knows or believes." **11–158**

[Add to end of paragraph] **11–159**

The meaning of "intimidation" was considered again by the Court of Appeal in *R. v ZN* [2013] EWCA Crim 989, where it was held that s.51(1) requires that the Crown prove that the "victim", whom the accused intended to be intimidated, was in fact intimidated. The *obiter* observations to the contrary in *Patrascu* were accordingly disapproved.

VIII. Common Law: Judges, Jurors and Legal Advisers

B. Interference with the jury system

2. *The current means of dealing with jury tampering*

[Add to end of paragraph] **11–191**

Section 24 of the Police and Criminal Evidence Act 1984 has now been amended by the Serious Organised Crime and Police Act 2005 s.110. A person who is guilty or reasonably suspected of an offence under s.51 may be arrested without a warrant if there are reasonable grounds for believing that the arrest is necessary *inter alia* in order to prevent the suspect causing physical injury to any other person, or to prevent him causing loss or damage to property, or to protect a child or other vulnerable person.

IX. Common Law: Interference with Witnesses

A. The mischief

[Add to note 417] **11–202**

See now also the express provision to this effect (unless the respondent's behaviour makes it impractical) in the Criminal Procedure Rules 2015, at r.48.5(2).

5. *"Improper" means or pressure*

[Add to note 467] **11–240**

The penultimate sentence of the quoted passage must now be read in the light of the decision in *R. v ZN* [2013] EWCA Crim 989. See above at 11–153 and 11–159.

11–240A *[Add new paragraph]*

The question of improper pressure was also considered in *Versloot Dredging BV v HGI Gerling Industrie Versicherung AG & 6 Others* [2013] EWHC 581. The claimants wished to obtain evidence from a surveyor retained by the defendants. The surveyor owed the defendants a duty of confidence and may have been privy to legally privileged information. The claimants contended that the defendants were seeking to restrict or impede their access to the surveyor by instructing or requesting him not to talk to them except in the presence of the defendants' solicitors. The court declined to grant an injunction. Having reviewed the authorities, including *Kellett*, Christopher Clarke J. stated the principle, at [19], that "it may be a contempt to interfere with attempts to interview a potential witness, or to prohibit the other side from getting the facts from him. Whether or not there is a contempt depends on whether the interference is improper". The judge continued:

> "21. Whether, however, there has been improper interference with a witness or the evidence-gathering process is fact sensitive. Because it is fact sensitive, it is not possible to be prescriptive as to what circumstances will, and what circumstances will not, constitute improper interference. Some matters can, however, be specified. Threats or promises made in order to persuade a witness to decline to be interviewed would be improper. But a solicitor for party A is entitled to raise legitimate concerns about questions of confidence and privilege, and indeed to tell a witness for party A, who may be about to be interviewed by the solicitor for party B, that he is not at liberty to break any confidence that he owes to party A or to reveal privileged information in respect of which party A alone can give a waiver.
>
> 22. What a solicitor is not entitled to do, or indeed a party, is to order or instruct a witness or a potential witness not to attend an interview with the opposing solicitor or to tell him that he has no real choice in the matter, or to put pressure on him not to comply. Nor must he make it appear that the witness can only be interviewed if the solicitor or his principal consents. Mr Jacobs accepted in the course of argument that any form of, as he put it, "strong persuasion" should be avoided, and in my judgment rightly so, for it is liable to be indistinguishable from improper pressure. Indeed, in determining whether or not there has been improper interference with a witness, the court will look at the reality of what has occurred."

7. *Contempt by threatening prima facie lawful action*

11–248 *[Add to note 482]*

See for example, the situation discussed in *Versloot Dredging BV v HGI Gerling Industrie Versicherung AG* [2013] EWHC 581, noted at 11–240A above, where Christopher Clarke J. held that, at the pre-trial stage, it would be legitimate for a party to tell a person whom the other side wished to interview that he was not free to break a duty of confidence or to reveal legally privileged information.

E. "Cheque-book" journalism

[Add to note 518] **11–272**

The Press Complaints Commission closed on 8 September 2014 and has been replaced by the Independent Press Standards Organisation ('IPSO'). IPSO has assumed responsibility for enforcing the Editors' Code of Practice formerly administered by the PCC. The wording of Clause 15 of the Code remains unchanged. However, the IPSO is not simply a replacement for the PCC. Not all newspapers have signed up to it or acknowledge its jurisdiction.

Possible reform of "cheque-book journalism"

[Add to end of paragraph] **11–281**

Concern was expressed by Sir Brian Leveson in the Report following his Inquiry into the Culture, Practices and Ethics of the Press (November 2012) as to payments made by journalists to sources, including police officers, but he did not identify payments to potential witnesses as being a specific problem and no recommendations were made in this respect: See Vol.2, Part F, Chapter 6, section 10, and Vol.2, Part G, Chapters 3 and 4.

X. Common Law: Litigants and Parties

B. Pressurising or intimidation

[Add to end of paragraph] **11–290**

In *Abbey v Gilligan* [2012] EWHC 3217 (QB), Tugendhat J. at [157] referred to *Martin* and to paragraphs 11–290 to 11–292 of the main text. Without making any finding as to contempt, he considered that, by analogy, the case supported the submission that making baseless threats to report a defendant to the police, in order to induce that defendant to settle a case otherwise than on the basis of its merits, could be an abuse of civil process.

D. The approach of the Phillimore Committee

[Add to note 566] **11–305**

But see now also the decision in *R. v ZN* [2013] EWCA Crim 989, where the *obiter* suggestion in *Patrascu*, that a person could be convicted of the full offence even though the alleged "victim" had not been actually intimidated, was disapproved.

G. Interference with legal advisers

11–316A *[Add new paragraph]*

The Supreme Court in Victoria had to consider, in *Legal Services Board v Forster (No.2)* [2012] VSC 633 what appears to have been effectively a case of harassment by Mr Forster of the counsel retained by the Legal Services Board (LSB). He sent her an email in which he threatened an application to restrain her from appearing in a particular case and stated that he intended to lodge a complaint against her with the Legal Services Commissioner. He also demanded from her to provide an itemised account and all the invoices rendered by her in connection with any matter involving him. The conduct was described, at [84]–[85], in these terms:

> "The offending email was Mr Forster's way of letting [counsel] know what he thought of her, and to signal to her that he would continue to 'niggle' her. In seeking to antagonise and annoy in this way, the offending email had a tendency to make [her] discharge of her duties as counsel for the Board much more difficult, whether or not it was actually likely to cause [her] to withdraw as counsel for the Board."

XI. INTERFERENCE WITH OFFICERS OF THE COURT

B. The provisions of the County Courts Act

11–319 *[Add to note 591]*

The relevant provisions of the Access to Justice Act 1999 have been repealed and public funding is now dealt with in the Legal Aid, Sentencing and Punishment of Offenders Act 2012, section 14 of which defines "criminal proceedings" in substantially the same terms. See 15–118 *et seq* below.

[Add new heading and paragraph]

3. *Procedure*

11–320A Where a person is alleged to have committed an offence under s.14, s.92 (rescuing or attempting to rescue goods seized in execution), or s.118, of the Act, but has not been taken into custody and brought before the court, the procedure is now governed by CPR r.81.34. The court will issue a summons which must be served on the alleged offender personally not less than seven days before the hearing. The procedure for a committal order in such a case is set out in CPR r.81.30.

C. Obstruction of enforcement officers and court officers executing process

[Add to note 598]

11–321 The reference to "a constable in uniform" has been removed from s.10 of the Criminal Law Act 1977.

2. *Interference with court-appointed receivers and sequestrators*

[Add new paragraph] **11–324A**

In *R. v Vasiliou* [2012] VSC 216, the court focussed on the issue of whether there was a tendency to interfere with the due administration of justice. There had been proceedings brought by a company against the trustee of the bankrupt estate of Mr Vasiliou, after which it was alleged that he sent an email to the judge's chambers and to the trustee which were intended, or had a tendency, so to interfere. It was held at [36]–[37] that:

> "I am satisfied beyond reasonable doubt that the email had a tendency to interfere with the due administration of justice. The email was calculated to place improper pressure on [the trustee] in his capacity as a party to the proceeding before Vickery J. Self-evidently, it constituted a threat of violence against at least [the trustee]. The statements in it ... were calculated to intimidate and improperly influence the decision of Vickery J if orders favourable to Mr Vasiliou were not made ... The email had a tendency to interfere with the administration of justice in that it had a tendency to dissuade [the trustee] from continuing to act as Mr Vasiliou's trustee in bankruptcy and a tendency to influence the decision of Vickery J."

3. *Interference with "enforcement officers"*

[Note 644] **11–333**

The final reference should read: Halsbury's Laws of England, 4th edn Vol 42 para.1130.

[Add to note 647] **11–334**

For warrants of restitution, see now CPR 83.26(8). For writs of restitution, see now CPR 83.1(2)(l)(iv) and CPR 83.13(5).

[Add to note 651] **11–336**

See now 11–320A above.

XII. INTERFERENCE WITH THE WARDSHIP OR *PARENS PATRIAE JURISDICTION*

B. Such interference treated as criminal contempt

[Add at end of paragraph] **11–342**

In MASM *v MMAM* [2015] EWCOP 3 at [47], Hayden J described the position in relation to wardship, as set out in paragraphs 11–338 to 11–342, as "largely anomalous, predicated as it is on the somewhat artificial premise that the court represents the Sovereign as *parens patriae* and cannot therefore be resolving contested issues as between parties in a non adversarial arena". He declined to extend the approach taken in wardship cases to a case in which, after the Court of Protection had made a declaration that it was in the First Respondent's best interests to reside and receive care in a specified residential home, the First Respondent's son arranged for her to be removed from the home and taken to Saudi Arabia. The son's conduct had frustrated the objectives of the litigation but, in the absence of an order prohibiting the removal, he was not exposed to contempt proceedings: [49]. See too *Re MN (Adult)* [2015] EWCA Civ 411. See also at 12–1 and 14–124.

XIII. THE SECRECY ATTACHED TO JURY DELIBERATIONS

A. Disclosing the deliberations of a jury: the background

11–359 *[Add to note 687]*

See also now Chapter 4 in the Law Commission's Consultation Paper No.209 and the discussion below at 11–408A and following. See also G. Daly and I. Edwards, "*Jurors Online*" (2009) 173 Criminal Law and Justice Weekly 261.

C. The text of s.8

11–361 *[Add to end of paragraph]*

The proposal of the Law Commission, canvassed in its Consultation Paper No.209, that a new statutory offence should be created in order to deal with cases of juror research, online or otherwise, would also embrace a different procedure; namely, that there should be trial on indictment. This would entail that the rules of criminal procedure would apply, rather than those of CPR Pt 81. It is thought that this would be more compatible with an accused's rights under arts 5 and 6 of the European Convention on Human Rights. (Relevant in this context also is *R. v Pouladian-Kari (Ramin)* [2013] EWCA Crim 158, where a conviction for unlawfully exporting goods which could be used for military purposes was quashed as being unsafe. The trial judge had failed to discharge the jury after a juror had written to him, following the prosecution opening, disclosing that he that was professionally employed in the customs sector, saying that there were "definite red signals" in the material presented by the prosecution, and that he was not sure that he could base a decision solely upon the evidence, as was his duty. See also at 2–147C above.) The Law Commission also saw additional advantages in a conventional trial on indictment; first as to the availability of legal aid and, secondly, by way of a route of appeal to the Court of Appeal (rather than to the Supreme Court, as at present, by reason of s.13 of the Administration of Justice Act 1960). In its final Report (no.340, December 2013, 4.71–4.77) the Commission recommended, for these reasons, that breach of s.8 should be triable only on indictment. In the event, s.8 has been abolished in England and Wales with effect from 13 April 2015 and a new indictable-only offence has been created (Juries Act 1974, s.20D). See 11–408A *et seq* below.

D. The compatibility of jury secrecy with the European Convention

[Add to end of paragraph] **11–367**

In *Seckerson v United Kingdom* (2012) 54 E.H.R.R. SE19, the European Court of Human Rights declared inadmissible applications by the defendants in *R. v Seckerson* which contended that their convictions and sentences were a disproportionate interference with their right to freedom of expression under ECHR art.10. Notably, however, the Court observed, at [45], that it was

> "not called upon in the present case to assess the compatibility with art.10 of s.8 in circumstances involving a conviction for research into jury methods. Nor is the Court concerned with a case where the interests of justice could be said to require the disclosure of the jury's deliberations: the applicants themselves argued that the disclosures did not seek to challenge or undermine the verdict in the particular case..."

F. Possible exceptions to the general exclusionary rule

[Add to note 712] **11–372**

The practice is likely to change in England and Wales in light of ss.20E to 20G of the Juries Act 1974 (as inserted by the Criminal Justice and Courts Act 2015 with effect from 13 April 2015). Those sections set out a detailed list of individuals and bodies to whom disclosure may be made and would permit, for example, a complaint received by the trial court after verdict to be passed directly to the police. The new provisions appear to contemplate that offences committed by or in connection with jurors will be investigated by the police or the Crown Prosecution Service, that contempts committed by or in connection with jurors will be investigated by the Attorney General, and that possible miscarriages of justice arising from alleged misconduct by jurors will be investigated by the Criminal Cases Review Commission. The new provisions are considered further at 11–408A below.

G. The meaning of "discloses" in s.8

[Add to end of paragraph] **11–373**

Section 8 has been abolished and replaced, with effect from 13 April 2015, with a new offence of disclosing a jury's deliberations (Juries Act 1974, s.20D). "Disclose" is not defined in the new offence and it is anticipated that the term will be given the same meaning as in s.8.

H. Offering to disclose

11–375 *[Add to end of paragraph]*

Section 8 has been abolished and replaced in England and Wales, with effect from 13 April 2015, with a new offence of disclosing a jury's deliberations (Juries Act 1974, s.20D). As with s.8, the new provision does not make it an offence for a juror to *offer* to disclose what had occurred in the jury room. However, since s.20D creates an indictable offence, there would seem to be greater scope for characterising such conduct as an attempt under the Criminal Attempts Act 1981.

I. The meaning of "deliberations"

11–380 *Add to end of paragraph]*

Section 8 has been abolished in England and Wales and replaced, with effect from 13 April 2015, with a new offence of disclosing a jury's deliberations (Juries Act 1974, s.20D). "Deliberations" is not defined in the new offence and it is anticipated that the term will be given the same meaning as in s.8.

J. Statutory exceptions: s.8(2)

11–381 *[Add to end of paragraph]*

Section 8 has been abolished in England and Wales and replaced, with effect from 13 April 2015, with a new offence of disclosing a jury's deliberations (Juries Act 1974, s.20D). Sections 20E–20G set out a number of detailed exceptions to the new offence. These are considered at 11–408A *et seq* below.

11–383 *[Add to note 728]*

It is submitted that Lord Slynn's analysis would be equally applicable to the new statutory offence under s.20D(1) of the Juries Act 1974. Moreover, s.20E(2) permits the trial judge to disclose information for the purposes of dealing with the case, or for the purposes of an investigation into whether an offence or contempt of court has been committed by or in relation to a juror in the proceedings. Section 20G makes it permissible to solicit disclosure for those purposes, or to obtain information by means of such disclosure. The new offence and its exceptions are considered at 11–408A *et seq* below.

[Add to end of paragraph] **11–384**

The position during the trial is now dealt with in s.20E of the Juries Act 1974, and the position after trial is dealt with in s.20F. These new provisions are considered further at 11–408A *et seq* below.

[Add to end of paragraph] **11–385**

The Law Commission's Consultation paper No 209 invited comments on whether s.8 currently inhibits legitimate research: see at paragraphs 4.61 to 4.62. In its final Report (No 340, December 2013), the Commission recommended that there be an exception allowing approved academic research into jury deliberations: see at paragraphs 4.31–4.57. In its response (Hansard, 30 July 2014: Column WS149) the Government said that it did not intend to take this recommendation forward for the time being, but would defer discussions until after the enactment of the Criminal Justice and Courts Bill. That Bill was duly enacted as the Criminal Justice and Courts Act 2015 and, with effect from 13 April 2015, repealed s.8 in England and Wales and introduced a new indictable offence of disclosing jury deliberations. See further 11–408A *et seq* below and see S Gilchrist, *Time for Real Jury Research* [2013] 177 JPN 171 and M Zander, *Research Should Not Be Permitted in the Jury Room* [2013] 177 JPN 215.

[Add to end of paragraph] **11–387**

In *R. v Connors (Josie)* [2013] EWCA Crim 368, a juror alleged that some of her fellows were racially prejudiced and were attempting to bully other jurors in order to secure a conviction. The trial judge declined to question the jury or to discharge them, since they appeared to him to be attentive and careful. His approach was approved by the Court of Court of Appeal.

K. Mens rea and s.8

[Add to end of paragraph] **11–388**

Section 8 has been repealed in England and Wales, with effect from 13 April 2015, with a new offence of disclosing a jury's deliberations (Juries Act 1974, s.20D). The new provision expressly states that any disclosure, solicitation or obtaining must be intentional. See further 11–408A *et seq* below.

[Add to end of paragraph] **11–396**

The Criminal Justice and Courts Act 2015 has introduced, by amendment of the Juries Act 1974, a number of new offences specific to jurors, viz, an offence prohibiting research by jurors (Juries Act 1974, s.20A); an offence of sharing research with other jurors (s.20B); an offence of engaging in other "prohibited conduct" (defined as "conduct from which it may reasonably be concluded that the [juror] intends to try the issue otherwise than on the basis of the evidence presented in the proceedings on the issue": s.20C); and an offence of disclosing jury deliberations (s.20D). Except for s.8 of the Contempt of Court Act 1981, which is repealed in England and Wales with effect from 13 April 2015, these offences supplement rather than replace the law of contempt applicable to jurors. See 10–181 *et seq.* Section 15A(7) specifies that it is a contempt for a juror to fail to surrender an electronic communications device in accordance with an order made by the trial judge.

The exceptions to the new offence of disclosing jury deliberations, set out in ss.20E–20G, are designed to address the difficulties considered in paragraphs 11–396 *et seq*. They do so by setting out a detailed list of disclosures which may be made for the purposes of raising concerns about possible jury misconduct, investigating those concerns, and conducting proceedings in respect of or occasioned by the alleged misconduct. See further 11–408A *et seq* below.

M. Jury secrecy and possible miscarriages of justice

11–396 *[Add to end of paragraph]*

The Criminal Justice and Courts Act 2015 has introduced, by amendment of the Juries Act 1974, a number of new offences specific to jurors, viz, an offence prohibiting research by jurors (Juries Act 1974, s.20A); an offence of sharing research with other jurors (s.20B); an offence of engaging in other "prohibited conduct" (defined as "conduct from which it may reasonably be concluded that the [juror] intends to try the issue otherwise than on the basis of the evidence presented in the proceedings on the issue": s.20C); and an offence of disclosing jury deliberations (s.20D). Except for s.8 of the Contempt of Court Act 1981, which is repealed in England and Wales with effect from 13 April 2015, these offences supplement rather than replace the law of contempt applicable to jurors. See 10–181 *et seq*. Section 15A(7) specifies that it is a contempt for a juror to fail to surrender an electronic communications device in accordance with an order made by the trial judge.

The exceptions to the new offence of disclosing jury deliberations, set out in ss.20E-20G, are designed to address the difficulties considered in paragraphs 11–396 *et seq*. They do so by setting out a detailed list of disclosures which may be made for the purposes of raising concerns about possible jury misconduct, investigating those concerns, and conducting proceedings in respect of or occasioned by the alleged misconduct. See further 11–408A *et seq* below.

11–408A *[Add new paragraph]*

The Law Commission in its consideration of the law of contempt ((Consultation Paper No 209) raised the possibility of a juror disclosing to appropriate authorities any information in the genuine belief that it might help to correct a miscarriage of justice. In its final Report (No 340, December 2013), the Commission recommended that there should be a specific defence where a juror discloses deliberations to a court official, the police or the Criminal Cases Review Commission ('CCRC') in the genuine belief that such disclosure is necessary to uncover a miscarriage of justice (4.15–4.30). With the exception of disclosures by jurors direct to the CCRC (as to which, see the Government's response: Hansard, 30 July 2014: Column WS149 available at *http://www.publications.parliament.uk/pa/ld201415/ldhansrd/text/140730–wms0001.htm*), these recommendations were adopted and expanded upon in the Criminal Justice and Courts Act 2015, which repealed in England and Wales s.8 of the Contempt of Court Act 1981 and created (by amendment of the Juries Act 1974) a new offence of disclosing jury deliberations, together with a series of detailed exceptions. Although the Commission had recommended that the exceptions should only apply in respect of jury misconduct in criminal trials, the new provisions apply to jurors in both criminal and civil cases, jurors in inquests (see s.75 and Schedule 13 of the 2015 Act), and lay members in a Court Martial (see s.76 and Schedule 14 of the 2015 Act). The new provisions came into force on 13 April 2015.

[*Add new Section*]

N. The new statutory provisions concerning disclosure of jury deliberations

[*Add new paragraph*] **11–408B**

Section 20D of the Juries Act 1974 provides as follows:

20D Offence: disclosing jury's deliberations

(1) It is an offence for a person intentionally—

(a) to disclose information about statements made, opinions expressed, arguments advanced or votes cast by members of a jury in the course of their deliberations in proceedings before a court, or
(b) to solicit or obtain such information,

subject to the exceptions in ss.20E to 20G.

(2) A person guilty of an offence under this section is liable, on conviction on indictment, to imprisonment for a term not exceeding two years or a fine (or both).

(3) Proceedings for an offence under this section may not be instituted except by or with the consent of the Attorney General.

[*Add new paragraph*] **11–408C**

Section 20D substantially replicates s.8(1) of the Contempt of Court Act 1981 and its terms are likely to be construed in the same way. The new provision states expressly that it is concerned with intentional disclosure, solicitation and obtaining of information, thereby resolving the doubt that existed over mens rea in respect of s.8 (as to which see 11–388 *et seq*). The principal difference is that the new provision creates an indictable offence, whereas s.8 classified the prohibited conduct as a contempt of court. The offence is subject to a number of exceptions, which are now considered in turn.

11–408D *[Add new paragraph]*

Section 20E provides:

20E Offence of disclosing jury's deliberations: initial exceptions

(1) It is not an offence under s.20D for a person to disclose information in the proceedings mentioned in s.20D(1) for the purposes of enabling the jury to arrive at their verdict or in connection with the delivery of that verdict.

(2) It is not an offence under s.20D for the judge dealing with those proceedings to disclose information—

(a) for the purposes of dealing with the case, or
(b) for the purposes of an investigation by a relevant investigator into whether an offence or contempt of court has been committed by or in relation to a juror in the proceedings mentioned in s.20D(1).

(3) It is not an offence under s.20D for a person who reasonably believes that a disclosure described in subs.(2)(b) has been made to disclose information for the purposes of the investigation.

(4) It is not an offence under s.20D to publish information disclosed as described in subs.(1) or (2)(a) in the proceedings mentioned in s.20D(1).

(5) In this section—

"publish" means make available to the public or a section of the public;
"relevant investigator" means—
(a) a police force;
(b) the Attorney General;
(c) any other person or class of person specified by the Lord Chancellor for the purposes of this section by regulations made by statutory instrument.

(6) The Lord Chancellor must obtain the consent of the Lord Chief Justice before making regulations under this section.

(7) A statutory instrument containing regulations under this section is subject to annulment in pursuance of a resolution of either House of Parliament.

11–408E *[Add new paragraph]*

Section 20E(1) substantially replicates s.8(2)(a) of the Contempt of Court Act 1981, considered at 11–381 *et seq*. Section 20E(2) puts the powers of the trial judge on a clear statutory footing. It permits the judge to disclose information directly to the police, the Attorney General, or other specified investigator for the purposes of an investigation. In this respect, s.20E(2)was more permissive than the procedure set out in the Practice Direction dealing with jury irregularities (Criminal Practice Directions 2014, CPD VI. 39M.13–39M.17). The Practice Direction was amended on the 16 July 2015 [2015] EWCA Crim 1253. PD 39 M.31 and 56 sets out the persons to whom such a disclosure may be made. If the jury has not been discharged, the judge should contact the Attorney General's office to consider police investigation (39 M.31). Where the jury has been discharged, it is not an offence for a judge of the Court of Appeal Criminal Division or the Registrar to disclose information about the jury's deliberations for the purposes of an investigation by a relevant investigator (39M.56). Investigators include the police, the Attorney General's office or the Criminal Cases Review Commission. The inclusion of the police as an investigator to whom disclosure may be made reflects the fact that jury misconduct may now amount to a distinct criminal offence as well as (or rather than) contempt of court.

[Add new paragraph] **11–408F**

Section 20F provides:

20F Offence of disclosing jury's deliberations: further exceptions

(1) It is not an offence under s.20D for a person to disclose information to a person listed in subs.(2) if—

- (a) the disclosure is made after the jury in the proceedings mentioned in s.20D(1) has been discharged, and
- (b) the person making the disclosure reasonably believes that—
  - (i) an offence or contempt of court has been, or may have been, committed by or in relation to a juror in connection with those proceedings, or
  - (ii) conduct of a juror in connection with those proceedings may provide grounds for an appeal against conviction or sentence.

(2) Those persons are—

- (a) a member of a police force;
- (b) a judge of the Court of Appeal;
- (c) the registrar of criminal appeals;
- (d) a judge of the court where the proceedings mentioned in s.20D(1) took place;
- (e) a member of staff of that court who would reasonably be expected to disclose the information only to a person mentioned in paragraphs (b) to (d).

(3) It is not an offence under s.20D for a member of a police force to disclose information for the purposes of obtaining assistance in deciding whether to submit the information to a judge of the Court of Appeal or the registrar of criminal appeals, provided that the disclosure does not involve publishing the information.

(4) It is not an offence under s.20D for a judge of the Court of Appeal or the registrar of criminal appeals to disclose information for the purposes of an investigation by a relevant investigator into—

- (a) whether an offence or contempt of court has been committed by or in relation to a juror in connection with the proceedings mentioned in s.20D(1), or
- (b) whether conduct of a juror in connection with those proceedings may provide grounds for an appeal against conviction or sentence.

(5) It is not an offence under s.20D for a judge of the Court of Appeal or the registrar of criminal appeals to disclose information for the purposes of enabling or assisting—

(a) a person who was the defendant in the proceedings mentioned in s.20D(1), or
(b) a legal representative of such a person,

to consider whether conduct of a juror in connection with those proceedings may provide grounds for an appeal against conviction or sentence.

(6) It is not an offence under s.20D for a person who reasonably believes that a disclosure described in subs.(4) or (5) has been made to disclose information for the purposes of the investigation or consideration in question.

(7) It is not an offence under s.20D for a person to disclose information in evidence in—

(a) proceedings for an offence or contempt of court alleged to have been committed by or in relation to a juror in connection with the proceedings mentioned in s.20D(1),
(b) proceedings on an appeal, or an application for leave to appeal, against a decision in the proceedings mentioned in s.20D(1) where an allegation relating to conduct of or in relation to a juror forms part of the grounds of appeal, or
(c) proceedings on any further appeal or reference arising out of proceedings mentioned in paragraph (a) or (b).

(8) It is not an offence under s.20D for a person to disclose information in the course of taking reasonable steps to prepare for proceedings described in subs.(7)(a) to (c).

(9) It is not an offence under s.20D to publish information disclosed as described in subs.(7).

(10) In this section—

"publish" means make available to the public or a section of the public;
"relevant investigator" means—
(a) a police force;
(b) the Attorney General;
(c) the Criminal Cases Review Commission;
(d) the Crown Prosecution Service;
(e) any other person or class of person specified by the Lord Chancellor for the purposes of this section by regulations made by statutory instrument.

(11) The Lord Chancellor must obtain the consent of the Lord Chief Justice before making regulations under this section.

(12) A statutory instrument containing regulations under this section is subject to annulment in pursuance of a resolution of either House of Parliament.

11–408G *[Add new paragraph]*

Section 20F concerns disclosures after the jury have been discharged. In order for any such disclosure to be lawful, the person making the disclosure must reasonably believe that an offence or contempt of court has been or may have been committed by or in relation to a juror in connection with the proceedings, or that the conduct of a juror in connection with those proceedings may provide grounds for an appeal against conviction or sentence. The list of those to whom a disclosure may legitimately be made by any person is set out in s.20F(2). Additional disclosures are permissible but only by a more limited class of person, or in specified circumstances. These are set out in s.20F(3)-(9). In contradistinction to s.20E(2), it appears that, once proceedings have concluded, the trial judge may not himself make an initial disclosure to an investigator other than the police. The same is true for jurors, other first instance judges, and court staff. Rather, the power to make initial disclosure to the other investigators listed in s.20F(10) is reserved to judges of the Court of Appeal and the registrar of criminal appeals (See also PD39 as amended: 39M.56). Since, where jury irregularities come to light after the jury has delivered its verdict, questions may arise as to whether the conviction is safe, the list of relevant investigators under s.20F(10) includes the Criminal Cases Review Commission, as well as bodies who may be concerned in the investigation or prosecution of criminal offences or contempts committed by jurors. At the time of writing, no additional investigators have been specified.

[Add new paragraph] **11–408H**

Section 20G provides:

20G Offence of disclosing jury's deliberations: exceptions for soliciting disclosures or obtaining information

(1) It is not an offence under s.20D to solicit a disclosure described in s.20E(1) to (4) or s.20F(1) to (9).

(2) It is not an offence under s.20D to obtain information—

(a) by means of a disclosure described in s.20E(1) to (4) or s.20F(1) to (9), or
(b) from a document that is available to the public or a section of the public.

[Add new paragraph] **11–408I**

Section 20G therefore permits a person to solicit a disclosure, or obtain information, where the disclosure itself would be permissible, or the information is obtained from a public document.

CHAPTER 12

CIVIL CONTEMPT

I. GENERAL PRINCIPLES

A. The nature of civil contempt

12–1 *[Add to note 2]*

And see *St George's Health Care NHS Trust v S* [1999] Fam 26, 60 and *MASM v MMAM* [2015] EWCOP 3, at [16], [20], [29]. The judge could have made an *order* to similar effect but, having chosen not to do so, he decided that it would not be open to him to commit for contempt. See additionally 11–43 and 11–342 above.

B. The public and private aspects of civil contempt

12–6 *[Add to note 12]*

As Sir James Munby P observed in *Jones, Re* [2013] EWHC 2579 (Fam) at [14],

> "It is quite clear, in my judgment, that the Law Officers have *locus* to apply for the committal of an alleged contemnor even if the contempt is civil and involves the breach of an order obtained, as in the present case, by a private individual in the course of proceedings between private individuals. The Law Officers act to safeguard the public interest and the administration of justice."

12–6 *[Add to end of paragraph]*

See also *Bedfordshire Police v RU and FHS* [2013] EWHC 2350 (Fam), [2014] 1 All ER 1062, [2014] Fam 69, at [30] *et seq*. It was held by Holman J that the police had no locus to apply for committal in relation to the alleged breach of a protection order made in respect of forced marriage. Sir James

Munby P expressed his agreement in *Jones, Re* [2013] EWHC 2579 (Fam), [2014] 1 FLR 852, at [16].

[Add new paragraph] **12–7A**

The public policy rationale underlying punishment for civil contempt was summarised by Jackson L.J. in *JSC BTA Bank v Solodchenko* [2011] EWCA Civ 1241 at [45], as follows:

> "The sentence for such contempt performs a number of functions. First, it upholds the authority of the court by punishing the contemnor and deterring others. Such punishment has nothing to do with the dignity of the court and everything to do with the public interest that court orders should be obeyed. Secondly, in some instances, it provides an incentive for belated compliance, because the contemnor may seek a reduction or discharge of sentence if he subsequently purges his contempt by complying with the court order in question."

The continuing value of the contempt jurisdiction was highlighted in *JSC BTA Bank v Ablyazov* [2012] EWCA Civ 1411; [2013] 1 W.L.R. 1331; [2013] 2 All E.R. 515; *The Times*, January 8 (discussed further at para.12.81A below) where Rix L.J. stated at [188] that:

> "The authorities demonstrate that it is vital for the court, in the interests of justice, to have effective powers, and effective sanctions. Without these, it would be possible for a defendant (or, in a different situation, a claimant) to flout the orders of the court, which are the court's considered means by which to keep the scales of justice for the parties even. If once it became known that the court was unable or unwilling to maintain the effectiveness of its orders, then it would lose all control over litigation of this kind, with terrible consequences for the administration of justice."

In Northern Ireland, the same point was made by McCloskey J. in *Quinn Finance v Lyndhurst Development Trading SA* [2013] NICh 2.

C. The jurisdiction to be kept separate from criminal proceedings

Double jeopardy

[Add to note 27] **12–11**

See also the discussion at 3–218 above and at 14–65 below.

[Add to end of paragraph] **12–11**

It was again emphasised in *Balli, Re* [2011] EWHC 1736 (Ch) that the court should avoid double punishment in respect of actions which constituted both contempt of court and a criminal offence under the general law. When sentencing for contempt, the court's concerns would be to mark disapproval of the breach of any relevant order, or other disregard of the rule of law, and in appropriate cases to ensure future compliance. In that case, a solicitor had acted in a professional capacity after his entitlement to practise had been withdrawn. He had thereby committed an offence under s.14(1) of the Legal Services Act 2007, but the court actually sentenced him to six months imprisonment for contempt of court in relation to that conduct. On the other hand, it is clear that the maximum penalty for contempt (two years) is regarded as wholly inadequate to address the level of wrongdoing involved in some activities, such as a serious case of child kidnapping by a parent in contravention of a court order: see e.g. *R. v Kayani; R v Solliman* [2011] EWCA Crim 2871, [2012] 1 WLR 1927, 2 All ER 647 and *R v Kenny (Mark)* [2013] Q.B. 896 discussed at 11–1 above.

12–14 *[Add to note 33]*

See the discussion in JAE Vervaele, "*The transnational ne bis in idem principle in the EU: mutual recognition and equivalent protection of human rights*", Utrecht Law Review 1, No 2 (2005); "*Ne Bis in Idem: Towards a Transnational Constitutional Principle in the EU?*", Utrecht Law Review, 2013; and (with S Gless) "*Law should govern: aspiring general principles for transnational criminal justice*" Utrecht Law Review, 2013.

12–14 *[Add to note 34]*

See too e.g. *Sergey Zolotukhin v Russia*, ECtHR App No 14939/03, 10 February 2009; *Zoran Spasic* C-398/12; *Kiiveri v Finland* [2015] ECHR 146; *Osterlund v Finland* [2015] ECHR 150. It was held in *Spasic* that Article 54 of the Convention Implementing the Schengen Agreement 1985 was not incompatible with the principle. In order to take advantage of it, it would be necessary to show that the criminal process in the other relevant jurisdiction had been completed. Spasic had paid the fine imposed in Italy but had not served the custodial sentence. This would appear to be compatible with the common law approach adopted in England: *R v Thomas* [1985] QB 604.

12–15 *[Add to end of paragraph]*

In *W (A Child) (Abduction: Committal), Re* [2011] EWCA Civ 1196, a father abducted his daughter who was a ward of court and refused to comply with orders to return her, and to provide information as to her whereabouts. The court did not expressly characterise the contempt as criminal, but in considering the penalty referred to the need for "regard to the likely sentence that might be imposed for similar conduct in the criminal court".

E. Committal and sequestration to be sparingly used

[Add to notes 46 and 47] **12–19**

Since October 1, 2012, the former RSC Ords 45.5–45.7 (setting out the procedure for the enforcement by the court of its judgments and orders in circumstances amounting to contempt) have been replaced by the provisions of CPR Pt 81. RSC Ord.45 has been replaced by CPR rr.81.4 (committal) and 81.20 (writ of sequestration). The Practice Guidance (Committal Proceedings: Open Court [2013] 1 WLR 1316 have been superseded by Practice Direction: Committal for Contempt of Court: Open Court [2015] 1 WLR 2195 (26 March 2015) at 15–16A. See Chapters 13 and 15 for further discussion about the changes effected more generally.

[Add to end of paragraph] **12–19**

Committal has been described as "the court's ultimate weapon in securing compliance with its orders": *JSC BTA Bank v Solodchenko* [2010] EWHC 2404 (Comm) at [15], Proudman J.

[Add to note 54] **12–23**

In *Sectorguard Plc v Dienne Plc* [2009] EWHC 2693 (Ch) Briggs J. accepted the thrust of counsel's argument that "failure to perform an impossible undertaking is not a contempt". It would be for the court, however, to determine whether compliance was indeed, in the circumstances, impossible. In that case, an undertaking had been given to identify a category of customers when the respondent had no list to enable it to do so. In a subsequent case, Males J. raised the question whether what he called "this principle of impossibility" should be extended to cover cases where compliance with the order or undertaking was not impossible but merely difficult or inconvenient: *Westminster City Council v Addbins Ltd* [2012] EWHC 3716 (QB); [2013] J.P.L 654. The answer, it is submitted, is that difficulty of compliance would go to penalty, rather than determining the issue of contempt or no contempt. There would always be the option of applying to the court for variation, extension or discharge.

[Add to note 57] **12–23**

See also para 3–195 on self-incrimination.

[Add to note 58] **12–24**

And see *Ipartner Pte Shipping Ltd v Panacore Resources DMCC* [2014] EWHC 3608 (Comm), Hamblen J.

F. Committal as a matter of "very last resort" in family proceedings

12–25A *[Add new paragraph]*

Practice Guidance was issued by the Lord Chief Justice and the President of the Family Division and the Court of Protection: [2013] 1 W.L.R. 1316. This emphasises the presumption that applications for committal for contempt of court in the Family Division and the Court of Protection will be heard in public. Only in exceptional cases, where it is necessary in the interests of justice, will the court sit in private. The fact that the committal application is being made in the Court of Protection, or in the Family Division in proceedings relating to a child, does not of itself justify the application being heard in private. Where an application is heard in private, the court is required to sit in public to state (a) the name of the respondent (b) in general terms, the nature of the contempt of court in respect of which the committal order is being made and (c) the punishment being imposed. The *Practice Guidance* also reflects the judgment in *Doncaster Metropolitan Borough Council v Watson* [2011] EWHC 2376 Fam (Sir Nicholas Wall P) where, in the context of a breach of an order issued to protect the confidentiality of child care proceedings, it was emphasised that committal proceedings were not issued to stifle free speech but to ensure obedience to orders of the court. See now also the decisions in the Court of Protection in *MASM v MMAM* [2015] EWCOP 3, Hayden J, and in *A Healthcare NHS Trust v P and Q* [2015] EWCOP 15, Newton J. A new *Practice Direction* came into effect in April 2015: *Practice Direction: Committal for Contempt of Court — Open court*.

12–30A *[Add new paragraph]*

In *Zuk v Zuk* [2012] EWCA Civ 1871, the Court of Appeal expressed doubt as to whether the approach in *M (Minors) (Access: Contempt: Committal), Re* [1991] 1 F.L.R 355 would be applied in proceedings brought in the Family Division under the Debtors Act 1869 where the burden of proving both the ability and a refusal to pay had been discharged by the applicant. Thorpe L.J. pointed out, at [16], that in such situations:

> "There are scant means of enforcement open to a person (usually a wife) who has achieved ancillary relief orders, unless there are assets within the jurisdiction against which the order can be readily enforced and it is important that the power to apply for committal under the Debtors Act should be seen by debtors as a real and lively threat."

See also his observations in *Mohan v Mohan* [2013] EWCA Civ 586; [2013] Fam. Law 959, set out below at 15–62. These passages were cited by Moylan J in *Prest v Prest* [2014] EWHC 3430 (Fam), at [62]–[65].

[Add new paragraph] **12–32A**

In *W (A Child) (Abduction: Committal), Re* [2011] EWCA Civ 1196; [2012] 1 W.L.R. 1036; [2012] 2 F.L.R. 133; [2012] Fam. Law 389; *The Times*, September 15, 2011, the Court of Appeal made clear that in an appropriate case, where a respondent makes repeated breaches of successive mandatory orders requiring positive action, s.14(1) of the Contempt of Court Act 1981 (which limits custodial sentences for contempt "on any occasion" to two years) does not prohibit successive custodial sentences being imposed. In a case where it could not be said with any certainty that the coercive effect of a custodial sentence would no longer serve any valid purpose, it was open to the court to impose a further penalty in respect of any further mandatory orders which it had made, and which had also been disobeyed. Courts should take a "proportionate, stage-by-stage, hearing-by-hearing approach". See also at 14–21A below.

[Add to note 74] **12–34**

See too *Sanchez v Oboz* [2015] 611 (Fam), Cobb J and (albeit in a commercial context) the discussion of principles in *Otkritie International Investment Management Ltd v Gersamia* [2015] EWHC 821 (Comm), Eder J. NB the correct reference to *Hale v Tanner* is [2000] 2 FLR 879.

G. Procedural steps to be rigidly enforced

[Add to note 75] **12–35**

It is provided by s.39A of the Child Support Act 1991 that:

> "(1) Where the [Child Maintenance and Enforcement] Commission has sought: —
>
> (a) in England and Wales to levy an amount by distress under this Act: or ... and that amount, or any portion of it, remains unpaid it may apply to the court [for an order of commitment to prison and disqualification from driving] under this section ...
>
> (3) On any such application the court shall (in the presence of the liable person) inquire as to ...
>
> (c) whether there has been wilful refusal or culpable neglect on his part ..."

The Court of Appeal considered applications to commit under these provisions and, because of their penal nature, applied a strict interpretation to the word "sought": *Child Maintenance and Enforcement Commission v Gibbons; Same v Karoonian* [2012] EWCA Civ 1379. It was held to be necessary for the Commission to show that distress had actually been attempted (not merely contemplated and rejected) and costs incurred.

12–35 *[Add to note 76]*

See para 3–69 *et seq* above.

12–35 *[Add to notes 78 and 79]*

See now the Practice Direction to CPR 81, referred to below.

12–35A *[Add new paragraph]*

The *Practice Direction on Committal Applications* formerly found at RSC 52 has been replaced with CPR Practice Direction 81 on contempt of court since October 1, 2012. Chapter 15 includes further detail on the new procedural rules. In *Giles v Tarry* [2012] EWCA Civ 1886; (2012) 156(38) S.J.L.B. 31, the Court of Appeal emphasised that the rules of procedure need to be followed properly, even where litigants were not represented by lawyers. Although formalities could be dispensed with where it was in the interests of justice (applying the reasoning of Judge L.J. in *Jolly v Hull* [2002] F.L.R. 69), the new Practice Direction required the court to have regard to the art.6 ECHR rights of the alleged contemnor. Where the defect in formalities was such that the alleged contemnor could not have a fair hearing of the allegations made against him, a finding of contempt or order of committal should be set aside. Practice Direction 81 para.16.2 preserves the ability of the court to waive procedural defects if satisfied that no injustice has been caused. See also *Westminster City Council v Addbins Ltd* [2012] EWHC 3716 (QB); [2013] J.P.L 654 referred to at note 80 below.

H. The safeguard of personal service of the notice of committal proceedings

12–36 *[Add to note 80]*

See now CPR Pt 81, and in particular r.81.8, which sets out the circumstances in which the requirement for personal service may be dispensed with. In *Westminster City Council v Addbins Ltd* [2012] EWHC 3716 (QB); [2013] J.P.L. 654, Males J. exercised the power on an application to commit a director where he had been clearly aware of the terms of the order when it had been made. See also *Ipartner Pte Shipping Ltd v Panacore Resources DMCC* [2014] EWHC 3608 (Comm), at [73]–[74].

I. Requirements as to service of the order said to be breached

12–38 *[Add to note 90]*

See now CPR r.81.9(2).

[Add new paragraph] 12–39A

See now CPR Pt 81 and in particular CPR r.81.5 which sets out the general requirements for service of any order or judgment for which enforcement by committal for contempt is sought. The changes to the rules are discussed further in Chapters 13 and 15.

[Add to notes 91 and 92] 12–39

See now CPR rr.81.5–81.8.

[Add to note 96] 12–41

See now CPR rr.81.9 and 81.25. In *Warner v Barnes* [2012] EWHC 4233 (Ch), the initial orders did not include penal notices; nor were they personally served. When compliance was not forthcoming, the applicant therefore applied for amended orders to include a penal notice and to set a deadline for compliance. This enabled the orders to be successfully enforced by committal.

[Add new paragraph] 12–42A

The rules governing the enforcement of orders against companies are now contained in the new CPR Pt 81. Where a committal order is sought against a company's director, he becomes a respondent pursuant to CPR r.81.3(c) and should normally be personally served with a copy of the order (although see *Westminster City Council v Addbins Ltd* [2012] EWHC 3716 (QB); [2013] J.P.L 654 discussed at note 80 above). Where enforcement is sought against a company's assets or the property of a director by means of a writ of sequestration, the relevant procedure is now set out in CPR rr.81.19–81.27: see below at 12–113A *et seq*. In the case of *Dar Al Arkan v Al Refai* [2014] EWCA Civ 715, [2015] 1 WLR 135, it was held that the sanctions available against directors under CPR 81, in respect of corporate contemnors, may legitimately be pursued against even those who are non-parties resident abroad. These changes are discussed further in Chapters 13 and 15.

[Add to notes 101–103] 12–43

CPR rr.2.11 (by agreement between the parties) and 3.1(2)(a) (by order of the court) allow for variation of any time period within which a positive act ordered by the court must be done. CPR r.81.15(1)(b) requires any order or agreement which varies the time period for compliance to be served on the respondent, in addition to the initial substantive order.

[Add new paragraph] 12–44A

If a judgment or order requires a person to deliver goods or alternatively to pay their assessed value, the judgment or order cannot be enforced by an order for committal under CPR Pt 81 unless the person entitled to enforce the judgment or order applies to the court requiring that the goods be delivered within a specified time, pursuant to CPR r.81.4(5). It is the order which specifies the time for performance which is enforceable by committal under Pt 81.

J. The criminal standard of proof: a further safeguard

12–47A *[Add new paragraph]*

In *JSC BTA Bank v Ablyazov* [2012] EWCA Civ 1411; [2013] 1 W.L.R. 1331; [2013] 2 All E.R. 515; *The Times*, January 8, 2013, the Court of Appeal stressed that, although the criminal standard of proof would apply on an application for committal, that did not necessarily require every single aspect of a case to be proved to that standard, but only that the necessary elements of the offence were so established. This was particularly so in a case based on circumstantial evidence, where the whole was stronger than the individual parts. In criminal cases, proof of intent to the criminal standard could be established having regard to the whole of the evidence, whether or not each individual fact which comprised that evidence could itself be proved beyond reasonable doubt (see *Shepherd v The Queen* (1990) 170 C.L.R. 573 (HCA) at 579/580).

K. Ambiguous or vague orders or undertakings

12–51 *[Add to note 120]*

See also *Jones, Re* [2013] EWHC 2579 (Fam), Sir James Munby P.

12–57 *[Add to note 133]*

And see *The Environment Agency v Hughes* [2014] EWHC 2484 (QB).

12–57 *[Add to note 134]*

See also *Att.-Gen. v Punch Ltd* [2003] 1 AC 11046, at [35] and *Rhodes v OPO* [2015] UKSC 32, at [79] and [100].

12–58 *[Add to note 137]*

And see the discussion in *Jones, Re* [2013] EWHC 2579 (Fam), [2014] 1 FLR 852, at [18]–[24].

12–60 *[Add to note 141]*

See now the provisions about "revenge porn" in the Criminal Justice and Courts Act 2015, ss.32–35.

L. The possibility of approaching the court for clarification

[Add to note 145] **12–62**

See further, on the courts' reluctance to grant declarations, *Nicklinson v MoJ* [2014] UKSC 38, [2015] AC 657 and *Bank St Petersburg v Arkhangelsky* [2014] EWHC 574 (Ch), at [11]-[12], where the judge rejected the idea of granting a declaration that an order had been breached instead of putting the claimant through the rigours of a committal application. See also C Draghici, *The blanket ban on assisted suicide: between paternalism and utilitarian justice*, [2015] EHRLR 286

N. The Court's discretion not to hear a contemnor until the contempt is purged.

[Add new paragraph] **12–68A**

It was emphasised in *JSC BTA Bank v Ablyazov* [2012] EWCA Civ 639, by Moore-Bick L.J., that it would only be in very rare circumstances that a contemnor would be precluded from arguing an appeal against an order for committal. He accepted, however, that the discretion to decline to hear a person in contempt had not been abrogated by art.6 ECHR. See also the discussion of this decision in C. Crifó, "*The Limits of Civil Contempt as a Measure of Compulsion: JSC BTA Bank v Ablyazov*" (2013) 32 C.J.Q. 14. In the subsequent hearing before the full Court of Appeal, [2012] EWCA Civ 1411; [2013] 1 W.L.R. 1331; [2013] 2 All E.R. 515; *The Times*, January 8, 2013, Rix L.J. confirmed, at [181], that there was a

> "plain distinction between the question of whether an unrepentant contemnor can appeal against the findings of contempt, and whether a contemnor (who has his appeal and, perhaps, the opportunity for relief against sanctions) can be made to face up to his responsibilities by means of unless orders."

And see *JSC BTA Bank v Ablyazov (Shalabayev intervening)* [2015] EWCA Civ 70, at [17]–[22].

[Add to end of paragraph] **12–81**

For an example of a "*Hadkinson* order" in the Court of Protection, see *A Local Authority v B, F and G* [2014] EWCOP B18 (COP), (2014) MHLO 70, Judge Cardinal.

[Add new paragraph]. **12–81A**

The criteria of fairness, necessity and proportionality lay at the heart of the Court of Appeal's decision in *JSC BTA Bank v Ablyazov (No.8)* [2012] EWCA Civ 1411; [2013] 1 W.L.R. 1331; [2013] 2 All E.R. 515; *The Times*, January 8, 2013. An order was upheld debarring a defendant from defending a claim unless he complied with the terms of a freezing order and surrendered himself to prison having been sentenced for contempt. The Court of Appeal undertook a comprehensive review of the authorities concerning art.6 ECHR and the right of a litigant to be heard in circumstances where he had failed to comply with court orders. Rix L.J. cited the reasoning of Arden L.J. in *Stolzenberg v CIBC Mellon Trust Co Ltd* [2004] EWCA Civ 827; (2004) 148 S.J.L.B. 824; *Independent*, July 2, 2004 at [161]:

> "the state can impose restrictions on the right of access to court provided that the restrictions serve a legitimate aim, are proportionate and do not destroy the very essence of the right. Here the legitimate aim in imposition a sanction is to secure compliance with court orders ... The imposition of a sanction is proportionate if it is reasonably necessary for achieving that aim. The essence of the right of access to court is not destroyed because the litigant has the opportunity to seek relief against the sanctions. The refusal of that relief is Convention-compliant if the same tests are satisfied. The legitimate aim remains the same. Proportionality will be met if the overriding objective is met. The essence of the right will not be destroyed even if refused, since the appellants always had the chance to comply with court orders ... "

Similarly, the Strasbourg jurisprudence showed that the right of access to court was not absolute, and could be subject to legitimate restrictions: *Z v United Kingdom* (2002) 34 E.H.R.R. 3. In considering how this applied to the position of a contemnor, Rix L.J. in *Ablyazov* stressed that a principal object of the contempt jurisdiction was to bring a contemnor to face up to what he had done by a process of sanction and encouragement. Rix L.J. summarised the reasons why it was appropriate for a court to debar a contemnor from defending an action unless he complied with previous orders and surrendered himself:

> "The court plainly has power, under its contempt of court jurisdiction, to order the imprisonment of a litigant found to be in contempt. That is the power that encroaches on the liberty of the subject. That power is held as part of the armoury of the court to ensure that justice can be done in civil litigation. Although it has a quasi-criminal aspect, the application for committal is typically made by one litigant against the other, in order to preserve the litigation. It would fatally undermine the power to commit to prison for contempt of court if the court were powerless to enforce its order in circumstances where the adjudged contemnor simply goes into hiding and, as has almost certainly occurred in this case, leaves the jurisdiction. The order of committal is made for the sake of justice in the litigation and to encourage the contemnor to abide by the orders of the court (not, as has been suggested, for the purpose of bringing an end to the litigation). Litigation is not a game, but I may perhaps use the metaphor of "playing by the rules". If an adjudged contemnor is able, whatever the circumstances, to hold an order for committal at nought *and yet at the same time* demand that the litigation continue as though nothing had happened, because the court is powerless to say that the fugitive contemnor should face up to his responsibilities by surrendering to custody and should do so as a condition of being able to continue with the litigation, then the utility of the contempt of court procedure can be destroyed and a significant factor in the checks and balances which operate in the field of civil litigation is lost. On any realistic view of it, a judge who makes such an order is not

> going further down the road of encroaching on the liberty of the subject than the order of committal that he has already made: rather he is attempting to preserve a just balance in the litigation which is before him in circumstances where the contemnor has sought to destroy that balance in his own interest. The court is entitled to seek to preserve that balance."

In such a situation, the court had denied a contemnor nothing except the ability to ignore the court's orders indefinitely. Where it was not just, fair or proportionate to permit a contemnor to avoid the consequences of his contempt, Rix L.J. stressed that the broader interests of justice required that the court be seen to maintain the effectiveness of its orders rather than permitting contemnors to "hitch a free ride to interminable litigation on the back of ill-gotten gains".

In his judgment, which dissented from the majority only on one point, Toulson L.J. expressed the view that it was inappropriate to require a contemnor to surrender himself to the court if he was to be permitted to defend the litigation, as this constituted an additional punishment: that would be "wrong in principle". Unlike the failure to give disclosure, which was necessary to ensure a fair trial, Toulson L.J. did not believe that the contemnor's failure to surrender himself to court was strictly necessary to ensure the fairness of the trial process. In cases which are less stark than *Ablyazov*, judges may therefore remain cautious in debarring contemnors from participation in proceedings in which they have failed to purge their contempt.

The reasoning and approach of Rix L.J. was applied in Northern Ireland by McCloskey J. in *Quinn Finance v Lyndhurst Development Trading SA* [2013] NICh 2.

[Add to note 188] **12–82**

See also *Mann v Mann* [2014] EWCA Civ 1674, at [24]–[25], where it was said that the authority of *Mubarak v Mubarik* had rightly not been challenged.

A. The traditional approach to mens rea in civil contempt

[Add to note 200] **12–84**

And see *Masri v Consolidated Contractors International Co Ltd* [2011] EWHC 1024 (Comm), at [353]-[354].

[Add to note 201] **12–85**

Spectravest was cited in *Specsavers International Healthcare Ltd v Asda Stores Ltd* [2012] EWCA Civ 494. And see *Ipartner Pte Shipping Ltd v Panacore Resources DMCC* [2014] EWHC 3608 (Comm), at [22] and *Public*

Joint Stock Company Vseukrainskyi Aktsionernyi Bank v Maksimov [2014] EWHC 3771 (Comm).

12–85 *[Add to note 202]*

The case was referred to and followed by Ryan J in *Reynolds v McDermott* [2014] IEHC 219. The Judge was satisfied beyond reasonable doubt that service had been effected according to the rules.

12–86 *[Add to note 205]*

Wookey v Wookey was cited in *Re B (A Child)* [2014] EWCA Civ 843, where an appeal was allowed on the basis that a penal notice should not have been attached to an order relating to someone under the age of 17, who could not be committed for contempt: *per* Sir James Munby P, at [36].

12–87 *[Add to note 207]*

The *CopyDirect* service has become more commonly used in England and Wales, as in Scotland, and is mentioned, for example, in the latest *Practice Direction: Committal for Contempt — Open Court* (26 March 2015) para 15. However, see also *P (A Child)* [2013] EWHC 4048 (Fam) on the limitations of Copy Direct and the fact that the system does not cater to all media organisations (discussed at 8–96 above).

II. THE MENTAL ELEMENT FOR CIVIL CONTEMPT

B. An apparent policy shift: the doubtful case of *Irtelli v Squatriti*

12–96A *[Add new paragraph]*

These authorities were reviewed in *Masri v Consolidated Contractors Intl Co SAL* [2011] EWHC 1024. Like Neuberger J. in *Bird v Hadkinson* and Jacob J. in *Adam Phones Ltd v Goldschmidt,* Christopher Clarke J. too felt bound not to follow *Irtelli* having regard to *Pioneer Concrete*. He commented at [155]:

> "In my judgment the power of the court to ensure obedience to its orders for the benefit of those in whose favour they are made would be inappropriately curtailed if, in addition to having to show that a defendant had breached the order, it was also necessary to establish, and to the criminal standard, that he had done so in the belief that what he did was a breach of the order — particularly when a belief that it was not a breach may have rested on the slenderest of foundations or on convenient advice which was plainly wrong."

The approach of Christopher Clarke J. was subsequently applied by Eder J. in *Templeton Insurance Ltd v Motorcare Warranties Ltd* [2012] EWHC 795 (Comm); by Teare J. in *JSC BTA Bank v Ablyazov* [2012] EWHC 237

(Comm); by Males J. in *Westminster City Council v Addbins Ltd* [2012] EWHC 3716 (QB); [2013] J.P.L 654; and by Tugendhat J. in *McCann v Bennett* [2013] EWHC 283 (QB), particularly in the context of the state of mind relevant to an alleged breach of undertaking. It was also applied in Northern Ireland by McCloskey J. in *Quinn Finance v Lyndhurst Development Trading SA* [2013] NICh 2. See also *Dar Al Arkan Real Estate Development Co v Refai* [2014] EWCA Civ 715, [2015] 1 WLR 135, at [33]; *Westwood v Knight* [2012] EWPCC 14, at [38] (Judge Birss QC).

D. The absence of "wilfully"

[Add new paragraph] **12–99A**

The replacement of RSC Ord.45 r.5 by CPR Pt 81 has not changed the substantive law of contempt, as PD 81 para.5.7 expressly makes clear. It is still incumbent upon an applicant seeking to begin proceedings for contempt to consider whether the incident complained of amounts to contempt and whether such proceedings would further the overriding objective.

III. WHO CAN BE LIABLE FOR CIVIL CONTEMPT?

A. Vicarious liability for civil contempt

[Add to end of paragraph] **12–103**

See now CPR PD 25A.

B. Corporations

[Add to note 247] **12–104**

And see *Back Office Ltd v Percival* [2013] EWHC 3776, at [18] and [39].

[Add to note 248] **12–104**

See also *Local Authority v HP and M* [2009] EWCA Civ 143; [2010] 1 W.L.R. 419; [2009] 2 F.L.R. 66; [2009] 2 F.C.R. 105; [2009] Fam. Law 387; (2009) 106(11) L.S.G. 19; (2009) 153(9) S.J.L.B. 28; *The Times*, March 19, 2009.

[Add to note 253] **12–106**

See also *Back Office Ltd v Percival and ors* [2013] EWHC 1385 (QB) at [66]–[70], Slade J.

12–106 *[Add to note 256]*

And see *White v Lynch* [2011] EWHC 1664 (QB), at [79], Edwards-Stuart J.

12–106A *[Add new paragraph]*

In *Back Office Limited v Percival* [2013] EWHC 1385 (QB) at [66]–[70], Slade J. decided, citing para.12–106 of the main text, that it was not a defence for a corporation merely to show that it had not authorised the alleged acts contempt or indeed that it had expressly forbidden them and taken reasonable steps to prevent them. Corporate liability could be established on the basis that the relevant employee or agent was acting in the course of his employment, even in dereliction of duty.

D. Directors

12–113A *[Add new paragraph]*

RSC Ord.45 r.5 formerly provided for enforcement of orders against corporations either by an order of committal against their directors or by a writ of sequestration against the property of a director or other officer of the corporate body. The equivalent provisions are now to be found in CPR Pt 81. CPR r.81.4(3) permits a committal order to be made against "any director or other officer" of a company. CPR r.81.20(3) provides that a writ of sequestration may "in addition be issued against the property of any director or other officer of that company or corporation".

12–115 *[Add to note 269]*

In *City of Westminster v Addbins Ltd* [2012] EWHC 3716 (QB), a director was held liable for breaches by his company even though he was not a party and had not been personally served with the order. The judge found that he had known of it, and indeed had given instructions not to oppose it. He was not prejudiced by the failure to serve him and, in the circumstances, permission was retrospectively given to dispense with service.

12–115A *[Add new paragraph]*

This approach was taken by Eder J. in *Templeton Insurance Ltd v Motorcare Warranties Ltd and others* [2012] EWHC 795 (Comm), and upheld by the Court of Appeal in *Templeton Insurance Ltd v Thomas* [2013] EWCA Civ 35. Citing the reasoning of Woolf L.J. in *Tuvalu,* the Court of Appeal took the view that liability of a director did not arise only where there had been active participation in the breach of an order, but also where there had been a failure to supervise or investigate, or wilful blindness, on the part of that director. (See also the summary of the relevant principles given by Hamblen J in *Ipartner Pte Shipping Ltd v Panacore Resources DMCC* [2014] EWHC 3608 (Comm), at [37].)

[Add new paragraph] 12–115B

In *Templeton*, liability for contempt was established against not only a director, but also a non-party who (together with his wife) owned the entire issued share capital in the company. The breach of the injunction took place in circumstances where the relevant act could only have taken place with his wilful forbearance. The rationale was summarised by Lord Hope in *Attorney General v Punch Ltd* [2002] UKHL 50; [2003] 1 A.C. 1046; [2003] 2 W.L.R. 49; [2003] 1 All E.R. 289; [2003] E.M.L.R. 7; [2003] H.R.L.R. 14; *The Times*, December 13, 2002; *Independent*, December 17, 2002; at [87]:

> "The power to commit for contempt ensures that acts and words tending to obstruct the administration of justice are prohibited. So a stranger is liable for contempt if his act constitutes a wilful interference with the administration of justice by the court in the proceedings in which the order was made. It has also to be shown there was an intention on his part to interfere with or impede the administration of justice. This is an essential ingredient, and it has to be established to the criminal standard of proof. But the intent need not be stated expressly or admitted by the defendant. As is the case where the question of intention, or mens rea, arises in criminal cases, it can be inferred from all the circumstances including the forseeability of the consequences of the defendant's conduct: *Attorney General v Newspaper Publishing plc* [1988] Ch 333, 374–375, per Sir John Donaldson MR."

The decision of the Court of Appeal in *Tuvalu* was also cited in *Back Office Limited v Percival and others* [2013] EWHC 1385 (QB), where Slade J. distinguished between the criteria necessary to establish liability for contempt by a company and those necessary in respect of a director. In order to establish liability on the part of a director, it was necessary to show that the director had either authorised the acts of contempt or could reasonably have foreseen the possibility of such acts and yet failed to take reasonable steps to prevent them. On the facts of *Back Office*, this distinction was sufficient for the applications against the directors to fail, but for those against the company to succeed.

[Add new paragraph] 12–115C

The approach in *Tuvalu* does not mean that the breach of an undertaking by a company automatically discloses a case to answer against all the directors. In *Sectorguard Plc v Dienne Plc* [2009] EWHC 2693 (Ch), Briggs J. held that the effect of the Court of Appeal's decision had been that an applicant for committal against a director of a company must show responsibility on the part of the director, either on the grounds of aiding and abetting or wilful failure to take reasonable steps to ensure that the order is obeyed. This was cited and applied in *Westminster City Council v Addbins Ltd* [2012] EWHC 3716 (QB); [2013] J.P.L 654 (Males J.). The director was held in contempt in circumstances where he knew that he acted or failed to act in a manner which meant that the order for the removal of advertisements could not be complied with. This was sufficient even though the director did not positively intend to breach the order: he knew that it was the probable or inevitable consequence of his failure to ensure a more determined effort to comply.

12–116 *[Add to end of paragraph]*

The passage in the main text was cited by Beatson LJ as accurately summarising the effect of the relevant rules: *Dar Al Arkan v Al Refai* [2014] EWCA Civ 715, [2015] 1 WLR 135, at [32].

12–118A *[Add new paragraph]*

The former RSC Ord.45 r.5 provided that enforcement could be pursued by "one or more" methods, including a writ of sequestration against the property of a director or an order for committal against a company's officer. This is replicated by the provisions of CPR Pt 81, where r.81.20(3) provides that a writ of sequestration may be pursued against the company and *in addition* against the property of any director.

12–119A *[Add new paragraph]*

In *Dar Al Arkan v Al Refai* [2014] EWCA Civ 715, [2015] 1 WLR 135, it was held that a judge had been entitled to permit service of committal proceedings out of the jurisdiction against a company director under CPR 6.36 and PD 6B, para 3.1(3), even though he was neither resident nor domiciled within the jurisdiction. Reliance had been placed *inter alia* on some words of Lord Diplock in *Air India v Wiggins* [1980] 1 WLR 815, 819, to the effect that any legislative provisions purporting to confer extra-territorial jurisdiction in a criminal or quasi-criminal context had to be "clear and specific". But the Court of Appeal held that CPR 81.3 and 81.4(1) and (3) are not to be regarded as criminal provisions: they represent "a vehicle and a mechanism for the court's disciplinary powers over corporate contemnors which are undoubtedly subject to its jurisdiction", *per* Beatson LJ at [32]. If the court were to take any other approach, its powers of enforcement in relation to directors would be rendered increasingly ineffective in modern international commercial litigation. (See also the discussion of extra-territorial jurisdiction at 3–233 *et seq* above.)

IV. BREACHES OF COURT ORDERS GENERALLY

A. Disobedience to a judgment or order requiring a positive act

1. *Where time for compliance is specified in the order*

12–128 *[Add to note 284]*

See now CPR r.81.4(3).

[Add to note 288] **12–128**

See now CPR r.81.2(3).

[Add to note 290] **12–128**

Cf *Kenneth Smith v Scottish Ministers* [2015] ScotCS CSOH 15.

2. *Where no time is specified in the order*

[Add to note 297] **12–131**

See also the discussion in *Jones, Re* [2013] EWHC 2579 (Fam) at [18]–[24].

[Add to note 304] **12–133**

The new CPR Pt 81 does not expressly contemplate the possibility that an order will be made without specifying a time for compliance.

3. *Other restrictions on committal*

[Add to notes 305–307] **12–134**

See now CPR r.81.4(5). An order for the delivery of goods can still be enforced by an application for writ of sequestration although no longer under CPR Sch 1, Ord 45.4, which is not included in the Schedule (with effect from April 2014). It is now necessary to address the provisions of CPR 81.20, which govern the procedure relating to sequestration.

4. *Disobedience to a judgment or order to give possession of land within a specified time*

[Add to end of paragraph and to notes 309–314] **12–136**

Unlike the changes to the rules for the enforcement of other court orders, the provisions relevant to giving possession of land remain in force, subject only to adjusting to the procedure now prescribed in CPR Pt 81.

5. *Disobedience to a judgment or order for delivery of goods within a specified time*

[Add to notes 316–319] **12–138**

RSC Ord 45 r.4 is no longer in effect. The current provisions corresponding to the former RSC Ord 45 rr.5 and 6 can be found at CPR 81.4.

B. Disobedience to a judgment or order to abstain from doing any act

12–139 *[Add to note 320]*

See now CPR r.81.2 which covers committal for breach of a judgment or order and CPR r.81.7 which addresses writs of sequestration.

12–141 *[Add to end of paragraph]*

CPR rr.81.4 and 81.20 state, respectively, that an application for committal or for a writ of sequestration may be made in respect of positive and negative orders.

C. Cases in which a judgment or order has been wrongly obtained

12–142 *[Add to note 326]*

Where an order has become final, principles of finality and legal certainty require that it should continue to be obeyed even in circumstances where a later decision has given the law a different interpretation such that an order would no longer be made in similar terms. That would not of itself justify re-opening or overturning such an order: see the decision of the Court of Appeal in *SOCA v O'Docherty* [2013] EWCA Civ 518, addressing the consequences for pre-existing orders in the light of the Supreme Court's (majority) decision in *Serious Organised Crime Agency v Perry (Nos 1&2)* [2012] UKSC 35; [2013] 1 AC 182. It has been reaffirmed (by a majority) in the Supreme Court of New Zealand that it will not be permitted on a contempt application to mount a "collateral challenge" to the original order alleged to have been breached. Where a member of the public was concerned that his freedom of expression was restricted by an order suppressing comment, and effective generally (i.e. *contra mundum*), his proper course was to apply to the court for a variation or rescission of that order; but it should be obeyed until set aside: *Siemer v Solicitor-General* [2014] 2 LRC 186. Elias CJ dissented in this respect: see at [23] and [26]–[27]. It was noted at [216] and [221] that the High Court of Australia had also confirmed that the ban on collateral challenges to superior court orders remained in effect: *Re Macks, ex p Saint* (2000) 204 CLR 158. On the other hand, the Supreme Court in Canada had recognised some limited exceptions to the principle: *Att-Gen of Quebec v Laroche* [2002] 3 SCR 708.

V. FREEZING AND SEARCH AND SEIZURE ORDERS

A. Freezing orders

12–147 *[Add to note 332]*

See 12–195A below. See also, generally, S Gee QC, *Commercial Injunctions*, 6th edn (due December 2015).

[Add to end of paragraph] **12–147**

In recent years, the law and procedure of contempt have been invoked increasingly in international commercial litigation, and especially in the context of fraud allegations. Sometimes, indeed, it would seem that the sanctions available in that jurisdiction have proved to be a significant attraction from a tactical point of view. Such litigation often begins with an application for a world-wide freezing injunction, including ancillary orders relating to the prompt disclosure of documents and assets. Where such an order is not fully complied with, there will arise an early opportunity to apply for committal against relevant individuals and to obtain corresponding advantages such as cross-examination or alternatively, where a respondent ignores the application, or fails to attend, it may be possible to accelerate the litigation by taking such steps as limiting the funds available for legal expenses, debarring the relevant defendant(s) from defending, or even obtaining summary judgment. Moreover, as was illustrated in the case of *Dar Al Arkan v Al Refai* [2014] EWCA Civ 715, [2015] 1 WLR 135, the sanctions available against directors under CPR 81, in respect of corporate contemnors, may legitimately be pursued against even those who are non-parties resident abroad. Pressures of this kind can be useful not only in speeding up the litigation process itself but also in encouraging negotiated settlement.

[Add to note 348] **12–157**

See now the example of a freezing injunction annexed to CPR PD 25A (updated in March 2014).

[Add to note 349] **12–157**

The wording in square brackets does not appear in the standard form, which otherwise remains the same in the current version (updated in March 2014). The decision of the Court of Appeal in *Kythreotis* is reported at [2011] 1 WLR 888.

[Add to note 350] **12–158**

See now the example of a freezing injunction annexed to CPR PD 25A. The wording cited remains the same in the version updated in March 2014.

[Add to note 351] **12–159**

See now *Archbold 2015*, paras 2–33–2–34.

[Add to note 355] **12–162**

See now *Civil Procedure 2015*, para.2A–162 and the example of a freezing injunction annexed to CPR Practice Direction 25A.

12–170A *[Add new paragraph]*

The fact that a director of a company which is in contempt may be resident abroad will not necessarily shield him from the disciplinary jurisdiction now embodied in CPR 81.3 and 81.4. In *Dar Al Arkan v Al Refai* [2014] EWCA Civ 715, [2015] 1 WLR 135, it was held that a judge had been entitled to permit service of committal proceedings out of the jurisdiction against a company director under CPR 6.36 and PD 6B, para 3.1(3), even though he was neither resident nor domiciled within the jurisdiction. The Court of Appeal held that CPR 81.3 and 81.4(1) and (3) are not to be regarded as criminal provisions: they represent "a vehicle and a mechanism for the court's disciplinary powers over corporate contemnors which are undoubtedly subject to its jurisdiction", *per* Beatson LJ at [32]. If the court were to take any other approach, its powers of enforcement in relation to directors would be rendered increasingly ineffective in modern international commercial litigation. (See also the discussion of extra-territorial jurisdiction at 3–233 *et seq* above.)

Freezing orders in aid of foreign proceedings

12–171 *[Add to note 368]*

See also *Blue Holdings v USA* [2014] EWCA Civ 11291, [2015] 1 WLR 1917, at [56] *et seq.*

B. Search and seizure orders

12–181 *[Add to note 385]*

Since October 1, 2012, RSC Ord.45 r.7 has been replaced by the provisions of the new CPR Pt 81. The requirement formerly set out at RSC Ord.45 r.7(4) for the order to be endorsed with a penal notice is now set out at CPR r.81.9 (application for committal) and CPR r.81.25 (application for writ of sequestration).

12–181 *[Add to note 386]*

See now CPR 81.8.

12–181 *[Add to note 387]*

See now CPR r.81.8 (application for committal) and CPR r.81.24 (application for writ of sequestration) which set out the circumstances in which a court may now dispense with service of a copy of an order.

[Add to note 396] **12–184**

The wording quoted remains the same in the current standard form attached to CPR PD 25A.

VI. BREACHES OF UNDERTAKINGS

A. Undertakings are equivalent to injunctions

1. *The general principle*

[Add to note 401] **12–186**

See now CPR r.81.9(2). A penal notice is not necessary in the case of an undertaking. In *McCann v Bennett* [2012] EWHC 2876 (Tugendhat J.) the court re-emphasised the principle that an undertaking was as binding and effective as an order of the court. The respondent was required to obey the undertakings until such time as they were actually varied or set aside, and was punished by committal for his failures to comply.

3. *Release from or variation of the terms of an undertaking*

[Add to note 414] **12–192**

See now CPR r.81.9(2).

4. *Breaches of undertakings: similar safeguards*

[Add to note 423] **12–195**

As to the need for a penal notice, see now CPR r.81.9(2).

[Add new paragraph] **12–195A**

The new CPR Pt 81, which sets out the procedure in respect of applications for committal, introduces some important provisions concerning the enforcement of undertakings to the court. CPR r.81.7 (in respect of an application for committal) and CPR r.81.23 (in respect of an application for a writ of sequestration) set out the formalities required for serving any undertaking on the person who has given it. PD 81 para.2.2 now provides that the court may decline to accept an undertaking or deal with any disobedience in respect of an undertaking by way of contempt of court proceedings unless the person giving the undertaking has made a signed statement to the effect that he or she understands the terms of the undertaking and the consequences of failure to comply with it. Failing to incorporate an undertaking in an associated order may hinder an applicant in meeting the necessary evidential requirements to show that a breach has been strictly proved: see *Pretorian v Vasile* [2013] All E.R. (D) 84 (Feb), Judge Seymour QC.

12–196 *[Add to note 425]*

See also *White v Lynch* [2011] EWHC 1664 (QB) and *Palmier Plc (In Liquidation): Sandhu v Kaur* [2012] EWHC 2679 in which close attention was paid to the wording of the obligations undertaken.

12–197A *[Add new paragraph]*

Note however that that under CPR rr.81.9(2) and 81.25(2) an undertaking which is contained in a judgment or order may be enforced by an application for committal or writ of sequestration notwithstanding that the judgment or order does not contain a penal notice.

5. *Undertakings given on behalf of persons without their knowledge*

12–203 *[Add to notes 435 and 436]*

See now CPR rr.81.20(3) and 81.4(3) respectively which replace the previous provisions of RSC Ord.45 r.5.

12–204A *[Add new paragraph]*

It is worth noting that CPR rr.81.4(4) and 81.20(4) both expressly state that the procedure in respect of committal and writs of sequestration applies to undertakings given by a party as they apply to judgments or orders.

B. The implied undertaking given upon disclosure of documents

1. *Introduction*

12–206 *[Add to end of paragraph]*

This contrasts with the position where a document which provides the basis for a libel claim is disclosed under compulsion, when the court may decline to permit its use in subsequent libel proceedings: see *McBride v Body Shop International Plc* [2007] EWHC 1658 (QB) and *White v Southampton University Hospitals NHS Trust* [2011] EWHC 825 (QB), also referred to at paragraph 12–239A below.

2. *The policy behind the implied undertaking*

12–209 *[Add to note 448]*

See too *Tchenguiz v SFO* [2014] EWCA Civ 1409, at [62]; *Alphasteel Ltd v Shirkhani* [2013] EWCA Civ 1272, at [13] and [17] *et seq.*

12–209 *[Add to note 449]*

And see *Tchenguiz v SFO* [2014] EWCA Civ 1409, at [61].

3. *The introduction of a specific rule*

[Add to note 464] 12–225

There continue to be regular reminders of the importance to be attached to open justice, both in relation to the Family Court and more generally. See e.g. at 7–4A and 7–22 *et seq* above.

At sub para 4, the reference to sub para ii) should be (2). 12–228

[Add to note 472] 12–229

And see *Nestec SA v Dualit Ltd* [2013] EWHC 2737 (Pat), where third parties were provided with copies of expert reports from an earlier trial.

[Add to note 473] 12–229

For subsequent case law on CPR 5.4C, see *G&G v Wikimedia Foundation Inc* [2009] EWHC 3148 (QB); *Pfizer Health Ab v Schwarz Pharma Ag* [2010] EWHC 3236 (Pat); *Various Claimants v News Group Newspapers* [2012] EWHC 397 (Ch).

[Add new paragraph] 12–230A

Although not directly applicable to the implied undertaking under CPR r.31.22, the clear tendency of the courts to make accessible documents deployed in court for the purposes of litigation, civil or criminal was recently demonstrated in the decision of the Court of Appeal in *R. (on the application of Guardian News and Media Ltd) v City of Westminster Magistrates' Court* [2012] EWCA Civ 420; [2013] Q.B. 618; [2012] 3 W.L.R. 1343; [2012] C.P. Rep. 30; [2012] E.M.L.R. 22. Toulson L.J., giving the leading judgment of the court, stressed that there was an increasing and expeditious practice of introducing documents without reading them fully in open court. In such circumstances, access to these documents for a serious journalistic purpose, namely stimulating informed debate about the way in which the justice system worked, was something which the court should assist rather than impede. In a case where documents had been placed before a judge and referred to in the course of proceedings, the default position should be that access should be permitted on the open justice principle, particularly when there was a serious journalistic purpose in seeking such information. It was not necessary for the court to declare that a document should be treated as having been read in open court.

5. *Does CPR r.31.22 inhibit the launch of libel proceedings?*

[Add to note 480] 12–234

See now *Civil Procedure 2015* Vol 1 31.22.1

12–235 *[Update to note 481]*

See now Hollander, *Documentary Evidence* 12th edn (2015) at para 27.46 and fn 147 and Matthews and Malek, *Disclosure* 4th edn (2012) at para 19.28 and fn 104. The decision in *Colbeck v Ferguson*, to which they both refer, was that of Sir Ian Kennedy dated 24 January 2002. See also http://www.5rb.com/case/colbeck-v-ferguson-another/ – where *Colbeck v Ferguson* is summarised. Sir Ian Kennedy there followed *Mahon v Rahn*.

12–239A *[Add new paragraph]*

In *McBride v Body Shop International Plc* [2007] EWHC 1658 (QB), it was emphasised that the purpose of the obligation of confidence in respect of documents disclosed by compulsion of law had always been to encourage full and frank disclosure. The courts recognised that the threat of being sued over a defamatory document would be a powerful disincentive to disclosure, and this was particularly the case where the document would be unlikely to see the light of day other than through the disclosure. Accordingly, where the publication in question was limited and had been obtained only through compulsory disclosure, the balance of justice required that the court make an order pursuant to CPR r.31.22 prohibiting the use of that document to start libel proceedings. See also *White v Southampton University Hospitals NHS Trust* [2011] EWHC 825 (QB) where the court declined to allow libel proceedings to be commenced based on compulsory disclosure of documents in employment tribunal proceedings.

6. *When will an order be made for "restricting or prohibiting the use of a document"?*

12–242A *[Add new paragraph]*

This result contrasts with the decision of Coulson J. in *Shlaimoun v Mining Technologies International Inc* [2011] EWHC 3278 (QB). In *Schlaimoun*, Coulson J. held that documents disclosed pursuant to a Norwich Pharmacal/Bankers Trust application were "disclosed" for the purposes of CPR r.31.2 and were therefore subject to the restrictions imposed by CPR r.31.22. However, since it was clearly envisaged on a Norwich Pharmacal/Bankers Trust application that the documents were sought for the purpose of launching or using in separate proceedings, the court was clearly giving consent to the use of those documents for the purposes for which the order was made. Consequently the use in associated foreign proceedings of documents disclosed in a Norwich Pharmacal/Bankers Trust application was not a breach of the collateral undertaking in CPR r.31.22 as the court had impliedly given permission for their use pursuant to CPR r.31.22(1)(b).

12–243 *[Add to note 490]*

See too *Tchenguiz v SFO* [2014] EWCA Civ 1409, at [62]; *Alphasteel Ltd v Shirkhani* [2013] EWCA Civ 1272, at [13] and [17] *et seq.*

C. Breach of undertakings given by strangers

[Add to end of paragraph] **12–248**

See now CPR r.81.9.

D. Undertakings by solicitors

[Add new paragraph] **12–253A**

In *Balli, Re* [2011] EWHC 1736, the court stressed that the importance of solicitors complying with the rule of law and the professional codes of conduct was a central feature of the administration of justice. This reflects the public policy rationale behind s.14 of the Legal Services Act which provides that practising as a solicitor when not authorised to do so is both a criminal offence and also separately a contempt of court.

[Add new paragraph] **12–263A**

The court's disciplinary jurisdiction over solicitors has recently been increased by a number of statutory measures. Section 14(4) of the Legal Services Act provides that practising as a solicitor when not authorised to do so is a contempt of court in addition to constituting a criminal offence. In *Balli, Re* [2011] EWHC 1736, a solicitor who had committed multiple offences of practising as a solicitor when he was not entitled to do so, was sentenced to six months' imprisonment for contempt of court. Similarly, s.149 of the Legal Services Act 2007 provides that a court may punish a solicitor as if he was in contempt, where it is satisfied that he has failed to comply, without reasonable excuse, with his obligations to provide information upon request to the Legal Services Ombudsman. In *Deputy Chief Legal Ombudsman v Young* [2011] EWHC 2923 (Admin); [2012] 1 W.L.R. 3227, Lindblom J. stated that for offences under this provision, comparisons with sanctions for civil contempt were not a helpful yardstick in sentencing, and that a £5,000 fine was an appropriate sanction to apply to a solicitor who had failed to comply with a disclosure request from the Ombudsman.

CHAPTER 13

JURISDICTION

I. GENERAL PRINCIPLES

D. Distinctions in jurisdiction between superior and inferior courts

13–7 *[Add to note 14]*

See additionally the scope of the amended definition of a county court judge in the County Courts Act 1984 s.5, following the enactment of Crime and Courts Act 2013, Sch.9.

II. SUPERIOR COURTS OF RECORD

B. The Supreme Court

13–12 *[Add to end of paragraph]*

According to Section 3 of UKSC Practice Direction 1 (r. 1.3.4), a contested application alleging contempt of the Supreme Court must be referred to a panel of three Supreme Court Justices and an oral hearing must be held.

C. Court of Appeal

13–13 *[Add to end of paragraph and Note 33]*

The rules previously contained in RSC Ord.52 and CCR Ord.29 have been replaced by the somewhat modified provisions of CPR Pt 81. These were inserted into the CPR by the Civil Procedure (Amendment No.2) Rules 2012 (SI 2012/2208) and came into force on October 1, 2012. There is no equivalent statement in CPR Pt 81 to that found in the former RSC Ord.52.1, to the effect (acknowledged by CPR r.81.2) that the substantive legal basis of the jurisdiction to punish contempt is derived from the common law and legislation and not from rules of court. It remains the position that the Court of Appeal and the High Court have the power to punish for contempt of court, including by way of committal. The power of the Court of Appeal to punish for contempt, specifically, is recognised in the general terms of CPR r.81.2(3).

An application for permission to commit for contempt in connection with proceedings before the Court of Appeal should be made to a Divisional Court of the Queen's Bench Division: see CPR r.81.13(1)(c).

[Add to end of paragraph] **13–14**

An application for permission to commit for contempt in connection with proceedings in the Court of Appeal (Criminal Division) should be made to a Divisional Court of the Queen's Bench Division: CPR r.81.13(1)(c).

[Add to end of paragraph] **13–15**

The Court of Appeal's jurisdiction in this regard was reaffirmed in *JSC BTA Bank v Solodchenko* [2012] 1 W.L.R. 350, where Jackson LJ emphasised, at [60] *et seq*, that "it would be wasteful of costs and serve no useful purpose" for the Court of Appeal to remit the issue of sentencing to the court below in circumstances where the first instance judge had been misled as to the material facts. The Court of Appeal was seized of the matter and in possession of all the relevant information. The proper course was for the Court of Appeal to determine the appropriate sentence in the light of the true facts as they had subsequently emerged.

E. High Court

[Replace note 42] **13–17**

Where contempt of court is committed in the form of interference with the due administration of justice in connection with any proceedings in the High Court (other than proceedings in a Divisional Court), an application for permission to commit must be made to a single judge of the Division of the High Court in which the proceedings were commenced or to which they have subsequently been transferred: see CPR r.81.13(1)(a).

[Replace note 43] **13–17**

Where contempt of court is committed in connection with any proceedings in the Divisional Court, an application for permission to commit must be made to a single judge of the Queen's Bench Division: see CPR r.81.13(1)(b).

[Add to note 44] **13–18**

Under CPR r.81.13(2), an application for permission to commit for contempt otherwise than in connection with proceedings may only be made to the Administrative Court. It should be noted that contempt by "scandalising" has now been abolished by s.33 of the Crime and Courts Act 2013, which came into effect from 25 June 2013: see 5–204 *et seq* above.

13–19 *[Add at end of first paragraph]*

The jurisdiction of the High Court in this regard is recognised in the general terms of CPR r.81.2(3). It should be noted that contempt by "scandalising" has now been abolished by s.33 of the Crime and Courts Act 2013, which came into effect from 25 June 2013: see 5–204 *et seq* above.

H. The jurisdiction of the Divisional Court over contempt of the Crown Court

13–24 *[Add at end of paragraph and to note 52]*

See now CPR rr.81.12(1) and 81.13(1)(e).

13–25 *[Add at end of paragraph]*

The issue of the concurrent jurisdiction between the High Court and the Crown Court needs now to be assessed by reference to the provisions contained in CPR Pt 81 (see the similar wording adopted in CPR rr.81.12(1) and 81.13(1)(e)).

The wording of RSC Ord.52 r.1(2)

13–26 *[Add at end of paragraph]*

The implication that the Divisional Court has power to deal with contempt of the Crown Court is sustained by the similar terms of the newly implemented CPR Pt 81. The combined effect of CPR rr.81.12(1) and 81.13(1)(e) is that a committal application in relation to interference with the due of administration of justice in connection with criminal proceedings may be made *only* to a Divisional Court of the Queen's Bench Division *except* where the contempt is committed in the face of the court or consists of disobedience to an order of the court or a breach of an undertaking to the court.

13–28 *[Add to end of paragraph]*

There is a similar distinction between the wording of CPR rr.81.12 and 81.13 and that appearing in s.12 of the Contempt of Court Act 1981. The same phrase "in the face of the court" which was used by RSC Ord.52 r.1, is now also used to define the exception contemplated by CPR r.81.12(1).

13–29 *[Add to end of paragraph]*

See now the equivalent references to "criminal proceedings" in CPR rr.81.12(1)(e) and 81.13(1)(e).

[Add to note 80] **13–35**

See now Pt 48 of the Criminal Procedure Rules 2015 (SI 2015/1490).

[Add to end of paragraph and replace note 79] **13–35**

See now the Criminal Procedure Rules 2015 (SI 2015/1490) in force with effect from 5 October 2015.

[Add new paragraph] **13–35A**

In *R v O'Brien* [2014] UKSC 23, [2014] AC 1246, the question arose whether a person who has been extradited for trial on a criminal charge could be punished for disobedience of a court order prior to his extradition even though it had not been the basis for his extradition. The appellant had been committed to prison for 15 months for contempt of court because he had disobeyed a restraint order under s.41 of the proceeds of Crime Act 2002. This was upheld by the Court of Appeal and by the Supreme Court. His argument was based on the speciality provisions of Part 3 of the Extradition Act 2003. It was held that s.151A did not preclude his being dealt with for civil contempt, since it applied only to criminal offences. Lord Toulson described it as "fallacious" to argue that disobedience to a court order amounts to a crime just because it was made by a criminal court. It depends on the nature of the conduct rather than upon the nature of the court. "To burst into a court room and disrupt a civil trial would be a criminal contempt just as much as if the court had been conducting a criminal trial. Conversely, disobedience to a procedural order of a court is not of itself a crime, just because the order was made in the course of criminal proceedings".

I. The Crown Court's own jurisdiction

[Add note 82A to end of paragraph] **13–36**

Similarly, the Crown Court has an inherent power to punish disobedience of an order made under the Terrorism Act 2000 and the Proceeds of Crime Act 2002 as a contempt of court: see Criminal Procedure Rules 2015 (SI 2015/1490) r.47.13 and 47.22 and *R v O Brien* [2014] UKSC 23; [2014] A.C. 1246, at [36].

2. *The Crown Court's power of committal to be sparingly used*

[Add new paragraph] **13–44A**

Similarly, in *Attorney General v Dallas* [2012] EWHC 156 (Admin); [2012] 1 W.L.R. 991, 994, Lord Judge C.J. emphasised, at [7], that in the context of alleged contempt of court by or affecting a juror or jury in the Crown Court "unless it is appropriate for the Crown Court to deal immediately with the contempt of its own motion (which in the light of many judicial warnings about the dangers inherent in a rushed process would be very exceptional), such cases of contempt should continue to be left to proceedings by the Attorney General ..."

It is clear that such an application would have to be made under the procedure now provided for by CPR r.81.13.

J. Inferior tribunals: the Divisional Court's role

13–45 *[Add to end of paragraph]*

An application for permission to commit for contempt in connection with proceedings in an inferior court may only be made to a single judge of the Queen's Bench Division: CPR Part 81.13(1)(d).

L. *Att Gen v BBC*

The "non-tests"

13–53 *[Add to note 119]*

This state of affairs is recognised in the terms of CPR Pt. r.81.2.

M. Employment Tribunals

13–66 *[Add to note 138]*

See now the Employment Tribunals (Constitution and Rules of Procedure) Regulations 2013 (SI 2013/1237).

13–67 *[Add to end of paragraph]*

Regulation 80 of the Employment Tribunals (Constitution and Rules of Procedure) Regulations 2013 (SI 2013/1237) gives the Tribunal the power to make a wasted costs order against a representative for any "improper, unreasonable or negligent" act or omission on his or her part.

P. Jurisdiction conferred on the Queen's Bench Division by statute

13–79 *[Add to note 159]*

The powers to commit for contempt formerly contained in the Army Act 1955 s.101, Air Force Act 1955 s.101 and Naval Discipline Act 1957 s.65 are now set out in the Armed Forces Act 2006, s.311. This specifies that the qualifying service court may certify any offence which would constitute a contempt of court to any court of law in the relevant part of the United

Kingdom having the power to commit for contempt (or to the High Court in England and Wales if the offence took place outside of the United Kingdom).

The powers formerly conferred on the Legal Services Ombudsman by the Courts and Legal Services Act 1990 have been replaced by the Legal Services Act 2007 s.149, which allows the ombudsman to certify a party's failure to provide information and documents. S 147 (1) of the 2007 Act provides that '[a]n ombudsman may, by notice, require a party to a complaint under the ombudsman scheme — (a) to produce documents, or documents of a description, specified in the notice, or (b)to provide information, or information of a description, specified in the notice.' Where the party to fails to do so, s 149 allows the ombudsman to 'certify the defaulter's failure to comply with the requirement to the court' (s 149 (2). S 149 (3) permits the court to look into the matter where such a failure has been certified under 149 (2). S 149 (4) provides that '[i]f the court is satisfied that the defaulter has failed without reasonable excuse to comply with the requirement, it may deal with—(a)the defaulter, and(b)in the case of a body, any manager of the body, as if that person were in contempt'.

Section 88 of the Charities Act 1993 has now been superseded by the similar provisions of s.336 of the Charities Act 2011, under which disobedience of an order of the Charity Commission may, on the application of the Commission to the High Court, be dealt with as for disobedience to an order of the High Court. An order on an application under s.336 may be made only by a single judge of the Chancery Division: see CPR Part 81.15(3).

[Add to note 160] **13–79**

See now CPR r.81.15.

III. OTHER COURTS OF RECORD

B. County Courts

1. *Introduction*

[Add to end of paragraph] **13–85**

Where contempt of court in connection with county court proceedings consists neither in contempt in the face of the court nor disobedience of a court order, it is punishable only by an application for permission to commit made to a single judge of the High Court in accordance with the provisions of CPR Part 81.13(d). See generally ss.3 and 8 of CPR Part 81.

[Add to end of paragraph] **13–86**

Brighton & Hove Bus & Coach Co Ltd v Brooks [2011] EWHC 810 (Admin) was not followed by the Court of Appeal in *Tariq Ali v Kayne* [2011] EWCA

Civ 1582; [2012] 1 W.L.R. 1868, where it was held that a single judge of the Queen's Bench Division had jurisdiction, under RSC Ord.52 r.1, to make an order for committal in respect of contempt of court committed in connection with any proceedings commenced in the county court, but subsequently transferred to the High Court, even where the contempt was committed prior to the transfer. The correct approach has since been restated formally in the revised wording of CPR Pt 81. CPR r.81.13(a) provides that where contempt is committed in connection with proceedings in the High Court, an application for permission may be made only to a single judge of "the Division of the High Court in which the proceedings were commenced *or to which they have subsequently been transferred.*" CPR r.81.13(d) provides that where contempt is committed in connection with proceedings before an inferior court, an application for permission may be made only to a single judge of the Queen's Bench Division. Similarly, CPR r.81.18(3) states that a committal application in relation to a false statement of truth or disclosure statement in connection with proceedings in the county court may only be made by the Attorney General or with the permission of a single judge of the Queen's Bench Division.

13–86A *[Add new paragraph]*

It is necessary also to consider the terms of CPR r.81.18, which is concerned with the contempt jurisdiction in relation to false statements of truth and to false disclosure statements. It is relevant both to High Court and county court proceedings. So far as the former are concerned, it is provided that an application may only be made by the Attorney General or with the permission of the court dealing with the relevant proceedings. As to the latter, on the other hand, a county court judge may *not* give permission — only a single judge of the High Court may do so. There is also express reference in r.81.18(5) to the court's power to refer a matter "with a request that the Attorney General consider whether to bring proceedings for contempt of court". In a case before the Patents County Court, it was argued that a county court judge did not even have the power to refer such a case to the Law Officers: *Utopia Tableware Ltd v BBP Marketing Ltd* [2013] EWPCC 28. (It so happened that it came before Birss J., a newly appointed High Court Judge.) It is difficult to see why a county court judge (or indeed anyone else for that matter) should not be able to refer a point to the Attorney General for his consideration. It was held that a county court in which the relevant proceedings had taken place could indeed make such a direction as is provided for in r.81.18(5). Furthermore, having considered the arguments in detail, he went on to do so.

2. *Assaults upon officers*

13–87

[Add at end of paragraph]

Minor amendments have been made to s.14(1) of the 1984 Act by the Crime and Courts Act 2013 (most notably replacing the "bailiff" with "officer" and "judge" with "court" in the last line). The procedure is now governed by CPR 81.34.

[Add to note 177] **13–88**

The broad definition of "judge" formerly contained in Courts and Legal Services Act 1990, s.14(3), has now been removed, having been rendered superfluous by the wider amendments to the County Courts Act 1984, ss.5–8: See the Crime and Courts Act 2013, Sch. 9.

4. *Wilful insults and interruptions*

[Add to end of paragraph] **13–93**

The wording of County Courts Act 1984 s.118 has been amended by the Crime and Courts Act 2013 and s.118(3) repealed in its entirety having been rendered superfluous. The procedure is governed by CPR 81.34.

[Add to end of paragraph] **13–94**

"Scandalising the court" has now been abolished with effect from 25 June 2013: see 5–204 above.

5. *The enforcement of injunctions in the county court*

[Add to note 203] **13–95**

CPR Sch.2 cc.29 has been revoked by the Civil Procedure (Amendment No.2) Rules 2012/2208. See now CPR 81.4.

[Add at end of paragraph] **13–97**

The power of a county court judge under s.38(1) of the 1984 Act and the former RSC Ord.52 r.5, to which Ward L.J. referred in *M (Minors) (Breach of Contact Order: Committal), Re* [1999] Fam. 263 at 277, is now acknowledged in CPR r.81.2(3).

6. *Witnesses*

[Add to end of paragraph] **13–98**

Pursuant to CPR 81.36, before or after imposing a fine under s.55 of the County Courts Act 1984, the court may direct that notice be given with a view to allowing the recipient a chance to demonstrate why a fine should not be or should not have been imposed.

13–99 *[Add to note 217]*

The penal and disciplinary provisions formerly contained in CPR Sch.2 cc.34.3 have now been revoked and replaced by the provisions contained in CPR 81.33 to 81.38.

13–99 *[Add to note 218]*

The penal and disciplinary provisions formerly contained in CPR Sch.2 cc.34.3 have now been revoked and replaced by the provisions contained in CPR 81.33 to 81.38.

7. *Corporations*

13–100 *[Add to note 219]*

CPR Sch.2 cc.29 has been replaced by the Civil Procedure (Amendment No.2) Rules 2012/2208. See now CPR 81.4(3). And see *Dar Al Arkan v Al Refai* [2014] EWCA Civ 715, [2015] 1 WLR 135, at [32], Beatson LJ.

8. *Undertakings of solicitors*

13–101 *[Add to note 221]*

CPR Sch.2 cc.29 has been replaced by the provisions of CPR 81.11. This however says nothing about the process to be followed where the court makes such an order of its own initiative.

9. *Penalty for non-attendance on a judgment summons*

13–102 *[Add to note 223]*

The provisions relating to the making of maintenance orders in respect of judgment debts which were previously contained in CPR Sch.2 cc27.17 were revoked by Civil Procedure (Amendment) Rules 2014/407 (SI 2014/407) Rule 39(p). In order to reflect that state of affairs, the corresponding provisions of CPR Sch.2 cc27.8 were also revoked by Civil Procedure (Amendment) Rules 2014, Rule 39(j). They relate to a failure by a debtor under maintenance order.

C. Coroners

13–103 *[Replace note 229]*

See now s.7(2)(a) of the Coroners and Justice Act 2009. The 2009 Act requires that an inquest into a death must be held with a jury if the senior coroner has reason to suspect that the deceased died while in custody or otherwise in state detention *and* that either the death was a violent or unnatural one or the cause of death is unknown. *Jervis on Coroners*, 13th edn (2014).

[Replace note 230] 13–103

See now s.7(2)(b) of the Coroners and Justice Act 2009. The formulation used in the 2009 Act is wider, encompassing any death resulting from "an act or omission" of a police officer or member of service police force.

[Add to note 231] 13–104

For a recent example of the risks of prejudicial reporting or online commentary which may arise in the context of a coroner's inquest see the advisory guidance issued by the Attorney-General in respect of the inquest into the Hillsborough tragedy (*https://www.gov.uk/government/news/attorney-general-issues-advisory-note-before-hillsborough-inquests-start*) [Accessed August 2015].

[Add to end of paragraph] 13–105

Schedule 5 to the Coroners and Justice Act 2009 now governs the powers of coroners to require evidence to be given or produced. Schedule 6 to the 2009 Act outlines a series of offences relating to jurors summoned to serve on a jury at an inquest and to the attendance of witnesses and evidence. Under paras 5 and 6 of Sch.6, a senior coroner may impose a fine not exceeding £1000 on a person who fails without reasonable excuse to do anything required by a notice under para.1 of Sch.5 or who, having been duly summoned as a juror at an inquest, fails without reasonable excuse to attend in accordance with that summons or attends but refuses without reasonable excuse to serve as a juror. Paragraph 9 of Sch.6 makes it clear, however, that the powers of a senior coroner in those respects "are additional to, and do not affect, any other power the coroner may have —

"(a) to compel a person to appear before him or her;
(b) to compel a person to give evidence or produce any document or other thing;
(c) to punish a person for contempt of court for failure to appear or to give evidence or to produce any document or other thing."

Paragraph 9(2) of Sch.6 maintains the qualification that a person must not be fined under paras 5 and 6 and also be punished under any additional power held by the coroner (including the power to punish for contempt of court).

IV. MAGISTRATES' COURTS

A. The nature of magistrates' courts

[Add to Note 238] 13–107

See now the Criminal Procedure Rules 2015 [SI 2015/1490) Part 48 and the Criminal Practice Directions 2015 [2015] EWCA Crim 1567 at CPD XI, 48A "Contempt in the Face of the Magistrates' Court".

V. APPELLATE JURISDICTION

A. The Administration of Justice Act 1960

13–121 *[Add to note 261]*

See e.g. *Kremen v Agrest* [2011] EWCA Civ 1482; [2012] 1 F.L.R. 414.

13–123 *[Add to note 276]*

See also *Giles v Tarry* [2012] EWCA Civ 1886; (2012) 156(38) S.J.L.B. 31, at [10]–[12].

13–123 *[Add to note 277]*

Permission to appeal is therefore required where the penalty imposed is not imprisonment, but a fine. In *Masri v Consolidated Contractors International Co SAL (No.3)* [2011] EWCA Civ 898; [2012] 1 W.L.R. 223, the Court of Appeal disapproved the *obiter* remarks of Wall L.J. in *Shadrokh-Cigari v Shadrokh-Cigari (Practice Note)* [2010] EWCA Civ 21; [2010] 1 W.L.R. 1311 (at [14]) which suggested otherwise. Maurice Kay L.J. noted, at [21], that the relevant authorities demonstrated that "the purpose behind the wording of CPR Part 52.3(1)(a)(i) was related to personal liberty" (at [21]). Accordingly, because a corporate entity cannot be committed to prison for contempt, an appeal by a company against a committal order may only be made with permission.

In *Thursfield v Thursfield* [2013] EWCA Civ 840, Lloyd L.J. noted that the issue of appeal as of right under CPR Part 52.3(1)(a)(i) may need to be revisited, and particularly so in cases where an appellant had refused to submit to the jurisdiction of the court and failed to attend the hearing in person.

13–126 *[Add to note 287]*

See also *Giles v Tarry* [2012] EWCA Civ 1886 at [10]–[12].

13–127 *[Add to note 288]*

For a decision on s.5 of the Debtors Act 1869, see *Kremen v Agrest* [2011] EWCA Civ 1482; [2012] 1 F.L.R. 414.

C. The prescribed appellate tribunals

13–137 *[Add to end of paragraph and note 310]*

With effect from 22 April 2014, Crime and Courts Act 2013, Sch.10(2) para.15(2), inserted a new s.13(2A) into the Administration of Justice Act 1960. This has the effect of disapplying the routes of appeal specified in s.13(2)(a) and (c) of the 1960 Act in respect of appeals against orders or decisions of the Family Court and states that such appeals shall lie to the Court of Appeal. This amendment, however, is subject to any provision made under Access to Justice Act 1999, s.56, or other enactment. Pursuant to the Access to Justice Act 1999 (Destination of Appeals) (Family Proceedings) Order 2014 (SI 2014/602) Art.2 an appeal will lie to the Family Court (and not the Court of Appeal) if it is made in respect of a decision or order of a judge referred to in Art.2(3). This "has effect subject to any requirement to obtain permission to appeal" (Art 2 (4).

[Add to note 316] **13–137**

In *Director of the Serious Fraud Office v B* [2012] EWCA Crim 901; [2012] 1 W.L.R. 3188, the Court of Appeal noted, in the light of the repeal by the Armed Forces Act 2006 of the reference to the "Court of Criminal Appeal" in s.13(2)(c) of the Administration of Justice Act 1960, it was not possible to read the reference to the Court of Appeal in that section as providing for an appeal from the Criminal Division of the Court of Appeal. The Court was "abundantly sure", however, that Parliament had not intended to remove that right of appeal in cases of contempt of court when enacting the 2006 Act. In the circumstances, the threshold test emphasised by the House of Lords in *Inco Europe Ltd v First Choice Distribution* [2000] 1 W.L.R. 586, HL(E) was met and the Court of Appeal were content to use common law principles of statutory construction to rectify the drafting error and reinsert words providing for a right of appeal from the Court of Appeal (Criminal Division) to the Supreme Court in cases of contempt of court. See also at 15–95 below.

[Add to note 320] **13–137**

See further the guidance given by the Supreme Court on the nature of the appellate court's function in *B (Algeria) v Secretary of State for the Home Department* [2013] UKSC 4; [2013] 1 W.L.R. 435, SC.

Chapter 14

SANCTIONS AND REMEDIES

I. General Introduction

14–1 *[Add to note 1]*

In *Attorney General v Norman Scarth* [2013] EWHC 194 (Admin); [2013] A.C.D. 41, the Lord Chief Justice, sitting in the Administrative Court, also referred to the related power contained in s.35 of the Mental Health Act 1983 to remand an accused person to a hospital specified by the court for a report on his mental condition.

14–2 *[Add to note 6]*

See also *Kenneth Smith v Scottish Ministers* [2015] ScotCS CSOH 15, where it was held that the finding against the Scottish Ministers that they were in breach of an undertaking (not to read a prisoner's mail) was in itself sufficiently serious that no other sanction need be imposed. A similar approach was taken in *Pinnacle Cloud Solutions Ltd v MacLellan Property Ltd* [2014] ScotCS CSOH 155 and in *Proceedings to determine whether CM and GL, Social Workers, Children's and Families Dept, City of Edinburgh Council* [2013] ScotSC 100.

II. Custodial Penalties

A. Historical use of imprisonment

14–5 *[Add to note 11]*

In *Willoughby v Solihull MBC* [2013] EWCA Civ 699, [2013] HLR 484, [2013] All ER (D) 233 (Jun) the Court of Appeal described a custodial sentence as the most serious sanction available to the court and observed that if such a sanction is to be imposed the appropriate period of custody is the least period which the seriousness of the offender's breaches can properly justify.

[Add to note 20] **14–6**

The reference should be to paragraph 3–122.

C. Section 14(1) of the 1981 Act

[Add to note 29] **14–9**

See also *Re Balli* [2011] EWHC 1865 (Ch).

[Add to note 30] **14–9**

See now, generally, for the functions and duties of the Official Solicitor, *Civil Procedure 2015* Vol.2 at para.9A–09 *et seq.*

E. Guidance as to the nature and length of penalty: civil contempt

[Add to note 34] **14–10**

See also *R v Curtis* [2013] 1 Cr. App. R. (S.) 28.

[Add to end of paragraph] **14–11**

RSC Ord.52 r.7(1) has been replaced by CPR r.81.29.

G. The application of section 14 to civil contempt

[Add to note 49] **14–14**

See also *JSC BTA Bank v Stepanov* [2010] EWHC 794 (Ch) at [23].

[Add to note 50] **14–14**

See also *Solicitor General v Dodd* [2014] EWHC 1285 (QB). In *Daltel Europe Ltd v Makki* [2014] EWHC 1411 (Ch) it was held that the same factors applied in considering whether to discharge a committal order before the contemnor has been arrested or committed to prison.

[Add new paragraph] **14–14A**

In *JSC BTA Bank v Solodchenko* [2011] EWCA Civ 1241 Jackson L.J. gave further guidance on practice where the court has in mind the coercive element of a custodial penalty, especially in the context of the disclosure provisions of a freezing order:

"56. In the case of a continuing breach, out of fairness to the contemnor, the court may see fit to indicate (a) what portion of the sentence should be served in any event as punishment for past breaches and (b) what portion of the sentence the court might consider remitting in the event of prompt and full compliance thereafter. Any such indication would be persuasive, but not binding upon a future court ...

67. In *Shalson* Neuberger J. made the point that the shorter the punitive element of the sentence, the greater the incentive on the contemnor to comply by disclosing the information required. I agree. On the other hand there is also a public interest in requiring contemnors to serve a proper sentence for past non-compliance with court orders, even if those contemnors are in continuing breach. The punitive element of the sentence both punishes the contemnor and deters others from disregarding court orders."

H. What is the "occasion" referred to in s.14?

14–15 *[Add to end of paragraph]*

In *JSC BTA Bank v Ablyazov (No.7)* [2012] 1 W.L.R. 1988, Gross L.J., giving the judgment of the Court of Appeal stated that the case of *Villiers v Villiers* [1994] 1 W.L.R. 493 was not authority for the proposition that all extant contempt allegations must be dealt with on the same occasion:

"While it is desirable, so far as possible, to consider on a single occasion all extant allegations of contempt of court, there is no fixed rule to such effect. The aim is desirable because of the wording of s.14(1), limiting the sentence for contempt of court which can be imposed on any occasion to a maximum term of two years imprisonment. Plainly the timetable should not be manipulated by the applicant with a view to multiple applications, in an attempt to procure a term of imprisonment in excess of two years; efforts to do so are overwhelmingly likely to fail. However and as made clear by Hoffmann L.J.'s wording ('so far as possible' at p.500), there is not and cannot be an invariable rule."

The application of the desiderata was said to be "a matter for the discretion or judgment of the judge on a fact specific basis": *Villiers v Villiers* [1994] 1 W.L.R. 493, 500; see too *Wilkinson v Anjum* [2012] 1 W.L.R. 1036, especially at [40]. As such, a decision, whether or not to leave over for future consideration extant allegations of contempt, is a case management decision of the judge, with which an appellate court should be slow to interfere, save on well-recognised grounds.

I. Guidance as to custodial penalties in family or domestic cases

14–19 *[Add to note 59]*

In *Prosser v Prosser* [2011] EWHC 2172, Vos J. observed at [121] that the guidance given by Baroness Hale may be applicable by analogy to cases of civil contempt.

[Add new paragraph] **14–21A**

In *W (A Child) (Abduction: Committal), Re* [2011] EWCA Civ 1196, a father abducted his daughter who was a ward of court and refused to comply with orders to return her, and to provide information as to her whereabouts. The court did not expressly characterise the contempt as criminal, but in considering the penalty referred to the need for "regard to the likely sentence that might be imposed for similar conduct in the criminal court". See at 12–8 and 12–32A above. See also the discussion in *R v Kayani* [2011] EWCA Crim 2871, cited at 3–85 above.

J. Imprisonment: powers of magistrates' courts.

Committal for debt

[Add to note 69] **14–23**

In *Woolley v United Kingdom* (2013) 56 E.H.R.R. 15 the European Court of Human Rights at [79]–[86] appeared to confirm that the existence of such a power did not constitute an infringement of the Convention.

[Add to note 70] **14–23**

The "stringent safeguards" were also considered in *R (on the application of Purnell) v Essex Magistrates' Court* [2015] EWHC 333 (Admin), [2015] 2 Cr. App. R. (S.) 4.

[Add to note 71] **14–24**

See also *R (on the application of Louis) v Ealing Magistrates' Court*[2009] EWHC 521.

K. The county court: powers of imprisonment

[Add to note 73] **14–25**

For the procedure, see now CPR 81.33 to 81.38 considered further at 15–83 of the main volume.

[*Add new paragraph*] **14–25A**

In *Ramet, Re* [2014] EWHC 56 (Fam), [2014] 2 FLR 1081, [2014] All ER (D) 156 (Jan), the President of the Family Division considered the position of an individual who during the course of court proceedings committed assault occasioning actual bodily harm against a litigant and common assault against a court clerk. These were offences which he admitted and for which he was given two concurrent sentences of twenty months and four months imprisonment. Accepting the submission that these sentences took account of the individual's contempt, the President declined to impose any additional sentence. He did, however, observe that "Those guilty of violent disorder in a court and those who resort to actual physical violence against a person in court can expect an immediate and lengthy custodial sentence" and went on, at [31], to criticise the limited powers contained in the County Courts Act 1984:

> "It is in this context that I have to express serious concerns about the adequacy — in fact, in my opinion, the utter inadequacy in modern conditions — of the statutory penalties available under the 1984 Act. So far as concerns the family justice system I accordingly invite the Family Procedure Rules Committee to consider whether there is some way in which, compatibly with the provisions of the Crime and Courts Act 2013 , District Judges, Circuit Judges and Recorders can be given powers more extensive than those currently available to them in these cases."

L. The power to discharge: superior courts

14–29 *[Add to note 87]*

For similar reasons, the note to CPR r.81.31 at 81.31.4, stating that "[t]he judge hearing the application has a complete discretion", must be treated with caution.

14–30 *[Add to end of paragraph]*

RSC Ord.52 r.8 has now been replaced by CPR rr.81.31(1) to (5). The general rule as now set out in CPR r.81.31(1) is in substance unchanged and states that: "Any person committed to prison for contempt of court may apply to the court to be discharged". The text of CPR rr.81.31(2) to (5) in relation to the requirements of such an application is as follows:

> "(2) The application must —
>
> (a) be in writing and attested by the governor of the prison (or any other officer of the prison not below the rank of principal officer);
> (b) show that the person committed to prison for contempt has purged, or wishes to purge, the contempt; and
> (c) be served on the person (if any) at whose instance the warrant of committal was issued at least one day before the application is made.
>
> (3) Paragraph (2) does not apply to —
>
> (a) a warrant of committal to which CCR Order 27 rule 8, or CCR Order 28 rule 4 or 14 relates; or
> (b) an application made by the Official Solicitor acting with official authority for the discharge of a person in custody.
>
> (4) If the committal order is made in a county court and —
>
> (a) does not direct that any application for discharge must be made to a judge; or

(b) was made by a district judge under s.118 of the County Courts Act 1984,

the application for discharge may be made to a district judge.

(5) If the committal order is made in the High Court, the application for discharge may be made to a single judge of the Division in which the committal order was made."

M. The power to discharge: "inferior" courts

[Add to end of paragraph] **14–32**

Under CPR r.81.31(4), unless a committal order made in a county court expressly states that any application for discharge must be made to a judge, the application may be made to a district judge.

[Add to end of paragraph] **14–37**

This statutory requirement needs to be considered alongside recent recommendations by the Court of Appeal that a judge, when fixing a penalty for contempt, might take the opportunity to indicate what proportion of a custodial term should be regarded as punitive in character and how much of it as primarily coercive: see e.g. *JSC BTA Bank v Solodchenko* [2011] EWCA Civ 1241, [2012] 1 WLR 350, at [56], *Thursfield v Thursfield* [2013] EWCA Civ 840, [2014] 1 FLR 389, [2013], [2013] All ER (D) 186 (Jun)at [25]–[26] and *Smith v Doncaster MBC* [2014] EWCA Civ 16, [2014] All ER (D) 105 (Jan) at [11], and 14–45 below. The purpose is to give guidance to any judge who is later called upon to address the issue of whether to discharge any part of the custodial term then outstanding (e.g. following late compliance with any relevant court order or other evidence of a change of heart). Whereas s.258 of the 2003 Act mandates unconditional release at the half way stage, it may still be open to the court to release the contemnor in respect of part of the term of imprisonment, so that he would not be liable to recall in the event of further misconduct. It is unlikely in practice that any such application would be made by a contemnor who has already been automatically released pursuant to the statute, but it may become necessary to think about how these two aspects of the law would interact. Certainly, the statutory provisions would come into play irrespective of any guidance given by the sentencing judge as to the division between the punitive and coercive functions of the penalty. The statute would surely operate in relation to the overall sentence: it would not be concerned with any such judicial (and, in any event, non-binding) apportionment.

O. No provision for deducting time spent on remand

[*Add to note 107]* **14–38**

This issue appears to continue to cause difficulty. In *R (on the application of James) v Governor of Birmingham Prison* [2015] EWCA Civ 58, [2015] All

ER (D) 90 (Feb) [2015] C.P. Rep. 20 the Court of Appeal drew attention to this paragraph and again had to express concern that the authorities, including particularly *Delaney v Delaney*, had not been drawn to the attention of the judge below or indeed referred to by counsel on appeal (at [33]). The Court went on to reject a submission that the judge was under a duty to give credit for time on remand on the basis of Articles 5 and 14 of the ECHR and s.3 of the Human Rights Act 1998.

P. The application of the Prison Rules

14–41 *[Add to note 115]*

Although amendments were made to a number of other paragraphs of Prison Service Order 6300 in June 2012, para.5.2 remains in its original form.

R. The power to suspend

14–44 *[Add to end of paragraph]*

CPR Sch. 1 Ord.52 r.7 has now been replaced by CPR r.81.29, which is in the following terms:

> "(1) The court making the committal order may also order that its execution will be suspended for such period or on such terms or conditions as it may specify.
>
> (2) Unless the court otherwise directs, the applicant must serve on the respondent a copy of any order made under paragraph (1)."

14–45 *[Add to end of paragraph]*

In *Doncaster MBC v Elizabeth Watson* [2011] EWHC 2376 (Fam) at [15], Sir Nicholas Wall P made such an order on an application to purge. After *Harris v Harris* had been drawn to his attention, on the same day, he handed down a further judgment: [2011] EWHC 2498. He substituted an order for the applicant's immediate and unconditional release. In *JSC BTA Bank v Solodchenko* [2012] EWCA Civ 1241 at [56], there was a suggestion, in the context of civil contempt, that a sentencing court might appropriately give an indication as to the portion of a custodial term which could potentially be remitted in the event of subsequent compliance with the relevant order.

14–46 *[Add to end of paragraph]*

See now CPR r.81.1(3), which also makes no mention of the Crown Court.

[*Add new paragraph*] **14–49A**

In *Baho v Meerza* [2014] EWCA Civ 669, [2014] 4 Costs LR 620, [2014] All ER (D) 43 (Jun), the Court of Appeal considered both cases and briefly summarised the position as follows:

> "If seems to me that the power to commit for contempt must be: (1) exercised with care and with due consideration of all of the circumstances of the case; (2) only exercised where there is intentional disobedience which, (3) involves some additional obstructive or obstinate dimension revealed by the evidence. It is for the judge to be satisfied to the criminal standard by the evidence."

S. The implementation of suspended sentences

[Add to end of paragraph] **14–50**

See now CPR r.81.29.

[Add to end of paragraph] **14–51**

Lindblom J. considered these general principles in *Deputy Chief Legal Ombudsman v Young* [2011] EWHC 2923 in relation to proceedings under s.149 of the Legal Services Act 2007.

[Add to note 144] **14–53**

See also *Deputy Chief Legal Ombudsman v Young* [2011] EWHC 2923, [2012] 1 WLR 3227.

T. Postponement of sentence

Judging whether a contemnor has "turned over a new leaf"

[Add to end of paragraph] **14–60**

See now CPR r.81.29.

[Add to end of paragraph] **14–61**

See now CPR r.81.29.

U. Consecutive sentences

[Add to note 159] **14–63**

R. v Anomo is reported at [1998] 2 Cr. App. R. (S) 269 and [1998] Crim. L.R. 356.

V. No one should be punished twice over

14–65 *[Add to note 162]*

See also *Ramet, Re* [2014] EWHC 56 (Fam), [2014] 2 FLR 1081, [2014] All ER (D) 156 (Jan), at 12–11 above and referred to in 14–25A above, and *Balli, Re* [2011] EWHC 1736 (Ch), [2011] All ER (D) 141 (Jul), discussed at 12–11 above.

W. The need for the presence of the alleged contemnor

14–66 *[Add to end of paragraph]*

CPR 81.28(6) acknowledges the court's power to make a committal order in the absence of the alleged contemnor. In *Companaia SUD Americana DE Vapores SA v HIN-PRO International Logistics Ltd* [2013] EWHC 987 (Comm), for example, a sentence of three months' imprisonment was imposed in the absence of the contemnor.

III. ATTACHING A POWER OF ARREST

C. The 1996 reforms

14–88 *[Add to note 202]*

See also *P v D* [2014] EWHC 2355 (Fam) which confirmed that there was "no doubt" that the court has the power in appropriate circumstances to make orders to continue indefinitely.

E. The Practice Directions

14–94 [*Add to note 210*]

Horgan v Horgan [2002] EWCA Civ 1371 was relied upon in the subsequent decision of *JM v CZ* [2014] EWHC 1125 (Fam) in circumstances where an order under s 45 (5) of the Family Law Act 1996 had failed to comply either with the statutory provisions, the decision in *Horgan* or the editorial comment in Family Law Practice 2013.

IV. NON-CUSTODIAL SENTENCES

A. Orders under the Mental Health Act 1983

[Add to note 233] **14–104**

See e.g. *Att Gen v Norman Scarth* [2013] EWHC 194 (Admin); [2013] ACD 41.

B. Community sentences

[Add new paragraph] **14–107A**

It seems likely from the issues canvassed by the Law Commission in its Consultation Paper No.209 that the legislature will take the opportunity to ensure that the full range of community penalties becomes available in contempt cases. Where Parliament has addressed reforms through introducing indictable offences (e.g. amending the Juries Act 1974), the usual range of sentencing options will automatically become available (subject to any specific statutory provisions) and these would include community penalties. We discuss the new statutory offences in chapter 11. The legislature has not chosen to make such penalties available for punishing contempt as such.

C. Fines: superior courts

[Add to note 241] **14–108**

And see *Deputy Chief Legal Ombudsman v Young* [2011] EWHC 2923, [2012] 1 WLR 3227.

[*Add to end of paragraph*] **14–108**

Breaches of the *contra mundum* orders made in *Venables and Thompson v News Group Newspapers Ltd* [2001] Fam 430, via social networking, were said to be so serious that a financial penalty would not have been appropriate: *Att Gen v Harkins and Liddle* [2013] EWHC 1455 (Admin) at [22].

D. Is there a power to suspend?

[Add to note 244] **14–109**

And see *Deputy Chief Legal Ombudsman v Young* [2011] EWHC 2923, [2012] 1 WLR 3227.

E. Fines: inferior courts

14–110 *[Add to note 245]*

See now CPR rr.81.33 to 81.38 considered further at 15–83 *et seq* below.

K. Sequestration

1. *Introduction*

14–119 *[Add to end of paragraph]*

The Civil Procedure Rules now formally distinguish between sequestration for the purpose of, on the one hand, executing a judgment (the rules relating to which are contained in CPR Pt 70 and RSC Ord.46) and, on the other hand, imposing a sanction for contempt of court where a party fails to comply with a judgment, order or undertaking (governed by CPR rr.81.19 to 81.27). CPR Pt 81 itself confers no power upon the Court to make an order for enforcement by a writ of sequestration: CPR r.81.2(1)(b). The wording of CPR r.81.20 would suggest that the power contemplated does not extend to third parties. The exception in CPR r.81.20(3) applies when the contemnor is a company or other corporation: the writ of sequestration may "in addition" be issued against the property of any director or other officer of the company or corporation. This provision may have been the basis for the applicant's initially seeking a writ of sequestration against a director's personal property in *Companaia SUD Americana De Vapores S.A. v HIN-PRO International Logistics Ltd* [2013] EWHC 987, but this aspect of the application was not pursued before the Judge. The director was in any event herself committed for contempt and sentenced to three months' imprisonment.

14–120 [*Add to note 270*]

Elliot v Klinger was referred to in *Bank St Petersburg v Arkhangelsky* [2014] EWHC 574 (Ch), [2014] All ER (D) 67 (Mar). The claimants sought declaratory relief in relation to an alleged breach of a freezing order rather than making an application for committal for contempt. The defendants sought to argue that they could not do so, on the basis that it had been established by *Elliot v Klinger* that in such circumstances the proper remedy was by way of motion for committal or sequestration. Hildyard J rejected the argument, distinguishing *Elliot v Klinger*, at least in part, on the basis that it concerned the position in relation to third parties. See also Hayden J in *MASM v Hackney LBC* [2015] EWCOP 3 [2015] 3 W.L.R. 190 discussed at 14–124A below, and Forbes J in *Webster v Southwark LBC* [1983] QB 698 discussed at 12–1 above.

14–123 [*Add to note 273*]

See also *Farnsworth v Lacy* [2013] EWHC 3487 (Ch)

[Add to end of paragraph] **14–123**

CPR r.81.20 applies in the county court: CPR 81.1(3).

2. *Enforceable order required*

[*Add new paragraph*] **14–124A**

In *MASM v Hackney LBC* [2015] EWCOP 3 [2015] 3 W.L.R. 190 the question arose as to whether a party who deliberately acts in defiance of a declaration of best interests in the Court of Protection could be held in contempt of court. The Official Solicitor submitted that "...it is the deliberate obstruction of the court's intentions that amounts to a contempt not the breach of any injunction (which need not, in any event, be a pre-requisite)." In declining to make such a general ruling, Hayden J referred both to *Webster v Southwark LBC* and *St George's Healthcare NHS Trust v S* [1999] Fam 26; a decision of the Court of Appeal in which *Webster* was referred to (very briefly) with apparent approval. See 11–43 above.

[Add to end of paragraph] **14–125**

Pursuant to CPR r.81.25(1) and (2), a judgment or order may not be enforced by a writ of sequestration unless a penalty notice is prominently displayed.

3. *The effect of a writ of sequestration*

[Add to note 296] **14–129**

For recent examples in which writs of sequestration have been granted against corporate bodies, see e.g. *Hin-Pro International Logistics Limited v Compania Sud Americana De Vapores S.A.* [2015] EWCA Civ 401, [2015] 2 Lloyd's Rep 1, [2015] All ER (D) 206 (Apr) and *IPartner Pte Shipping Ltd v Panacore Resources DMCC* [2014] EWHC 3608 (Comm).

[Add to note 303] **14–131**

See now CPR 81.20(1), which has replaced CPR Sch 1, Ord 45.5.

M. Costs

[Add to note 328] **14–142**

In *Jones, Re* [2013] EWHC 2579 (Fam) at [41], Sir James Munby P declined to "follow the event" on costs. Even though the Solicitor-General had failed to discharge the burden of proof in establishing the breach of an order, he had been "fully justified in bringing the application" and in having the evidence tested before a judge.

14–142 *[Add to end of paragraph]*

This was discussed by Lindblom J. in *Deputy Chief Legal Ombudsman v Young* [2011] EWHC 2923. The respondent was fined £5,000 and ordered to pay the applicant's costs. The level of fine took into account both the respondent's means and the impact of the order for costs.

Costs on a contemnor's successful appeal

14–144 *[Add to end of paragraph]*

For the discretion on costs, see now CPR r.44.2.

Responsibility for the costs of proceedings to which one is not a party

14–148 *[Add to note 347]*

See also now Practice Direction (Costs in Criminal Proceedings) 2015 [2015] EWCA Crim 1568.

CHAPTER 15

PRACTICE, PROCEDURE AND PUBLIC FUNDING

I. COMMITTAL: THE HIGH COURT

C. Committal

[Add to note 1] **15–1**

In relation to the "unique constitutional position" of Law Officers and judicial review proceedings, see 2–201 *et seq.*

[Add to end of paragraph] **15–4**

CPR Pt 81 (SI 2012/2208) has replaced RSC Ord.52, CCR Ord.29 and CCR Ord.34 in their entirety and parts of RSC Ords 45 and 46, though not CCR Ord.28 (Judgment Summonses). CPR Pt 81 provides rules of procedure only. It does not confer on the court the power to impose any sanction for contempt of court: see CPR r.81.2(1). It applies to the Court of Appeal, the High Court and the county courts: see CPR r.81.1. CPR Pt 81 is arranged in sections according to the nature of the contempt liability concerned, with each section providing a distinct procedural framework. The rule does not seek to define the respective jurisdictions of the courts to which it applies.

D. Applications to the Divisional Court

1. *Applications to the Divisional Court*

[Add to end of paragraph and to notes 15 and 16] **15–9**

See now CPR Pt 81. There is no specific provision setting out the jurisdiction of the Divisional Court, but see CPR 81 PD para.10: "Court to which applications should be made and levels of judiciary". CPR rr.81.13 and 81.18 indicate the circumstances in which the application must be made to the Divisional Court. These include interference with the administration of justice in any proceedings, including criminal proceedings, and contempt proceedings brought by or with the consent of the Attorney General against publishers of material in breach of s.2 of the Contempt of Court Act 1981. The term "judge in chambers" used under CPR Sch 1 Ord 52.2 has been replaced with the term "single judge" in relation to applications for permission in all courts to which Part 81 applies (see CPR 81.13).

15–10 *[Add to notes 18–21]*

See now CPR r.81.28 for general rules governing committal applications, orders for committal and writs of sequestration.

As to the procedural steps to be followed in seeking permission to make a committal application for interference with the due administration of justice, see CPR r.81.14. Any such application must be made by Part 8 Claim Form, accompanied by a detailed statement of the grounds for bringing the application and an affidavit setting out the supporting evidence (exhibiting relevant documents).

CPR r.81.14 (3) requires the respondent to acknowledge service and file any evidence within 14 days of service of the claim form. CPR r.81.15(1) requires that when issuing the claim form or application notice for committal, the applicant must obtain a date for the hearing from the court. This should generally be not less than 14 days after service: CPR r.81.15(2).

Personal service

15–11 *[Add to note 22]*

See now CPR r.81.14(2), which sets out the requirement in each case for personal service and the power to dispense with such service.

15–11 *[Add to note 24]*

CPR 5.4 (2) now provides that "Any person who pays the prescribed fee may, during office hours, search any available register of claims".

E. Application to a court other than the Divisional Court

15–12 *[Add to notes 25 and 26]*

See now CPR Part 81 which identifies the appropriate originating process in respect of each category of contempt liability. The Rules of the Court of Judicature (NI (1980) updated May 2013 retain the difference in procedure for different types of contempt which gave rise to the *cri de coeur* in *McKinney, Re* [2008] NIQB 3.

Personal service

[Add to note 31] **15–13**

See now CPR r.81.10(4) and (5) (in the case of committal for breach of a judgment, order or undertaking); CPR r.81.14(2) (in the case of applications for permission) and CPR r.81.26(4) (in the case of writs of sequestration). These set out the requirement in each case for personal service and the court's power to dispense with such service.

F. Special provisions relating to applications in the Family Division

[Add new paragraph] **15–16A**

The Family Procedure Rules 2010, Part 33 provide that the procedure for committal applications in the High Court applies also in family proceedings. Part 37.27.5 provides that the 'general rule' is for the committal application to be heard in public unless one of the circumstances set out in 37.25.5 (a)–(g) applies. In *B (Contempt: Evidence), Re* [1996] 1 FLR 239, it was recognised by counsel that it would be appropriate for the evidence to be heard in open court. Yet the Court of Protection and (in proceedings relating to a child) the Family Division (now the Family Court) had a discretionary power to hear a committal application in private: see r.188 of the Court of Protection Rules 2007/1744 and the Family Procedure Rules Part 37.27.5 (a)–(g). Even if the evidence is heard in private, the court is required to state in public the name of the respondent, in general terms the nature of the contempt, and the length of the period of the committal order (see FPR 37.27.6, CoPR 188 (3)). The Practice Guidance (Committal Proceedings: Open Court [2013] 1 WLR 1316 have been superseded by Practice Direction: Committal for Contempt of Court: Open Court [2015] 1 WLR 2195 (26 March 2015). It is there emphasised that the discretion to sit in private should be exercised only in exceptional cases where it is necessary in the interests of justice. The fact that a committal application is being made in the Court of Protection, or in proceedings relating to a child, does not of itself justify the application being heard in private [9]. Nor does the fact that the hearing of the committal application might involve the disclosure of material which ought not to be published, provided that the publication of such material can be restrained by an appropriately drafted order [9]. The requirement to give details of the respondent, nature of the contempt and period of committal is mandatory and there are no exceptions [11]. These details should be provided to the National Media via the Copy Direct Service and to the judicial office for publication on the web site of the Judiciary of England and Wales judicialwebupdates@judiciary.gsi.gov.uk [13 (1) (i)–(iv)]. A judge deciding to sit in private should give a judgment in public setting out the reasons for doing so; and transcripts of any judgment given should be prepared at public expense and published on the BAILII website [15]. However, see also *P (A Child)* [2013] EWHC 4048 (Fam) on the limitations of the Copy Direct Service and the fact that the system does not serve all media organisations, discussed at 8–96 above.

15–17, 15–18 and 15–19 *[Delete paragraphs]*

G. The contents of the notice or claim form

15–20 *[Add to note 52]*

See also *Environment Agency v Hughes* [2014] EWHC 2484 (QB), [2014] All ER (D) 203 (Jul) where the notice of application to commit was said to be "woefully lacking in particularity" [19] and the nature of the alleged breach "simply too vague" [26] so that the application to commit failed. In *Group Seven Ltd v Allied Investment Corporation Ltd* [2013] EWHC 1509 (Ch), it was held by Hildyard J that although an application notice "did not adumbrate as clearly and comprehensively as it should have all the grounds relied on by the Claimant...[the Defendant] and his advisers were aware of the allegations and arguments that they had to meet". The circumstances were exceptional and his conclusions were "not to be taken as any dilution for the future of the rule that a committal application must give clear and fair notice of the breach alleged and the basis of the allegation; and ordinarily any defect cannot be cured by reference to the supporting affidavit, still less a subsequent skeleton argument". [45]

15–20 *[Add to note 53]*

See now CPR 81.28(1). In *Invideous Ltd and Ors v Thorogood and Ors* [2013] EWHC 4644 (Ch) an application to permit amendment to an application for committal was refused by Rose J on the basis that "they would be rapidly followed by a further request for extra findings and extra contempt committals, and that any hearing would raise more and more issues".

15–20 *[Add to note 54]*

See also *Westwood v Knight* [2012] EWPCC 14, where the Judge declined to sentence the respondent in his absence, indicating that he would issue a bench warrant if the respondent failed to attend the handing down of judgment when the court would consider the appropriate penalty. A similar approach was taken in *QRS v Beach* (22 May 2015) [2015] EWHC 1489 (QB), [2015] All ER (D) 03 (Jun) where the court adjourned more than once to ensure the presence of the respondent before addressing the issue of penalty on the 26 June 2015 (see at [2015] EWHC 2019 (QB)).

15–22 *[Add to note 58]*

See *Practice Guidance: Interim Non-Disclosure Orders* [2012] 1 WLR 1003.

See now CPR r.81.28(1).

I. Dispensing with service of a mandatory order

[Add to note 59] **15–23**

See now CPR r.81.5(1) (which can be contrasted with CPR r.81.8(1) dealing with prohibitory orders). See also the discussion of the provisions in respect of both mandatory and negative orders by Briggs J. in *Thomas v Jakes* [2012] EWHC 525, [2012] All ER (D) 131 (May).

[Add to end of paragraph] **15–24**

A helpful summary of the authorities is to be found in *Masri v Consolidated Contractors International Company SAL* [2010] EWHC 2458 (Comm) at [40]:

> "(8) However the case law establishes that the power of dispensation is not limited to the circumstances dealt with in r.7(6). By r.7(7), the court may dispense with service of a copy of an order if it thinks it just to do so. This power is general and is exercisable as regards mandatory orders as well as prohibitory orders (*Davy International Ltd v Tazzyman* [1997] 1 W.L.R. 1256 , Morritt L.J.).
>
> (9) Since the court has power to dispense with service of the order, it has power to proceed to consider a proper notice of application to commit notwithstanding the absence of a penal notice (*Jolly v Hull* [2002] 2 FLR 69, CA, at p. 75C, Judge LJ, *Knowlden v Tehrani* [2008] EWHC 3636 at [13], Lewison J).
>
> (10) The modern approach is that such discretion must be exercised in a way which in all the circumstances best reflects the requirements of justice (*Nicholls v Nicholls* [1997] 1 WRL 314 at 326, Lord Woolf MR, at [47], Neuberger J). This is reflected in paragraph 10 of the Practice Direction to RSC O.52, by which 'the Court may waive any procedural defect in the commencement or conduct of a committal application if satisfied that no injustice has been caused to the respondent by the defect'.
>
> (11) In principle however the jurisdiction should not be exercised too readily, lest what should be a dispensing power for use in exceptional cases may gradually undermine the express requirements of the rule (*Jolly v Hull* , ibid, p.75D, Judge LJ)."

[Add to note 63] **15–25**

See also *Prosser v Prosser* [2011] EWHC 2172 (Ch) (dealing with a consent order).

[Add to end of paragraph] **15–26**

In *Serious Crime Agency v Hyas and others* [2011] EWHC 3599 (QB), Parker J applied RSC Order 45.7 (6) in holding that personal service of an order could be dispensed with where the Defendant had been notified of its terms and the penalties that could follow in the event of breach. So too, in *City of Westminster v Addbins Ltd* [2012] EWHC 3716 (QB), where a director was held liable for breaches by his company even though he was not a party and had not been personally served with the order. The judge found that he had, at the time it was made, given instructions not to oppose it. He was thus not prejudiced and, in the circumstances, permission was retrospectively given to dispense with service. Similarly, he decisions in *Davy International Ltd and Others v Tazzyman and Others* [1997] 3 All ER 187, [1997] 1 WLR 1256 [CA] and *Hydropool Hot Tubs Ltd v Roberjot and another* [2011] EWHC 121 (Ch) were followed by Hildyard J in *Group Seven Ltd v Allied Investment Corporation Ltd and others* [2013] EWHC 1509 (Ch).The circumstances warranted dispensation with personal service of the order where the defendant and his representatives were fully aware of the terms of the freezing order and the consequences of breaching it, and no injustice would be done to the Defendant. 'The overriding objective would not be served by requiring proper service purely as a matter of form. Nor would it be proportionate to stand over to enable a formal application for dispensation' [37].

J. The need for a penal notice

15–27 *[Add to note 66]*

See now CPR r.81.9 (judgments and orders) and CPR r.81.25 (writs of sequestration). There must be a prominent warning as to the consequences of disobedience: CPR r.81.4. See also *FW Farnsworth Ltd v Lacy* [2013] EWHC 3487 (Proudman J) at [11]–[16]. CPR 81.9 (2) provides that an undertaking to the court in lieu of an injunction to do or not to do an act contained in a judgment or order may be enforced under 81.4 even if there is no penal notice, and can be waived in any event if no injustice is caused to the Respondent.

15–27 *[Add to note 67]*

The court declined to sanction the inclusion of a penal notice on an injunction which was to prohibit the use or disclosure of private information. An order addressed to third parties was not shown to be proportionate or necessary and it was doubtful whether the inclusion of a penal notice would in itself have rendered the order enforceable against third parties (as opposed to an express order *contra mundum*): *Ambrosiadou v Coward* [2013] EWHC 58 (QB). In *Serious Organised Crime Agency v Hyas and others* [2011] EWHC 3599 (QB), it was held that where no penal notice had been attached to a further order (although attached to the original order) no injustice would be done to the Defendant given that he was fully aware of the consequences of the breach of the original order and the subsequent order simply included further assets. The circumstances fell within RSC Order 45.7 (6) and there was no good reason why the order, as varied, should not be enforced against him. See at [10]–[11] and 15–30 below. By contrast, in *Environment Agency v Hughes and Others* [2014] EWHC 2484 (QB), [2014] All ER (D) 203 (Jul) it was held that although the court had the power to dispense with the need for penal notices in certain circumstances, it would be 'wholly inappropriate to exercise it retrospectively' in circumstances where a Defendant had not been aware that he might be personally liable as an officer of a company and subject to committal proceedings for contempt [31].

K. Recommended wording for penal notices

[Add to note 69] **15–29**

See now CPR r.81.9, which sets out the requirement for a penal notice on judgments and orders (and the prescribed wording in *Civil Procedure 2013* at 81.9.2). CPR PD 81 para.1, requires the inclusion of a penal notice in the following words or words to substantially the same effect: "If you the within-named [ ] do not comply with this order you may be held to be in contempt of court and imprisoned or fined, or your assets may be seized". This form of words was considered by the Court of Appeal to be insufficient in the case of a harassment injunction, because the notice did not inform the recipient that disobedience also risked prosecution for a criminal offence under the Protection from Harassment Act 1997: *Jeffries v Robb* [2012] EWCA Civ 1149.

CPR 81 also sets out the required form of penal notice for application notices at CPR 81 PD Annex 3:

> "IMPORTANT NOTICE The Court has power to send you to prison, to fine you or seize your assets if it finds that any of the allegations made against you are true and amount to a contempt of court. **You must attend court** on the date shown on the front of this form. It is in your own interest to do so. You should bring with you any witnesses and documents which you think will help you put your side of the case. If you consider the allegations are not true you must tell the court why. If it is established that they are true, you must tell the court of any good reason why they do not amount to a contempt of court, or, if they do, why you should not be punished. If you need advice, you should show this document at once to your solicitor or go to a Citizens' Advice Bureau or similar organisation."

[Add to note 77] **15–30**

And see also *Serious Organised Crime Agency v Hymans* [2011] EWHC 3599 (QB), where a variation order (incorporating further assets into the original freezing order) had not been endorsed with a penal notice but was nevertheless held to be enforceable.

L. Enforcement of undertakings

[Add to note 78] **15–31**

See also *McCann v Bennett* [2013] EWHC 283 (QB). See also 12–186 above.

15–31 *[Add to note 79]*

CPR r.81.9 now makes clear that an undertaking can be enforced without the need for a penal notice. And see *FW Farnsworth Ltd v Lacy*, [2013] EWHC 3487 (Proudman J).

M. The power to sit in private

15–32 *[Add to note 82]*

See now CPR 81.28(5) and, in relation to family proceedings, the Family Procedure Rules 2010 rule 33.27.5 and the Practice Direction: Committal for Contempt of Court: Open Court [2015] 1 WLR 2195 (26 March 2015) discussed at 15–16A above. See also the remarks of Sir Nicholas Wall P as to the "myth" of secret justice in *Doncaster MBC v Elizabeth Watson* [2011] EWHC 2376 (Fam).

15–32 *[Add to end of paragraph]*

CPR 81.28(5) does not in itself confer a power to sit in private, but recognises implicitly that such a right exists. It sets out the matters to be mentioned in public in circumstances where a committal order has been made following a hearing in private: see 15–34 below. See also *JTR v HNL* [2015] EWHC 2298 (QB) [28 (7)], EWQ v GFD [2013] EWHC 3231 (QB) [14] and Practice Direction: Committal for Contempt of Court: Open Court [2015] 1 WLR 2195 (26 March 2015).

Matters to be stated in open court

15–34 *[Add to note 87]*

See now CPR 81.28(5). This requires that the court should sit in public to state certain matters: (a) the name of the respondent; (b) in general terms, the nature of any contempt in respect of which a committal order is being made; and (c) the length of the period of committal. See also *JTR v HNL* [2015] EWHC 2298 (QB) [28 (7)], EWQ v GFD [2013] EWHC 3231 (QB) [14].

15–35 *[Add to note 89]*

See now CPR Part 81 PD17.

N. Procedural safeguards at committal hearings

15–36 *[Add to note 90]*

See *Archbold 2015*, para 28–92 *et seq* and Criminal Procedure Rules 2015(SI 2015/1490) in force with effect from 5 October 2015, r.48.5.

[Add to note 91] **15–36**

See the Practice Direction attached to CPR Pt 81, and, in particular, CPR r.81.28. And see *Daltel Europe Ltd (In Liquidation) v Makki (Committal for Contempt)* [2006] EWCA Civ 94; [2006] 1 W.L.R. 2704; *The Times*, March 8, 2006, where the court found that High Court committal proceedings were not criminal proceedings for the purposes of admitting hearsay evidence under the Criminal Justice Act 1988 (ss.23 and 24); nor did the fact they were subject to art.6 of the European Convention preclude the admission of hearsay evidence. In *Forresters Ketley v Brent and anr* [2012] EWCA Civ 324 it was held at [24] *per* Lewison LJ that because an application for committal is classified as "criminal" for the purposes of Article 6, it does not follow that that the procedure to be adopted should be that contained in the Criminal Procedure Rules as opposed to the CPR.

[Add to note 92] **15–36**

In *Westwood v Knight* [2012] EWPCC 14, the Judge declined to sentence the respondent in his absence, indicating that he would issue a bench warrant if the respondent failed to attend the handing down of judgment when the court would consider the appropriate penalty. See also *QRS v Beach* [2015] EWHC 1489 (QB), [2015] All ER (D) 03 (Jun) where the court adjourned on several occasions to enable the respondent to attend and in the end issued a warrant for his arrest so as to enable him to address the matter of penalty and introduce medical evidence if he wished.

[Add to note 94] **15–36**

Where a judge had sentenced a contemnor in his absence (to the maximum of 24 months) the Court of Appeal dismissed an appeal: *Thursfield v Thursfield]* [2013] EWCA Civ 840. The court upheld the judge's approach, in treating the Respondent's second failure to attend as aggravating factor, observing that it was "repugnant to the proper administration of justice that a contemnor can flout orders of the court, then absent himself from the committal hearing, then avoid serving whatever prison sentence is imposed and then finally avail himself of the procedures of the Court of Appeal, whilst enjoying the shelter of some safe haven overseas". At [44]–[49], the question was canvassed whether contemnors, or at least those who refused to submit to the jurisdiction of the court, should continue to be free to appeal without the need to apply for permission.

[Add to note 95] **15–36**

See now CPR r.81.28(1).

[Add to end of paragraph] **15–36**

A respondent was committed to prison for eight weeks in his absence, having claimed that he was not well enough to attend the hearing. The

Court of Appeal approved the approach adopted by Norris J in *Levi v Ellis-Carr* [2012] EWHC 6 (Ch) towards considering medical evidence. An adjournment was not to be seen as there for the asking: *Forrester Ketley v Brent* [2012] EWCA Civ 324. See also *Yazdanparast v Yazdanparast* [2013] CSIH 27 and 16-130 A and the safeguards suggested in *Robertson & Gough v HMA* 2008 SCCR 20, at [90]–[95] and *Scottish Ministers v Smith* [2010] CSIH 44.

15–37 *[Add to notes 96 and 97]*

See now CPR Part 81 PD16.

15–38 *[Add to note 98]*

See now CPR Part 81 PD16.

15–39 *[Add to note 99]*

See now CPR r.81.28(2). See also the general discussion of self-incrimination by Roth J. in *Milsom v Ablyazov* [2011] EWHC 1846 (Ch) at [9] *et seq.* See also *NFU v Tiernan* at 15–47 below.

15–39 *[Add to note 103]*

See now CPR Part 81 PD 15.

An opportunity to meet the "charges"

15–40 *[Add to note 104]*

See also *ABC v Def* [2014] EWHC 3346 (QB), at [27] *per* Stuart-Smith J, relating to the cross-examination of witnesses under CPR 81.28 (4). There is no automatic obligation for witnesses who have provided affidavit evidence to attend for cross-examination, but anyone who wishes to cross-examine a witness may apply for directions requiring the witness to attend.

Legal representation: art.6 of the Convention

15–45 *[Add to note 111]*

See also *McCann v Bennett* [2012] EWHC 2876 (QB). See also the discussion as to funding at 15–118 below.

15–47 *[Add to end of paragraph]*

In *NFU v Tiernan* 16 July 2015 (unreported) the National Farmers' Union had obtained an injunction preventing the harassment of farmers and others involved in the culling of badgers. They brought contempt proceedings against the Appellant who was part of the Coalition of Badger Action Groups, an unincorporated association opposed to the cull. The contempt proceedings were adjourned to enable the Appellant to obtain legal representation. He was also alerted to the possibility of obtaining legal aid and the seriousness of the proceedings. After five months, the Appellant was still unrepresented. The breaches were found proved and he was committed to prison for six months suspended for two years. The Court of Appeal found that there had been no breach of Article 6 of the European Convention of Human Rights. The Appellant had been adequately informed of desirability of being legally represented and the availability of legal aid. The case was not so complex that the Appellant could not represent himself. The privilege against self-incrimination had been referred to in the NFU skeleton arguments and the Appellant exercised his right to remain silent. There was no basis for interfering with the decision because the Appellant had not been told about the adverse inferences that could be drawn, applying the decision in *Radford v Kent County Council* (18 February 1998, [1998] EWHC Admin 199). Where no adverse inference is drawn, a failure to warn is of no consequence. The Court of Appeal did note however that CPR 81 PD does not refer to the right to silence and it would be better if it did. There was no abuse of process and the judge was entitled to find the breaches proved to the criminal standard.

Q. The effect of a committal order

[Add to note 131] **15–54**

See now generally CPR r.81.30.

II. COMMITTAL IN THE COUNTY COURT

A. The changes in the rules

[Add to end of paragraph] **15–57**

The increasing convergence of practice as between the High Court and county courts is now completed with the coming into effect of CPR Pt 81. There are common rules of procedure for dealing with the various forms of contempt liability. Section 9 of Pt 81 expressly covers the penal, contempt and disciplinary provisions under the County Courts Act 1984. See also at 13–86 above. It is necessary specifically to consider the terms of CPR r.81.18, which is concerned with the contempt jurisdiction in relation to false statements of truth and to false disclosure statements. It is relevant both to High Court and county court proceedings. So far as the former are concerned, it is provided that an application may only be made by the Attorney General or with the permission of the court dealing with the relevant proceedings. As to the latter, on the other hand, a county court judge may *not* give permission — only a single judge of the High Court may do so. See the consideration of *Utopia Tableware Ltd v BBP Marketing Ltd* [2013] EWPCC 28 at 13–86A above.

The Debtors Act and committal: the family law context

15–62 *[Add to note 145]*

See now RSC Ord.28 and the Family Procedure Rules 2010/2955. For a decision under s.5 of the Debtors Act 1869, see *Kremen v Agrest* [2011] EWCA Civ 1482. In *Mohan v Mohan* [2013] EWCA Civ 586; [2013] Fam. Law 959, Thorpe L.J. noted, at [34], the tenor of modern cases in the family context, since the coming into effect of the HRA in October 2000, whereby the courts had

> "sought a balance between the Article 6 right of the judgment debtor not to be compelled and the legitimate search of the judgment creditor for the recovery of the debt."

(See e.g. *Corbett v Corbett* [2003] EWCA Civ 559, *Rundell v Rundell* [2005] EWCA Civ 1764, *Zuk v Zuk* [2012] EWCA Civ 1871 and *Karoonian v Child Maintenance and Enforcement Commission* [2012] EWHC 3633 (Fam).) Moreover, safeguards had been established against the risk of a debtor being imprisoned, which are now to be found in the Family Procedure Rules 2010 at 33.14. At around the same time, there was "simplification of the tangled mechanisms for the enforcement of maintenance orders". There was introduced the "general application", which might result in the making of one or more from a menu of five possible enforcement mechanisms — not including the judgment summons which seeks a debtor's imprisonment. The key question in the *Mohan* appeal, as identified at [4], was whether the judge had been right to exclude documents and statements produced by the husband in the course of complex proceedings to enforce a financial remedy in the wife's favour. He had served a Form E and a sworn statement, as ordered, and at that point the wife and her advisers changed tack and to request the issue of a judgment summons. It was argued that it is not, in general terms, permissible to rely at the hearing of a judgment summons upon any statements made by a debtor in prior or contemporaneous proceedings resulting from a "general application" (i.e. for enforcement by non-penal means). The court accepted, unlike the judge below, that a distinction could be drawn between a criminal case, such as *R v K* [2009] EWCA Crim 1640, [2010] Q.B. 343, where the husband was being prosecuted for tax evasion (and his evidence in prior ancillary relief proceedings had been held inadmissible), and the instant case concerning *only* enforcement proceedings. The court struck the balance between the rival interests differently. In *Mohan*, it had not been suggested that the relevant evidence disclosed any criminal offence on the husband's part. It was held that the judge had been right to exclude his statements from the Debtors Act proceedings but not as to the documents disclosed. Even though the general application might well have been motivated by a desire to obtain documents for use in the Debtors Act proceedings (since the "general application" was in itself unlikely to yield much in the case of " a mobile international entrepreneur with no assets within the jurisdiction"), that did not necessarily mean that the product of that strategy was to be excluded when the court came to consider the Debtors Act summons.

In *Young v Young* [2012] EWHC 138 (Fam); [2012] 3 W.L.R. 266, the court considered s.6 of the Debtors Act and noted the intention of Parliament to the effect that the debtor's liability was to be limited:

> "(i) The power to impound a passport pending the disposal of a financial remedy claim exists in principle in aid of all the court's procedures leading to the disposal of the proceedings.
> (ii) But it involves a restriction of a subject's liberty and so should be exercised with caution. The authorities emphasise the short-term nature of the restraint. The law favours liberty.
> (iii) A good cause of action for a substantive award must be established.
> (iv) The applicant must establish that there is probable cause for believing that the respondent is about to quit the jurisdiction unless he is restrained.
> (v) And the applicant must further establish that the absence of the respondent from the jurisdiction will materially prejudice her in the prosecution of her action.
> (vi) Provided that the principles in (i)–(v) are carefully observed a passport impounding order will represent a proportionate public policy based restraint on freedom of movement founded on the personal conduct of the respondent."

The decision in *Young* was applied in *JSC Mezhdunarodniy Promyshlenniy Bank and another v Pugachev* [2015] EWHC 1586 (Ch) (Hildyard J) at [40] where it was accepted that there was a need for caution and that the court had to to be satisfied that there was risk sufficient to justify the incursion into liberty [40].

C. The need for strict compliance with the rules

[Add to end of paragraph] **15–72**

On the day after the new rules contained in CPR Pt 81 came into effect, Moore-Bick L.J. made the following remarks in *Giles v Tarry* [2012] EWCA Civ 1886 at [24]:

> "The circumstances which have given rise to this appeal emphasise the importance of paying proper attention to the rules of procedure, which are designed to ensure as far as possible that the rights of all parties to proceedings are respected. Enforcement of an order [of] the court is normally obtained by means of an application to commit a person to prison for contempt of court. However, if such an application is successful, it may have serious consequences for the person against whom it is made, even if the court does not make an order for his immediate imprisonment. For that reason the rules of the court lay down stringent conditions that must be observed before such an application can be considered and determined. An order for committal is the principal way in which the court can seek to enforce compliance with its orders and also provides a means of punishing those who have failed to comply in the past."

E: Can a defective order be corrected on appeal?

The guidance in Nicholls v Nicholls

15–82 *[Add to note 184]*

The *Nicholls* guidelines were also applied in the case of *S v O (Committal: Non-attendance of Respondents)* [2015] EWHC 235 (Fam) at [32] *per* Cobb J where it was said that "not every instance of non-compliance will render the committal invalid and that (see PD 37A para 13.2) the court may in any event waive any procedural defect 'if satisfied that no injustice has been caused to the Respondent by the defect'".

F. Enforcing the county court's statutory jurisdiction

15–83 *[Add to end of paragraph]*

CCR Ord.34 has been revoked. Equivalent provisions are now contained in CPR Pt 81, s.9. In CPR rr.81.34 and 81.35, the time limit for serving the summons has been reduced from eight to seven days.

III. APPLICATIONS FOR SEQUESTRATION

A. Mode of application

15–84 *[Add to notes 187–191]*

RSC Ord.45 rr.5 and 7 (only) have now been replaced by s.7 of CPR Pt 81. CPR rr.81.19 to 81.27 now set out the procedural rules relating to writs of sequestration, which now correspond to those applying to writs of execution. The new rules expressly extend to breaches of undertakings (CPR r.81.20(4)) and are also expressed to be available for judgments and orders "to do or not do an act" (CPR r.81.20(1)). The same requirements as to penal notices (set out in CPR r.81.25) apply as in s.2 of CPR 81 (Committal for breach of a judgment, order or undertaking to do or abstain from doing an act): see CPR PD 81 para.1. Applications for permission to issue a writ of sequestration are governed by CPR r.81.26. The application notice must set out the grounds for the application in full, separately and numerically listing each alleged act of contempt: CPR r.81.26(3)(a). It must be supported by affidavits containing all the evidence relied upon: CPR r.81.26(3)(b). Personal service of the application is required, but may be dispensed with or replaced with service by an alternative method if the court thinks it just: CPR r.81.26(5).

CPR Sch 1 Ord 46 has been repealed by the *Senior Courts of England and Wales County Courts, England and Wales: The Civil Procedure Amendment Rules 2014* (SI 2014/407), r 37. The process is now governed by Parts 83–86 .

B. Hearing usually in open court

[Add to note 192] **15–85**

See now CPR Part 81.28(5) and 15–16 above. See also Practice Direction: Committal for Contempt of Court: Open Court [2015] 1 WLR 2195 (26 March 2015).

C. Function of the court at hearing

[Add to note 198] **15–86**

See also *Deputy Chief Legal Ombudsman v Young* [2011] EWHC 2923 (Admin); [2012] 1 W.L.R. 3227. See also paras 14–108 and 14–142 above.

D. Formalities following the grant of permission

[Add to end of paragraph] **15–87 and 15–88**

CPR Sch 1 Ord 46 has been repealed by the *Senior Courts of England and Wales County Courts, England and Wales: The Civil Procedure Amendment Rules 2014* (SI 2014/407), r 37. The process is now governed by Parts 83–86.

E. Duration of Validity

[Add to note 205] **15–89**

CPR Sch 1 Ord 46 has been repealed by the *Senior Courts of England and Wales County Courts, England and Wales: The Civil Procedure Amendment Rules 2014* (SI 2014/407), r 37. The process is now governed by Parts 83–86.

[Add to note 206] **15–89**

See now Parts 83–86 of the CPR.

F. Sequestration will not lie against the Crown

[Add to end of paragraph] **15–91**

See now CPR Pt 81.

G. The property sequestered

[Add to note 208] **15–92**

See now CPR Parts 83–86.

H. Discharge of sequestration

15–94 *[Add to notes 214 and 215]*

See now CPR Parts 83–86.

IV. APPEALS PROCEDURE

A. Introduction

15–95 *[Add to end of paragraph]*

These matters are now governed by CPR Pt 81. It is necessary to note, however, the observations of the Court of Appeal in *Thursfield v Thursfield* [2013] EWCA Civ 840, raising the issue for consideration as to whether it was any longer appropriate to maintain a right of appeal, generally, in relation to committals (i.e. without the need to obtain permission). See also at 15–36 above.

In *Director of the Serious Fraud Office v B* [2012] EWCA Crim 901; [2012] 1 W.L.R. 3188, the Court of Appeal noted, in the light of the repeal by the Armed Forces Act 2006 of the reference to the "Court of Criminal Appeal" in s.13(2)(c) of the Administration of Justice Act 1960, that it was not possible to read the reference to the Court of Appeal in that section as providing for an appeal from the Criminal Division of the Court of Appeal. The Court was "abundantly sure", however, that Parliament had not intended to remove that right of appeal in cases of contempt of court when enacting the 2006 Act. In the circumstances, the threshold test emphasised by the House of Lords in *Inco Europe Ltd v First Choice Distribution* [2000] 1 W.L.R. 586, HL(E) was met and the Court of Appeal were content to use common law principles of statutory construction to rectify the drafting error and reinsert words providing for a right of appeal from the Court of Appeal (Criminal Division) to the Supreme Court in cases of contempt of court. See 13–137 above.

15–95 *[Add to note 218]*

In *R. v Haw* [2007] EWHC 2960 (Admin) [2008] Q.B. 888; [2008] 3 W.L.R. 465; [2008] 2 All E.R. 326; (2008) 172 J.P. 122; [2008] A.C.D. 22; (2008) 172 J.P.N. 309; *The Times*, December 31, 2007 the court determined that, in cases of a conviction or sentence under s.12(5) of the Contempt of Court Act 1981, there was no right of appeal to the Crown Court from the magistrates' court under s.13. of the 1960 Act. The correct procedure was to take the ordinary route of appeal for convictions in the magistrates' court. See also at 10–120, 10–122, 10–124, 13–134 and 13–137 of the main text.

[Add to note 221] **15–95**

Wood v Collins [2006] EWCA Civ 743 was disapproved in *Poole Borough Council v Hambridge* [2007] EWCA Civ 990. See also *JSC BTA Bank v Anatoly Ereschenko* [2013] EWCA Civ 829 at [38], where the court described the prospect of an appeal from a judge's refusal to commit as "legally possible", but "very rare".

[Add to note 222] **15–95**

See now CPR Pt 81 and *Giles v Tarry* [2012] EWCA Civ 1886 at [11]–[12].

[Add to note 223] **15–95**

A company would require permission to appeal, since a corporation cannot be subject to a committal order: *Masri v Consolidated Contractors International Co SAL* [2011] EWCA Civ 898; [2012] 1 W.L.R. 223; [2011] CR Rep 44.

B. The terms of s 13 of the Administration Act 1960

[Add to note 226] **15–97**

There are outstanding changes due to s 13, brought about by the Crime and Courts Act 2013. Schedule 9 is concerned with the introduction of a single county court in England and Wales. Para 52, when it comes into effect, will change "a county court" to "the county court". Schedule 10 of the 2013 Act is concerned with the consequential changes following from the introduction (in April 2014) of the Family Court. Para 15(2) of the schedule inserts a new s.13(2A) which disapplies paras (a) to (c) of s.13(2) to any contempt appeals under the section from the Family Court and those appeals are assigned to the Court of Appeal. Para 15(3) of the same schedule will amend s.13(5)(a) of the AJA to insert the words "family court" after "High Court".

C. Appeals to the Court of Appeal

[Add to note 231] **15–99**

See note 221 above.

[Add to end of paragraph] **15–102**

See now CPR Pt 81.

[Add to end of paragraph] **15–103**

See now CPR Pt 81.

15–103 *[Add to note 234]*

See also *Giles v Tarry* [2012] EWCA Civ 1886 at [11]–[12].

15–105 *[Add to end of paragraph]*

See now CPR Pt 81.

15–106 *[Add to end of paragraph]*

See now CPR Pt 81.

The power to grant bail

15–109 *[Add to end of paragraph]*

The Court of Appeal has recently confirmed, in *JSC BTA Bank v Ablyazov (No.8)* [2012] EWCA Civ 1411; [2013] 1 W.L.R. 1331, that it has inherent jurisdiction to do what is just, convenient and necessary to give effect to its own orders and to the interests of justice. In the absence of any specific provisions, it is surely likely that the Court would similarly acknowledge an inherent or implicit power to grant bail.

15–110 *[Add to notes 244–245]*

See now CPR r.81.29(10); power to suspend execution of a committal order. See also CPR r.81.31(1), which permits a contemnor to apply for discharge.

D. Appeals to the Supreme Court

15–111 *[Add to end of paragraph]*

It was pointed out in *OB v Director of SFO* [2012] EWCA Civ 501 that the Parliamentary draftsman had mistakenly included wording within s.378 and Sch.16 para.45, which had the effect of abolishing the long standing right of contemnors, under s.13 of the Administration of Justice Act 1960 (as amended), to appeal from the Court of Appeal Criminal Division to the highest court in the jurisdiction (i.e. now the Supreme Court). The court was satisfied that this important change, which had been "entirely unheralded", had not been intended by the legislature. Accordingly, it was decided that the Court of Appeal was in these unusual circumstances entitled to exercise the power to rectify obvious legislative errors: see *Inco Europe Ltd v First Choice Distribution* [2000] 1 W.L.R. 586 and *R. (on the application of CPS) v Bow Street Magistrates' Court* [2007] 1 W.L.R. 291. Thus it is now clear that this right should be treated as having survived. See also R. Munday, *Appealing Contempt of Court: Parliament's Homeric Nod*, (2012) Statute Law Review, 33(3), 354–362. The 2006 Act is due to expire at the end of 2 November 2016 (see Armed Forces Act (Continuation) Order 2015).

[Add to end of paragraph] **15–113**

See now CPR r.81.18.

V. Legal Services Commission: Advice, Assistance and Representation

B. The Access to Justice Act 1999

Public Funding

[Add to end of paragraph] **15–118**

The relevant provisions of the Legal Aid Act 1988 and of the Access to Justice Act 1999 have been largely replaced by the Legal Aid, Sentencing and Punishment of Offenders Act 2012. Sections 14, 15, and 16 cover the provision of advice and representation in criminal proceedings, which are defined at s.14(g) to include "contempt committed, or alleged to have been committed, by an individual in the face of the court". Contempt in the face of the court has always been recognised as criminal in character (see chapter 10), but is only one of many forms of contempt. It certainly would not, on a natural interpretation, embrace breaches of a court order or undertaking, which is the classic form of civil contempt. One would expect that if legal aid is to be made available for civil contempt it would have to come within some other statutory provision. Section 14 (h) makes reference to "such other proceedings, before any court, tribunal or other person, as may be prescribed." The Criminal Legal Aid (General) Regulations SI 2013/9, reg 9 (in force 31 July 2015) "Criminal proceedings" provides that "[t]he following proceedings are criminal proceedings for the purposes of s.14(f) of the [2012] Act...(v) "any other proceedings that involve the determination of a criminal charge for the purposes of Article 6 (1) of the European Convention on Human Rights". This appears on the face of it capable of encompassing forms of contempt other than contempt in the face and this is how this provision has been interpreted in a series of decisions discussed at 15–122 A below.

Sections 15 and 16 of the 2012 Act provide, respectively, for regulations to be made in respect of "advice and assistance" and "representation". In relation to choice of representative, provision has been made in the Criminal Legal Aid (Determination by a Court and Choice of Representative) Regulations 2013/614. It should be noted that by s.17 of the Criminal Legal Aid (Financial Resources) Regulations 2013/471 contempt proceedings in a magistrates' court are exempted from the requirement for the court to make a determination in respect of a respondent's financial resources. See also at 10–10 above. Reg 39 of the Financial Resources Regulations, with effect from the 27 January 2014, makes provision in relation to '[r]epresentation in other criminal proceedings' and provides that '[i]n any criminal proceedings other than — a) magistrates' court proceedings; and b) Crown Court proceedings; the relevant authority must make a determination that the individual's financial resources are such that the individual is eligible in accordance with s.21 (1) of the [2012] Act for representation under s.16 of the Act'. Section 21 of the 2012 Act provides that '(1) A person may not make a relevant determination that an individual qualifies under this Part for services unless the person has determined that the individual's financial resources are such that the individual is eligible for the services (and has not withdrawn the determination)'. The legislative scheme thus appears to suggest that if legal aid were to be available in committal proceedings for contempt in the High Court, that it is to be subject to a means test.

15–121 *[Add to end of paragraph]*

Section 19(1) of the Legal Aid, Sentencing and Punishment of Offenders Act 2012 provides that the relevant authority (a caseworker, or a court seised of the criminal proceedings) must determine whether an individual qualifies for representation for the purposes of criminal proceedings (whether provisionally or otherwise) in accordance with s.21 (financial resources) and regulations under that section, and the interests of justice. The relevant criteria echo the previous legislation, namely whether, if any matter arising in the proceedings were to be decided against the individual, the individual would be likely to lose his or her liberty or livelihood or to suffer serious damage to his or her reputation; whether the determination of any matter arising in the proceedings may involve consideration of a substantial question of law; whether the individual may be unable to understand the proceedings or to state his or her own case; whether the proceedings may involve the tracing, interviewing or expert cross-examination of witnesses on behalf of the individual; and whether it is in the interests of another person that the individual be represented.

15–122 *[Add to note 267]*

The decision in *Hammerton v Hammerton* [2007] EWCA Civ 248 has been relied upon in a series of subsequent decisions dealing with the statutory regime for legal aid set out at 15–118 above, see *Jones, Re* [2013] EWHC 2579 (Fam); *King's Lynn and West Norfolk Council v Bunning* [2013] EWHC 3390 (QB), [2014] 2 All ER 1095; *Ramet, Re* [2014] EWHC 56 (Fam); *Inplayer Ltd v Thorogood* [2014] EWCA Civ 1511.

15–122A *[Add new paragraph]*

In *Hammerton v Hammerton* [2007] EWCA Civ 248, [2007] 3 FCR 107, [2007] 2 FLR 1133, [2007] All ER (D) 393 (Mar) Wall, LJ at [51] expressed the view that a litigant in person liable to be sent to prison for contempt should have access to legal advice and representation, if necessary at public expense. It seems to be the springboard of a series of subsequent decisions under the new statutory regime even though *Hammerton* was decided before the current legislative scheme was in force. The legislative changes took place under the 2012 Act after the decision in *Hammerton*, when Parliament presumably would have been aware of Article 6 and what judges were saying about it. Nevertheless, it seems that courts are still taking the view that the reasoning in *Hammerton* is to be applied even though there is a new statutory regime.

In *Jones: Re* [2013] EWHC 2579 (Fam), a decision before the current statutory regime came into force,, the alleged contemnor was subject to committal proceedings following an application by the Attorney General who alleged that she had, in breach of a mandatory order, failed to deliver up her children to the care of their father. That application was unsuccessful. The mother had not been able to obtain public funding for her representation in the proceedings because her share of two properties in Spain meant that her capital exceeded the statutory limit of £8, 000, and she was not able to release her share within the short time frame of the proceedings. It was said that there was no other basis upon which public funding could be obtained. Sir James Munby P said that: "*If* this is really so, it might be thought that something needs to be done, not least bearing in mind the requirements of art 6(3)(c) of the Convention and the learning expounded in *Hammerton v Hammerton* [2007] EWCA Civ 248, [2007] 3 FCR 107, [2007] 2 FLR 1133."

[Add new paragraph] **15–122B**

In *King's Lynn and West Norfolk Council v Bunning* [2013] EWHC 3390 (QB), [2014] 2 All ER 1095, the council had commenced proceedings for contempt in the High Court against the defendant for breaching an order which prohibited her and persons unknown from residing on certain land without obtaining planning permission. It was held, following the decision in *Hammerton v Hammerton* [2007] EWCA Civl 248, [2007] 3 FCR 107, that committal proceedings for breach of a court order were criminal proceedings for the purpose of s.14(h) of the 2012 Act and reg 9 (v) of the General Regulations. Blake J held as follows:

> "[14] Mr Rimer refers me to a decision of the Court of Appeal in *Hammerton v Hammerton* [2007] EWCA Civ 248, [2007] 3 FCR 107, [2007] 2 FLR 1133 per Moses LJ at [9] to the effect that at committal proceedings (in that case in the Family Division for breach of an injunction granted in the course of family proceedings) are proceedings that involve the determination of a criminal charge within the meaning of the jurisprudence of the European Court of Human Rights. In doing so the Court of Appeal approved the decision of the Family Court in *Re K (Contact: Committal Order)* [2002] EWCA Civ 1559, [2003] 2 FCR 336, [2003] 1 FLR 277 at 21 p 282.
>
> [15] In these circumstances it is not necessary for this court to review the jurisprudence of the European Court of Human Rights or to reach its own independent conclusion upon how the Strasbourg Court would classify proceedings for committal for disobedience to a court order. The guiding principles have been given in *Benham v United Kingdom* (1996) 22 EHRR 293 at 324, [1996] ECHR 19380/92. It is clear that the European Court examines whether proceedings give rise to a criminal charge, independently from the way that proceedings are characterised in national law generally.

> [16] I am satisfied that reg 9(v) refers to the jurisprudence discussed in *Hammerton v Hammerton* and there is no material difference between committal proceedings for breach of a court order in the Family and Queen's Bench Division."

In *Bunning* a representation order was granted on the basis that there were 'no financial requirements for a High Court application for legal aid' [31]. However, this decision was made before the Financial Resources Regulations came into force.

15–122C *[Add new paragraph]*

Bunning was considered further by Sir James Munby P in *Ramet, Re* [2014] EWHC 56 (Fam) at [32]–[33]. The respondent had, during the course of a hearing concerning contact arrangements for his child, assaulted both the mother and the court clerk who had attempted to assist. The committal application was unsuccessful because the respondent had been convicted for assault occasioning actual bodily harm (for his attack on the mother) and common assault (for his attack on the court clerk) and he could not be punished twice for the same conduct. Referring to *Jones, Re* and the limited availability of public funding in contempt cases, Sir James Munby stated that '[w]hatever the limitations of *civil* funding, public funding in contempt cases is available under the *criminal* scheme.' Relying on reg 9 (v) of the General Regulations, and the effect of the decision in *Hammerton*, he said that public funding is available for "all proceedings for contempt of court, whether criminal or civil in nature and whether arising in the context of criminal, civil or family proceedings". Because it was *criminal* public funding, it could be ordered by the court. The decision in *Bunning* was followed in *Inplayer Ltd v Thorogood* [2014] EWCA Civ 1511. The First Defendant had been committed to prison for 42 days for providing affidavits that were untruthful. Jackson LJ held that he should have been informed of his entitlement to legal aid, and that the failure to do so amounted to a breach of the common law principles of fairness, as well as the Appellant's rights under Article 6.3 ECHR.

15–122D *[Add new paragraph]*

The entitlement to legal aid for committal proceedings in the county court was confirmed in *Brown v LB Haringey* [2015] EWCA Civ 483, where the Appellant applied for permission to appeal out of time against the decision of the County Court at Central London to commit him to prison for 18 months for breaches of two injunctions granted in the course of possession proceedings. There had been some confusion as to whether he was entitled to legal aid for contempt proceedings in the county court, with the result that he appeared unrepresented. An application for legal aid had been submitted to Westminster Magistrates' Court but was returned stating that the form was submitted by mistake because the matter was a civil matter. McCombe LJ held that this was an error. The Appellant was entitled to legal aid for the contempt proceedings in the county court under reg 9 of the 2013 Regulations and following the decision in *Bunning*. The county court does not have the power to make a representation order in relation to contempt proceedings: a previous power under s.29 of the Legal Aid Act 1988 to grant legal aid in contempt proceedings was repealed by the Access to Justice Act 1999 and not replaced. However, the Appellant's application should have been considered by the Director of the Legal Aid Agency under s18 of the Legal Aid, Sentencing and Punishment of Offenders Act 2012. McCombe LJ held at [36] that "[u]nfortunately, although nothing could be simpler, there is no clear legislative provision providing in straightforward terms that applications for publicly funded representation for committal proceedings in the County Court are to be made to the Director."

The issue of means tests for legal aid applications has however been left open. In the recent decision in *NFU v Tiernan* 16 July 2015 (unreported) the court did not consider it necessary to determine whether a defendant to a committal application in the High Court is entitled to legal aid as an absolute right. Reg 21 of the Criminal Legal Aid (General) Regulations 2013 (SI 2013/9) does not appear to provide for a merits test, but reg 39 of the Criminal Legal Aid (Financial Resources) Regulations 2013 SI 2013/471 suggests that a means test should be applied.

CHAPTER 16

SCOTLAND

I. CONTEMPT IN SCOTS LAW BEFORE 1981

A. The principles underlying the jurisdiction

16–1 *[Add to note 2]*

For a discussion of developments in the Scottish Criminal Justice process since *Cadder*, see Pamela R. Ferguson and Fiona Raitt, "A Clear and Coherent Package of Reforms? The Scottish Government Paper Upon the Carloway Report" [2012] Crim. L.R. 909. See also D. Giannoulopoulos, "'North of the Border and Across the Channel': Custodial Legal Assistance Reforms in Scotland and France" [2013] Crim. L.R. 369. Following the decision in *Mackay and BBC Scotland v The United Kingdom*, Application No.10734/05, discussed in 16–383, 16–384, the Scottish Civil Justice Council has published its *Consultation Paper on Draft Court Rules in Relation to Reporting Restrictions* (July 2013), which was accompanied by draft rules for the Court of Session. After the decision in *A v BBC* [2014] UKSC 25 and the responses to the consultation paper, the Act of Sederunt (Rules of the Court of Session and Sheriff Court Rules Amendment No 3) (Reporting Restrictions) 2015 was brought in. The Act amended the Rules of the Court of Session, the Ordinary Cause Rules and the Summary Application Rules concerning the restriction of the reporting of proceedings.

C. The relationship between "dignity" and "authority"

[Add to note 10] **16–6**

The reasoning in *Robertson* was followed in *Scott v The Procurator Fiscal, Alloa* [2014] ScotHC HCJAC 134, where it was held that the mere fact that the applicant was late for court because he had overslept could not in itself be characterised as contempt of court. His conduct had not been wilful or defiant. The same principles were applied, but a different conclusion reached, by Sheriff Kathrine Mackie in *Proceedings to determine whether CM and GL, Social Workers, Children's and Families Dept, City of Edinburgh Council* [2013] ScotSC 100.

J. The Lord Justice-General's Memoranda on Contempt

[Add new paragraph] **16–46A**

The problem was addressed in due course by a Scottish statutory instrument (No 388), the Act of Sederunt (Contempt of Court in Civil Proceedings) 2011, which came into effect on 28 November of that year and applied to certain types of contempt committed in the Court of Session or the Sheriff Court. It was confined by art.2(2) to "an alleged contempt directed at a member of the court personally or any other contempt that it would be inappropriate for that court to deal with" The procedure to be adopted in such cases provides for another court to deal with the matter, within three court days of the occurrence, by reference to a "statement of facts" prepared by "the first court" and intimated by it at least 24 hours before the hearing to all relevant persons, including "the other court" and the Lord Advocate: see art.5. If, however, the Lord Advocate intimates an intention to bring criminal proceedings in respect of the alleged contempt, then those instigated under the Act of Sederunt are to cease and the person concerned would no longer be subject to any remand in the proceedings: art.6. Otherwise, further provision is made for the conduct of the proceedings before "the other court" by rules 7 to 11 of the Act. It was held in *Petition of Leanne Martin to the Nobile Officium of the High Court of Justiciary* [2014] ScotHC HCJAC 15, at [29]–[30], that the mere fact that a contempt issue has had to be determined by another judge "does not mean that fresh or separate proceedings were instituted".

K. Summary Jurisdiction to be used with restraint and discretion

[Add to note 82] **16–52**

In *ADM, In Petition to the Nobile Officium* [2013] Scot CS CSIH 69, it was held that the contempt jurisdiction should not be used to short circuit the prescribed statutory procedure under ss.3 and 4 of the Civil Imprisonment (Scotland) Act 1882.

L. The continuing need for a summary procedure

16–58 *[Add to note 88]*

Wylie was followed in *Stephanie Bowie v The Procurator Fiscal, Paisley* [2014] ScotHC HCJAC 65, where Lord Carloway, the Lord Justice Clerk, decided in a case of prevarication that the Sheriff had been "best placed" to judge the matter and dismissed the petition. This was despite some undue haste by the Sheriff in the procedure adopted, since a finding of prevarication was almost inevitable. Shortly thereafter, a similar approach was adopted by Lord Brodie in *Owen Hood v HMA* [2014] ScotHC HCJAC 85. It is important nevertheless to bear in mind the safeguards identified in *Robertson & Gough v HMA* 2008 SCCR 20 at [90]–[95] (and listed at 16–130A below). A failure to comply with these requirements led to a finding of contempt being set aside by Lady Paton and Lady Smith in *Petition of Leanne Martin to the Nobile Officium of the High Court of Justiciary* [2014] ScotHC HCJAC 15.

P. The approach to "mens rea" or "dole" at common law

1. *Constructive contempts*

16–82 *[Add to note 122]*

And see *Scott v The Procurator Fiscal, Alloa* [2014] ScotHC HCJAC 134

16–84 *[Add to note 125]*

See *Haney (Catherine) v HMA* HCJAC 144; 2013 SCL 54. The initial failure of a witness to attend a trial, together with her behaviour when she did attend, was treated as contempt of court. On the other hand, in *Cryans v Robertson* 2009 S.C.C.R. 620, failure to attend was reasonably explained on the basis that the witness was on medication following the death of her mother.

II. DIRECT CONTEMPTS INVOLVING JUDGES

B. Abusing or "murmuring" judges

16–89 *[Add to end of paragraph]*

The form of contempt known as "scandalising" has been abolished in England and Wales by s.33 of the Crime and Courts Act 2013. The statute received the royal assent on April 25, and came into effect on June 25 2013. Nonetheless, the history remains of significance not least because the notion survives in other jurisdictions addressed in 5–262 and following. Similar provision has been made in Northern Ireland in s.12 of the Criminal Justice

Act (Northern Ireland) 2013. The Scottish concept of "murmuring", which is also discussed at 16–288 and following of the main text, has not been affected by legislation either at Westminster or Holyrood.

III. Misbehaviour in Court

C. Non-attendance: the common law supplemented

[Add to note 179] **16–117**

See *Haney (Catherine) v HMA* HCJAC 144; 2013 SCL 54. The initial failure of a witness to attend a trial, together with her behaviour when she did attend, was treated as contempt of court.

D. Other forms of misbehaviour in court

[Add to end of paragraph] **16–120**

In *Haney (Catherine) v HMA* HCJAC 144, 2013 SCL 54, the initial failure of a witness to attend a trial , together with her behaviour when she did attend which included interrupting counsel during cross examination and behaving in a hostile and offensive manner towards him, was treated as contempt of court. See also *Yazdanparast v Yazdanparast* [2013] CSIH 27.

[Add to end of paragraph] **16–120**

See also *HMA v McAllister* [2014] ScotHC HCJ 111, in which it was argued in a drugs case that the defendant had only acted under the threat of violence. Lord Boyd of Duncansby was of the view that it had not been shown that it was necessary for this reason either to clear the court or to make an order under s.11 of the Contempt of Court Act 1981 preventing identification.

[Add to note 191] **16–120**

Robertson was considered and followed in *Scott v The Procurator Fiscal, Alloa* [2014] ScotHC HCJAC 134, where it was held that a finding of contempt could not be allowed to stand in circumstances where he applicant had been late for court because he had overslept, but without any wilful defiance.

IV. PREVARICATION

B. Prevarication as a constructive concept

16–130A *[Add new paragraph]*

It is appropriate in such cases to apply the safeguards identified by Lord Gill in *Robertson & Gough v HMA* 2008 SCCR 20, at [90]–[95]: (i) A judge should not find anyone to be in contempt without giving an opportunity to receive legal advice, to be represented in court and to be heard (see *R v K* (1984) 78 Cr App R 82, 87; *BK v The Queen* (1995) 129 DLR (4th) 500); (ii) The judge should give adequate time to consult legal representatives in private and to prepare a response. In due course, there should be an opportunity to make representations on fact and law and, if necessary, to adduce evidence before determining whether a contempt has been committed; (iii) Having heard any submissions, the court has to make a judgment on the matter — the facts sometimes being capable of more than one interpretation. In a case of prevarication, the trial judge is best placed to decide, from the nature of the witness' evidence and from his demeanour, whether the unsatisfactory aspects of the evidence are explicable on some alternative basis; (iv) Then the court must decide if the facts establish contempt (to the criminal standard); (v) Where there is a finding of contempt, the contemnor must be given an opportunity to apologise and to prepare and make any representations on penalty.

VI. MEDIA CONTEMPTS

I. Reporting court proceedings

16–203 *[Add to note 299]*

The Scottish Civil Justice Council has issued a *Consultation Paper on Draft Court Rules in Relation to Reporting Restrictions* (July 2013) and the Act of Sederunt (Rules of the Court of Session and Sheriff Court Rules Amendment No 3) (Reporting Restrictions) 2015 was brought in following the decision in *A v BBC* (see para 16–1 above).

1. *Contemporaneous reports of proceedings in open court*

16–205 *[Add to note 302]*

These words of Lord President Inglis were cited by Lord Reed in *A v BBC* [2014] UKSC 25 at [25].

[Add to note 304] **16–207**

In *A v BBC* [2014] UKSC 25, at [28] and [33], Lord Reed referred to the Court of Session Act 1693 and to the corresponding Act passed on the same day, which made similar provision for the High Court of Justiciary ("Advising Criminal Processes with Open Doors"). He noted that "... the two Acts formed part of the Revolution Settlement, and bore testimony to a determination to secure civil liberties against judges as well as against the Crown".

3. *Reproducing pleadings through the media prior to a hearing*

[Add to note 318] **16–221**

The judgment of Lord President Inglis was quoted by Lord Reed in *A v BBC* [2014] UKSC 25, at [25], as illustrating the long established link between the principle of open justice and the freedom of the media to report court proceedings.

VII. BREACH OF INTERDICT OR UNDERTAKING

A. Breach of a court order

[Add to note 353] **16–238**

The principles explained in *Gribben v Gribben* 1976 SLT 266 were followed and reaffirmed in *British Sky Broadcasting Group plc v Avalonbar Ltd* [2014] ScotCS CSOH 39.

[Add to end of paragraph] **16–239**

This form of contempt has recently fallen to be considered in a number of cases involving child contact orders which have been disobeyed: see e.g. *M v S* 2011 SLT 918; *G v B 2011 SLT 1253; JB v AG 2012 WL 6774694; JDE v SDW [2014] ScotSC 86; CAF v MLH (AP)* [2014] ScotSC 84; *GOT v KJK* [2014] ScotSC 81.

B. Breach of an undertaking

[Add to note 359] **16–241**

Graham was considered, and the principle reaffirmed, in *Pinnacle Cloud Solutions Ltd v MacLellan Property Ltd* [2014] ScotCS CSOH 155, at [38] and [39].

C. The mental element in breach of interdict

16–246 *[Add to note 369]*

See also *Pinnacle Cloud Solutions Ltd v MacLellan Property Ltd* [2014] ScotCS CSOH 155 at [39].

D. Is breach of interdict properly described as "contempt"

16–252 *[Add to note 386]*

See also *British Sky Broadcasting Group plc v Avalonbar Ltd* [2014] ScotCS CSOH 39.

E. Breach of interdict as "quasi-criminal"

The standard of proof

16–260 *[Add to note 403]*

And see *British Sky Broadcasting Group plc v Avalonbar Ltd* [2014] ScotCS CSOH 39.

G. Breach of interdict: procedure

16–267A *[Add new subheading and paragraph]*

The court's discretion

The Court's jurisdiction under s.1 of the Administration of Justice (Scotland) Act 1972, broadly similar to that of search and seizure in England and Wales, may occasionally give rise to an application to commit for contempt if there is obstruction or disobedience, but whether it is appropriate to invoke that jurisdiction will depend on the circumstances. A doctrine of proportionality was developed and explained by Lord Reed in *Sovereign Dimensional Survey Ltd v Cooper* [2008] CSOH 85, at [29]–[34], and more recently applied in *Martin & Co (UK) Ltd, Re Administration of Justice (Scotland) Act 1972* [2014] ScotCS CSOH 33. It was emphasised that the rationale of the contempt jurisdiction is to uphold the rule of law by protecting or enforcing the authority of the court. Reference was made to *HMA v Airs* 1975 JC 67, at p.69, and to the words of Lord Diplock in *Att.-Gen. v Times Newspapers Ltd* [1974] AC 273, at p. 312, to the effect that it is for the court to decide whether the jurisdiction should be invoked in the light of the particular facts and that "... the court's discretion in dealing with a motion for committal is wide enough to entitle it to dismiss the motion with costs , despite the fact that a contempt has been committed, if it thinks that the contempt was too venial to justify its being brought to the attention of the court at all". It is a question of where the public interest lies. The factors to be taken into account are likely to include such matters as the extent to which the contempt proceedings would be likely to promote the authority of the court and the administration of justice and/or whether their discontinuation would run the risk of encouraging parties to treat the court's orders as being of little importance. They may include the relationship between the contempt application and other proceedings; whether for example the progress of the substantive proceedings would thereby be likely to be disrupted or give rise to a need for the duplication of evidence. Also, of course, there may be an unacceptable call on court time and resources. To put it another way, the court is likely to have well in mind what is called, south of the border, the "overriding objective". In a case where there is initial resentment or bluster when the commissioners arrive, out of the blue, but no substantial obstruction to the carrying out of the order, it is unlikely that it will be thought appropriate to proceed by way of contempt.

H. Presence of the defendant required

[Add to note 423] **16–268**

And see *CLA v MLH* [2014] ScotSC 84 at [23]. See also *QRS v Beach* (22 May 2015) [2015] EWHC 1489 (QB), [2015] All ER (D) 03 (Jun) and *Westwood v Knight* [2012] EWPCC 14 discussed at 15–20 and 15–36 above.

VIII. THE PHILLIMORE RECOMMENDATIONS FOR SCOTLAND

I. Scandalising the court

[Add to end of paragraph] **16–288**

The form of contempt known as "scandalising" has been abolished in England and Wales by s.33 of the Crime and Courts Act 2013. The statute received the royal assent on April 25, and came into effect on June 25, 2013. Similar provision has been made in Northern Ireland in s.12 of the Criminal Justice Act (Northern Ireland) 2013. The Scottish concept of "murmuring", which is also discussed at 16–88 and following of the main text, has not been affected by legislation either at Westminster or Holyrood.

IX. THE CONTEMPT OF COURT ACT 1981: APPLICATION TO SCOTLAND

A. Closing the gap between Scotland and England

6. *The test for restraining publication*

16–337A *[Add new paragraph]*

It was re-emphasised in *Massie v McCaig* [2013] CSIH 14; 2013 S.L.T. 373 that the court should apply s.12 of the Human Rights Act, and carry out the appropriate balancing exercise, when asked to grant an interim interdict in the context of defamation, whereas in England and Wales it would, at least for the time being, still be right to give priority to freedom of speech in accordance with *Bonnard v Perryman* [1891] 2 Ch. 269. See too at 6–8 above.

X. THE CONTEMPT OF COURT ACT 1981: A COMMENTARY

F. Reporting court proceedings

2. *Section (4) 2*

16–383 *[Add to note 604]*

The case is reported at *Mackay and BBC Scotland v UK* (2010) 53 EHRR 671. In relation to developments after the consultation paper, see 16–1 above.

16–384 *[Add to note 605]*

The case is reported at *Mackay and BBC Scotland v UK* (2010) 53 EHRR 671. See now the discussion in *A v BBC* [2014] UKSC 25 at [67]–[68]. In relation to developments after the consultation paper and *A v BBC*, see para 16–1 above.

3. *Section 11*

16–390 *[Add to end of paragraph]*

The Lord President considered in *BBC, Applicants* [2013] CSIH 43 at [37]–[38], the inherent jurisdiction of the Court of Session to withhold the name of a party in appropriate circumstances, by way of "fulfilling its duty to do justice by all men", and the use of s.11 of the Contempt of Court Act 1981 to prevent reporting thereafter. He stated that the inherent jurisdiction lay at the heart of the court's constitutional function. The other members of the Court agreed with him and rejected the interpretation of s.11 by Lord Brailsford in *SRC v Kemp* [2013] CSOH 56 (who had interpreted s.11 as rather limiting any inherent jurisdiction). They all concluded, however, that the procedures available in Scotland for addressing the legitimate concerns of the media had proved inadequate and suggested that the Scottish Civil Justice Council should consider the matter and make proposals for improvement. See also at 7–38, 7–110, 7–118A and 7–140A. The appeal before the Supreme Court was dismissed: *A v BBC* [2014] UKSC 25. It was held that although the Article 10 rights of the BBC were engaged, the restrictions imposed by the s.11 order and by the continuance of A's anonymity were justified by reference to Article 10(2). The tribunal was seeking to protect his physical wellbeing and right to life, if he was deported, because of a real risk on his return to his country of origin. Publication of his identity would thus frustrate the court's intention and the order was, therefore, necessary to uphold the authority of the judiciary — quite apart from the need to protect the countervailing rights of A under Articles 2 and 3. In relation to developments in Scotland following this judgment see para.16–1 above.

[Add to note 611] **16–391**

See *HMA v McAllister* [2014] ScotHC HCJ 111, where it was held that the circumstances did not warrant an order to clear the court or to prevent the publication of a name under s.11 of the Contempt of Court Act 1981. It was argued in a drugs case that the defendant had only acted under the threat of violence.

[Add new paragraph] **16–391A**

It was argued in *A v BBC* [2014] UKSC 25 that before a s.11 order was made it would have been appropriate to give notice to the media in accordance with s.12(2) of the Human Rights Act 1998. But, at [66], Lord Reed rejected the submission, since no there was no person against whom any remedy or relief was being sought. Directions made under s.11 operate on a blanket basis: there is no respondent who should be notified or who might be present or represented at the hearing.

K. Photography, sound recordings and television in the vicinity of the court

2. *Tape recorders*

[Add to end of paragraph] **16–425**

Section 9 of the Contempt of Court Act 1981 has been amended by s.31 of the Crime and Courts Act 2013: see para.10–197 above.

3. *The Television Practice Direction*

[Add new paragraph] **16–430A**

In July 2013, there took place a broadcast of recorded (and heavily edited) coverage of a criminal trial in the High Court in Edinburgh, for which permission had been sought and obtained in accordance with the current practice. The Practice Note had been supplemented by Lord Hamilton in January 2012, but in October of that year the new Lord President, Lord Gill, announced that it was in his view time for an extended review of the existing practice in the light of the many technological developments in the intervening years. No further applications for filming in the courts would be considered until the outcome of the review was known. In Scotland, Lord Gill announced in January 2015 (and appropriately on television) the outcome of the consultation on the subject and of the enquiry carried out under Lady Dorrian. The central conclusion reached was that there should be wider opportunities for coverage, especially of appellate proceedings, but that clear guidelines should be worked out and especially for the protection of vulnerable witnesses.

The experience of television in court rooms in New Zealand has not so far been auspicious, as emerges clearly from the discussion in *Law Talk*, October 26, 2012 (a journal published by the New Zealand Law Society). The problems have clearly been noted by Elias C.J., who on August 9, 2013 instituted a review by a panel of judges of "in-court television coverage, photography and sound recording by mainstream media". It will address current guidelines, any changes that may be required in the light of continuing developments in the available technology, and whether appropriate safeguards are in place to protect the fair trial process. On 20 July 2015, a final Report to the Chief Justice on In-Court Media Coverage was published. The Report concluded that it did not recommend any fundamental changes to the existing system, saying at [6] that "We consider it better to have the present coverage than none at all. There is room for improvement, particularly in the procedures, and the quality and detail of the publications. Lawyers and judges want more accuracy and balance in reporting". New "In-Court Media Coverage Guidelines 2015" have been produced to reflect these aspirations. See further the discussion of these issues at 10–213 above.

L. Penalties for contempt after the Act

16–431 *[Add to end of paragraph]*

In *Gorrie v Haddington* [2014] HCJAC 10 a non-custodial penalty was substituted in the High Court of Justiciary after the Court made reference to the observations of Lord Judge CJ in *HH v City of Westminster Magistrates' Court* [2012] UKSC 25 at 125–132 and, specifically, to the need to balance Article 8 considerations of the impact of imprisonment on the family members of the contemnor when addressing the possibility of imposing a custodial sentence. This should only be done if the judge is satisfied that it is necessary to override those considerations in the circumstances of the case.

16–433 *[Add to end of paragraph]*

There is the power to remit proceedings to the Court of Session under s.37(2A) of the Sheriff Courts (Scotland) Act 1971 if it is thought that the case warrants consideration in the light of the greater sentencing powers. It is provided by ss.1(1), 5(1)(b) and 5(2)(a) of the Prisoners and Criminal Proceedings (Scotland) Act 1993 that a contemnor who is given a custodial penalty shall normally be released on serving half the term. This was taken into account as a relevant factor when making an assessment of the likely impact upon a child of his mother being imprisoned for contempt: see *CAF v MLH* [2014] ScotSC 84 at [30].

M. Lack of a specific appeals procedure

[Add to note 674] **16–438**

In solemn criminal cases, it would appear that a petition to the *nobile officium* is the only competent route available by which to challenge either a finding or a penalty imposed in respect of contempt: see Mayer v HMA 2005 JC 121 and *CAF v MLH* [2014] Scot SC 84.

[Add to note 679] **16–440**

For recent examples, see *Stephanie Bowie v The Procurator Fiscal, Paisley* [2014] ScotHC HCJAC 65 and *Owen Hood v HMA* [2014] ScotHC HCJAC 85.

APPENDIX 3

EXAMPLES OF PENALTIES IMPOSED

I. CRIMINAL CONTEMPTS

19–1

NAME OF CASE	NATURE OF CONTEMPT	PENALTIES
Re Balli [2011] EWHC 1736	The respondent was found guilty of disciplinary offences by the SRA and struck off the roll of solicitors. He nonetheless continued to hold himself out as a solicitor and provided legal services in an ongoing case. Upon discovering this, the judge hearing the case initiated contempt proceedings. Although the respondent's clients were aware of the situation, the Court, Counsel, and the other side's legal representatives had all been deceived.	Six months' imprisonment. In his favour, the respondent was young (26), relatively inexperienced, co-operated early, made a sincere apology to the court and was of otherwise good character. The court emphasised that the sentence was only for contempt, and separate criminal proceedings under the Legal Service Act 2007 might yet follow.
Att-Gen v MGN Lt & NGN Ltd [2011] EWHC 2383	Following the murder of a young woman in Bristol, her landlord was arrested. The *Daily Mirror* and *The Sun* published articles about the landlord after his arrest which amounted to "vilification" of him. Although he was subsequently released without charge, the newspaper publications were found to amount to a breach of s.1 CCA 1981. The landlord subsequently pursued separate defamation claims against the newspapers. Neither newspaper pleaded guilty or admitted their contempt.	£50,000 (MGN) and £18,000 (NGN) fines imposed. MGN's larger fine reflected the fact it had published two articles and continued to maintain that it had been entitled to contest the prosecution. NGN had published only one article and had apologised after judgment was given on liability. It was an aggravating feature that the Att-Gen had given warnings to the newspapers before the offending articles were published. The settlement in the defamation claims was irrelevant.

R v Curtis [2012] EWCA Crim 945	Two women, C and M, attended a friend's criminal trial and then followed three of the jurors on to a bus at the end of the day. They sat immediately beside the jurors on what was an otherwise empty bus and C staged a conversation on her mobile phone, the clear implication of which was that if the jury convicted the defendant it would be the fault of the jury rather than the defendant or his barrister. The jurors were unsettled and shaken, and got off the bus and returned to court. The women accepted their wrongdoing and admitted that they knew the passengers were jurors only at the third contempt hearing. Although no direct threat was made to the jurors, the conduct had been intended to and did intimidate them. The jury did not have to be discharged.	M — three months' imprisonment; C — five months' imprisonment; both upheld on appeal. C's sentence reflected the fact she had played the leading role. The women were single mothers with young children but they had deliberately followed the jurors, intentionally threatened them, and only made a very late admission of guilt.
Att-Gen v Dallas [2012] EWHC 156	Dallas was a juror in a criminal trial. During the trial she looked up information about the defendant, and discovered he had a previous conviction for his involvement in a rape. She told the other jurors. The jury was accordingly discharged and the defendant re-tried. The court did not believe her evidence that she had simply 'stumbled' upon the information about the defendant or that her English was not good enough to understand the directions to the jury not to seek information from the internet — she was articulate and highly	Six months' imprisonment. Mitigating features included her lack of personal gain, good character, considerable achievements, consequential resignation from her job and her apology. However she had failed to make any admission of guilt.

	intelligent and her actions were a deliberate disobedience.	
Att-Gen v Pardon [2012] EWHC 3402 (Admin)	P was a juror on a criminal trial. After the jury returned a guilty verdict for two of the defendants, P visited one of them at work. He apologised for the verdict and disclosed the jury's reasons for it and the deliberations they had gone through. Subsequently, after the jury were unable to return a verdict on a third defendant, P attempted to pay him a similar visit. P's disobedience was deliberate and occurred in circumstances where he had been told by the court of his duties as a juror, that jury discussions were confidential, and warned not to visit any places associated with the case.	four months' imprisonment. P was of good character, genuinely remorseful and co-operated fully with the police investigation.
Att-Gen v Scarth [2013] EWHC 194	The respondent was the defendant in a criminal harassment case. At a hearing of the case the respondent recorded the proceedings without the leave of the court, and had subsequently published that recording online. This was not the first time the respondent had done this, and the offence was deliberate.	28 days' imprisonment suspended for 12 months for each of the two counts of contempt.
R v Ahmed Balogun [2013] EWCA Crim 479	The appellant was a member of the public in a courtroom during a criminal case. When the defendant became argumentative, the appellant stepped forward, pointed at the Recorder in an aggressive manner and shouted "you are corrupt, a corrupt judge like all British Justice".	28 days' imprisonment upheld.

Att-Gen v Harkins; *Att-Gen v Liddle* [2013] EWHC 1455 (Admin)	The respondents posted photographs on Twitter and Facebook which were said to show James Bulger's killers, Jon Venables and Robert Thompson, as adults. Thompson and Venables had been given new identities on leaving prison and there was a worldwide injunction on publishing details of them, or publishing any photographs taken of either of them after 1993. Both the respondents' posts made it clear they knew they should not post the photographs. Harkins had 141 followers, but his post resulted in over 20,000 shares with other people. Liddle had 915 followers.	nine months imprisonment suspended for 15 months. Aggravating factors included the potential consequences to Thompson, Venables and those who might be mistakenly identified as them; the respondents' knowledge of the injunction; and that the publications were part of a deliberate campaign on the 20th anniversary of Bulger's death which they freely participated in. In mitigation, both had good character, had removed the photographs when told to do so, apologised and had made admissions. Liddle in particular had strong personal mitigation linked to his charitable work and care for his deaf son.
R v Ivanov [2013] EWCA Crim 614	The jury complained that the appellant, a defence witness, had been filming them on his mobile telephone. Although he initially denied it, on being asked to produce his phone it was apparent he had taken three photographs of the defendant and recorded one minute of the judge's summing up. The jury was discharged and a fresh trial ordered. The appellant had previously been in court and was aware that filming and photography were prohibited.	Eight months' imprisonment, reduced to five months' on appeal. The judge had accepted the appellant's apology and claim that he had not intended to derail the trial. Sentenced reduced in light of the appellant's age (22) and mother's illness.
Att-Gen v Kasim Davey; *Att-Gen v Joseph Beard* [2013] EWHC 2317 (Admin)	Two jurors committed for contempt after their cases were heard together. Davey posted a Facebook message about a case he was trying, including the words "I've always wanted to Fuck up a paedophile & now I'm within the law". Beard conducted research on the	Each given two months' immediate imprisonment.

	internet despite judicial directions.	
Att.-Gen. v Dallas [2012] EWHC 156 (Admin); [2012] 1 WLR 991	Juror disobeyed instructions and sought information about a defendant she was trying, on a charge of grievous bodily harm, and informed her fellow jurors that he had been involved in an earlier case of alleged rape. This had been excluded by the judge.	Six months' imprisonment
HM Solicitor General v McEvoy [2015] EWHC 4788 (Admin)	The respondent was a juror. After being discharged from serving on a particular jury she deliberately spoke to other members of that jury to try to influence them against the defendant. The jury had to be discharged. This was a grave consequence of a serious and deliberate contempt.	12 months' imprisonment, suspended for 12 months. The suspension was unusual but appropriate because the respondent had eventually admitted her contempt and apologised, was 67 years old with a previously blameless life, and the sole carer of her elderly and infirm mother.
R v Savva [2014] EWCA Crim 1386	S and L were the victims of a violent assault who gave statements to police. They refused to comply with witness summons and to give evidence at trial, as a result of which the trial collapsed. Both were found to have made up their minds not to attend trial before receiving the witness summons and made no attempt to engage with police about protection that could be offered.	S — £3000 fine. L — £5000 fine. Both subject to a three month custodial sentence in default of payment. Upheld on appeal. S had less significant means than L, and had taken his lead from him. He had no previous convictions, whilst L had previous convictions for theft and related sentences.
R v John Rogers [2014] EWCA Crim 1080	The appellant was a defendant in criminal proceedings. As he walked into court for a PCMH he called another man, who was a defendant to a sexual abuse allegation, a "fucking wanker". They were overheard by the usher, but not by a barrister in the public gallery.	Six months' imprisonment, reduced to seven days' imprisonment on appeal. The verbal abuse was directed only at another defendant, not a witness, juror, judge or member of court staff. It was not so loud that it could be heard through the court room. The defendant to whom it was directed was undisturbed by it, and may

		not even have understood it was directed at him.
R v Sherlock [2014] EWCA Crim 310	The appellant was a prisoner, on trial for offences of rioting in the prison. During the trial he had threatened a prison guard who was giving evidence by leaning forward, putting a finger on his neck and mouthing "you dirty lying bastard". This was a serious contempt — it was an attempt to intimidate a crucial witness whilst he was giving evidence in a very serious case. It was likely that the appellant would have come into contact with the prison officer again or that his associates would have done.	12 months' imprisonment, upheld on appeal.
Attorney General v Baines [2013] EWHC 4326 (Admin)	The respondent was from the same community as the family of James Bulger. In breach of an ongoing and world-wide injunction, he tweeted photographs of a man he said was Venables, one of Bulger's murderers, as an adult. The respondent knew of the injunction and knew what he was doing amounted to contempt. Moreover, when this was pointed out to him by other Twitter users, the respondent heaped scorn and abuse on them, and later retweeted the images. When questioned, he first said the Twitter account was not his, then served a statement admitting the postings were his but denying any knowledge of the injunction. Two days before the committal hearing he admitted he had been aware of the injunction all along and admitted his contempt. The breach was flagrant, he	14 months' imprisonment, suspended for 15 months. He was 27 years old and of previous good character. His link to the Bulger family gave some explanation for his conduct, and he did admit the breach, albeit very shortly before the hearing. He was also ordered to pay £3000 towards the Attorney General's costs.

	displayed complete contempt for authorities and the court, and it was a persistent course of conduct aimed at harming Venables.	

II. CIVIL CONTEMPTS

NAME OF CASE	NATURE OF CONTEMPT	PENALTIES
Nield v Loveday [2011] EWHC 2324 (Admin)	N brought a personal injury claim which was subsequently found to have grossly overstated his injuries. He had verified his claim and supporting witness statement with a statement of truth, and his solicitor had warned him of the consequences of signing a false statement. It was clear he had known what his witness statement had said and any injuries he had sustained did not affect his capacity in this regard. His wife, W, made a statement corroborating his false account of his injuries, which also carried a statement of truth.	N — Nine months' imprisonment. W — six months' imprisonment suspended for 18 months. Both were of previously good character. W had admitted her contempt but N had not, and had continued to fabricate in his oral evidence. However, his real injuries, and the effect of prison on them, were taken into account in sentencing.
South Wales Fire and Rescue Service v Smith [2011] EWHC 1749 (Admin)	The respondent made a false claim for loss of earnings following an accident at work. The claim was supported by a total of four false statements of truth. The dishonesty was persistent and deliberate. He admitted his claim was false and repaid some of the money he had received. Approximately £10,000 remained outstanding.	12 months' imprisonment, suspended for two years, provided that the respondent repaid the outstanding £10,000. For reasons unconnected with the parties, there had been a substantial delay in hearing the contempt proceedings, and it would be inappropriate to commit the respondent to prison now.
JSC BTA Bank v Solodchenko [2011] EWCA Civ 1241 (reversing [2010] EWHC 2843 (Ch))	The respondent failed to comply with a freezing injunction and disclosure order. Before the committal hearing he disclosed certain material and was sentenced	21 months' imprisonment, of which nine months was punitive.

	on the basis that his contempt had been purged. He was accordingly ordered only to pay the costs of disclosure on an indemnity basis. On appeal it was held that this was incorrect. The purported disclosure was misleading and contained false evidence. This was a case of continuing non-compliance.	
Lane v Shah [2011] EWHC 2962 (Admin)	Shah had sought damages from the applicant insurer following a road traffic accident. Despite carrying signed statements of truth, her witness statements and schedule of loss (also verified by her husband and daughter) falsely claimed that she was wholly unable to work as a result of the accident. She was covertly filmed working full time and without her claimed disabilities. On being confronted with the footage the applicant, her daughter and husband admitted their deception and their solicitors wrote to the court.	six months' imprisonment for Shah and three months' imprisonment for each of her husband and daughter. They were of previously good character and had admitted their contempt, but it was an aggravating factor that shah had been advised about the consequences of signing false information.
Alstom Power Ltd v Somni Impianti [2011] EWHC 3941 (TCC)	The respondent gave an undertaking in the course of litigation that it would deliver specific documents to another company by a specific date and not cause or permit any damage of any kind to the documents, or lose or otherwise dispose of them. The undertaking was breached and an order imposed by the court requiring the respondent to return those documents in its possession or control, serve an affidavit explaining the whereabouts of any others and restraining the respondent from causing or permitting any damage to the documents or losing,	£40,000 fine imposed. Half of this was to reflect the breach of the undertaking, and half the breach of the injunction. The court explicitly said it would be prepared to consider an application to reduce the fine but only where the injunction was complied with promptly.

	selling or otherwise disposing of them. The respondent breached the order. The breaches were committed deliberately and were serious.	
Doncaster MBC v Watson [2011] EWHC 2376; [2011] EWHC 2498	The respondent breached an order prohibiting the disclosure of details about a child in care proceedings. She viewed herself as a "campaigner for justice" and had written about the case on websites and emailed third parties. She had been aware of the order because she sent a copy back to the court, disputing its validity. She refused to attend the committal proceedings, despite an order to do so.	nine months' imprisonment imposed. On an application to purge her contempt, the sentence was suspended for two years. Although the respondent's acts were deliberate and knowing, by the time of the application to purge she had expressed contrition and done what she could to remove the material from the internet. She further gave an undertaking to use her best endeavours to remove the material from the internet. Later, in the light of the Court of Appeal decision in *Harris v Harris* (see 14-45 of the main text), she was unconditionally released.
Bar'yudin v Pilipenko [2012] EWCA Civ 1524	The appellant failed to comply with a possession order and an order to leave the matrimonial home on the breakdown of the marriage. The failure was resolute, based on the appellant's contention that the order was wrong.	14 days' imprisonment, suspended for 12 months, upheld — "an entirely suitable coercive penalty".
Liverpool Victoria Insurance Co v Bashir [2012] EWHC 895 (Admin)	The respondents were members of a family who brought a fraudulent personal injury claim following an alleged car accident. R1 had visited a doctor to get a false medical statement in support of the claim. However, they all admitted their fraud and explained it was arranged by a third party who ran a claims company and who had paid them to make the bogus claim.	Six weeks' imprisonment for R1 and R2; six weeks' imprisonment suspended for 12 months for R3 and R4 (who were R1's elderly parents). Although they were all 'foot soldiers' in a greater fraud, their conduct had to be deterred and custody was entirely appropriate. The court's initially considered penalty of 12 months' imprisonment was reduced in light of the admissions made and very considerable

		assistance given to the insurance company about the third party. Suspended sentence was appropriate for the elderly parents who had some disabilities and ill health.
Law Society of England and Wales v Otobo [2012] EWHC 754 (Admin)	The respondent, a former solicitor, breached an injunction restraining him from disclosing a confidential report to third parties. Although he initially sought to avoid addressing the contempt proceedings, for which he spent a night in jail, the respondent subsequently admitted the breach, accepted his obligation to deliver up copies of the report, and regretted what he had done.	Six months' imprisonment suspended for two years. The respondent's admission and history of psychiatric problems meant immediate custody was not appropriate.
Thomas v Jakes [2012] EWHC 525 (Ch)	The respondents put it out of their power to comply with a court order to deliver up company shares to a liquidator, by disposing of them to a third party. This was deliberate, premeditated and designed to put an end to enforcement of the court order. The respondents subsequently lied to the court about it at a hearing.	Twelve months' imprisonment each
Havering LBC v Bowyer [2012] EWHC 2237	B brought a personal injury claim against the local authority, which was only discovered to be fraudulent upon disclosure. Witness statements were provided by R (B's father) and J (his friend) in support of the false account.	B — two months' imprisonment, R — four months' imprisonment, J— 1 months' imprisonment. Each had good character and B and J had admitted their contempt. R had attempted to exculpate himself but had in fact been the driving force behind the continued attempt to deceive.
Colchester BC v Pryke [2012] EWCA Civ 1809	The appellants breached an injunction preventing them from developing a field in an area of outstanding	Four months' imprisonment, suspended on the condition they cease to live in the field, upheld.

	natural beauty or placing any mobile home or structure on it.	
Warner v Barner [2012] EWHC 4223 (Ch)	The respondents were a husband and wife involved in bankruptcy proceedings. They were ordered to disclose documents about their assets and bank accounts but failed to do so. Committal proceedings were commenced by the trustee in bankruptcy and adjourned due to the respondents' alleged ill-health. The hearing finally took place 14 months after the disclosure order was made, during which time they had still not instructed their lawyers to release the documents.	£500 fine imposed on each of the respondents, and costs of the application awarded against the respondents on the indemnity basis. The motive of the respondents was irrelevant but their alleged state of mind and depression could not excuse the failure to comply for such a long period of time.
Oxfordshire CC v Wyatt Brothers (Oxford) Ltd [2012] EWCA Civ 1921	The appellants were directors of a company which failed to comply with waste removal planning orders. The orders dated back to ten years previously, and in 2010 suspended sentences of four and six months' imprisonment were imposed on the directors for contempt. After there were still no efforts made to comply with the orders, the Council applied to activate the sentences.	Activation of the suspended sentences of four and six months' imprisonment, upheld. Court orders had to be complied with and it was irrelevant that the planning harm to the community was said to be limited. The limited information as to the directors ill-health and old age was not persuasive.
University of Southampton v Mohtasham [2012] EWHC 3795 (QB)	Southampton University obtained an interim injunction against the respondent, a former student, on the grounds of harassment. After trial but prior to judgment, the respondent breached the injunction by sending further emails to the University. She was well aware of the terms of the injunction and the consequences of breach.	Eight weeks' imprisonment suspended for one year with the condition that the respondent comply with the terms of the final injunction against her. The breaches were deliberate and intentional. It was difficult to find any mitigation in light of her oral evidence making it clear she had no intention of complying with the order.

Giles v Tarry [2012] EWCA Civ 1886	The respondent breached an order made in the context of a neighbours dispute, by failing to remove items from his drive and trespassing on his neighbours' land. On appeal it was held that the allegations of trespass ought not to have been considered by the judge as various procedural requirements (including the need for affidavit evidence on the breach) had not been complied with.	£2,500 fine, reduced on appeal to £750, to reflect the fact the respondent should not have been sentenced for the trespass.
Phonographic Performance Ltd v Fletcher, Chancery Div, 22 June 2015, (unreported)	The respondent played music in his nightclub without a licence. The music licensing company applied for an injunction to prevent this, which was granted and then subsequently breached by the respondent. He also failed to make promised payments towards acquiring a licence. The respondent's actions did not amount to a single breach, but to a sorry history of failure by him. The contempt could only have been deliberate, and although it was his first offence, it passed the threshold for a custodial sentence.	28 days' imprisonment, suspended for 12 months. It was appropriate to suspend the sentence on the condition that the respondent cease infringing the claimant's copyright. The respondent was also ordered to pay (i) damages, summarily assessed, for the copyright infringement; and (ii) costs of the application on the indemnity basis.
Intercity Telecom Ltd v Solanki, Queen's Bench Division, 15 June 2015 (unreported)	The respondent gave an undertaking to the court for delivery up of certain documents before trial, with which he materially failed to comply. He then gave a second undertaking and signed a witness statement saying he had delivered up relevant material to his solicitors. At trial, it was found that he had deliberately destroyed critical evidence and that his sworn witness statement	£1,250 fine for each breach. Although the respondent submitted he would not be able to pay a financial penalty, it was likely that he had some means beyond those revealed to the court.

	was untrue. The contempt had been a deliberate interference with the court process and the respondent's behaviour had been deplorable.	
QRS v Beach and Others [2015] EWHC 1489 (QB)	First Defendant: 16 breaches of orders designed to prevent harassment on the internet.	First Defendant: Six months imprisonment on each to run concurrently. Third Defendant: Four months' imprisonment on two 'counts' of aiding and abetting the breach, to run concurrently. Suspended for two years.
Birmingham City Council v Wale, Birmingham County Court, 12 May 2015,	The respondent had committed six breaches of an interim antisocial behaviour order. Three of these had been in the immediate days after being served with the order. One was particularly aggravating as it amounted to verbal abuse directed at a neighbour - an escalation in the nature of the respondent's antisocial behaviour. The respondent had also attended court immediately before some of the breaches, when the seriousness of the proceedings and the injunction had been made abundantly clear to her. The respondent had failed to attend court for the committal hearing or show any remorse.	14 days imprisonment for each breach, to run concurrently. The breaches did not amount to actual or threatened violence against the respondent's neighbour, and were, in the main, items of noise nuisance.
Revenue and Customs Commissioners v Munir [2015] EWHC 1366 (Ch)	The respondents were two directors and the secretary of a company, which was the subject of an order appointing a provisional liquidator following £7.7m unpaid VAT. In breach of the order, substantial payments were made to one of the company's suppliers on the day of the liquidator's appointment	All received sentences of six months' imprisonment. In mitigation, they had not been directly lining their own pockets, were of good character and had admitted their default. Although the secretary payment was of a lesser sum, it was premeditated to a greater extent. The fact the proceedings had been

	and the following day. Although liability was denied at first, the directors later admitted involvement in two payments, and the secretary admitted involvement in one. The conduct was a serious and deliberate breach of the order which the respondents knew would deprive the order of effect. There was no prospect of receiving the money subsequently, and a clear message had to be sent to the commercial community that such conduct had serious consequences.	prolonged before the contempt was admitted would be taken into account in costs and not sentence.
BG International v Umali [2015] EWHC 1702 (QB)	The respondent was the fourth defendant in a fraud claim. He had repeatedly failed to comply with the disclosure requirements of a freezing injunction, or to appear in court to be cross-examined in proceedings designed to find out what had happened to the money. He had clearly and deliberately decided not to engage and his contempts were serious, flagrant and persistent. The victim had suffered prejudice as a result of the respondent's failure to comply and had been unable to recover the money. An immediate custodial sentence was necessary to mark the seriousness of the contempt.	Nine months' imprisonment. Five months of that was imposed punitively and the balance might be remitted in the event of full and prompt compliance.
Otkritie International Investment Management Ltd v Gersamia [2015] EWHC 821 (Comm)	Committal for contempt was sought against G and J following a trial. Three grounds were alleged against G, including breaching a freezing injunction by deliberately dissipating assets and failing to disclose information. These were deliberate and	G — 12 months' imprisonment, suspended on terms that G repay the remainder of his share of the proceeds of the fraud within 120 days. He had admitted the contempts, had not been imprisoned before and had co-operated to some extent in the recovery of assets.

	contumacious, and there was no excuse for them. As they had had occurred repeatedly over a long period of time, they demonstrated an ingrained attitude of continual non-compliance with court orders. Four grounds were alleged against J including disclosure of fake documents, concealment of relevant ones, making false statements in a statement of case and non-compliance with disclosure obligations of a freezing injunction. J was found to be in persistent and contumacious contempt of the court's orders and had not apologised or sought time to comply. The breaches had persisted over a long time and some were continuing, and there was no evidence that she was acting under pressure or for anything other than a wicked motive.	J — 20 months' imprisonment.
Royal & Sun Alliance Insurance Plc v Fahad [2015] EWHC 1092 (QB)	The respondent made false statements in a claim for damages following a staged road traffic accident, including that the accident was caused by the other driver's negligence, and that he did not know her. In fact, they were in a serious and long-term relationship. The respondent had knowingly and deliberately set out defraud his insurance company of £15,000, and in doing so had sought to interfere with the administration of justice. The fraud was planned and carried out over a long period of time. The impact of false claims on society is great and those who commit such offences	12 months' imprisonment. The respondent was of previous good character and had expressed remorse.

	can expect to be sent to prison.	
Sanchez v Oboz [2015] EWHC 611 (Fam)	The respondent father had breached an order to return his child to this jurisdiction from Poland. Untold damage is caused to children who are 'spirited away' from one country to another without warning, and parents who remove their children in this way cannot go unpunished. The respondent was fully aware of the terms of the order but had chosen to turn his face against English law. Although sentencing was adjourned to allow him to return the child or come to court, he did not do so.	12 months' imprisonment.
Richmond LBC v Howell [2015] EWHC 104 (CH)	The respondent mother failed to deliver up her and her child's passports, as required by a court order. The court did not accept her evidence that she did not know where the passports were and found she was not engaging with the proceedings.	Seven days' imprisonment.
National Farmers' Union v Tiernan [2015] EWHC 69 (QB)	Nine breaches of an injunction intended to prevent interference with a badger cull. Appeal dismissed.	Six months' imprisonment on each to run concurrently, suspended for two years.
R (on the application of Saleem) v Serwan [2015] EWCA Civ 123	The appellant made false statements in a Particulars of Claim and witness statement about a road traffic accident which had never occurred. The fraud was only admitted by the appellant after trial and at the committal hearing. The contempts were persistent and repetitive and impugned the integrity of her co-claimant who had confessed the fraud. She had shown no remorse.	Eight months' imprisonment, upheld on appeal.

Aziz v Ali [2014] EWHC 4003 (QB)	The four respondents commenced personal injury proceedings in respect of an alleged road traffic accident. Six months before the start of trial K contacted the insurer and confessed the claim was fraudulent. She gave evidence at the trial that there had been no accident. By contrast X and S gave evidence maintaining their stories, and J did not attend at all. The claim was dismissed, and at the subsequent committal proceedings X and K admitted their contempt. J and S initially denied it, but admitted it part way through the hearing. The court held that giving false statements in legal proceedings undermined the administration of justice and public confidence in the justice system. They were so serious that only a custodial sentence was justified.	X — six months' imprisonment. J and S — eight months' imprisonment. J and S had only admitted their contempt at a late stage and could therefore only get limited credit for the admission. K — 12 weeks' imprisonment suspended for six months. K had admitted the fraud and expressed genuine remorse.
Bank of Ireland v Shah [2014] EWHC 4839 (QB)	The respondent had been evicted from a property following a possession order with a penal notice. He subsequently broke back in, in flagrant breach of the penal notice. That was a serious contempt showing a total disregard for court orders.	Three months' imprisonment
Bate v Aviva Insurance UK Ltd, Queen's Bench Division, 18 November 2014, Unreported	The respondent had created or colluded in the creation of false documents in support of an insurance claim.	Nine months' imprisonment, suspended for two years. The respondent's age (71), poor health and previous good character were all mitigating factors.
Joint Stock Company VTB Bank v Skurikhin [2014] EWHC 4613	Following summary judgment being entered for the applicant, the Court had made an order under CPR Pt 71 for the	16 months' imprisonment, of which 12 months was for failing to comply with the freezing injunction and four months was for the failure

	respondent to attend for oral examination about his means. The respondent failed to do so, and subsequently failed to provide details of his assets in accordance with a freezing injunction. The contempts were knowing and deliberate, with the aim of preventing the applicant from entering judgment. Freezing injunctions were made for good reason and any substantial breach was a serious matter which normally merited a prison sentence. A long sentence should be considered where the failure to comply was continuing, although court had to be careful before using the *JSC BTA Bank v Ablyazov* [2012] EWCA Civ 1411 as guidance. In that case the contempt had been particularly egregious.	to attend the means hearing.
C v F [2014] EWHC 3346 (QB)	The respondent sent abusive and threatening emails, made abusive phone calls and published derogatory comments about the applicant online, in breach of a harassment injunction. The conduct amounted to a serious and sustained breach of the injunction, and was aggravated by the fact he had previously been imprisoned for similar breaches and been warned about the possibility of future imprisonment.	Seven months' imprisonment suspended for two years. The respondent suffered from mental health problems which may have led to some of the breaches. The applicant would be best protected if the respondent was able to reach a robust and stable mental state. This was most likely to happen outside prison.
Yellow Van London Ltd v Driver [2014] EWHC 3094 (Ch)	Breach of an injunction restraining passing off, infringement of trade marks and copyright. The respondent admitted the breach but remained in contempt. His attitude to the injunction had been extremely casual.	£10,000 fine. A jail sentence was threatened for any future breaches.

Liverpool Victoria Insurance Co Ltd v Thumber [2014] EWHC 3051 (QB)	The respondent had brought a fraudulent insurance claim involving a false witness statement, and had sought to gain money by perjury. The fraud was discovered before trial, but he failed to attend court at the subsequent committal application and falsely claimed this was due to mental health problems.	12 months' imprisonment
Suffolk CC v H [2014] EWHC 2830 (Fam)	The respondent breached a harassment injunction, which had been imposed for the benefit of council employees after his child was taken into care. He threatened a member of court staff, uploaded a threatening video to the internet which he tweeted to celebrities, politicians and media organisations, and sent letters to the council employees. The respondent accepted the breaches, but they were so serious that an immediate custodial sentence was required. The breaches had had a serious effect on council employees who were professional people doing their jobs and entitled not to be abused or threatened.	Two months' imprisonment for the contempts listed in the committal application, and a further one month imprisonment for contempt in the face of the court. Sentences to run consecutively. One month later D made an application to purge his contempt, apologised and promised there would be no recurrence. He was released from custody.
Khan v Khan [2014] EWCA Civ 913	The appellant signed a consent order to destroy all private photographs of the claimant which were in her possession, and to swear an affidavit to confirm the same. After signing the consent order, the appellant wished to resile from it, but made no application to the Court to this effect. The order was sealed, and the appellant breached it by failing to swear the affidavit. She was given 48 hours to comply before the committal hearing but	three months' imprisonment, reduced to 28 days on appeal. Costs of the hearing to be paid by the appellant on the indemnity basis.

	again failed. The Court of Appeal overturned the Judge's finding that she had not destroyed all the images, and allowed her to swear an affidavit during the course of the appeal hearing. Nonetheless, she had still persisted in her contempt until the last moment, and the Judge had been entitled to reach the conclusion she had simply decided not to comply with the terms of the consent order after signing it. The appellant did not purge her contempt before the Judge at first instance.	
Wokingham BC v Dunn [2014] EWCA Civ 663	The appellants failed to comply with an injunction to clear a site, restore the land by topsoiling and reseeding and not permit further occupation of the land. The breaches had been flagrant.	Four months' imprisonment, reduced to a financial penalty of £20,000 on appeal. By the time of the appeal the appellants had fully complied with the injunction, accepted responsibility and apologised.
Solicitor General v Dodd [2014] EWHC 1285 (QB)	The respondent had concocted false documents to bolster a claim and lied under oath.	Six months' imprisonment, reduced to eight weeks on appeal. The appellant had been sent to Pentonville, a category B/C prison where he had suffered lockdowns and lived in fear of violent inmates. He was of previous good character, might now lose his job and was undoubtedly suffering. The effect of the conditions of imprisonment had thus been greater than anticipated when sentenced was passed. It was appropriate to release him after eight weeks had been served, rather than wait for him to serve half the six month sentence.
Tower Hamlets LBC v Ali [2014] EWHC 845 (Fam)	The respondent father failed to comply with a location order in respect of	Four months' imprisonment.

	his children. He knew or suspected that the mother of his children had taken them to Bangladesh in breach of an interim supervision order, but had denied knowledge of their whereabouts to police and social services. The contempt was serious. Untold damage was done to children who were spirited away without warning or preparation, and parents who removed children in their way could not go unpunished. Parents who sought to protect those who did this, who deliberately obstructed the administration of justice and knowingly breached court orders should expect to be punished appropriately.	
Surface Systems Ltd v Wykes [2014] EWHC 422 (QB)	The respondent was the claimant in a personal injury action who made false statements in his particulars of claim. The defendant had conducted video surveillance of the claimant and found him using his arm normally. He discontinued the proceedings, and the defendant applied to commit him for contempt. He pleaded guilty on the first day, explaining that he had initially been injured as alleged but had failed to say anything when he began to recover. The aggravating factors were the size of the damages sought (£1.9m), and the extent of the deception — nearly all of the professionals involved had been repeatedly deceived. It had been a deliberate attempt to cheat the insurance company.	Six months' imprisonment. The respondent was only 19 at the time of the accident and of good character. He was the sole carer for his son and did have some genuine physical and psychiatric injuries. The claim was not fraudulent from the outset and he had admitted his contempt, but the sentence could not be suspended.

Sunguard Systems Ltd v Ponomareva, 5 February 2014, unreported	The respondent breached a restraining order, imposed following unsuccessful employment tribunal proceedings, by placing highly defamatory and hurtful material online. She had willfully embarked on a campaign to cause trouble and upset the company and its employees. There had been more than one breach, but the psychological harm caused was not of the most serious type.	Three months' imprisonment, suspended for two years. There were some concerns about the respondent's mental health.
Hope v Krejci, 31 January 2014, unreported	The respondent husband breached a financial remedy order, made in divorce proceedings, to transfer property worth £16,000 to his wife. The relevant background context was that very substantial sums were still owed to the wife and the husband had substantial undisclosed resources, although this could not bear on the appropriate sentence for this particular contempt.	Two months' imprisonment, suspended for six weeks to allow the husband to pay the value of the property to the wife's solicitors. The wife should not have to come back to court if the money was not paid.
BTA Bank v Zharimbetov [2014] EWHC 108 (QB)	The respondent was the deputy chairman of the applicant bank's management board. He breached a court order not to leave the jurisdiction and to deliver up his passports, and another court order to return to the jurisdiction. He failed to attend the committal hearing. The breaches were serious, and imprisonment was necessary. The respondent was continuing to breach the orders, the breaches had been deliberate, and they had caused the bank significant prejudice.	15 months' imprisonment.
Smith v Doncaster MBC [2014] EWCA Civ 16	The respondent failed to comply with the terms of an order requiring him to	Release was refused and that decision was upheld on appeal. Persistent failure to

	remedy breaches of planning restrictions on his land. A sentence of imprisonment was imposed but suspended for 28 days to allow him to comply. He again failed to do so, and was sentenced to 9 months' imprisonment. Two months into that sentence he gave up possession of the land. He therefore applied to be released on the basis that the sentence no longer had any coercive element.	comply with an injunction, including after sentence, aggravated the gravity of the conduct. The lack of a coercive element did not mean the respondent had to be released, the judge had properly reviewed his conduct as a whole to see whether it justified release, and had been entitled to conclude that it did not.
EWQ v Jansen [2014] EWHC 894 (QB)	The respondent voluntarily gave undertakings to the court to settle an action brought against her. She subsequently committed 17 breaches, which were only admitted to the court at the start of the committal proceedings.	Two months' imprisonment, suspended for 18 months. The respondent had made clear that she acknowledged the wrongfulness and harmfulness of what she had done. She had not put the applicant to the trouble and distress of a full committal hearing.
Russian Commercial Bank (Cyprus) Ltd v Khoroshilov [2013] EWHC 443 (Comm)	The respondent had breached a worldwide freezing order by transferring ownership of his yacht, so that he could not meet a $291m judgment debt against him. He had then disappeared and was not present at the committal hearing. The breach had been deliberate, the sums involved were large, and he had legal representation until recently. There was no possibility of purging the contempt. The contempt was so serious that imprisonment was required.	18 months' imprisonment. There was no mitigation which could be offered, and no one to offer it in the respondent's absence.
Button v Salama [2013] EWHC 4152 (Fam)	The respondent father had taken his daughter to Egypt, and after his return to the jurisdiction had failed to comply with a series of orders requiring him to reveal her whereabouts and	There had been no change since the last committal order. Although there could lawfully be successive terms of imprisonment for further and repeated breaches of orders, it was for the court

	procure her return. He was the subject of a series of orders committing him to prison for contempt but still refused to comply. When the respondent had been in prison for almost two years, the mother applied for a further 12 months to be imposed, arguing that the continuing failure to comply was an aggravating factor.	to determine on each application whether a further term was necessary and proportionate. The Court should not lose sight of s.14 Contempt of Court Act 1981 which provided that a term of imprisonment for contempt should not exceed two years, or attempt to subvert that by imposing aggregate sentences of longer periods. The respondent could not be further punished, and imprisonment seemed to have lost all coercive effect. It was therefore not proportionate or justifiable to commit the respondent to any further term of imprisonment.
Re Hartmayes Ltd [2013] EWHC 4624 (Ch)	The respondent was the former sole director of a company in liquidation. He failed to attend a private examination under the Insolvency Act 1986 and was brought before court. He gave an undertaking to deliver up all paperwork and company information under his control. He failed to comply with this, or a subsequent order from the court to deliver up documents relating to a particular company he had purchased and a linked property sale. Although the respondent had sworn two affidavits before the committal hearing, these were perfunctory and failed to provide sufficient information. It was beyond belief that the respondent could not remember the details of the deal — he was a professional property dealer and it had involved a substantial development. He had shown a lamentable	Four months' imprisonment for each of the two breaches, with the sentences to run concurrently. However, the sentences were suspended so that they would only be activated if he failed to file and serve an affidavit which fully complied with the order within a set period of time; and that activation could only occur after the conclusion of the criminal proceedings against the respondent. The respondent was heavily involved in the preparation of his defence in the criminal proceedings.

	disregard for his duties as a director of a company in liquidation over a long period of time, and had only ever disclosed the minimum he considered necessary on any occasion. His offence merited a term of imprisonment.	
Back Office Ltd v Percival [2013] EWHC 3776 (QB)	A company and one of its employees had breached undertakings to the court that they would not solicit or deal with certain clients of another company within a period of eight months. Although a breach soon after the giving of undertakings would have been an aggravating feature, it was no mitigation to say the breach had been at the very end of the eight month period. The company was liable because of the actions of its salesmen, which was less contumacious than if the company had ordered or encouraged a breach. The employee's breach had occurred in the course of dealing with a complaint about the salesmen's behaviour.	The company was ordered to pay a fine of £5,000, and the costs of the committal application. These were to be assessed on the indemnity basis from the date of giving evidence. Although one of the company directors had apologised to the court, he had shown disdain for the proceedings and sworn an affidavit that misrepresented the financial position. The employee was ordered to pay a fine of £1,200. The employee's breach was opportunistic and he had regretted his breach and apologised to the court.
Homes for Haringey v Fari [2013] EWHC 3623 (QB)	A husband and wife had lied in a personal injury claim brought by the wife. She had deliberately exaggerated her symptoms, and her husband had colluded in her deceit by signing a false witness statement. Both had maintained their lies through the trial, and contested every allegation.	The wife was sentenced to three months' imprisonment. Although she had children with disabilities who relied on her and whose Article 8 rights would be adversely affected if she went to prison, that was proportionate and necessary. The sentence length reflected that no damages had been paid out as a result of her fraud and she had been in the media spotlight. The husband was sentenced to two months' imprisonment, suspended

		for 12 months. He had played his part in the pretence such that imprisonment was appropriate, but the sentence was suspended to enable him to look after the family whilst his wife was in prison.
Brown v Davies [2013] EWHC 3523 (Fam)	A mother had removed her child from the jurisdiction and the child's father sought her return. The respondents were the maternal grandparents and another family member. They had refused to provide the judge with details of where the mother was living, despite knowing where she was and having the means to contact her. The maternal grandmother had indicated on oath that she had no means of contacting the mother, but had sent her text messages only a few hours later. However, since their evidence, the mother had contacted the courts and agreed to return to the jurisdiction with the child.	12 days' imprisonment each. The fact that the mother had agreed to return to the court helped their cases. They were of previous good character, the grandparents were elderly, and the other family member had young children and was in poor health.
JSC BTA Bank v Ablyazov, 28 October 2013, unreported	The respondent was subject to a disclosure order in respect of assets owned by a third party, which also required him to hand over any document that would permit travel outside of the jurisdiction. On his arrival in the UK he refused to hand over his passport. The disclosure order was found to be too wide and onerous and was discharged by the court.	14 days' imprisonment, suspended for 12 months. The fact the court had ruled the disclosure order should be discharged was no answer to the contempt — the law required compliance with court orders unless and until they were set aside. However, it was relevant to the question of sanction. No prejudice had been caused to the applicant by the failure, and the passport had been subsequently delivered up.

Ealing LBC v Connors [2013] EWHC 3493 (Fam)	The respondent mother failed to deliver up two of her children who were the subject of emergency protection orders. When she was brought before the court she confessed she had hidden the children with family members, and asked to be allowed to contact them to bring them back. The court was satisfied that she knew where the children were, but that her evidence was inherently unreliable and that her expressed intentions of future compliance rang hollow. It was an extremely serious matter when the court was unable to trace children. There was no basis for a suspended sentence where there had been no recent co-operation or reliable information.	28 days' imprisonment.